The Spirit Driven Church

The Spirit Driven Church

Signs of God's Graceful Presence

Terje Hegertun

☙PICKWICK Publications · Eugene, Oregon

THE SPIRIT DRIVEN CHURCH
Signs of God's Graceful Presence

Copyright © 2017 Terje Hegertun. All rights reserved. Except for brief quotations in critical publications or reviews, no part of this book may be reproduced in any manner without prior written permission from the publisher. Write: Permissions, Wipf and Stock Publishers, 199 W. 8th Ave., Suite 3, Eugene, OR 97401.

Pickwick Publications
An Imprint of Wipf and Stock Publishers
199 W. 8th Ave., Suite 3
Eugene, OR 97401

www.wipfandstock.com

PAPERBACK ISBN: 978-1-5326-1717-1
HARDCOVER ISBN: 978-1-4982-4167-0
EBOOK ISBN: 978-1-4982-4166-3

Cataloguing-in-Publication data:

Names: Hegertun, Terje.

Title: The spirit driven church : signs of God's graceful presence / Terje Hegertun.

Description: Eugene, OR : Pickwick Publications, 2017 | Includes bibliographical references and index.

Identifiers: ISBN 978-1-5326-1717-1 (paperback) | ISBN 978-1-4982-4167-0 (hardcover) | ISBN 978-1-4982-4166-3 (ebook)

Subjects: LCSH: Holy Spirit. | Church.

Classification: BT122 .H33 2017 (print) | BT122 .H33 (ebook)

Manufactured in the U.S.A.   06/13/17

Scripture quotations are from the New Revised Standard Version Bible, copyright © 1989. Division of Christian Education of the National Council of the Churches of Christ in the United States of America. All rights reserved.

*Dedicated to my dear family,
my colleges at MF Norwegian School of Theology,
And those within all churches
who confess Jesus as Lord and Savior*

Contents

Acknowledgments | ix
Preface | xiii

1. The Church, Fruit of the Third Article | 1
2. The People of God's Presence | 23
3. The Gifted Church of the New Testament | 54
4. The Gift of the Spirit | 84
5. God's New Reality | 108
6. Shaped by Pentecost | 138
7. A Life of Worship | 162
8. Graceful Gifts | 183
9. The Church Spells Relations | 216
10. Unified and Missional | 252

Epilogue | 279

Bibliography | 281
Index | 297

Acknowledgments

FIRST AND FOREMOST, my deepest appreciation goes to my wife because of her patience, understanding, love and encouragement during the demanding time it has taken for realizing a work like this one. I owe her more than I can truly express. So I only say, thank you, my beloved Rigmor! My thanks also go to the rest of my family: our three sons, Andreas, Kristian, and Nikolai; our daughters-in-law, Veronica, Heidi, and Ingrid; and our ten lovely grandchildren. Thanks for your support and care, and for your kindly interest in the project.

Throughout my life, I have belonged to the Pentecostal movement of Norway, which has brought me both delights and concerns. Most of all, the Pentecostal movement welcomed me with great confidence and open arms from the time I was a young man until well after I became ordained for ministry. The leadership of my local assembly—farmers and fishermen—prayed for me by their laying on of hands, and graceful blessing has followed me since. We are all shaped by our contexts, and I think that a tree usually grows best where it is planted. Notwithstanding, thanks to the ecumenical winds by which the worldwide church has been affected for a long time, my Christian family has grown much broader and deeper.

I had been part of that blowing for years even before I began my theological studies and became a part of the dedicated and excellent academic staff at MF Norwegian School of Theology. To this specialized university, my feeling can be summarized by paraphrasing Paul, I give thanks to my God because of you (1 Cor 1:4). By catching the sign of the times, MF has abandoned outdated confessionalist positions. Without losing its Lutheran self-understanding, MF has created a theological environment, which is a thrilling workshop and a unique laboratory for new ecumenical insights, relations, and groundbreaking experiences.[1]

Thus, I appreciate the support of the management team, specifically rector and Professor Dr. Vidar L. Haanes and Dean of Research, Professor Dr. Jan-Olav Henriksen, for giving me the opportunity to have periods of deep, drilling research. Professor Harald Hegstad and the staff at the department of systematic theology are also included in my gratitude. Thank you for your open-minded attitude and for your interest and favor. Here I also include the goodwill from the library staff, who were always ready to support me with an endless number of resources. Many thanks go to Marissa Ortiz and Seth Villegas for their excellent proof-reading of the manuscript and to Jo Bertil Værnesbranden, Tormod Engelsviken, and Roar G. Fotland for reading selected parts of the text. Though not involved in this project specifically, I still appreciate engaging in theological conversations with persons like Veli-Matti Kärkkäinen, Mel Robeck, Amos Yong, Olav Fykse Tveit, Tony Richie, Frank D. Macchia, Steven J. Land, Joel Green, William K. Kay, Jean-Daniel Plüss, Matthias Wenk, Joel Halldorf, Silje Kvamme Bjørndal, Karl Inge Tangen, and Cheryl M. Peterson, to name a few.

Surrounded by a crowd of devoted persons within the strange fellowship called Pentecostalism—made up of ordinary men and women, old and young—I have been formed, cultured, and refined like clay in the hands of the potter, hopefully in the way that seemed best to him (Jer 18). Concealed in the hand of the LORD, I have been travelling on an ecumenical pilgrimage I could not have imagined possible earlier in my life. I have been enriched by the theological treasures I recovered when I entered the threshold of those within the great family of God who have given important contributions to many of the issues reflected in this work. Theological research is to be exposed to an abundance of encounters; men and women from all the major streams of world Christianity who have influenced my theological formation and spirituality, nurtured my visions, fostered my respect for diversity and helped me to address common positions as well as shared challenges.

This pilgrimage has been synchronized with major shifts in global Christianity, not the least of which is the expanding influence of Spirit-sensitive church identities transcending old confessional borders. Among those arenas, the Global Christian Forum has been important because of its search for alternative ecumenical approaches, new creative dialogues, and space for expressing spiritual unity in ways previously unthinkable. Other forums, like the World Council of Churches and various local ecumenical networks, have given me a glimpse of "what the Spirit says to the churches"

---

1. Hegertun, "When a Theological Institution Becomes Ecumenical," 364–71.

(Rev 2:7). It is a blessing to be part of a passionate longing for the realization of a Spirit-directed contemporary church which is shaped by God's graceful gifts and nurtured by a humble attitude of hospitality.

I belong to those who take into account the possibility of a renaissance of the church in the midst of a postmodern and secularized age. In the future, I think the church will prove to be more than a socialization of a conviction.[2] The dividing lines will be changed, cultural expressions will be transformed, conditions will be altered, new challenges will be raised, and networks and alliances will appear and disappear. Much of the work within the church's world is contingent, but the word of the Triune God endures. On the rock of the great confession that Christ is the Son of the living God, the church is built, now and forever (Matt 16:16).

In fact, the church is the people of the Spirit. So let's dance!

---

2. Curiously, church as concept—understood as an open-minded and inclusive fellowship—seems to be such an excellent idea worldwide that a "jealousy" initiative has been taken among agnostics and atheists to establish church-like communities without having any religious framework. *The Sunday Assembly, a Global Phenomenon for Wonder and Good,* has a vision to establish a "godless congregation in every town, city and village that wants one." They profile themselves as "a secular congregation that celebrates life." Following a motto to "live better, help often, wonder more," they yearn to help everyone find their potential and celebrate life. http://www.sundayassembly.com/.

Preface

WOMEN AND MEN ARE human beings concerned for community and shaped to live in relationship with God. In the midst of society, there is a yearning for committed belonging and for a deeper and more relational faith. The rise of new-religious spirituality within the larger culture seems to indicate a hunger for genuine spirituality in the secular society. There is a longing for something that transgresses the pattern of consumption and a searching for more than we physically may observe. Though there are persons who ask "why the church," I consider her to be the real answer of the longing for spiritual life. The church is a dwelling in which God lives by his Spirit (Eph 2:22). She is shaped by the good news for humans, in order to be a place where devoted disciples are formed. She is a reality which allows me to be surprised by love. She gives me a glimpse of something deeper, larger, and broader; and acts as a reminder of Christ, incarnated in the world.[1] As an expression of God's empowering presence, the church is not a proud executor but a glad recipient: a mother of faith offering new life by the work and influence of the Holy Spirit.[2] Thus, the doctrine of the church is based on what it is that constitutes the church.

The Holy Spirit is described as the heartbeat of the Christian and the life-blood of the Christian church.[3] But how is the pneumatological nature of the church to be described? What does it mean that the church exists

---

1. According to McCarthy, spirituality is a fundamental component of our human beingness, rooted in natural desires, longings, and hungers of the human heart. McCarthy, "Spirituality," 196.

2. Hütter, "The Church," 23.

3. Doctrine Commission of the General Synod of the Church of England, *We Believe in the Holy Spirit*, 1. See also Suurmond, *Word and Spirit*, 189.

in accordance with the Creed, by which we declare, "I believe in the Holy Spirit?" In both the Bible and in church traditions of various kinds, the construal of the body of Christ has been considered as just the genuine work of the Spirit. A variety of ecclesial identifications are displayed in the contemporary church. Regardless of diversities in structures and cultures, all churches are deeply dependent on the Spirit. They are created by the Spirit and continually sustained and renewed by the Spirit's ongoing impulse. Church is not something we express, but something we are given, by grace alone.

In the New Testament and in the Christian tradition, the reality of the church is manifested as a concrete reality and as the body of Christ. This is in line with the Christian faith which has experiential, practical, and rational dimensions. My position is that this real, empirical church needs to be a theologically relevant church through the way she appears to those people in society and to those people in need of the other. However, the church does not consist only of local fellowships composed of concrete human beings. Those fellowships have their significance only because of their relation to the salvation event in the sacrifice and resurrection of Christ. The dwelling of Jesus in the midst of the church is made manifest by the Holy Spirit. But this making visible of the Spirit is nothing more mysterious than the gospel of Jesus practiced in its breadth and fullness. The Spirit thus imparts the presence of Christ as a persistent experience.

In his writings, Harald Hegstad ascertains what makes the church a church: the presence of Jesus. Because there is no presence of Christ without the Spirit, there is no church without the gift of the Holy Spirit. Hegstad writes, "The fact that the church presupposes the Spirit in order to be a church is not to say that the Spirit is a part of the church, or the spirit of the church. The Spirit is not a property of the church. Continuously she must pray for the presence of the Spirit and trust in the promise that Jesus will be present wherever two or three are gathered in his name."[4] In fact, the church is what she always has been, a cracked image of Christ. That's why we have our treasure in jars of clay (2 Cor 4:7) because the all-surpassing power comes from God, not from ourselves. And—as a miracle of grace— the church is given the ministry of reconciliation (2 Cor 5:18). The New Testament is clear: all believers are marked with the seal of the promised Holy Spirit (Eph 1:13). The church is really a place to meet God.

My presupposition is that to be a Christian is to have the Spirit. All are baptized into the body of Christ by the one Spirit, who is given to all and experienced by all, though in different ways. The charismatic gifts can

---

4. Hegstad, *Real Church*, 24.

be described not as toys but as channels of grace, love, and blessing. So, driven by my ecumenical instinct, my hope for this work is to give a modest contribution for a further revitalization of the church by pointing to the deep connection between the Spirit and the church, through which we are given a fellowship which is both charismatic and sacramental. Not the one without the other.

An economist normally says that you are what you do. A theologian, however, answers that you do what you are. So please, let the church be church in the fullness of God's grace.

> *The yearning survives the absence of God. But in the depths of this emptiness*
>
> *there lies a feeling, that far beyond all appearances, And far past the final boundary of the probable, Prayers from restless souls reach their secret address and say,*
>
> *Our Father in heaven . . .*
>
> *And when these meet—our yearning for God and God's yearning for us—*
>
> *When these meet at the point of the centre of the cross, light flows toward us. As gospel.*
>
> *If I had to give an answer as to what gives me the courage to enjoy life*
>
> *and why it is that my faith has survived the wanderings of a long life*
>
> *Then the shortest formula is, Never alone! The paradoxical within the Christian faith*
>
> *is that I sometimes have to enter the shadows to see the light of Christ.*
>
> *I have to find solitude to feel the mystery of the presence of Christ.*
>
> *I have to admit my own betrayal to find His grace.*[5]

---

5. Kolnes, "Ralphs femte brev," 19. My translation.

1

The Church, Fruit of the Third Article

> *Everything that one believes, reflects, and says about God the Father and God the Son in understanding the first and second articles would be demonstrated and clarified through God the Holy Spirit.*[1]

Introduction

THEOLOGY IS SOMETHING SCHOLARS and church leaders are doing in a reflective, concrete, and practical way. Though Christian theology as a conceptual science is the study of God, it is at the same time a qualified reflection about Christian life and experience. Therefore, ecclesiological and pneumatological studies seem to be more and more relevant in the field of systematic theology. Because of the potential of both constructive and critical interpretation inherent in theological considerations, the need for a comparable study of the Spirit in the context of the church is reasonable.[2] New experiences and reflections on the reality of the Holy Spirit have led to considerations about how a theology of the Third Article can be more than just a supplement to theological studies in general. The third person of the Trinity cannot be regarded as just an appendix or an underrated topic of theological conceptions. Rather, the Spirit is a key concept in constructing the doctrine of God, just as Christ and Spirit are mutually related. That is why we may ask: Is God the Spirit doing something fresh in our age?

---

1. Karl Barth in Bolli, *Schleiermacher-Auswahl*, 311.

2. This study combines perspectives from both systematic and practical theology. It searches for a coherent and inclusive understanding of the Christian faith in light of Christian traditions, as they come to the fore in the context of historical and contemporary thought and different church practices.

Church traditions crosswise underline the unifying factor of the Spirit. Not only is the Spirit the bond of love in the economy of the Trinity, as said by Augustine. The Spirit is also a central agent in the dialogical processes between churches and denominations in their honest seeking of the unity for which Christ prayed (John 17:21). To be enriched by other insights, we need a breadth of outlook and considerations which go beyond our own tradition. The crossover capacity lying behind comparably oriented studies is obvious and in some ways corresponds to the Spirit as one who blows wherever he wills (John 3:8). The field of pneumatology thus represents a common ground for further ecumenical victories. Consequently, the possibilities for making a path for an ecumenical innovation should be within reach.

Why This Book?

The aim of this work is to contribute to a greater elaboration of an ecclesiology formed by the Spirit. I will argue in favor of the substantial, inseparable, and organic relationship which truly exists between the Spirit and the church, according to a large number of New Testament passages and theological reflections within different layers of the church's widespread diversity. Moreover, a pneumatological ecclesiology, which gives attention to the economy of the Spirit, will contribute to an ecumenical comprehension of what it means to foster open and graceful fellowships, beloved by the Trinity. This fostering of a mutual understanding in terms of spirituality, faith, and practice is hardly possible without a joyful feeling of being surprised by God's love and touched by the Godhead's undeserved grace.[3]

However, to avoid a technical and anemic definition of spirituality, I defer to a broad understanding that includes both diaconal virtues and concrete expressions of our Christian belief. Christian spirituality is fused into the believing community as a social, charismatic, and sacramental fellowship. This points in the direction of fostering a congregational oriented spirituality. Such a spirituality is rooted in discipleship as a way of life and a combination of contemplative awareness and creative action and discernment. Accordingly, the link between spirituality and theology seems to be obvious. Knowledge of God is inseparable from the love of God, deepened in prayer.[4]

---

3. Remark the slogan of the Lutheran World Federation and the marking of the 500 years of Reformation in 2017: "Liberated by God's Grace."

4. McKenna and Sheldrake, *Spirituality and Theology*, 36. Fee, "Renewed Presence of God."

The church exists as a gift of the Spirit, or as said by Edmund Schlink, the church is the proper work of the Holy Ghost.[5] But how is the presence of the Holy Spirit to be perceived within the life of the church, and what is the interplay between Spirit and church? The understanding of the Spirit (pneumatology) and the perception of the church (ecclesiology) is defined in different ways within different church traditions. While normally the study of the church has followed strict confessional lines, today we observe a tendency to construe an ecumenical understanding of the church in general. To do this, it is appropriate to bring different scholars and traditions together in dialogue. This work aims to do so by putting different voices in conversation with one another. So, what can we learn from each other and what kind of theological insights do other traditions have which may contribute to, and even expand, our own understanding?[6] Faith is a gift. It is wonder and experience but also delivering of new knowledge.

In the Apostolic Creed the church is understood as a fruit of the Holy Spirit and as the center of the Spirit's activity among humans. In the original text, the central statement in the third section of the Creed reads simply, "I believe in the Holy Spirit." The section refers at first to the Holy Spirit as God's agent in forming a community of those who believe in Christ and thus as another chapter of the story of Christ. According to Ratzinger, the remaining statements of the third section of the Creed are intended to be nothing more than a development of the basic profession that I believe in the Holy Spirit. The communion of the saints and the forgiveness of sins are concretizations of the way the Spirit works. The statement has a directly sacramental meaning, operating through the Eucharist and baptism, respectively, and produces a distinct theocentric understanding of the church.[7] However, the third part of the Creed also reckons the church as a Spirit-filled community that is open for the gifts and fruits of Spirit, in line with how these fellowships are construed in numerous passages of the New Testament.[8] Thus, the conceptions of church and Spirit are connected in the Apostles' Creed as one joint section of belief, pointing to the church's distinctive charismatic and sacramental character. In a fundamental way, the church's being and activity are dependent on the presence of the Spirit within her midst.

---

5. Schlink, *Coming Christ and Coming Church*, 96.

6. This is an approach which during the later years has been designated as receptive ecumenism. See Murray, *Receptive Ecumenism*.

7. Ratzinger, *Introduction to Christianity*, 331–36.

8. See Acts 1:8; 2:4,38; 4:31; 8:17; 10:45; 13:52; Rom 5:5; 8:9; 1 Cor 3:16; 12:13; 14:12; Eph 5:18.

Ratzinger regrets that the church's charismatic and pneumatological nature has been ineffectual during the ages. Teaching about the church must commence with teaching about the Holy Spirit and his gifts, not the other way around, as is the norm in the history of dogma. The former President of the Pontifical Council for Promoting Christian Unity, Walter Kasper, admits that modern theology describes pneumatology as a function of ecclesiology. Then the Spirit has become a guarantor of the church as an institution, and pneumatology has become the ideological superstructure on top of ecclesiology.[9] Nicolas M. Healy asserts that it is the Spirit who makes the church's witness true and effective. The Spirit upbuilds the church in a way beyond the possibility of human activity.[10] This theological uniqueness is implied when the church is designated as the Body of Christ and the temple of the Spirit (1 Cor 12:27; 6:19). As such, she may be understood in terms of the presence and the acts of the Spirit. Hence, the doctrine of the church must begin with a consideration of how she is constituted.

The church as a spiritual reality has been constructed in various ways within different church traditions. The *filioque* controversy and the following break between the Eastern and Western Church reinforced the notion of a subordinate role of the Spirit in relation to the Father and the Son, in order to avoid any kind of speculative pneumatologies. Eastern orthodoxy has accused the West of replacing the unmediated relationship between the individual believer and the Spirit with the use of mediated agencies such as church, sacraments, and clergy. Orthodox theology defends, at least theologically, the relative independence of spiritual experience to any ecclesiastical institutionalism, even though it has to be tested by the church. Thus, the emergence of pneumatology has implications not only for the subject matter of theology in general, but also for the approach to methods and expressions.

Approach

In this work, I analyze the church as a Word-anchored graceful fellowship.[11] My aim is to present and elucidate in what way the church as Spirit-driven can be recognized and qualified as a lived reality with recognizable fruits. Consequently, a working definition and an overall perspective for this work

---

9. Ibid., 333. Kasper, *The God of Jesus*, 138.

10. Healy, *Practical-Prophetic Ecclesiology*, 9–10.

11. The extensive use of Scripture references is a deliberate decision based upon my methodological presuppositions where my reflections are in a continuous interplay with how I understand various text-passages.

is as follows: by going behind the different external and structural frameworks that normally define different church identities, I designate the church as a composition of the Spirit. This comes to the fore in the fact that she is pneumatologically founded and thus exists by an identity which includes both charismatic and sacramental elements. As a dwelling place for God's Spirit, her dual identity characterizes what it means to be church. The Spirit is her DNA. It marks the church as a fellowship shaped by graceful gifts and gracious relations, both of which reflect the presence of God. It is time to reconsider the notion that the church is either charismatic or sacramental. She has the privilege to be both. Thus it is imperative to construct a sustainable environment based on both the subjective and objective dimensions of Christian faith and practices.

In discussions of the nature of the church, the Spirit functions as a substantial theological subject, permeating and governing our talks about God and our approach to the topic of church growth. Spirit-related fellowships need to be rooted in a trinitarian appearance of the church and governed by an intrinsic relationship between Word, Spirit—and community.[12] So I ask, how can this relationship be described, and what characterizes a church designated as a spiritual fellowship? Which kind of mature pneumatological perspectives and linguistic recourses may be activated in the comprehension of the church as the pneumatological body of Christ? To what extent do the figurants in this work provide important resources in formulating an ecumenical theology of a church, made and filled by the Spirit? My overarching goal is to give substance to a common theological understanding that provides the building blocks for an ecumenical theology of the church as a fellowship, made by the Spirit.[13]

Normally, research on theological issues requires a combination of empirical observations and normative claims. The perspectives presented here go in a practical-theological direction, but are at the same time marked by transparent normative standards, because of the need to secure the quality of the scholarly discussion. However, no one person can assume exclusive responsibility and privileged knowledge. Everyone's hand is needed. Together we can learn from each other's experiences and benefit from each

---

12. Here I am in accordance with Orthodox ecumenist Boris Bobrinskoy, who writes that the theology of the Holy Spirit is not so much one specific chapter of Christian theology as an essential dimension of every theological view of the church and of its spirituality and liturgical and sacramental life. Bobrinskoy, "Holy Spirit," 470.

13. In this work, I limit my consideration to the sphere of the church, without going into further deliberations about the work of the Spirit in areas which transcend the field of ecclesiology. These include the potential for establishing a dynamic theology of creation and the possibility of constructive dialogue with traditions of other religions, as well as the big questions of peace, hope and justice.

other's wisdom. Only together we are able to witness to the full gospel held by the whole body of Christ (Eph 3:17–19).[14]

Different Perspectives

By drawing from across the spectrum of Christian traditions, my aim is to consider the reciprocal interplay between these two doctrinal loci: the Spirit and the church. My interlocutors, coming from different traditions within the global church, render the church as fellowship, created and sustained by the Spirit. In spite of the distinctions that normally separate churches from each other, it is still possible to describe the church as a composition of the Spirit. And though there are different spiritual expressions of life and gifts within the church, the Spirit serves as a comprehensive principle of Christian unity across denominational lines. So, in order to examine how the relationship between the Spirit and the church is designed, different figurants are introduced for imagining what characterizes a church with ambitions to be a healthy and spiritual fellowship. Thus, the book offers various reflections which may represent resources for use in ecumenical circles as well as in theological studies.

My topic may be seen from different angles. Unlike most classical Western theology, the ecclesiology of Eastern Orthodoxy is permeated with pneumatology. This tradition has scarcely reflected upon the nature of the church independent of the unitary bond between Christ and of the Spirit. As such, she appears with two distinctive aspects: she is the body of Christ, a body which represents the fullness of the Spirit. John D. Zizioulas underlines the nature of the church as *instituted* by Christ; the christological perspective (1 Cor 3:11), and *constituted* by the Spirit; the pneumatological perspective (1 Pet 2:5).[15] Orthodox theology is described as a Spirit-sensitive theology,[16] though still closely related—and in some way also restricted—to the performance of the liturgy. That is why she defines herself as a charismatic church.

---

14. This perspective is reflected by many denominations, such as The United Methodist Church in their Basic Christian Affirmation: "With Christians of other communions we confess belief in the triune God-Father, Son, and Holy Spirit." See also the formulation that "we share a common heritage with all Christians." http://www.umc.org/what-we-believe/our-christian-roots-god.

15. Zizioulas, *Being as Communion*, 140; Lossky, *Mystical Theology*, 174. The difference between the prepositions *in-* and *con-* refers to the fact that institution is something that is given us as a fact, while the constitution is something that involves us by our partaking in its very emergence.

16. Kärkkäinen, *Pneumatology*, 69.

In the Roman Catholic Church, the Spirit plays a role not only within a broader ecclesiastical framework, which includes the activities of the clerical ministries and the magisterium, but also within the spiritual life of the individual believer. Vatican II urged theologians and lay people to revive the focus on the Spirit and consequently to reframe their ecclesiology based on the idea that the church is made visible because of the Spirit. In the Protestant tradition, the Spirit is understood primarily as an agent of conviction connected to the proclamation of the Word and to the administering of the sacraments, though the Spirit is not only restricted to the activities of the church.[17] Among the Pentecostals, the Spirit is the Spirit of encounter, giving power for prayer and ministry in order to stimulate religious and personal progress. Today, a more communal orientation seems to affect this tradition, preserving the movement from an individualism which otherwise would be a contradiction to the ecclesiologically oriented model of the Book of Acts. The interrelatedness between free churches and historical churches, charismatic experiences and liturgical adventure, spontaneity and order, east and west, points to the comprehensiveness of approaches needed. In order to answer the question of how to facilitate the constitutive role of the Spirit in the representation of the church as a Spirit-driven fellowship which fosters a dynamic-sacramental identity, I am in dialogue with theologians and writers who provide various theories for understanding the doctrine of the Spirit in the church based on a charismatic-sacramental identity.

An Outline of This Work

For a brief synopsis, this work consists of ten chapters. In chapter 2, I focus on who the church truly is. As a community of the Holy Spirit, she is characterized by signs. The church is visible in her highly different embodied and concrete manifestations. The essence of the church is not to be found in her organizational sophistication but rather in her clear confession of Christ. The focus is also on her apostolicity, which requires a broader perspective than the traditional lens of apostolic succession.

In the third chapter, I draw a picture of the pneumatological characteristics of the church, as they seem to appear within the Lukan and Pauline text corpus. Their understanding of what it means to be a faith

---

17. Art. 5 of the Augsburg Confession identifies the work of the Spirit as foundational to the proclamation of the Word of God and to the effects of the sacraments. Through these elements "the Holy Ghost is given, who works faith; where and when it pleases God." However, the charismatic renewal within the mainline protestant churches has stimulated a more abundant range of spiritual approaches, and a richer pneumatological language has been established. See Bittlinger, *The Church is Charismatic*.

community stems from a common experience of having received the eschatological Spirit as it became visible on the Day of Pentecost and in the time thereafter. Furthermore, when anchored in the spiritual life of the congregation, the question of "the gift of the Spirit" becomes crucial. May we here have the key to understanding the inner life of the church? I take up this topic in the fourth chapter. Using a cluster of theologians from different traditions, I discuss the understanding of this term. Here I also make use of of biblical sources.

This work presents some specific figurants from different church traditions. All of them share an interest in the theological nature of the church. As such, in the fifth chapter, I present the ecclesiological position of John Zizioulas from the Orthodox tradition and the thinking of Roman Catholic Yves Congar. I also discuss some of the ecclesiological and pneumatological aspect given by Reformed theologian Jürgen Moltmann and the Lutheran perspective of Wolfhart Pannenberg. The sixth chapter allows for different Pentecostal voices to be heard regarding their understanding of the church community as shaped by the Pentecost narrative.

In the chapters that follow, I draw upon insights presented so far in order to identify some selected perspectives of church life which can be considered as characteristics and as results of the Spirit giving gifts to the church. These gifts emerge as sustainable and passionate attitudes and virtues, important for the church's public reputation. The seventh chapter deals with the formative role of a life expressed as worship. The term signifies a form of life that is shaped by an orientation to the world prior to what is given through conceptual reflections alone. All elements of life are fused together by virtue of the same agenda: to be embraced by God's free acts of mercy. The eighth chapter goes on to present some of the graceful gifts by which the church defines herself. The relationship between the Spirit and the church becomes clearest in the sacraments. In their essence, the sacraments are pneumatic gifts because of what they proclaim and what they affect when received. By communicating divine grace to undeserving humans, they are holy liturgical practices with clear christological and pneumatological distinctiveness.

The two last chapters are preoccupied with aspects of the church as she acts and behaves in a broader context. A Spirit-driven church expresses herself as church when her attitudes and actions are shaped by the gospel and influenced by the crucified and resurrected Christ. The confessional profile, as well as her charismatic and sacramental life, needs to be distilled through the content of the gospel. A spiritual church does not communicate her spirituality, but the good news of the incarnated Christ. So, in the ninth chapter I underline the virtues of hospitality, friendship and graceful relationship as fruits of a pronounced pneumatological profile of the church. Cheerful inclusiveness has the theology of love as its source. Love is the concrete and ultimate expression of Pentecost, because it shapes the church with a cross-marked power. The last chapter of this work can be summarized as my reflection about the unifying and missional character of the church. Unity is a matter of love, not of mutual convergence. It is influenced by the Christ narrative and it promotes a reconciled community distinguished by a radical inclusiveness.

Aspects of Clarification

When working theologically with the relationship between Scripture and contemporary church experiences, methodological and hermeneutical considerations are actualized. First, the notion that the church is Spirit-driven should not at all be perceived as an exclusive term. I strongly oppose any tendency to ecclesial triumphalism. Nothing should be more alien to a fellowship saved by grace. The church is Spirit-filled strictly because she is a result of God's redemptive, diaconal, graceful, and concrete acts in the world (Rom 8:5, Eph 5:8). None other than the triune God has caused the existence of the worldwide church (Matt 16:18). This is a foundational description, independent of culture and modes of expression. Accordingly, some substantial thesis can already be given: the church must be understood christologically (Matt 18:20; Eph 5:23), pneumatologically (Acts 2:33), sacramentally (1 Cor 11: 23–26), eschatologically (Matt 21:41), and missiologically (1 Pet 2:9). These fundamental aspects lead to a balanced pneumatological ecclesiology emphasized by the signs of God's graceful presence. The church is both charismatic and sacramental insofar as she, in her practices and congregational life, is infused by the gift of the Spirit for the purposes of seeing the kingdom of God realized in a proleptic way. We may talk about an empirically established sacramental identity in and through her material and embodied experiences of being the body of Christ because of the Easter event and the Day of Pentecost.[18]

When I state that the church is both charismatic and sacramental, it is a fundamental position which presupposes a broad understanding of the charisms. A charismatic fellowship may have an identity where gifts such as speaking in tongues do not have a prominent place in public worship. High visibility of charismatic gifts does not make the church as such more spiritual than a church environment with a more sensitive approach. Here, I challenge pastors and leaders to be creative in terms of finding good and

---

18. Yong, *The Spirit Poured Out on All Flesh*, 156.

varied forms that stimulate the more spontaneous aspect of congregational spirituality. This can be done by creating alternative venues for the operation of the Spirit's gifts such as smaller gatherings and bible studies.

Another assumption is the issue of the empirical character of the church because of the Spirit's activities in the concrete. My conception is that the church is in fact church by virtue of her visible reality and her multitude of expressions. In her breadth, depth and diversity, the church's being in the world as God's ecclesia is a visible fellowship that is part of the greater cultural existence of humans within society. As such, all churches are actual manifestations of the contextuality of Christian theology. As such they are not places for mysterious theological experiences. By their differences and interdependence, they carry the seed for new theological insights.

As acknowledged, we make theology under constantly changing conditions with the assumption that the result should be empirically verifiable. In order to qualify the church's life theologically, it is imperative to understand not only the nature of the church and her commission, but also to admit both her constituents' sin and holiness. Social and cultural elements complicate every attempt to place God exclusively in the realm of transcendence. God works in and through ordinary people, living their ordinary lives in the ordinary world.[19]

Furthermore, the empirical shift in the field of systematic studies to a pragmatic, rather than idealized, approach to the account of the church has influenced the questioning of methods and perspectives. It demands a double task: interpreting Scripture in light of the practical experiences of the church members and assessing that praxis in the light of Scripture.[20] Hence, a fundamental ecclesiological reflection is based on the conditional aspect of positions that are coming into existence in the mold of history. The hermeneutical premise behind different theological distinctions recognizes that no perceptions of the relationship between church and Spirit are cemented forever. As different ecclesial discourses develop, the structures of religious, political and cultural power need to be revisited and even challenged in light of new empirical insights. The reality of the theological and ecclesiastical inheritance embedded in every theological tradition is a part of the reason why theology is understood in different ways. The church is presented with both a devotional and a professional theological language. The latter is reflexive and of second order, while the

---

19. That is a main topic for Norwegian theologian Harald Hegstad and his empirically and practically oriented church perception. Hegstad, *Real Church*.

20. By making use of the proposals of Charles Peirce and Josiah Royce, the Catholic Donald L. Gelpi argues for a turn to experience that is triadic, realistic and communitarian in nature. Gelpi, *Turn to Experience*.

church is the concrete, empirical, and researchable topic which points to the useful dimension of theology.

These immanent and pragmatic elements in construing theology entreat us to ask how theological positions really function in light of our daily life and spirituality. One of the critical tasks every church needs to face is how to introduce these new theological insights so they can be an essential part of ordinary people's way of living. Healthy theology does not exist without reflection on context and function.[21] The need for a closer integration between theory and practice may secure a more church-identifiable theology, which in turn may foster a broader gallery of ecclesiological resources. It seems to be more and more difficult to talk about the church as something quite different than the actual church which is perceptible for people in their daily life and locality. A lack of such recognition will complicate the feeling of responsibility in the endeavor to build healthy local fellowship. An ecclesiology informed by social insights will open closed fellowships and give competence to release conflicts.

On the other side, a theology with ambitions to say something about God has other interests than those perceptible in the empirical arena. The ways in which different churches are talking and acting in the public sphere are, in fact, our contemporary speech about God. No church can evade the ambitious attempt to explain what the truth may be. But that is not only a question of statements, but also of experiences, of acts, of language, of arts, and of shared reality. The everlasting predicament is how church leaders and scholars can constructively steer between relativism and fundamentalism, give new life to the general application of important dogmatic statements, and interpret specific theological claims in ways which are relevant and intelligible to people of our own time. According to the Swiss Catholic writer Hans Urs von Balthasar, Christian faith is always a confession of the ecclesial community, made possible by the Holy Spirit before the world. Since theology cannot be anything else but a meditative clarification of this confession of faith, it must be grounded and unfolded by a careful treatment of Scripture illuminated by the Holy Spirit.[22]

Parts of the theological debate seek to relate the results of biblical exegesis to the more contemporary systematic-theological enterprise. Within modern scholarship, people such as Joel Green and Max Turner talk about a bridge-building hermeneutic by which the gulf separating contemporary

---

21. This pragmatic perspective does not threaten the normative character of Christian belief, as long as the overall intention is to identify and resolve specific problems. By using the phrase "judge for yourselves" (1 Cor 2:15; 10:15; 12:10), Paul encourages the reader to make use of different kinds of discernment.

22. Balthasar, *Spirit of Truth*, 3, 367. Cited in Innerdal, "Spirit and Truth," 271.

Christians and the biblical text may be regained through a transformative discourse.[23] This book is written in the same spirit. The reader will observe that I combine scriptural references with more systematic-theological reflections, observations, and comments. Though there indeed are a variety of voices within the New Testament, my position is that they nevertheless have a unique and prescriptive influence on theological reflection. After all, our positions become anchored to the great salvation story and qualified as Christian theology in a genuine sense in order to instruct and illuminate reflection on being church in a secular age.[24] I am arguing for the biblical-theological relevance of a given position by integrating the New Testament witness and stories as more than just a foggy backdrop. The number of voices and consciously chosen references used in this book contribute to the fulfillment of that ambition. To understand the church, we look to a story of the church's life within Scripture and history rather than through the exclusive use of descriptions of order and structures.[25]

That is why I have no reluctance for using figurants and sources from a wide range of church confessions and from different periods of time. Their value is not connected to the length of their long standing but to my assessment of their relevance. Though systematic theology continuously has contemporarity in view, theological reflections are at the same time released from the accidents of time and space because of the heritage of faith and the treasures received throughout the great Christian tradition. Presumably this helps to preserve the church from the temptation of self-sufficiency. Selfishness never suits the church.[26] My position concurs with that of the Lutheran theologian Cheryl M. Peterson: the church receives her particular identity and purpose through the Holy Spirit, which, in the Book of Acts, is promised by Christ and received at Pentecost.[27] In an act of affirmative response, the church ties her faith and identity to the New Testament sources.

---

23. Green and Turner, *Two Horizons*, 1–14. See also O'Collins and Kendall, *Bible for Theology*, 2.

24. Wall, *Why the Church?*

25. Peterson, *Who is the Church?*, 101.

26. G. K. Chesterton posits this issue in a characteristic way: "Whatever else is true, it is emphatically not true that the ideas of Jesus of Nazareth were suitable to His time, but no longer suitable to our time. Exactly how suitable they were to His time is perhaps suggested in the end of His story." Cited in: Dawn, *Reaching Out*, 297.

27. Peterson, *Who is the Church?*, 105. You will observe my use of the feminine pronoun when referring to the church. By pointing to values that may replace the conceivable patriarchal image of the church, my particular purpose has been to revive and broaden the understanding of the church's nature and to underline her dependence on God alone. Admittedly, both masculine and feminine metaphors about God are used in Scripture. Trinitarianism cannot be read in terms of a "three men" analogy but rather

Methodological Considerations

It is a matter of fact that the notes are not the music, just as theology is not the church. Just as the sum of the instruments is needed to create a symphony, so too are the people of God and the graceful gifts necessary to create church. The congregational life is motivated by hermeneutical questions of how to live as spiritual beings and how different kinds of spiritual practices and formations can identify the church as Spirit-driven. There is a richness of meanings and convictions in the worldwide church, as well as in other cultural and religious traditions. However, our reading and interpretations of texts and traditions are never neutral. Our insights are partial. We read and write and reflect from our own place, time, culture, and social setting. Our perspectives are like snapshots of what Christian faith seems to look like when incarnated in a specific place at a particular time.

A charismatic-sacramental ecclesiology is formed by the Word, construed within an overarching trinitarian framework, and adjudicated by various communities of interpretation. In other words, we talk about a context in which spirituality can be healthily expressed and lived through highly different communities of faith. Because theological perspectives are inevitably connected to a living, local community informed by the broader Christian tradition, it can be described as a hermeneutical trialectic, consisting of interpretive acts (the Spirit), interpretive objects (the Word), and interpretive contexts (the communities). As such, Spirit and Word mutually interpenetrate and inhere within the community, which together function as the framework for the believer's experiences of God and of the reflective dealings of theological positions. Church is interpretive practice.[28] A mature pneumatology insists on an intentional trinitarianism, which is especially necessary for those who have ambitions to bring forth an appropriate interpretation of those various traditions exposed in the global church today. The work of the Spirit in the community of faith becomes normalized by the lived, spoken, written and traditioned Word. As Amos Yong suggests, the intention of sola scriptura cannot proceeds apart from Spirit and community; the community needs to be transformed by the Spirit and checked by the Word.[29] All theological reflections are directed toward discerning ecclesial praxis.

Hence, the understanding of the Bible can be grasped as a practical reasoning driven by virtues, habits, traditions, concerns, practices, and

---

in terms of an inclusive image of God (Gen 1:27; Isa 49:15; Gal 3:28). See also Tanner, "On Being Church."

28. This hermeneutical approach is outlined in Yong, *Spirit-Word-Community*.

29. Ibid.

ways of living by the faithful community. Both biblical and theological symbols transform the souls of believers as they are living within specific socio-historical contexts and cultural and religious traditions. With Yong, theological reflection should translate into meaningful praxis since object and subject, text and context, interpreter and community all coinhere and are informed by each other. The main function of theology seems to be the reflective understanding of the claims of Christian faith and the intellectual analysis of religious experience.

Proposals about the Role of Scripture

However, is it possible to refer to a reality beyond our experiences? Is theology able to elaborate reliable truth-claims about domains of reality that lie beyond human limitations? And what is the epistemological status of the Bible in the theological reflection? These are questions that also need to be raised in a work like this. More than everything else, the Bible communicates a revelation which has the utmost authority within the contextually oriented and hermeneutically based theological enterprise. In can be stated, as J. Wentzel van Huyssteen does, that the different understandings of Scripture are transconfessional issues linked to the credibility of Christian faith and to the ultimate quest for meaning in life.[30] In a similar way, the canonical-linguistic approximation of Kevin J. Vanhoozer determines the postfoundationalist rationality as following maps.[31] You recognize the priority of the canonical text as a canonical atlas, in line with the relationship between reality and our use and reading of it. The collection of maps variously renders the way, the truth, and the life. However, Scripture is over against the church because of the role of Scripture to address, edify, and confront her in the midst of her limited perceptions and susceptibility to error. When embracing doctrinal truths as a dramatic story about life and existence which includes the framework of the church, the proper end of that drama is wisdom and lived knowledge, a performance of the truth.[32]

The position of Huyssteen and Vanhoozer combines two perspectives, 1) a deep respect for the reality and authority of the canonical text; and 2) the need for critical reflection and the evaluative dimension in providing a rationale for the way one thinks, chooses, acts, and believes. This is in accordance with both the consecutive and the break-up dimensions of the church tradition. The strength of a critical realist position is connected

---

30. Huyssteen, *Postfoundationalist Theology*, 124–61.
31. Vanhoozer, *Drama of Doctrine*, 294.
32. Ibid., 21.

to its insistence that the object of religious belief lies beyond the range of literal description. Or as said by van Huyssteen: "Because believers regard themselves as making meaningful assertions about reality that humans can and do encounter in faith experience, religion and religious experience has always been and still is regarded as a way to reality, that is, as referring to a reality beyond our experience."[33] What evokes genuine faith experiences leads back to the basic role of the biblical text and to its construing of what may represent the content of Christian life. Faith experiences, the language of faith, and the theoretical language of theological reflection presuppose the existence of the biblical text as essential for interpreting Christianity to people today. Hence, the Bible has a decisive role to play in the mapping and exposition of theological statements.

Critical realism acknowledges the possibility of human imagination in the formation of theories but also admits the existence of reality structures not created by the human mind. However, there is no uninterpreted access to reality. That's why the role of metaphors in the process of interpretation is so central to indirectly redescribing reality. Critical realism represents a model of rationality where theological concepts are both partial and provivional while at the same time being necessary for referring to the reality called God and Godhead's relation to humanity.[34] None of our models are literal pictures, neither are they fictions. The metaphorical language of the biblical texts and the propsitional models coming as a result of the reflection upon this language provide us with resources that otherwise would not have been available to us. It has equipped the Christian tradition with indispensable images, visions, symbols, metaphors, narratives, propositions, assertions, and conceptions.[35] These biblical resources are represenational for a reality beyond the experience and thus anchor any further reflection of the faith commitment to the assumption of God as the outmost reality.[36] Theological-methaphorical language and religious experiences become interpreted on the basis of the classical texts of Christian faith. Thus the realism of the biblical text itself becomes a reality that functions epistemologically as an exclusive access to the reality of God and contributes to the question of the

---

33. Huyssteen, *Postfoundationalist Theology*, 132.

34. For this position, see McGrath, *Science of God*, 100–42.

35. Huyssteen, *Postfoundationalist Theology*, 135.

36. Within the theories of Huyssteen, there is a clear link between the formulation of models in both science and theology. Both partake of the nature of discovery and of increasing intelligibility. In science, it is the entities and structures of the natural world that are discovered and rendered intelligible. In theology, it is the human's search and longing for ultimate meaning within the realm of Christian faith that is correspondingly rendered intelligible. Ibid., 136.

authority of the Bible.[37] Our epistemic access to God goes through central metaphorical concepts of the Christian tradition, while we are supplied at the same time with the reality behind the biblical texts.

For everyone who seeks, belongs and acts, the Bible is a crucial part of a theological argument. However, Scripture supports a surprising variety of theological and ecclesiological positions.[38] That is why the question of authority cannot be resolved apart from asking: what is the essence of Christianity? Apparently, the root-metaphor of Christian faith is the redemption work of Christ. In other words, we need to seek those critical realist arguments that allow for the complexity of hermeneutical interpretations of text positions that evoke the potential of religious experience which is excluded neither from long traditional lines nor from metaphorical references to the redemptive work of Christ. The biblical text has the ability to be a reality in its own right and, as such, does more than just establish a conversation process between writer and reader. During the process of redescribing reality, the text lives through an extension of meaning in the relation to the reader, thus becoming an imaginative experience within its own inner patterns and limits. As a creative and constructive process, reading is giving new life to a text while respecting it in a kind of productive but consciously responsible pluralism.[39] In one respect, the reader is inscribed and encoded in the text, though the different texts appear as a pluriform witness of God.

Rightly understood, the biblical text is not completed until it has been received by the reader. The reference process must therefore be analyzed in light of the world of the reader. But more importantly, since the biblical texts refer to God and to the redemptive work of Christ as the recurrent theme, it seems clear that Jesus Christ, as an authorized authority, alone authorizes the Bible. This is a redemptive and christological authority for a life in faith and commitment.[40] The Bible is and will always be the classic model for understanding God and the main resource for a reliable life of the church. In a broader sense, the question of authority can be traced back to the referential and proleptic stucture of the living Christian faith that precedes the establishing of the New Testament canon, modelled by the ancient church. Later expressions of faith have always related to the classical models of faith expressed in the biblical texts. The faith was "Christian" because it referred to Jesus, the Son of God. Thus the Bible is an exclusive epistemological access to the faith reality.

37. Ibid., 138.
38. Barr, *Holy Scripture*, 32.
39. Huyssteen, *Postfoundationalist theology*, 148.
40. Ibid., 154.

The notion of inspiration is predominantly a quality of the biblical text, which is connected to both the writing and the reading of the text. Received from the Holy Spirit as the giver of life, inspiration is made accessible as an ontological reference of the written text and of its redemptive authority (2 Tim 3:16). Since the inspiration of the Spirit was a reality among the people of God before, under and after the writing process and the establishing of the New Testament canon, the term cannot be restricted to a text as a final product. By referring to a reality that is powerfully revealed through the text, the faith community can see inspiration as the quality of the text and as the referential power of the text under the guidance of the Spirit. The same Spirit who was at work in the community that created the text, is also present in the community that recreates the text by reading and interpreting it for people of today.[41] The believing community thus recognizes, as a matter of fact, that the text of the Bible as inspired.

However, the hermeneutic role of the Spirit must be seen in a perspective that encompasses both the question of the original biblical text as well as the capacity for giving new interpretation within the contemporary landscape. A model of a Spirit-sensitive text interpretation may be defined as controlled liberty.[42] Anchored within the biblical canon, this model implies a combination of careful exegesis, an honoring of the original, historical meaning, and serious attentiveness to the potentiality of an interpretation directed at the present. According to Clark Pinnock, "without the former, meaning could collapse into hopeless pluralism; without the latter, reading could become an academic exercise without transforming power."[43] The controlled liberty role of the Holy Spirit within the ongoing interpretive enterprise implies ongoing scriptural revelation.

The notion that the interpretation process is not a private enterprise points to the corporate interpretive contexts which exist within and between the church and responsible theological fellowships (2 Pet 1:20). As Pinnock points out, the history of the early church is indeed the history of a movement willing to break free from Judaic restrictions, de-stigmatize pagan cultures, generate a universal faith, and risk new understandings. Loyalty to the truth was not tantamount to loyalty to traditional approaches and attitudes but rather to insights that shaped a new future.[44] From these

---

41. Ibid., 159–60.

42. Pinnock, "Work of Holy Spirit," 9. His point of departure is 2 Tim 3:16, that "all Scripture is God-breathed."

43. Ibid., 10. This would be in line with Ricoeur's concept of a world behind and a world in front of the text as well as the call for the writer to negotiate both worlds.

44. Ibid., 19. Pinnock refers to Charles H. Kraft and his claim that the dynamic of Christianity is not the sacredness of cultural forms but the venturesomeness of

particular perspectives, it is preferable to allow historical exegesis to interact with prophetic openness to the Spirit of God, which is itself marked by a spirituality facilitating transformative encounters with Scripture.[45]

Based on the Salvation Story

In sum, these reflections state that the Bible is the main source of the revelation of God throughout history. As such, it is the primary document for faith communities across confessional lines. In its substantial structure and proportion, it is a given and finalized revelation. However, according to John 16:12 the instructions of Jesus open a wider process for understanding the course of history. New insights and wider perspectives can be developed in order to fulfill the traditional positioning known through the course of history. Obviously, our perceptions are historically limited and, at the same time, exposed for their own potentialities.[46] The Bible was written by vulnerable people and thus is marked by the stamp of human's limited enlightenment on some secondary issues. It should be read for what seems to be the main purpose of Scripture: to be the womb of the salvation story.

According to Peter (1 Pet 1:10), the writers realized that the prophets spoke about things that later on would be given to the church as a salvation story. The gospel came to the church by the Holy Spirit sent from heaven (v. 12), and, as such, the message could not be a matter of negotiation (John 17:3). God revealed Godself definitively through Christ, though Godself did so contextually in a particular place and in a particular time. The church was then given the commission to communicate and translate this very salvation story for new generations in new times and cultures. Objectively, the revelation is clear and distinct. Subjectively, the revelation needs to be justified and accounted for in the midst of highly different historical periods and shifting cultural circumstances.

An interesting approach to a theological prolegomenon can be described as revelational-pneumatic, appealing to the divine revelation of the intervention of God through salvation history in the person of Jesus Christ,

---

participating with God of contemporary cultural forms to serve more adequately as vehicles for God's interaction with human beings. Kraft, *Christianity in Culture*, 382.

45. For an overview, see Thiselton, *New Horizons*, and Osborne, *The Hermeneutical Spiral*. Among the groundbreaking environments which have created new interpretive traditions by their alternative reading of Scripture are liberation theology, feminist theology and pentecostal theology. See Kristiansen and Rise, *Theological Thinkers*.

46. Normally we may talk about two levels of meaning: firstly, what is my position (the concrete, actual position), and secondly, what I mean about my meaning (the metaphorical level where I am open to the fact that I may miscalculate).

as recorded in Scripture. In his reflection on the presence, reality, and ministry of the Holy Spirit, Donald G. Bloesch holds that the decisive point with regard to the question of interpretation is neither experience nor language, but rather the divine-human encounter.[47] A revelational-pneumatic theology gives priority to the personal relationship between the giver and the receiver of the revelation based on the Spirit's communication of the objective revelation. In its abundance, it cannot be captured in concepts and categories but is stated in reformable and open-ended affirmations.

A theology of Word and Spirit will subordinate propositional knowledge to the knowledge of acquaintance rooted in an I-Thou-relationship, a conviction of being personally addressed by the living God. In fact, the source of faith is the gracious result of the sanctifying work of the Spirit in the heart of the believer that is tied to the redeeming work of Jesus on the cross. No one can rightly seek God's righteousness unless one is already grasped by the power and love of Christ.[48] This revelational-pneumatic approach is a position that may be described as trans-modern, because the source and content lies in the revelation of Christ. It does not arise out of culture as such but breaks into human culture and history from the outside.

This approach calls for a devotional commitment to Christ as the way, the truth, and the life (John 14:6). However, the position does not deny that Christ manifests his presence through the Spirit outside the parameters of Christian faith and community.[49] While we, in one sense, may affirm a "hidden" church in people's search for religious consciousness and intuition, Christ's community in the world has always been the visible church. She does not arise out of human experience but is created by the Spirit and filled with the Spirit in the midst of human culture. That is why she is sometimes in dialogue and sometimes in confrontation with modern and postmodern conceptions. A theology of Word and Spirit is an alternative to both narrational and propositional theology, though the Bible obviously contains both narratives and propositional truths.[50] This approach

---

47. Bloesch, *The Holy Spirit*. This is an alternative approach to the three theological typologies of George Lindbeck, the cognitive-prepositional, the experimental-expressive and the cultural-linguistic. Bloesch proposes an intratextual theology of social embodiment, designed to help Christians draw from the resources available within their own traditions.

48. Ibid., 25.

49. Ibid., 31.

50. A Pentecostal scholar cannot be regarded as a pure propositional theologian because one appeals not to Scripture alone but to Scripture as illuminated by the Spirit. One becomes a theologian of Word *and* Spirit because one's appeal rests in the dialectical interplay between the present work of the Spirit and the past revelation given in Scripture. All spiritual utterances and charismatic activities must be assessed in light of Scripture.

seeks to transcend the divide between dogmatism and mysticism, logos, and mythos. In the dramatic unfolding of salvation history, we perceive the unity of logos and mythos. The fact that the Bible testifies to Christ, as Luther said, reveals a commitment to the role of the Spirit in leading us beyond the natural meaning of the text to the transcendent reality of the gospel. This kind of theology will see faith as both intellectual assent *(credentia)* and trust in God's mercy *(fiducia)*.[51]

Come, Thou Holy Paraclete!

According to the Creeds, the church is an arena for the influence of the Spirit. The growing interest in pneumatology has given the doctrine of the Spirit a place at the theological table. Thus today the doctrine of the Spirit serves an integrating function, governing the general talk about God. New experiences of the reality of the Spirit are dependent on language and thoughts which are integrated within the context of the Christian community, rooted in Scripture, and framed by a trinitarian image of God. Human beings are not humans in their abstraction but in the concrete historicity in which they experience the revelation of God, as mediated by Christ through the Spirit.

A savory fruit of the experiential part of the life of the Spirit is the expanding and visible unity between different church bodies, which can be described as a manifestation of unity in diversity. Oneness seems to be growing from below in ways that are both extensive and deep-rooted; manifested like a pilgrimage guided by the Spirit. No church tradition has any kind of monopoly on the Spirit. In a deep sense, the Holy Spirit—as God's unvisible presence in the world—is affiliated to the whole church. As ecclesial bodies, believing fellowships are shaped by God's spiritual activities in the world in order to reflect and serve God in their own right and multiplicity. The result is a Christian spirituality which can be interpreted as the lived experience of Christian belief. There need to be a continuous dialogue between theology as faith declaration and theology as Christian practice and faith experience.[52] Those two dimensions are closely linked together as underscored by Philip Sheldrake: "All human statements about God have practical implications; we live what we affirm. Ineffective or even destructive spiritualities inevitably reflect inadequate theologies of God."[53]

---

51. Bloesch, *The Holy Spirit*, 46.

52. Concurring with Vanhoozer, I contend that doctrine is one of the principal means God uses to build up his church. Vanhoozer, *Drama of Doctrine*, 29.

53. Sheldrake, *Spirituality and Theology*, 15.

In our attempts to make a picture of a God who is always greater and a church who is more beautiful and more vulnerable than we normally imagine, our experience of reality is too confined, our conceptions are too limited and our languages are too restricted. But we have our inducements, our symbols, metaphors, and stories. The prevailing images of God are shaped by doxological praise and adoration. Why do I say this? Because the issue of the spiritual life is not about spirituality, it is about God. The Godhead has the source of life in God's hands and carries the weight of the world (Job 34:14–15). The triune God is the name of a fellowship which opens itself to the world in everlasting love. Jesus completes God's love story to the world. Through Christ, the mystery within the Trinity has a visible face and a confirmed story. It is a story made to communicate and a language fitted to open those dimensions within a reality that no language is able to contain. In the shadow of the cross and throughout history, Christians have prayed, Come, thou holy Paraclete!

Hopefully, this work unveils that there is a consensus among the people of God regarding the work of the Spirit within the church which is grounded in worship and ministerial formation. It combines and interrelates with spirituality, academic excellence, mission, justice, peace, the formation of the Christian character, and pastoral sensitivity and competence.

The church lives because of the life which flows from Christ through the Spirit. Thus, the church will always be shaped by the gospel. So, let her have:

> *The ear to hear God's word and the cry of God's people;*
>
> *the heart to heed and respond to the suffering;*
>
> *the tongue to speak to both the weary and the arrogant;*
>
> *the hands to work with the lowly;*
>
> *the mind to reflect on the good news of the gospel;*
>
> *the will to respond to God's call; the Spirit to wait on in the prayer,*
>
> *to struggle and wrestle with God, to be silent in penitence and humility*
>
> *and to intercede for the church and the world;*
>
> *the body to be the temple of the Holy Spirit.*[54]

In the coming three chapters I address different preconditions for the intrinsic link between the church and the Spirit. I start by writing about the nature of the church in a more general sense. Then I give a presentation of different aspects of church life portrayed in the New Testament before

54. World Study Report, "Challenges and Opportunities," 5.

asking whether the the gift of Spirit or "Spirit baptism" may function as a key metaphor for an appropriate understanding of the life of the church.

Firstly, I deal with the church as the people of God's presence. One definition is that she is a community of the Holy Spirit marked by three distinguishing signs: she anticipates the kingdom of God by her worship *(leitourgia)*, she proclaims the gospel by her witness *(martyria)*, and she serves humankind by her deeds *(diakonia)*.

2

The People of God's Presence

> *I will live in them and walk among them, and I will be their God, and they shall be my people . . . I will welcome you, and I will be your father, and you shall be my sons and daughters, says the Lord Almighty.*[1]

Introduction

ONE OF THE MOST beautiful expressions of the church comes from the Apostle Paul. We are being built together to become a dwelling place in which God lives by his Spirit (Eph 2:22). Identifying the church as a graceful reality and as a place for living in communion with God through Jesus Christ in the Holy Spirit has been met with extensive approval by very different church bodies.[2] The church is an actually existing local group, a concrete reality situated in history and instituted by the triune God.[3] By the Spirit, the global church is united as a single body through which Christ once again has become incarnate in the world. As an ordered fullness, living and organic, the church in her totality is more than a collection of different elements and greater than the sum of her parts. The church is the very community in which the faith, as the good treasure entrusted to us (2 Tim 1:14), is shared relationally throughout time and space with the help of the Holy Spirit. The unity between past, present, and future is rooted in this pneumatological understanding of the church. This section aims to outline several key intersections of pneumatology and ecclesiology. Scholars from various traditions are brought into

---

1. 2 Cor 6:16, 18.
2. World Council of Churches, *BEM*, 20.
3. Nikolajsen, *Identity of the Church*, 15.

conversation concerning the nature of the Spirit-driven church, that is, the church founded by Christ and animated by the Spirit. A mutual affirmation is that she is the communion of the Spirit (2 Cor 13:13); one, holy, catholic, and apostolic, according to the Nicene Creed. That includes a dynamic-sacramental potential.[4]

The Presence of God

The dwelling of God is a key concept throughout the Bible. The people of Israel were the people of his presence (Deut 14:23). As an identification marker, the glory of God's presence was more important than circumcision, the Law, and the Sabbath. The primary symbol was defined in this way: The glory of the Lord filled the tabernacle (Exod 40:35). Of the coming Messiah it was said that the Spirit of the LORD shall rest on him (Isa 11:2). In the Old Testament God's dwelling place is described as lovely (Ps 84:1), the place where God has promised to be with them as their God and Savior (Ezek 37:27). By the Spirit we have access to God's very presence. These perspectives are pursued and reinforced in the new covenant (2 Cor 3:1–18; Eph 2:22).

Properly understood, the church is a community of the Holy Spirit with three distinguishing signs. She anticipates the kingdom of God by her worship *(leitourgia)*, she is charged with proclaiming the gospel by her witness *(martyria)*, and she serves humankind by her deeds *(diakonia)*.[5] In other word, the nature of the church cannot be ascertained apart from her relationship to the community in which she is placed. We cannot reflect upon the church in abstraction from its concrete appearance and visible identity. The church serves as a real expression of the undeserved grace and gift in the midst of human existence. As beloved children, we can comprehend the church rightly through her diversity of embodied manifestations. She is the living presence of the Spirit.

This relates to the notion that Christ's mission in the world is trinitarian. The Father sends his Son into the world (John 3:16). Christ leads people back to relationship with God (14:6), in the power of the Spirit (Luke 4:1;

---

4. The great British missiologists, Lesslie Newbigin, says that the question of where Church is cannot be legitimated answered without the reference to the Spirit. Newbigin, *The Household of God*, 95. Likewise, Catholicos Aram I states that the church is a community of faith, a confessing community, a healing community and a missionary community; not a fixed institution but a dynamic reality. Aram I, *Ecumenical Vision*, 58–60.

5. Wainwright, "Church," 159.

Acts 10:38) and by the church as instrument. In the missionary work of the church, the Spirit glorifies Christ (John 16:12–15). At the same time Christ builds his church (Matt 16:18; Eph 2:20) and purposes to empowers her by ministerial and charismatic gifts (Eph 4:11–13; 1 Cor 12–14) in order that she become a dwelling place in which God lives by his Spirit (Eph 2:22). The Spirit is the breath of Christ who is reflected through the church's gifts, ministries, and practices. At the same time, she is sensitive and vulnerable. On this background, the appeal of Paul is legitimate, "do not quench the Spirit" (1 Thess 5:19; cf. Col 1:9), and "be filled with the Spirit" (Eph 5:18). Since the basic identity of the Spirit is spelled out in relation to church, we hardly can talk about the Spirit without also talking about the church.

Ralph del Colle writes in the affirmative that the Holy Spirit is associated with ecclesiology to such an extent that ecclesiology is best understood when it is a branch of pneumatology.[6] Because of the gift of the Spirit, the church is the locus of God's presence on earth (Eph 2:18–22). She exists purely by the outpouring of the Holy Spirit.[7] According to another ecclesiologist, Simon Chan, the Spirit and the church clarify each other's identity:

> The Spirit is the third person precisely in his relation to the Church; and the Church is what it is essentially in relation to the third person of the Trinity: it is the body of Christ indwelled by the Spirit, making it the temple of the Holy Spirit. (. . .) As the temple of the Holy Spirit, the Church's chief act is the worship of God, through Jesus Christ, in the power of the indwelling Spirit (1 Pet 2:5).[8]

In short, the church is pneumatologically conditioned. The Spirit appears to be the bond of love between Christ and the church. Because of the Spirit, the church is christologically shaped into the body of Christ and pneumatologically linked to Christ. The Spirit who comes from beyond history now has released the church from every historical-linear limitation or succession. That is why Pentecost is a repeated event. The Spirit has come and continues to come when the church prays for Godhead's presence in the worship and the epiclesis.[9] According to Reinhard Hütter, without the realization that the church is the creation of the Spirit in time, the action of the Spirit is found everywhere and nowhere.[10] Under the dynamic guidance of the Holy Spirit,

---

6. Del Colle, *Christ and Spirit*, 25.

7. Del Colle, "The Outpouring of Spirit," 249.

8. Chan, "Jesus as Spirit Baptizer," 145.

9. With Emil Brunner, the Body of Christ is nothing other than a fellowship of Christ and the Spirit. This fellowship signifies a common participation of a community of life, given by the Spirit. Brunner, *The Misunderstanding*, 10–11.

10. Hütter, *Suffering Divine Things*, 127.

the church is a community on the move. This process is beyond our control. The capacity of the Holy Spirit to transform lives in the here and now manifests in diverse expressions, corresponding to the richness and diverseness of human personalities.

So, to what extent may the church today expect or hope that the conditions of the Spirit's operation among the first generation will be reproduced among us? It may be argued that the Book of Acts as well as the Gospels were written in order to establish a particular pattern of church life for generations to come.[11] Furthermore, contemporary spiritual experiences invites to a better understanding of some of the New Testament passages. And conversely, the lack of particular experiences also affects one's understanding of Scripture. The risk is that which is not experienced can be discarded as unnecessary.

A Corporate Dimension

It is common to conceptualize the church as a historical occurrence or as an entity within the larger creation. But Simon Chan proposes that the church must be understood as chosen in Christ prior to the creation of the world (Eph 1:4). As the living body of Christ, the church is ontologically linked to Christ, the head of the church (Col 1:18), while its historical existence was initiated by the Holy Spirit on the Day of Pentecost (Acts 2).[12] This embodied church is built upon the commitment of those who confess Christ as LORD (Matt 16:16; Acts 2:41–47). In her, Christian faith is expressed in liturgy, creeds, worship, testimony, prayer and theological reflections. She exists dynamically and develops in order to be properly manifested within current and highly different social and cultural contexts.

As a general description of Old Testament pneumatology, The Anglican Doctrine Commission states that the Spirit is breathed by God into human beings for their very life, for the empowering of individuals with respect to particular tasks, and for the act of prophecy.[13] With respect to the New Testament narratives, it is reasonable to understand the early church as a loving and suffering fellowship that provided an important context

---

11. See also Robinson and Wall, *Called to be Church*.

12. Chan, "Church and Doctrine," 63. Chan seems to mean that an ecclesiology that is intimately linked to an ontological and pneumatological understanding of the church promotes the church as an interpretive community and gives authority to the church's regulative role of the Christian tradition. To the extent that the link between Spirit and Church is weak, the result will be a weakened view of dogma. Ibid., 61.

13. Doctrine Commission of Church of England, *We Believe in the Holy Spirit*, 6.

for different pneumatic experiences (Acts 5:41; 1 Pet 4:12–14.). The good news was communicated in a powerful way in order to enact the reshaping of lives associated with a Christian conviction. The church's existence was shaped by her dependence on the power of her message; i.e., the power of the Spirit. Thus we are not meant to be isolated nor assimilated disciples, but communities incorporated into the Spirit-filled Body of Christ. Our experiences with God are corporate, shared experiences, sustained by community.[14] Human life is always co-human. The corporate dimension of the church is fundamental also in the light of society in general. Her presence as mediator of grace is a necessary part of God's restoration of a world full of broken relationships.[15]

The church takes its root identity from a central category in the proclamation of Jesus: the coming near of God's kingdom in grace and power (Mark 1:15), but also in weakness and vulnerability (2 Cor 12:9–10). The church was not that kingdom in its full sense, but from the beginning she understood that she would include the outpouring of the Spirit, the inauguration of the world mission, and the formation of the end-time people. In accordance with the gospel narratives, Jesus envisaged a holistic liberation through forgiveness and rehabilitation of the whole person. It became evident through his sign activity that the kingdom of God was going to be realized. The faith community thus became a new social reality. Their legitimacy was not their worldly power, but the fact that God testified to their message of salvation "by signs, wonders and various miracles, and by gifts of the Holy Spirit, distributed according to his will" (Heb 2:4). These activities served as a pneumatological interpretation of the gospel (Mark 2:1–12).[16] Motivated by an understanding of God as a loving and relational person, the shared life within the congregation is an intrinsically social relationship. By sharing the glory of God (John 17:24–26), the church mirrors God's existence as triune community in a self-giving love. In this regard the church cannot be anything but an inclusive community of liberated humans, reconciled to God and to each other in a common calling to serve the world.[17] Reinhard Hütter argues that the church does not need to be demarcated by walls. More constructively, we can talk about her distinct identity as the public sphere of the Holy Spirit where her ground and telos are qualified by her core practices:

14. Pinnock, "Church in the Power," 150.

15. See Nicolas M. Healy, and particularly his presentation of an inclusivist ecclesiology which may help the church acting responsibly for the other and promote genuine particularity. Healy, *Practical-Prophetic Ecclesiology*, 129–53.

16. See Pinnock, "Interpretation of the Holy Scripture," 3–23.

17. Pinnock, "Church in the Power," 155.

> As the public of the Holy Spirit, the church is constituted not through "boundaries" but through a "center" that in the core practices (as proclamation, baptism, Eucharist etc.) creates "space" and "time" and is expressed authoritatively in doctrina. This center is of an utterly christological nature, and as such also does indeed demarcate the one 'boundary' the church never transcends.[18]

This is close to the position that the essence of the church, who she really is, may be termed by help of this statement: she is charismatically open-minded and sacramentally well-founded. Upon these two feet the church goes forward in the twenty-first century.[19]

Ecclesial Interpretations

The word *koinonia*, normally translated as fellowship, often means sharing together as a community which could include not only life but interests, decisions, or property. Lesslie Newbigin states that the church is, in the most exact sense, a common sharing in the Holy Spirit.[20] The many-sided nature of *koinonia* is seen in the apostolic writings (Acts 2:42-44; Gal 2:9; Phlm 1:5; Heb 10:25). A deeper comprehension of this conception is participation (1 Cor 1:9; Phlm 3:10; 1 Cor 10:16). To be a Christian is indeed to share one's life along with fellow believers in the communal life of Christ. A complementary way of understanding the church is to consider her as the body of Christ (1 Cor 12:12), wherein Christians are equal members through faith and baptism. In the Pauline letter to Ephesians, a drama of the Spirit and the body unfolds (Eph 1:21-22), reaching a climax where the reader is exhorted to practice the fellowship to which they are called (4:4-6). This in turn leads to the description of some important gifts and ministries (vv. 11-12) whose purpose is to equip members for ministry in order that the church may fulfill her goal (v. 13).

According to the position rendered in *BEM* of WCC from 1982, the concept of *koinonia* was a major, though not exclusive, ecclesiological category in the report responses coming from the churches worldwide.[21]

---

18. Hütter, *Suffering Divine Things*, 165.

19. Note the formulation of Jan-Olav Henriksen, stating that the church is constituted by those who participate in the community gathering around the promises present in the sacraments; thus linking together nature and church. Henriksen, *Live, Love & Hope*, 323.

20. Newbigin, *The Household of God*, 90.

21. Thurian, *Churches Responses*, vol. 1, 1-27.

The notion stems from the triune life of the Godhead (John 17:17; 1 John 1:2–10; 2 Pet 1:4; 1 Cor 1:9). The church participates in the gospel and in the apostolic faith, in suffering and in service (2 Cor 8:4). It is a life in Christ through baptism, (Rom 6:1–14; Gal 3:26–28) nurtured by the Eucharist (1 Cor 10–11). Each local community is related in *koinonia* with other Christian communities as a missionary fellowship sent to bear witness to God's love and solicitude for humans. The *koinonia* model is characterized by seeing the church a) as a gift of the word of God, b) as a mystery or sacrament of God's love for the world, c) as the pilgrim people of God, and d) as a prophetic sign of God's coming kingdom. Hence, the totality of the gospel constitutes the church.

Connected to the understanding of the church is the acknowledgement that none of us lives for ourselves alone (Rom 14:7). This is the experience and the belief lying behind the phrase "the communion of the Holy Spirit."[22] The latter phrase is used twice by Paul; once in the greeting of blessing to the Corinthians (2 Cor 13:13), and once in an appeal to the believing community in Philippi to pursue true unity in mind, heart, attitude, and action (Phlm 2:1–7). In these two passages, both fellowship and participation are used with respect to the Holy Spirit. The faith fellowship thus has divine roots in God's love, Christ's mind, and the fellowship of the Spirit. According to Paul, the risen Christ works through the Holy Spirit to mold the lives of Christians into being the medium of his own activity, the body of his risen life (1 Cor 6:19; 12:13; Rom 7:4–6; 8:11–12). Union with the risen Christ is union with all who are his members.[23] One can hardly imagine a better ecumenical incentive for the searching of visible unity.

Another image of the church is that of a spiritual house or temple (1 Cor 3:16). According to Paul, in Christ the whole building is joined together and rises to become "a holy temple in the Lord" (Eph 2:20–22, cf.1 Pet 2:4–5). Here the relationship to the Holy Spirit is readily expressed. The church as a temple is composed not of stones and wood as in the old covenant, but of ordinary lives of ordinary people, indwelt by the Holy Spirit. They are the people of God, the new covenant people, God's ecclesia. The local communities of Christians in any place are representing the one people of God (1 Cor 1:2; 1 Pet 2:9). The unity of Christians is basically that of a common spiritual birth and brotherhood, creating a people distinguished in the world by its call to holiness. So in all the many concepts Christians have called upon to describe *koinonia*—be it fellowship, participation, body,

---

22. Ramsey, *Holy Spirit*, 75.
23. Ibid., 77.

temple, or people of God—the Holy Spirit is the determining agent for both the sustaining and renewal of the church.[24]

The conspicuous lack of female voices in the doctrine of pneumatology and ecclesiology is unfortunately reflected in this work. Two exceptions are Cheryl M. Peterson and the Pentecostal Daniela S. Augustine. As an alternative to emphasizing church strategies and purpose—what the churches do—Peterson and Augustine wants to reclaim a theological understanding of who churches are, by focusing on their identity as fellowships created by the Spirit.[25] According to Peterson, ecclesiology begins from below as a web of social practices animated by the Spirit that define the church's agency as well as the church's identity. The activity of the Holy Spirit is grounded in the *missio Dei* (the mission of God) that gives the church her distinctive identity. The church finds her self-understanding in the fullness of the trinitarian God. Without ending in "a theology of glory" Peterson explores the church's story from the viewpoint of the Acts of the Apostles and the Pentecost narrative, showing that the Spirit and the church are utterly intertwined.[26]

In Accordance with Early Christian Thoughts

When reflecting about the church as the visible dwelling place of the Spirit, extensive insights can be drawn from certain formative periods of her history. One of our guides in that respect, Robert Louis Wilken, depicts some

---

24. In his book about the great changes in how to define the church in the contemporaneous in order to build revitalizing congregations, Eddie Gibbs proposes nine areas in which these changes and renewals are observed: from living in the past to engaging with the present, form being market driven to being mission oriented, from bureaucratic hierarchies to apostolic networks, from schooling professionals to mentoring leaders, from following celebrities to encountering saints, from holding dead orthodoxy to nurturing living faith, from attracting a crowd to seeking the lost, from belonging to believing, from generic congregations to incarnational communities. Gibbs, *Church Next*.

25. For a presentation, see Peterson, *Who is the Church?* The perspectives of the Pentecostal Daniela S. Augustine are reflected a couple of places in this work.

26. For an introduction of the ecumenical involvement in female ecclesiology, see Crawford, "Women and Ecclesiology." See also the important contribution of Dame Mary E. Tanner in: Tanner, "On Being Church." Tanner refers to Gen 1:27 and Gal 3:28 for biblical passages which encouraging a global exploration and conversation on women's ecclesial experiences. In her article she holds that within ecumenical study groups the question was not so much about the liberation of women, positions of power and authority, the issue of ordination and so on, but rather the strict theological question about a rediscovering of the feminine and inclusive images of God, which the Christian community as the church of solidarity really needs in light of her searching for wholeness and holiness. Ibid., 65.

patterns of Christian thinking as they took shape in the early church. His approach is that even though the believing community through the centuries has been a thinking fellowship, Christian theology may have been too preoccupied by formulating the faith along conceptual lines. Studies of Christian thinkers show that the main mission of the early church was to win the hearts and minds of men and women in order to change their lives.[27]

Early Christian thinkers appealed to a deep level of human existence and experience. "The Bible (. . .) poured forth treasures of words that created a new religious vocabulary and cornucopia of scenes and images that stirred literary and artistic imagination as well as theological thought," Wilken states.[28] The resurrection of Jesus was the overarching story and became the focal point of Christian devotion. Upon that miraculous event the church was founded. Christianity entered the historical scene not only as a messenger of love, reconciliation and hope, but as a community whose communal life reflected love, reconciliation and hope. The leaders in the early church were gifted thinkers. The vitality and imaginative power of their thoughts came from within, from the person of Christ, and from the biblical texts in their variety, abundance, and pluriformity. But they drew from sermons, liturgies, and practices as well. Christian thought developed through reflections about the means of grace, ministries, and virtues, from worship, arts, music, and from the life of the church.[29] The church's spirituality and her devotional practices became the well from which Christian thinking was nurtured. Thus, the early church gave us a broad tradition of gifted thinkers whose lives were interwoven with their thought.[30]

Concerning the pneumatic character of the church, the Eastern concept of the mystical communion (*communio sanctorum*) was more sophisticated in the Greek tradition than in West, because there the heritage of Late Platonic mysticism remained alive as a particular spiritual approach.[31] Cyril of Jerusalem (313-386) looked upon the church as a spiritual society. Cyril of Alexandria (378-444) emphasized the importance of unity in faith as the marker of the oneness of the church, while Theodore of Mopsuestia (ca. 350-428) described the union of believers and the constituting of

27. Wilken, *Early Christian Thought*.
28. Ibid., xiv-xv.
29. Ibid., xvi.
30. Throughout his book, Wilken turns consistently to four writers from the early church: Origen, living in the third century, Gregory of Nyssa in the fourth, Augustine in the fifth, and Maximus the Confessor in the seventh century. According to Wilken, these four are the most rewarding, the most profound, and the most enduring of the Christian thinkers, with Augustine at the summit. Ibid.
31. Evans, "Church in Early Christian Centuries," 29.

the body of Christ as a result of both water baptism and the action of the Spirit.[32] However, the mystical union was threatened by arguments about who was in and who was out of the community, and the common life was frequently disrupted by disagreements about details of shared practices and beliefs in the community.[33] But after all, the ancient church considered herself to be a vehicle and instrument of God's free-acting grace rather than as an institution.

Many of the early Christian thinkers were familiar with Greek and Roman philosophy and engaged comfortably with the prevalent intellectual thinking of their time. But they were also men of prayer, knowing Christ not as a historical memory or as a subject of doctrine, but through experience, made present in liturgy and worship. They continuously referenced the Bible and participated in the church's worship regularly and extensively. What they learned was confirmed by how they prayed. Accordingly, faithfulness was of greater value than originality for those theological intellectuals who also served as bishops, living with the believing community before their eyes.[34] They moved effortlessly between the study chamber and the sanctuary. Wilken writes:

> If we are to enter into the spirit of early Christian thinking, then, we must consider not only what early Christian thinkers thought but also what they did when they lifted up their minds and hearts to worship God, the Father, Son, and Holy Spirit.[35]

Here Wilken is indebted to Justin Martyr, who provides us with a detailed account of how the communion service was practiced in the second century. Though the following quotation is well known, it affords outstanding insight into early Christian worship. Observe not only the rhythm between the liturgical components, but also the values, priorities, and diaconal virtues within the faithful community. The description also gives us a glimpse of some ordained gifts of ministries, as well as the system of voluntary financial collection:

> On the day called Sunday all who live in the cities or in the country gather at one place and the memoirs of the apostles or the writings of the prophets are read as long as time permits. When

---

32. Swete, *Theodore of Mopsuestia*, 99–108.

33. For further insights in the diversity of the early church, see Kaufman, "Diverging Trajectories."

34. In *Against Heresies* 4.18.4–5, Irenaeus declares that his teaching is "consonant with what we do in the Eucharist and the celebration of the Eucharist establishes what we teach." The following description is based on chapter 2 of Wilken 2003.

35. Wilken, *Early Christian Thought*, 28.

the reader has finished, the one who is presiding instructs us in a brief discourse and exhorts us to imitate these noble things. Then we all stand up together and offer prayers for ourselves (. . .) and for all others everywhere (. . .). When we have finished the prayer, bread is brought forth, and wine and water, and the presiding minister offers up prayers and thanksgiving to the best of his ability, and the people assent, saying the Amen; after this the consecrated elements are distributed and received by each one. Then the deacon brings a portion to those who are absent. Those who prosper, and who so wish, contribute what each thinks fit. What is collected is deposited with the presiding minister who takes care of the orphans and widows, and those who are in need because of sickness or some other reason, and those who are imprisoned, and the strangers and sojourners among us.[36]

As suggested, the early Christian liturgy was a celebration of the presence of the living Christ, symbolized concretely in the Eucharist meal when the bishop prayed that the Holy Spirit would sanctify the elements that they might become the body and blood of Christ.[37] Another notable feature of early Christian thought is its distinctly narrative structure. The liturgy kept intact the biblical narratives, all the way from creation through the giving of the Law to the people of Israel, and on to include the coming of Christ, his death and resurrection, and his coming again. By recounting the story of Israel and Christ in ritual form, the liturgy confirmed the classic salvation story of a God who reveals Godself through historical events. But more than a pure recollection of ancient history is at work here. Early Christian thought is concerned with the remembrance of Christ's life-giving sufferings, as displayed in the second part of the Apostolic Creed. The Greek word *anamnesis* is usually translated as remembrance, to recall by making present, which carries a clear connotation of the Jewish Passover. To love is to remember, and to remember is to keep in living memory together with all those who are alive in Christ everywhere and at all time.[38] Wilken writes:

---

36. *Apology*, 61, 65–67, in ibid., 28–29.

37. See *The Apostolic Tradition* of Hippolytos, a book with prayers for the Eucharist, baptism and ordination, reflecting the practice in Rome at the end of the second century. The prayer connected to the Lord's Supper finishes with an invocation of the Holy Spirit: "We pray that you would send your Holy Spirit upon the offerings of your holy church." Bradshaw et al., *Apostolic Tradition*, 40–41. In the new liturgy of Church of Norway, the *epiclesis* (the invocation of the Holy Spirit) is part of the various Eucharist prayers. One version sounds like this: "We pray: Send over us your Spirit and your gifts so that we may receive Jesus Christ in the bread and the wine." *Gudstjeneste for Den norske kirke*, 2.71.

38. Tarasar, "Worship, Spirituality and Biblical Reflection," 220.

> Remembrance is more than mental recall, and in the Eucharist the life-giving events of Christ's death and Resurrection escape the restriction of time and become what the early church called mysteries, ritual actions by which Christ's saving work is represented under the veil of the consecrated bread and wine. (. . .) What was once accomplished in Palestine is now made present in the action of the liturgy. (. . .) Liturgy is always in the present tense. The past becomes a present presence that opens a new feature.[39]

The repeated and celebrated elements of the service brought the participants into a relationship with Christ built not on a historical memory but on the fact of experience. This is an inspiration for churches of today not only to seek the sacrament of baptism, but to encourage the whole congregation to take part in the Eucharist meal. Related to this, Wilken states:

> Before there were treatises on the Trinity, before there were learned commentaries on the Bible, before there were disputes about the teaching on grace, or essays on the moral life, there was awe and adoration before the exalted Son of God alive and present in the church's offering of the Eucharist. This truth preceded every effort to understand and nourished every attempt to express in words and concepts what Christians believed.[40]

From its inception, Christianity has been anchored in elements that accompany daily life. By apprenticing themselves to the church's inner life, the bishops acquired fluency in the church's language, discovered the implications of biblical images by trafficking in a world of things that could be seen and touched, and learned that what they taught had to do not only with words and ideas but palpable realities.[41] It appears that the early Christians had a strong feeling of being a community made by the Spirit, despite what we can observe of a radical discontinuity.[42] Some scholars talks about the first century as a period of wandering-charismatics. In the absence of established ecclesiastical structures, Spirit-led teachers, apostles, and prophets travelled around, encouraging the churches by using their gifts in ministry but instructing the assemblies to follow severe instructions. The sense of being a *koinonia*-oriented community among the first Christians was so pronounced that they addressed each other by using familial terms (Matt

---

39. Wilken, *Early Christian Thought*, 34.
40. Ibid., 36.
41. Ibid., 42.
42. *Didaché*, chapter 11. See also Milavec, *The Didache*.

28:10; John 20:17; Luke 22:32).⁴³ The main substance that contemporary churches share with primitive Christianity is the desire to gather around the teaching of Christ and to share the good news of his death and resurrection. The sharing of table fellowship and the practice of baptism found their roots in the life and ministry of Jesus (Matt 28:19; John 3:22–26; Acts 2:38–41) and represented the pneumatologically oriented center of the earliest communities.⁴⁴

In any case, the theological foundation of the doctrine of the church must be understood and defined in pneumatological categories as a lived reality. Long before her outward structures were fixed, the church had already emerged as a diverse and living fellowship.

A Story of God's Action

The notion that the church is Spirit-driven makes this fellowship truly a living tradition, because of the vertical dimension of the church.⁴⁵ This living tradition is the center for the transmission of the message of the fourfold gospel, for the preservation of core practices and for the continuing interpretation of faith. There are rich possibilities for doctrinal development when we consider the church not just as an agent for the gospel but also as part of the gospel story itself. As the temple of the Spirit, the church eucharistically bears the presence of Christ. She is a dynamic event in the world, an ongoing action of the Spirit.

As will become evident through this work, the church is influenced by the regulative teaching by which the Spirit links the gospel events past and the gospel events yet to come with the gospel event of the present, in

---

43. Among the most utilized descriptions are brothers and sisters (Acts 11:29), saints (Rom 12:13), disciples (Matt 9:19), Christians (Acts 11:26), the Way (Acts 24:14), the body of Christ (1 Cor 12:27), priesthood (1 Pet 2:5), the elected (1 Pet 2:9), and the household of God (1 Tim 3:15). It appears that the early Christians were fumbling to find words and images to describe themselves both internally and externally. On the other side, the great variety of names implies a surprising well-articulated diversity. As such, it indicates remarkably non-uniformed stage of church history.

44. In his attempt to reconstruct the different elements in the worship of the early church, J. T. Burtchaell, suggests that the Lord's Supper was *the* central moment in the church service. Burtchaell, *From Synagogue to Church*, 282.

45. Chan clearly states that worship practices and the gospel keeps doctrine alive, while the theologians reflects on those practices in line with doctrinal norms and reappropriate them in new contexts. To do that in a proper way, theologians need to be accountable to the church by being part of the worshipping community. They cannot operate as only consultants to the church. Chan, "Church and Doctrine," 67–72.

which she exists as a contemporary reality.[46] Or said in another way, the development of doctrine within the framework of the whole church can be understood as the progression of a plot, an ongoing story of God's action in the world. The story of the church is in fact the story of the Spirit *within* her. The gospel in its actual content is fixed, though in a pluriform way through the different NT sources. But the whole story to tell is not yet finished. Through ecclesiology and pneumatology, the gospel story continues. In all likelihood, the best time for the church worldwide is yet to come. Chan declares:

> We must maintain that ecclesiology is an intrinsic part of the doctrine of the gospel of Jesus Christ, not an administrative arrangement for the sake of securing practical results. The story of the Church is what it is because it is the story of the Spirit who constitutes it. Ecclesiology and pneumatology, therefore, cannot be separated, as can be seen in the way Spirit and Church are linked in the third article of the Nicene-Constantinopolitan Creed.[47]

The creedal marks of the church function as an expression of the pneumatological nature of the church. She is one because she is united to Christ, the head, by the one Spirit who indwells her. She is holy because she is the temple indwelt by the Spirit, and she is apostolic because the Spirit guides her into all truth and to the teaching of the apostles in an unbroken succession. The Spirit's relationship to the church is what marks the distinctive role of the Spirit in the triune economy of salvation.[48] From the Day of Pentecost, the third person of the Trinity took an ecclesial form and was revealed as divine presence (John 16:13–15).

In a similar manner, Lesslie Newbigin writes that the church is the company of people whom it has pleased God to call into the fellowship of the Godhead's Son. It is not segregation but congregation, and the power by which she is constituted is no less than the work of the Spirit.[49] In addition

---

46. Ibid., 73.

47. Ibid.

48. Regarding the prospect of an ecumenical dogma on the church, Chan regrets that the twin dogmas of the Spirit and of the church have remained unelaborated in the ecumenical creeds. However, here Chan seems to underrate different dialogue reports and present ecumenical documents. Contrary to the position of Chan, I consider new ecumenical texts to be quite promising. Pneumatology and ecclesiology, and the link between them, has become an integrated element in the church conversations within WCC/Faith and Order and other ecumenical bodies. See the two documents from World Council og Churches, "The Church: Towards a Common Vision," and "Together Towards Life."

49. In Weston, *Lesslie Newbigin*, 128. See also Newbigin's statement that what the

to the narrative of creation, fall, redemption, and consummation, Karl Inge Tangen contends that early Pentecostalism was driven by a specific vision of being a Spirit-embowered church.[50] This vision manifests as gratitude expressed in the practice of worship, in love, and in witnessing to God's deeds. As a worshipping, witnessing, forming, and reflective whole, she is committed to God's vision of humanity and of a transformed world.[51]

Among the elements discovered in my investigation, is the fact that theology is perceived as the discerning reflection upon the living reality of divine-human relations. From the time of Wesley's field preaching, worship and daily life gave experiential validity to theology.[52] We might think of the church as a garden in which walking by the Spirit cultivates Christ-like transformation (Gal 5:16). Steven Land writes about this fellowship as discerning participation:

> The church is a communion of diversity and unity in the Spirit. Just as God is one in three so the church is one and many in God. The church as eschatological trinitarian fellowship is a communion in God—a people of God, a body of Christ and thus a communion in the Holy Spirit. What is fellowship but participation? In this fellowship, gift and office should coincide and theology should be the discerning reflection of the whole as each offers his or her gift, recognizes the other's gifts and is built up to disciple and love the neighbor.[53]

Obviously, he is inspired by the writings of Paul. The graceful relationship to the Trinity provides the fruit of the Spirit, visible as love, joy, peace, patience, kindness, generosity, faithfulness, gentleness, and self-control (Gal 5:22–23). Being part of the church is being part of one another, as we all are part of the body of Christ. Through baptism, Paul says, we are baptized in the one Spirit so as to form one body (1 Cor 12:13).

An Ecclesiology in the Concrete

In our reflections on the church as a dwelling place for the Spirit of God, we may ask: How is the life and ministry of the Spirit to be understood in light

---

Lᴏʀᴅ left behind Him was not a book, nor a creed, nor a system of thought, nor a rule of life, but a visible community. Newbigin, *The Household of God*, 27.

50. Tangen, *Ecclesial Identification*, 8.
51. Ibid., 9.
52. Land, *Pentecostal Spirituality*, 34.
53. Land, "Passion for the Kingdom," 38.

of God's redemptive purposes in the world? One answer is that the church brings about an encounter with the Spirit of God, living in the midst of a people who are created and formed into a unique, but vulnerable, community.[54] However, we may also observe a growing emphasis on making the ministry of the church responsive to a continuously changing context, confronted by the complexities of modern life and the emerging postmodern culture. This approach proceeds from the temptation to view a church's ministry as functional, defining her primarily in terms of what she does. But a pure functional approach leaves unaddressed basic questions about the nature of the church. Her nature is always deeper than her functions and structures.[55]

Even if the church of tomorrow needs to be culturally relevant and organizationally sound, a thorough understanding of her nature must be grounded in extensive theological consideration before it turns to social sciences.[56] The church is a spiritual communion that has a social structure.[57] The question is whether the church is able to carry out a ministry consistent with her inner nature. So in order to stimulate the development of the church, she needs to be empowered to be what she is called to be and do what she is called to do.[58] My reflection is that to a certain degree the church does what she is when she knows who she is.

In order to situate myself within the discussion of how to eschew a triumphalistic attitude in depicting the church, I turn to the writings of Nicholas M. Healy. He proposes an ecclesiology that is practical and prophetic in orientation. What we say about the church will be said primarily in order to make a case for how to do ecclesiology.[59] Tracing this aspect, Healy considers the context of ecclesiology to be everything that affects the life and the

---

54. Van Gelder, *Essence of the Church*, 11–15.

55. Examples of functional approaches are so-called seeker-sensitive churches, purpose-driven churches, user-friendly churches, seven-day-a-week churches, small-group-churches, and so on. On the other hand, there is a similar focus on the organizational structure of the church, diagnosing weaknesses and restructuring decision-making processes, informed by different organizational theories. These inclinations to treat the church in functional, sociological, or organizational terms may reduce the church to a set of human activities and ministries administered through management skills for maintaining effectiveness, or to an organization designed to accomplish certain instrumental oriented goals. The church is always more than this. Ibid., 21–23.

56. For alternative ecclesiological perspectives launched recently, see Belcher, *Deep Church*, and Nikolajsen, *Identity of the Church*.

57. Congar, *Word and Spirit*, 55.

58. This normative definition of church development is given by Harald Hegstad in: Birkedal et al., *Menighetsutvikling i folkekirken*, 12.

59. Healy, *Practical-Prophetic Ecclesiology*, 1.

work of the church. Thus the purpose for ecclesiology is to help the church respond to this context in an appropriate way by reflecting theologically and critically upon her concrete identity and effectiveness. The preference for describing the church in her historical and concrete shape are related to a concern for developing ecclesiology into a social practice that reflects theo-dramatically upon the church's concrete identity.[60] The theological aspects of the church, including the presence of the Holy Spirit, are constitutive of the concrete religious body. This by no means intends to invalidate different theoretical approaches to the question of what a church is. In her great pluriformity, the church is always more than we are able to observe in the visible. There may be many possible definitions yet to be realized.

As Healy describes, the church is a distinctive way of life made possible by the gracious action of the Spirit.[61] Together with Hans Urs von Balthasar, Healy argues for an image of the church that is fully constituted by both divine and human agency. That permits theological reflections upon the concrete church, including the formation of the individual Christian's distinctive identity. Her identity is constituted both by the activity of the Holy Spirit and by the activity of her members when they live their life as agents of hope and charity. Healy writes:

> It is therefore not enough to discuss our ecclesial activity solely in terms of its dependent relation upon the work of the Holy Spirit. The identity of the concrete church is not simply given; it is constructed and ever reconstructed by the grace-enabled activities of its members as they embody the church's practices, belief and valuations.[62]

From this, it follows that the church is called to bear witness to God's formation of a covenant people of disciples through Christ (2 Cor 3:6; 16–18). However, if it were to be shown that following Christ within the communal life of the church is impossible, she would be blamed for deception. That is why Gregory Jones, referenced by Healy, argues that true discipleship involves practices that testify to the costliness of what God has done for us in the Spirit, as well as practices that confess our failures and embody our need for individual and corporate forgiveness.[63] The implications of this insight offer a revision of the "blueprint" ecclesiologies of more idealistic definitions of the church, which result in abstract reflections severed from

---

60. Ibid., 22.
61. Ibid., 4–5.
62. Ibid., 5.
63. Ibid., 14. See Jones, *Embodying Forgiveness*, xii.

her concrete historical identity.[64] A more heuristically oriented definition of the church is given by Joseph A. Komonchak, who describes the object of ecclesiology as the set (or sets) of experiences, understandings, symbols, words, judgments, statements, decisions, actions, relationships, and institutions which distinguish the group of people called the church.[65] This is an effort to construct an ecclesiology on the basis of a concrete anthropology. The starting point for a church in the concrete is the actual persons, socially and culturally located, subjected to sin and open for healing from above.

This approach situates the church's identity in her factual location, grounded in concrete narratives.[66] This narrative is not so much her doctrine or distinctive theological character as compared to other churches, but her history more generally, and the reflections about her contextual and confessional identity based on that particular history. In this respect, the narratives demand more than simply telling the history of the church. They require judgments to be made about that history. Such a story is about transitions as much as it is about traditions. Theological and sociological constructions, judgments and critiques are integrally related. Shane Clifton asserts that theological assessment will take into account the ecclesially constitutive elements generally addressed in ecclesiological analysis. It includes appropriation of Scripture, charismatic orientation, structures and authorities, and the missionary mandate, together with elements important to specific communities. But because the church is a human institution which interacts with society, ecclesiology will need to appropriate the social sciences in order to properly understand its object.[67]

Sociological studies have conceptualized the interaction between individual intentionality and symbolically mediated values of society using five categories: vital, social, cultural, personal, and religious values.[68] This set of values may function as a useful heuristic tool to describe the dimensions of a church. A hallmark of a church is her religious values, mediated by God's grace, which are understood to facilitate personal integrity. The cultural values within a church are influenced by more transcendent values, while biblical motifs and metaphors form her ecclesiological understanding and missionary nature.

However, we cannot fully grasp the identity of the church without addressing the reality of sin. A church permeated by grace is still a human

---

64. Healy, *Practical-Prophetic Ecclesiology*, 26.
65. Komonchak, *Foundations*, 57.
66. Clifton, "Pentecostal Ecclesiology," 218.
67. Ibid., 219.
68. Doran, *Theology and Dialectics*, 94.

institution and subject to destructive forces. Religious values may be distorted, individuals transgress, the culture can become inauthentic, and the church may ignore groups in need of attention.[69] The reality of sin is essential to acknowledge if we are to understand the church in her contingency and honesty. So despite her dependence upon the Spirit, the church activity is at times sinful. The eschatological "not yet" reminds her members that as imperfect people, they constitute an imperfect church (cf. the phrase *ecclesia semper reformanda;* the church is always in need of being reformed).

In Paul's letter to the Corinthians, the members of the church were characterized as "those who are sanctified in Christ Jesus" and "called to be his saints" (1 Cor 1:2), although the church evidently was judged because of the many divisions among the leaders (1 Cor 1:10–13). They were still of the flesh (3:3), there was jealousy and quarreling among them (v. 3), and they were acting like merely humans (v. 4). They were accused of destroying God's temple (v. 17), and of arrogance and boasting (4:18; 5:6). They were called to account for sexual immorality of a kind that even pagans did not tolerate (5:1), and for being proud of that (v. 2). In all this, Christ had become divided among them (1:13). Christ is not only the LORD of the churches; he is also their Judge. However, through all this they were still unmistakably identified as the church of God in Corinth (1 Cor 1:1).

With Paul, we may consider the church part of the problem as well as part of the solution. She is part of the problem if she gives the impression of knowing all the answers and possessing all the power and glory. "To glory in anything other than Jesus Christ crucified can result in idolatry, or, if one glories in something of which one is a part, is sinful pride," Healy contends (Gal 6:14).[70] Prideful exclusivity in the church is an obstacle to the activity of the Spirit. God works through those who are humble and vulnerable (1 Cor 1:28). Christ alone has become our wisdom, righteousness, holiness, and redemption (v. 30). Constructive criticism of the church is a legitimate part of our concern for her well-being in the world.

When a specific church is referred to in a rather exclusive and triumphalistic way, one has to realize that salvation is not limited to the church, just as God is not dependent on a particular church. To be honest, there have been times when the church has acted in ways that perhaps have complicated the door of salvation. Furthermore, Christ reveals himself even in places outside the church (see Matt 25:34–36; cf. Joel 2:28–29). This requires us to

---

69. Healy, "Church in Modern Theology," 37. Healy observes that in the blueprint approach to church identity, the sinfulness can be considered as an insignificant distortion of the church's abiding fundamental reality, rather than an ever-present aspect of her concrete identity.

70. Healy, *Practical-Prophetic Ecclesiology*, 12.

differentiate between the church's uniqueness and the notion of the church's superiority. Her "superiority" can only be rightly understood in light of her uniqueness. The presence of the Spirit is not restricted to the church in any exclusive way. Yet the church enjoys a unique Spirit-empowered orientation to Christ and to the Triune God.[71] It is her specific christological orientation, together with her specific confession (Matt 16:16), that makes the church unique. The claim to superiority is never about the church but about that which she is witnessing: the crucified and resurrected Christ.

The Grace of God at Work

By this modest adaptation, we can define the church as the community where the grace of God is at work by the influence of the Spirit. Through the healing of the wounded and the transformation of humans she acts as a sign, steward, and instrument of God's design. Using this logic, we can now address the distinctiveness of the church. The church derives her identity from what she has received, and from her agency as a sacrament for God's saving work. In a dialogue between Lutherans and Methodists, a mutually satisfying agreement was achieved by the following text: "The church is the community of Jesus Christ called into being by the Holy Spirit. Those who respond in faith to the gospel of Christ, proclaimed in word and sacrament, are brought into a new relationship with God and with one another."[72] However, the tendencies to give idealized accounts of the church may be problematic, since there seems to be a plurality of ways of talking about her within the New Testament itself.[73] Rather than talking about definitive *models*, we are presented with a variety of imaginative visions of who the church is.[74] Healy writes:

> If different perspectives on the church are necessary as well as permissible, then not only are claims for a supermodel unwarrantable, the very search for them unwarrantably contracts our ecclesiological horizons. Models should instead be used to discover and explore imaginatively the many facets of the Christian church.[75]

---

71. Healy, *Practical-Prophetic Ecclesiology*, 17.

72. The dialogue between the Lutheran World Federation and the World Methodist Council resulted in 1984 in the document called "The Church: Community of Grace."

73. See different models presented in Brown, *Churches the Apostles Left Behind*.

74. Peterson, *Who is the Church?*

75. Healy, *Practical-Prophetic Ecclesiology*, 36.

This imaginative exploring emerges from the writings of Paul. His theology about the church is grounded on two insights. Firstly, that the salvation of people comes through the saving power of the resurrection of Christ (Rom 1:4). Secondly, that this is effected through the proclamation of the gospel and by baptism of the faithful into Christ's body, the church. By using the metaphor of the body, Paul privileges the nature of Christian life, spiritual coexistence, and the interdependence of all members of the community (Eph 4:1–6).

The first generation of Christians established bonds of community with one another and with God through the celebration of the Eucharist, understood both as a sacred meal and as a contribution to the community's common memory (1 Cor 11:23–29).[76] As a result of the baptismal initiation into this mystical participation in Christ's salvation story, their ecclesiological consciousness arose gradually because of the work of Spirit through the sacramental activities. The church is not only an accumulation of individuals but a new relational reality that confers identity upon those who enters into its life.[77] The Greek term *ekklēsia* indicates the same: a condition of being called out by the power of the Spirit in order to be part of the community of believers.

As a fellowship of the Spirit, the church is located where the Spirit is present by virtue of the communicated Word of God, the spiritual gifts, and the sacraments.[78] Because God is an operational verb through the presence of the Spirit, both charismatic and sacramental distinctives are natural features of the fellowship's response to God's incarnated reality. Given the fact that the church is a gifted and discerning community, the so-called preternatural elements (charismatic gifts, intersession, the laying on of hands, anointing, healing, worship, etc.) are more natural than often supposed. They are genuine expressions of the fact that nobody owns the church but the LORD (Jas 5:13–20; Matt 16:18). And what often is perceived as more ordinary sections of the liturgy (confession, kyrie, Word of God, creeds, prayers, and benediction) are as spiritual as the former, shaped over the centuries and given life by the Spirit (Col 3:15–17).

---

76. Gaillardetz, *Global Church*, 20.

77. Ibid., 22.

78. According to Hippolytos and *The Apostolic Tradition*, the members of the church shall be zealous to go to the church, because there is the place where the Spirit flourishes. Bradshaw et al., *Apostolic Tradition*, 178.

Shaped by Narratives and Judged by Discernment

The Bible tells stories. Personal identities are formed by life stories great and small. The very consciousness of being a Spirit-led church takes narrative shape through the story of God's work for the salvation of humans. When it comes to defining communal identities, personal identities are embedded in the stories that are shared by the members of a community.[79] Christian communities are both formed and informed by these stories, and they respond in accordance with their own values and self-understanding.[80]

Amos Yong refers to communitarian ethicists who have sought to retrieve the category of narratives: "One might describe this central focus on local stories, indigenous narratives, and communal traditions as representing the reaction of the postmodern mind against the hegemony of Enlightenment values such as universality, abstraction, and fact."[81] The account of Jesus' life, learnings, and attitudes serve to shape the identity and the activities of the church. Yong continues, "the given datum of the gospel narratives is thereby transposed through the act of imagination such that they serve to symbolize just who it is we are and what it is we are about."[82] This teaching serves as a guide for shaping contemporary attitudes for the church towards topics such as gender relationships, peace-making, forgiveness, and reconciliation.[83]

These formative narratives contribute to the church's identity and her ethical character. Biblical narratives and church traditions are told and retold because they mediate a soteriological experience, recognized in our daily life. These stories then become the source for our theological reflection, which serves to transform the believing community to live according to her conviction. In the Book of Acts, the narratives of Luke verify the pneumatological conditioning of the church. He bears witness to the Spirit transforming a collective of individuals into the living communion of the believers. Gaillardetz writes:

> Without this pneumatological dimension, there is a danger of the concept of communion degenerating to secular conceptions

---

79. Yong, *Spirit-Word-Community*, 277.
80. Hauerwas, *Character and Christian Life*. Hauerwas, *Community of Character*.
81. Yong, *Spirit-Word-Community*, 279.
82. Ibid.
83. Ibid., 285. Anthony Thiselton operates with a similar concept when presenting his hermeneutics of hope, which aim to grasp the transformative power of theological interpretation while avoiding rigid objectivity or rank subjectivity. The position derives from the communicative acts of Scripture, declarations, proclamations, appointment, commands, worship, and promise. Thiselton, "Communicative Action," 222.

that ignore the way the believer is configured in communion with other believers and with God. Luke's pneumatological perspective provides him with a more universal scope in his presentation of Jesus' mission. It is the power of the Spirit that allows the message of Jesus to transcend its Jewish context, and it is the Spirit that impels the church outward to bring the gospel to the world.[84]

This community of brothers and sisters has become a fraternity (*adelphos*), a spiritual house, a royal priesthood, and God's people who has received mercy (1 Pet 2:4–10). These images of the church create a communal identity not attached to kinship or ethnicity (Mark 3:31–35) but to the spiritual bond established through discipleship and a common vocation marked by the cross (1 Cor 1:18; Gal 6:14). The spiritual character of the church is confirmed in the narratives of Acts, specifically the story of the Pentecost event (Acts 2), as will be emphasized in the coming chapter. The dramatic outbreak of the Holy Spirit followed by the promise of an outpouring of the Spirit on all people (v. 17) suggests an essential ecclesiological principle: the Holy Spirit does not erase difference but renders difference non-divisive. Since the church is born and driven by the Spirit of God, it is from its beginning open to diverse languages and cultures.[85] It is a concrete church which, as Healy says, living in and for the world, performs its tasks of witness and discipleship within particular, ever-shifting contexts.[86]

Seeing the church like this corresponds with the idea of church as an event. The church is a gathering of believers in which the gospel is purely preached and the sacraments are administered according to the gospel, as stated in *Confessio Augustana* (§ 7).[87] This view of the church, focusing upon concrete practices rather than upon structures, has the advantage of allowing for repeated adjusting. Its emphasis is on the contingent aspects of church's being in the world. She becomes visible in her concreteness and thereby in her need of God's grace and Spirit, through the elements and gifts at work during the service.

The attractiveness of an ecclesiology that sees the church as a sacramental banquet open to the world, resides in its perception of the inviting character of the gospel and the welcoming nature of the church. Gradually, the receiving community becomes part of a reflecting and communicating community. What she reflects and communicates, however, is not the

---

84. Gaillardetz, *Global Church*, 24.
85. Ibid., 38.
86. Healy, *Practical-Prophetic Ecclesiology*, 39.
87. Tappert, *Book of Concord*, 32.

church but Christ and his gift of grace. The result is a practice-oriented spirituality, based on the faithfulness of God, through whom we were called into fellowship with his son, Jesus Christ our LORD (1 Cor. 1:9). The character of the church transcends social or political networks. It is a fellowship beyond any borders; a unity that does not undermine the colorful diversity of the global Christianity.

In the time of the New Testament, the question of belonging was not restricted to a technical question about certain models of membership. For Paul, fellowship was a question of functional character. Everybody has to find his or her place as a limb on the Body of Christ, according to gifts given by the Spirit (1 Cor 12–14). The universal dimension is obvious: no church traditions ought to regard themselves as exclusive of or isolated from other churches that share the same firm belief in Christ. This all-encompassing feature of the church transcends any narrow particularity and corresponds with her open, welcoming, and dialogical character. As a fellowship of inclusive grace, there is room for everyone who wants to belong to Christ in confidence and faith.[88] Yet the event character of the church exists within and is formed by the concrete contexts of time and place.

These various contexts consist of all that bears upon and contributes to the shape of the church's embodiment: her own history and background, social status of her members, theological profile and character, networks, ecumenical approach, styles of worship, etc. The construal of one's ecclesiology is also influenced by the theological imagination within the leadership and how a distinct community understands itself in light of church history in general and her present culture specifically. Normally the leadership constructs imaginaries and develops these interpretive narratives as their answer to the theological and ecclesiological resources and obstacles within their particular horizon.

Of course, this calls for distinct elements of discernment. The Spirit as giver and distributer knows what is for the common good (1 Cor 12:7; cf. Phil 1:9). Therefore, through the Spirit "someone is given the utterance of wisdom, and to another the utterance of knowledge according to the same Spirit," and "to another the discernment of spirits" (vv. 8–10). Paul assures the congregation of Corinth that all these are the work of one and the same Spirit, and he distributes them to each one, just as he determines (v. 11). In his final instructions Paul urges to the congregation of Thessalonians not to quench the Spirit. The prophecies shall not be treated with contempt but

---

88. For further reflections about a Trinitarian theology of love and grace, see Yong, *Spirit of Love*, 147–64.

rather become tested. Afterwards, you have to hold on to what is good (1 Thess 5:19–21; see also 1 Cor 14:39–40).

Those examples from Paul are grounded in his conviction that the members of the congregation were being built together into a dwelling in which God lives by his Spirit (Eph 2: 22). This should not be a place for charismatic chaos and triumphalistic individualism, as was the case in Corinth. It was necessary to develop corporately beneficial structures with order and mutual respect, balanced by the gifting of individuals. A Spirit-driven church does not mean there is no place for office. Church structures can be seen as gifts from the Spirit as well. From the time of the early church there were regular ministries that served the community consistently using various gifts of guidance (1 Cor 12:28). A well-informed ecclesiology takes for granted that any pattern of collective behavior that becomes habitual will also be in need of institutional structure. However, the institutional dimension must be functional and accommodated to its proper goal. Though the Spirit is far more fundamental for the church than her structures, all contemporary communities open to the influence of the Spirit are dependent on workable structures that are culturally viable and temporally flexible.[89]

Authenticity and Apostolicity

A central aspect of the church's existence is the issue of episcopacy and authenticity, as well as of the apostolicity of the church. At its foundations, the church is birthed and sustained by the power of the gospel and the genuine revelation of Christ (Acts 4:12). But in another sense she is a political society, a sphere of visible human fellowship with a specific calling and shared life. Official patterns of ministries have emerged by virtue of the self-organizing power of the gospel. In accordance with the writings of Webster, I agree that office as such does not usurp the work of Christ and the Spirit as long as the task of overseeing preserves the overarching unity and apostolic authenticity of the testimony of the church.[90]

Thus, every ministry is bound directly to the church's identity in the gospel. In the deepest sense there is only one overseer of the church, Christ himself (1 Pet 2:25), which makes episcopacy contingent and relative to the headship of God (Eph 4:15). Admittedly, the role of the overseer's ministry is ostensive. Without the consciousness of these limitations, Christ would be pushed into inactive transcendence, and the Spirit would be reduced to simply the immanent animating power of an institution, according to

---

89. Hütter, *Suffering Divine Things*, xiv.
90. Webster, "Episcopacy and Community Formation," 187.

Webster.[91] The oneness of the church becomes visible when the episcopacy points away from itself, directing its own attention towards Christ and towards the unity which is already given by the proclamation of the gospel through word and sacrament.[92] The episcopate publicly serves, represents, and testifies to that unity. This function is undertaken in a variety of ways within different church traditions. However, this apostolic unity is a theological statement inasmuch as the body of Christ is one, filled with one Spirit, confessing one hope, one LORD, one faith, one baptism, and one God (Eph 4:4–6). The need for a ministry of unity seems to be uncontested from a broad range of church traditions within Christianity.

From an ecclesiological point of view, this introduces a broader understanding of apostolic succession. Roman Catholics consider the apostolicity of the church in terms of historical succession, while Protestants have aimed to restore apostolic doctrine. But the Free Church movement has been preoccupied with recovering the apostolic *mission*. As an element of the marks which defines the church essence, apostolicity must be anchored to the whole spiritual life of the church. It is a dimension to be fulfilled ever anew in history. All Christians have the Spirit and as such they all are a royal priesthood (1 Pet 2:9). Thus we hear their witness, believe their message, and imitate their work in the same spirit of the historical apostles. Thus the church continuously becomes an apostolic community (Eph 2:19–22). This does not depend upon pure historical preconditions, but on her present expression and operation.

In this respect, the overseer is by no means in possession of something other than the truth of the gospel.[93] A leader forms a congregation in a proper way only to the extent that she or he already has been formed by Christ's revelation of God. The question of unity and leadership is close related to the issue of apostolicity.[94] This has less to do with transmission than with identity and authenticity. Leaders must expect to be met with critical evaluation of whether they give an authentic account of the church's teaching and mission. Episcopal office is not a condensed form of apostolicity. The ministry presides over the event in which the church becomes apostolic by consenting to the apostolic gospel of the resurrection, and gives itself to the apostolic mission of proclamation and service.[95] It is the church who has the apostolic character and the superior mandate. A minister may

---

91. Ibid., 189.
92. Ibid.
93. Ibid., 190.
94. Ibid.
95. Ibid., 191.

have an apostolic task, but it is based upon the church's calling, apostolicity, sanctification, and her empowerment to know, to live, and to speak the gospel. A church is given the freedom to order her ministerial life appropriately in light of her calling and mandate: that in every circumstance, the gospel must be proclaimed and God must be adored. Here the understanding of apostolicity deserves a reflection.

Christian tradition identifies four marks of the church in the creeds: oneness, holiness, apostolicity, and catholicity. The latter mark is the subject of continuous debate between different church traditions, and it needs to be discussed in light of the gospel rather than of the succession. In the eyes of the Roman Catholic and Orthodox churches, Free Church ecclesiology normally represents the quintessence of what is *not* apostolic. However, it is appropriate to look a little bit closer to the term "apostolic." Is it possible that apostolic church ministry legitimately may take several forms? In his overview of various theological traditions and denominations, Charles J. Conniry presents several major views of apostolicity, which he considers complementary. *Ecclesial* apostolicity emphasizes apostolicity as a means of establishing the institutional authority of the church. *Biblical* apostolicity tries to identify the apostolic character of the church in order to define a norm by which the legitimacy of subsequent accretions is determined. *Pneumatic* apostolicity appeals to the charismatic nature of the church and the ongoing work of the Spirit, in line with the first century of the church's history. By this perspective, apostleship is a charisma of the Spirit. *Kerygmatic* apostolicity sees the church's apostolic character actualized in the faithful pursuit of its mission, so apostolicity is understood in light of the church's missional nature.[96]

Thus the question of apostolicity cannot be reduced to a matter of succession in office or apostolic succession. Kärkkäinen identifies the following six facets of apostolicity that should be broadly affirmed among Christians: 1) Apostolicity involves continuity with the life and the faith of the apostolic church and the New Testament. 2) Pneumatological and charismatic life and worship are an essential part of apostolicity. 3) Mission and the proclamation of the gospel are an indistinguishable aspect of apostolicity. 4) The Scriptures of the New Testament are themselves apostolic and give the norms of apostolicity. 5) Apostolicity is a dynamic concept. It is not only or primarily a question of juridics but a question of life and vitality, of obedience, service, and everyday discipleship. 6) Apostolicity concerns the whole people of God, not only the clergy.[97] These various aspects are

---

96. Conniry, "Apostolic Christianity," 247–48.
97. Kärkkäinen, "Pentecostals and Apostolicity," 63.

also summarized in the old Christian treatise called *The Apostolic Tradition*, followed up in *BEM*. The following refers to the Creed where the church is confessed to be apostolic:

> The Church lives in continuity with the apostles and their proclamations. The same LORD who sent the apostles continues to be present in the Church. The Spirit keeps the Church in the apostolic tradition until the fulfillment of history in the Kingdom of God. Apostolic tradition in the Church means continuity in the permanent characteristics of the Church of the apostles; witness to the apostolic faith, proclamation and fresh interpretation of the Gospel, celebration of baptism and Eucharist, the transmission of ministerial responsibilities, communion in prayer, love, joy and suffering, service to the sick and the needy, unity among the local churches, and sharing the gifts which the LORD has given to each.[98]

The concept of apostolicity in the New Testament is already pneumatologically and charismatically loaded. This is evident in the birth of the church at the outpouring of the Spirit on the Day of Pentecost and in the apostles' ministry in and through the Spirit (Acts 1:8; 2:4; 4:8; 6:5; 11:12, 15; 20:22, 28). According to 1 Cor 12:28, ministry is itself a charism. The apostles were church-founding charismatics and their ministries were made visible, among other aspects, by their healing activities (Mark 16:12–13).[99] Hence, seeking an ecumenical consensus of apostolicity that includes charismatic expression, means continuity with the spirituality and faith of the church, given in the apostolic writings.

This continuity may be ascertained in different ways and allows for several complementary orientations. No single church can claim monopoly on the definition of being apostolic. For apostolicity refers not only to the content of the faith but also to the spiritual vitality, the missionary dimension, and to the sacramental aspect of the church worldwide. Roman Catholic writer Avery Dulles admits that there are criteria other than only the episcopal succession when talking about the church as apostolic. Unity, holiness, catholicity, and apostolicity are dynamic realities that depend on the foundational work of Christ and on his continued presence and activity through the Holy Spirit. A strong statement from Dulles reflects an ecumenical climate of respectful affirmation of other churches:

---

98. World Council of Churches, *BEM*, 28.

99. This is the position of the Lutheran theologian, Edmund Schlink in his ecumenical dogmatics: Schlink, *Ökumenische Dogmatik*, 591.

Evangelical communities that excel in love for Jesus Christ and in obedience to the Holy Spirit may be more unitive, holy, catholic, and apostolic than highly sacramental and hierarchically organized churches in which faith and charity have become cold.[100]

It seems possible also to argue for a more functional and dipolar relationship between ordained ministers and the whole congregation. This mutual service is just one corner of an even greater vision of the church as a polycentric ministry of many gifted members who submit to one another in order to build the church in love and mutual respect (Eph 4:15–16; Eph 5:21).[101] Ordained ministers can be considered as a charism of the Spirit, governed by the norm of the gospel. Though everyone received the Spirit on the Day of Pentecost, the apostles modeled a legitimate need for appointed leadership. They held by their responsibility for unity in the body of Christ and for clearing the way for the good news to flow freely to all nations in ages to come.[102]

Constructive Reflections

As a worshipping, witnessing, and serving communion, the church is a concrete reality. She is founded upon the commitment of those who confess Christ as LORD (Matt 16:16). She is visible in her highly different embodied manifestations. Because of the unique promise of Christ (v. 18), the church is built and empowered by structural, sacramental, and charismatic gifts. As such, the doctrine of the church may be seen as a branch of pneumatology, not the other way around.[103] The church is a graceful reality whose existence is based on the inauguration of the Spirit on the Day of Pentecost. We can hardly talk about the Spirit without at the same time talking about

---

100. Dulles, "One, Holy, Catholic, and Apostolic," 27.

101. See Macchia, *Baptized in the Spirit*, 234. See also Volf, *After our Likeness*, 231.

102. The relation to the Petrine office will not be discussed in its breadth within the framework of this book. I share the position of Frank D. Macchia, holding that the role of the Pope in the coming years perhaps may be regarded in another light than before, compared to *Lumen Gentium* §22 where the Pope is given the "full supreme, and universal power over the church." Ironically, at the same time as the Petrine office symbolizes the unity of the Roman Catholic Church, it represents one of the greatest barriers to a broader unity with other church bodies. However, the Pope is indeed mouthpiece for more than the Catholics when the Petrine office with boldness stands up for valuable and vulnerable treasures in the Christian tradition, when he talks for the role of Christianity in the current European secular culture, and when he emphasizes the spiritual unity between churches worldwide. Macchia, *Baptized in the Spirit*, 239.

103. Newbigin, *The Household of God*, 95.

the church, and vice versa.[104] The church as the people of the Spirit is pneumatologically construed. Pentecost is—rightly perceived—a repeated event. When she prays for the presence of Christ in worship and epiclesis, the Spirit continues to come to the church on the move. Indeed, this is a process beyond our control. Hence, the essence of the church is not connected to her organizational sophistication but to her confessional clarity. Her role as mediator of grace is one of the prerequisites for fulfilling God's calling to restore the many broken relationships featured in society.

The church is a Spirit-driven *koinonia*, a sign of the approach of God's kingdom in grace and power, in weakness and vulnerability. Her apostolicity is anchored to the whole spiritual life of the congregation. In light of this, a wider notion of apostolic succession leads us to a rediscovering of the apostolic mission. An apostolic community is not only based on the church's historical preconditions, but also on her prevailing faithfulness to operate in grace and power. It is fair to assume a wide range of spiritual marks and expression in the life of the contemporary church. However, her spirituality will always be balanced by her vulnerability.

Furthermore, it is legitimate to reflect upon the nature of the contemporary church by looking to the writings of early Christians. The mission of the early church was to change lives, not only illuminate minds. Her leaders were gifted thinkers, men and women of prayer. Many of them were both intellectuals and bishops, living close to the believing community. The imaginative power of Christian thoughts arose from within: from the use of the biblical texts, from liturgies and practices, and from their devotional life. The ancient church regarded herself as an instrument of God's free-acting grace. Recounting and remembering the life of Christ gave their thoughts a narrative structure that formed the church's symbolic worldview.

An ecclesiology which regards the church as a sacramental banquet open to the world emphasizes the inviting and welcoming nature of the church. If the church really is a gifted and discerning community because of the Spirit, elements like charismatic gifts, laying on of hands, anointing, and healing are more natural than often supposed. A gifted church is a reminder that nobody owns the church but the LORD. The gift of discernment guards the fellowship against charismatic chaos and triumphalistic individualism, and it fosters behaviors of accountability, order and mutual respect. In that light we may consider that different structures are Spirit given as well. This is among the insights that have emerged from recent ecumenical convergence texts and documents concerning the purpose and nature of the church.

The preference for describing the church in her concrete, historical, and actual shape rather than in her idealist version is founded on a vision

---

104. Volf and Lee, "Spirit and Church," 382–409.

of a practical and prophetic fellowship, formed by grace-enabled activities in order to face the need of humans in the contemporary society. To glory in anything other than Christ is an obstacle to the activity of the Spirit. My concluding remark is in line with the position of von Gelder and Healy: the visible church, with all its sinfulness, brokenness, conflicts, and lukewarmness, still is the creation of the Spirit.[105] Her nature will always be deeper and more important than her functions and outward framework.

It is through continuity with the spirituality and faith of the apostolic church that consensus about apostolicity is to be found. This question cannot be reduced to merely a matter of succession in office. With Dulles and Kärkkäinen, I hold that apostolicity involves continuity with the life, vitality, and faith of the church, as well as with the everyday discipleship. Apostolicity requires the whole people of God, not only with the clergy and professional part of the church structure. The church of the Spirit does not grow and spread through uncontrolled outbursts of raw energy for an experience of high-voltage emotional release. Instead, a sensitive presentation of the gospel presupposes a refining of the gifts of the Spirit in accordance to their distinctive character. When church members act in ways that are grace-filled and edifying, they contribute to a community of graced relationships, marking the church as a sign of the goodness and beauty in the world. The baptismal waters would be lifeless, the Eucharist empty, Scripture meaningless and the charismata nothing, were it not for the constituting activity of the Spirit. That gives us a gospel shaped ecclesiology, labelled by a mature understanding of spirituality, a conscious practice of the sacraments and a devoted oriented worship.

In the subsequent chapter, I survey the many voices of the New Testament to paint a picture of the distinctive character of church, focusing on the writings of Luke and Paul. Just as charismatic elements pervaded the ministry of Jesus, so dynamic activity of the Spirit characterized the corporate life of the earliest Christians. Gradually this developed into the first pattern for the worldwide church. For the disciples, the Pentecost event was synonymous with the coming of the gift of the Spirit. An affirmation of these insights may expand our horizons and inspire a broadening of the contemporary ecclesiological dialogue. To anchor her ecclesiology as an expression of God's very presence where the Spirit abides, the church depends upon the narratives and instructions of the New Testament.

---

105. Van Gelder, *Essence of the Church*, 105–12.

3

The Gifted Church of the New Testament

> *The event of Pentecost serves as contextual origin, dialogical anchor, and continual source of inspiration and challenge.*[1]

Introduction

THE NEW TESTAMENT CAN be described as the first real church history. NT *is* ecclesiology. To understand the essence of the church, we read the New Testament as the story of the various communities that came to be defined as assemblies (Matt 16:18). From ancient times, the work of Christ and the life of the Spirit have been linked together as a two-fold and equal divine economy in the doctrine of Easter and Pentecost. The church is only an instrument of something bigger than herself. As an inseparable part of the salvation history, the church has always been confessed the Spirit, in her Creeds. Especially in the East, the church holds special reverence for the role of the Spirit in the constitution and the inner sacramental life.[2] Orthodox theologians have observed the work of Christ as establishing the unity of the church while the Spirit ensured the diversity in the church. The former establishes her unchangeable and sacramentally anchored nature, while the latter sustains her dynamic, experiential qualities. But what about the New Testament witness? What are the ecclesiological implications of Pentecost? How do we understand Luke and Paul when it comes to the question of church and Spirit?[3] This chapter aims to offer some possibilities.

1. Augustine, "The Empowered Church," 157.
2. Kärkkäinen, *Pneumatological Theology*, 83–95.
3. While Luke is a valuable but in some sense undiscriminating guide to the experiences, activities and expressions of the early church, Paul is the writer to answer *how* charismatic activities are to be assessed and evaluated.

Christ and the Spirit

Various NT passages reveal the emergence of the church, established on the Day of Pentecost as the concrete result of the outpouring of the Spirit. Conversion, baptism, and the promise of the Spirit were given as collective and individual gifts, together with a commission to mission (Acts 2:38–41; John 16:7–15; Matt 28:18–20). The Holy Spirit was the nerve centre of Christian life, marking one as a Christian.[4] Being in Christ and in the Spirit were parts of the same reality (Phlm 2:1; Rom 8:1). The church was one because of the divine life pulsing through her, not because of how she was structured. Though the role assigned to the Spirit has been treated in different ways throughout history, it seems clear that the pneumatic ramifications of ecclesiology cannot be construed apart from christological and trinitarian orientations. In the New Testament, Christology is not depicted apart from the Spirit. Christ as the Spirit-bearer (John 3:34) precedes his role as the Spirit-giver (Acts 2:33).[5] Even if there is no formal doctrine of the Trinity in the New Testament, there is a rich triadic teaching which has been reappropriated by scholars. A shallow understanding of the scriptural witness on the Holy Spirit gave rise to factions in the earliest centuries and continues today. Within the rhythm of the economic Trinity, the Spirit exercises a contact function and a hermeneutic role which corresponds with the New Testament material.

The position that the church was born out of the womb of the Spirit as a result of the Spirit's outburst on the Day of Pentecost, is widely acknowledged.[6] However, this does not fully satisfy the question of how to perceive the relationship between the Spirit and the church. Miroslav Volf and Maurice Lee hold that the work of the Spirit cannot be limited to the vivification of the church. For the very identity and mission of Christ were fundamentally shaped by the Spirit, as recorded in the narrative of his baptism and the descent of the Spirit upon him (Luke 3:21–22).[7] Rather, we talk about the triplicity of relations: the relationship between the Spirit and the church, the

---

4. Macchia, "Kingdom and Power," 115.

5. McDonnell holds that it would be difficult to separate theology from a personal and communitarian confession of faith, simply because this profession, if it partakes of the full character of faith in the sense of the New Testament, is elicited by the Holy Spirit (1 Cor 12:3). By reason of faith, the Lord opens to the believer a horizon where the Spirit operates in a unique way, within which revelation is appropriated. God touches human knowing as faith understanding. McDonnell, "A Trinitarian Theology," 221.

6. For a broader and historical oriented introduction, see Thiselton, *The Holy Spirit*.

7. Volf and Lee, "Spirit and Church," 384.

relationship between Christ and the church, and the relationship between the Spirit and Christ, who is both the bearer and the giver of the Spirit.

According to Heribert Mühlen, the church can be conceived of as the continuation of Christ's anointing by the Spirit.[8] Jesus considered his calling and proclamation of the kingdom of God as driven by the eschatological Spirit of the prophets (Matt 12:18–21, 28; see also Luke 3:4–6). The reign of God required a people of God, which from the beginning was represented by the community of disciples around Jesus. They became authorized by the same Spirit as Jesus, and they were given the capacity to do the same deeds (John 14:12). This gathering and sending in the power of the Spirit gave impetus to the emergence of the church.[9] And the outpouring of the Spirit first on the disciples of Jesus and later on all believers on the Day of Pentecost shaped the pneumatological profile of the church from its beginning and was a central aspect of her original identity. However, the interplay of both identicality and non-identicality are important in order to avoid the temptation of triumphalism. Volf and Lee states:

> The presence of the Spirit in Jesus' ministry was immediate: the Spirit had descended upon him and made him into the Messiah of God while the presence of the Spirit in the church is mediated through Jesus. (. . .) Jesus was given the Spirit "without measure" (John 3:34); in the church, the Spirit operates "according to the measure of faith" (Rom 12:3). In the terminology of later tradition, Jesus was endowed with the Spirit "by nature"; the church is endowed with the Spirit "by grace."[10]

As we pursue both relevance to a pluralistic age and faithfulness to the biblical witness, we thus begin the task of theology with the doctrine of the Triune God. Pentecostal theologian Steven Land reflects on the intrinsic relationship between the Spirit and the Word in light of trinitarian relations:

> The Spirit who inspired and preserved the Scripture illuminates, teaches, guides, convicts and transforms through the Word today. The Word is alive, quick and powerful, because of the Holy Spirit's ministry. The relation of the Spirit to Scripture is based on that of Spirit to Christ. Even as the Spirit formed Christ in Mary, so the Spirit uses Scripture to form Christ in believers and vice versa.[11]

---

8. For a deeper presentation, see Mühlen, *Una Mystica Persona*.
9. Volf and Lee, "Spirit and Church," 387.
10. Ibid., 391–92.
11. Land, *Pentecostal Spirituality*, 100.

Land makes use of the phrase "Spirit-Word" when it comes to the way God is guiding the Godhead's church.[12] As Spirit-Word, Scripture directs the everyday life and witness of individual believers as well as of the church. Spirit and Word are fused together and can only be separated at great peril to the same believers or churches. Because of the Spirit, the Word comes in more than words. It comes in power and manifestations of the Spirit as guide and interpreter. The call to practice discernment requires a church to be informed by the Word, shaped in the Spirit and directed by the will of God (1 Cor 12:10).

It is worth considering how this understanding of the Spirit informs our view of the distinctive character of Christ as head of the church. In his extensive study of the religious and charismatic experience of Jesus and the first Christians, James D. G. Dunn claims that Jesus was charismatic in the sense that he manifested a power and authority which was not his own. He received this power by virtue of the Spirit's endowment on the day of his baptism at Jordan (Luke 3:21–22).[13] However, this power did not possess him against his will. It was not a compulsion which filled him, but a power which he could exercise in response to faith. The power to act came from his relation to God and from his insight into the mission of God. Healing and proclamation of the good news to the poor were charismata which Jesus specifically attributed to the Spirit. Thus Jesus' experience of God embraced both rational and non-rational elements, all regarded alike as manifestations of the Spirit of God. According to Dunn, it is imperative to hold together these two sides of Jesus' self-understanding:

> As he found God in prayer as Father, so he found God in mission as power—these are but two sides of the one character, of the one experience of God. In this two-fold experience of Jesus we see closely interwoven both the ethical and the charismatic, both the obedience of the Son and the liberty of the prophet. Jesus can be presented neither simply as moralist nor simply as an ecstatic. It is the interaction of sonship and Spirit that gives Jesus' ministry its distinctive character.[14]

---

12. Question 54 of the Heidelberg Catechism states that the community of the elected destined for eternal life is upholded through His Spirit and Word. As Moltmann observes, the mention of the Spirit before the Word is surprising in a Reformation catechism but is correct in view of the breadth of the Spirit and the abundance of the Spirit's gifts. Moltmann, *Church in the Power of the Spirit*, 69. See also Kubac, *Splendour*, 37, 147.

13. Dunn, *Jesus and the Spirit*, 87. However, Dunn refuses to designate Christ as ecstatic, though some experiences where of high exultation (Mark 9:1–8; Luke 10:18). I owe thanks to Dunn for parts of the delineation given in this chapter.

14. Ibid., 90.

By his mighty deeds Jesus probably regarded himself more as a manifestation of grace than as a witness to faith. He demonstrated the eschatological presence of the kingdom (Matt 12:28) and to some degree he shared his authority and charismatic power with his disciples (Luke 10:19), just as he sought to share his relationship with his Father (Luke 22:29–30). Jesus lived out of a consciousness of sonship and power, of commission and authority.[15] So we speak of the divinity of the historical Jesus in the light of his relationship with God as Son and with the Spirit working in him with authority and power.[16] George S. Hendry declares that there is no reference in the New Testament to any work of the Spirit apart from Christ.[17]

So, Christ is present and active in the church as the Spirit, the vicar of Christ and the mediator of the presence of the exalted LORD within the community. In the Pauline texts, the image of the Spirit is presented as the unifying element in the church. The church actually *is* a body filled with the Spirit of life (Rom 12:3–8; 1 Cor 12:12–31). In this respect, it is inappropriate to draw a sharp distinction between the more charismatic and sacramental elements of the church daily living.

The Experience of the Risen LORD

From being the subject of religious experiences before the resurrection, Jesus featured as the object of religious experiences among his followers. There was a clear charismatic element in the ministry of Jesus, as it was among the earliest believers. The balance between the ethical and charismatic elements in the ministry of Jesus also appears in the teaching of Paul. These transfer motives gave birth to the identity of the first church. Jesus is called a life-giving spirit (1 Cor 15:45). Resurrection appearances and Pentecostal appearances were running together (John 20:22). For Paul, the appearance of Christ (Acts 9) became for him a commission (Gal 1:15–16), and the revelation of Christ was understood as the gospel itself (Gal 1:1, 11).

Despite difficulties of conceptualizing the various encounters with the resurrected Christ—listed in the gospels and Acts—it is clear that these revelations of Jesus became the foundation of both the conversion and ministry in the early church. The experience of the risen LORD became the driving force in their lives, the touchstone of the hermeneutic, and the norm for their gospel.[18] On the Day of Pentecost the disciples experienced divine

15. Ibid., 91.
16. Ibid., 92.
17. Hendry, *Holy Spirit*, 26.
18. Dunn, *Jesus and the Spirit*, 133–34.

THE GIFTED CHURCH OF THE NEW TESTAMENT   59

power which was unexpected in its givenness and fullness. The formulations "like the rush of a violent wind" and "a tongue rested on each of them" (Acts 2:2–3) expressed this unexpectedness. Although the Day of Pentecost represented an initial experience of getting the gift of the Spirit, the outpouring of power was repeated on both individuals and groups throughout the book of Acts.

Pentecost was the great event by which the friends of Jesus were drawn together into a living community. Obviously it was an enthusiastic fellowship within first-century Judaism. Their sense of community stemmed from a common experience of having received the eschatological Spirit. Their worship combined both ritualistic and spontaneous elements. It was, according to Dunn, primarily charismatic and enthusiastic rather than institutional and structured,[19] and the aura of the numinous made this infant church awful, attractive, and expanding. Their identity stemmed from their understanding of Jesus as source and object of their experiences and actions.[20]

Reformed theologian Michael Welker describes the Spirit's role of enlightening the minds of Christians so they are able to discern all things (1 Cor 2:15). However, it is reasonable to ask whether we are able to conceptualize the activity of the Spirit at all by academic defense of the biblical claims. Are its dimensions simply too deep for words (Rom 8:26–27)? According to Welker, the Spirit of the New Testament traditions is an utterly empathetic personality with a multi-contextual presence.[21] The Spirit is not a power that acts in the same way in every context (1 Cor 12:11) but reveals itself by various gifts and miracles, according to its own will. And it does so without measure (Heb 2:4; John 3:34). The Spirit is context- and individuality-sensitive, perfectly compatible with the assurance that where the Spirit of Lord is, there is freedom (2 Cor 3:17). From this it follows that the people of God is called into the fellowship with Godhead and into a substantial unity with the Divinity (Rom 8:9, 15; 1 Cor 1:8; 6:17; Gal 4:6). The presence of the Spirit is described as an entrance into the reign of God (Gal 6:8). Thus it represents a multicontextual and polyphonic existence connected to several different phenomena within the biblical tradition.

In the scriptures, the Spirit is responsible for various different actions, such as, a) the canonical coherence of the biblical traditions who speaks as the one voice in and through the different voices of the canon (Mark

---

19. Ibid., 188.

20. Jesus was not only a sort of archetypal Christian charismatic. More significantly, the miracles were performed in the name of Jesus (Acts 3:6), as was their teaching (4:18) and their baptizing (Acts 2:38). The authority exercised in the church was understood as derived from him. Ibid., 195.

21. Welker, *Work of the Spirit*, 225.

12:36; Acts 1,16; 4:25; 11,28; 20:28); b) the pouring out of the Spirit with the insistence that male and female, young and old, masters and slaves of all nations, language, and cultures, should be endowed with prophetic insight and power (Joel 3:1ff; Acts 2:17ff; Gal 3, 28); and c) the presence and power that gives voice to the persecuted and oppressed in contexts of trial and danger (Mark 13:11).[22]

Understanding the Book of Acts

Questions have been raised whether the Book of Acts is to be regarded as a blueprint for church organization (the Restorationist view), or a sketch of the immediate consequences of the outpouring of the Spirit within a specific context, without any normative aspirations (the classical view). According to Anthony C. Thiselton, the first perspective seems extrinsic to biblical writings and lacks biblical validity.[23] Recent studies of Acts no longer separate history from theology, since God works both in and through history.[24] While Conzelmann criticized pristine Christianity as an idealized age, Thiselton's position, however, by no means implies that the Book of Acts has nothing to say to the contemporary church. As Christ identified himself with the church (Acts 9:4), the new fellowships drew their inner life of praise, teaching, baptism, and the breaking of bread from the presence of the Spirit they had received (Acts 2: 42–47). The reality of the Spirit embraced all the believers and formed God's people to be one fellowship (1 Cor 12:13). As the body of Christ, organically linked together in community based on the events of Pentecost, all participated together in these various religious experiences. Before sophisticated cognitive representations were elaborated, there was a corporate encounter with the Holy.

The Day of Pentecost had its own liturgy. The Petrine use of the prophecy of Joel to describe the phenomena made visible on the Day of Pentecost represents a central point for some theologians. The Old Testament hope for a universal presence of the Spirit had now been inaugurated to the people of the new covenant. As a fulfilment of Joel's prophecy, as a milestone in God's saving history (1 Pet 1:10–12), and as the birth of the church, Pentecost is a unique occurrence. By relating the Pentecost occurrence to the Jewish written tradition (Acts 2:14–36), the apostles revealed the crucial role which the Spirit had to play as guarantor of the continuity between the established tradition of the Spirit-filled prophets and the completion of that tradition

---

22. Ibid., 228.
23. Thiselton, *The Holy Spirit*, 496.
24. See the introduction parts of Marshall, *Luke*.

by the risen Messiah.[25] The parallelism between the Spirit's action in the life of Jesus and the Spirit's action in the church thus became uncovered. The Spirit-created Christ in the stomach of Mary is the same Spirit who created the church at Pentecost. The manner by which the Spirit descended upon Jesus at his baptism (Luke 3:22) is comparable to the spiritual equipment that introduced the mission of the apostles.

And now, because the church lives in the post-Pentecost era, the time of waiting and prayer is over. The Spirit has come. Now the church is not called to pray for a new Pentecost but to walk by the Spirit (Gal 5:16) and to keep in step with the Spirit (v. 25). However, the proper order is not without relevance: The Spirit did not come until the work of Jesus was completed (John 20:19-23; Acts 2:33). The function of the Spirit, therefore, is subsequent and instrumental to that of Jesus, whom the Spirit glorifies (John 16:14) and to whom the Spirit bears testimony (John 15:26).

The Pentecost had epochal significance. As an historical event, the breakthrough of the new age had come and could not recur. However, in another sense the Pentecost can be anyone's personal experience, as an element of the conversion-initiation process and as the fulfillment of the mission of Jesus.[26] Thiselton understands the baptism of the Holy Spirit on the Day of Pentecost (Acts 1:8) as a communal initiatory baptism which was experienced together with all the members of the new-born church of Jerusalem (Acts 2:2-4). As individuals, however, the experience of the Spirit cannot be linked to a uniformed scheme for how the Spirit must be received. Every filling with the Spirit is founded on what was given by Christ once and for all on Pentecost (Acts 2:33), forming a participatory ecclesiology for the purpose of building up (1 Cor 14:26). Though there are highly different individual experiences of the presence of the Spirit, the understanding of Pentecost does not need to be the object of an individualistic interpretation. As a paradigmatic event in the salvation story, Pentecost was the communal announcement of the promise of Christ (Acts 1:4). Rightly understood, the Spirit came both from above and from within (Luke 24:49). The Day of Pentecost brought about a complete filling of the Spirit, which was neither partial nor conditional.[27] Because of Pentecost, Paul could announce, " . . . be filled with the Holy Spirit, as you sing psalms and hymns and spiritual songs" (Eph 5:18-19). The events of Pentecost made the church Spirit born, Spirit shaped, and Spirit-driven.

---

25. A broader presentation is given in Wenk, *Community-Forming Power*.

26. Dunn, *Baptism in Spirit*, 53.

27. Thiselton, *The Holy Spirit*, 56. See also Bruner, *A Theology of the Holy Spirit*, 155-224.

Spanning the Gulf

God communicates and interprets Godself to the world by the mediation of both Word and Spirit in a healthy combination. While the Spirit is a reality which not only informs but also transforms, a partial focus only upon the communicative role of the Spirit in prophecy and ecstatic utterance is not satisfactory. In the Spirit we identify with the Son in his death and resurrection. We share in the fruits of God's work because of the Spirit. From the perspective of the New Testament, emphasis on the gifts of the Spirit is balanced by emphasis on the life of the Spirit with its moral and relational fruits (Gal 5:22–23). To Rowan Williams, the most important event in the life of the church with which the Holy Spirit is linked, is the forgiveness of sins (John 20:23; Acts 2:38–39). The test of the Spirit's presence is the confession of Christ's coming in flesh (1 John 4:2).[28]

Another much-neglected pneumatological doctrine is the notion that the Spirit is not pointing to the Son outside of the human world. The Spirit affects the formation of Son-like life in the world by pointing to the forgiven and justified life that is already given by Christ. To share Christ's relation to the Father is to share in his sufferings. Union with Christ may involve an absence of manifested power,[29] illuminating the tension between action and contemplation within Christian spirituality. As in Gethsemane, the absence of God's manifest power is bound up with a decision to embrace powerlessness rather than domination of the world by manipulation. This is not an escape into passivity or disengagement, but a choice to live within the potentially hurtful and destructive bounds of the world. It requires a decision to stay in a contemplative receptivity to *humanum* as gift, renewal, and life.

Thus the role of the Spirit is to span the gulf between suffering and hope. Is it really possible to regard the church as a Spirit-filled community whose values which become visible in the tension between security and powerlessness? Williams answers in the affirmative. The Spirit is active amidst broken flesh and shed blood, as the sign and promise of human wholeness through union with God the Father. A significant part of the manifestation of the Spirit is the growth of human persons to the fullness of their particular identities. The result is that Spirit work ceases to be confined to only extraordinary events but becomes an intrinsic quality of a Christian human being. If there should exist a face of the Spirit, it would be "the assembly of redeemed human faces in their infinite diversity."[30]

---

28. Williams, *On Christian Theology*, 119.

29. Ibid., 122.

30. This is a quotation from Vladimir Lossky, referred by Williams in his *Wound of Knowledge*, 173.

Through incarnation and Pentecost, the Spirit has related God and the world to each other. Jesus' work as mediator between God and human (1 Tim 2:5) is inseparable from the work of the Spirit in the church through proclamation of the gospel, reception of the sacraments, and empowering believers with spiritual gifts and fruits. The Spirit seems to be that very relational medium that makes possible the paschal mystery, based on Jesus' relationship with his Father (John 10:30).[31] As such, the Pentecostal outpouring may be regarded as the fulfilment of the promised saving work of Christ. But by its horizontal work in the world, the Spirit becomes the agent of relational reconciliation. Despite how racially and socially segregated many churches are, it must be underlined that the baptism of the Spirit into one body of Christ reconciles people across ethnic, gender, racial and social lines (Acts 2:5–11; Gal 3:28). In the letters of Paul, the pneumatological relation between God and human is described in terms of justification, sanctification, and glorification (Rom 5:1). The love of God has been poured into the hearts of the believers through the Spirit. This calls forth affective, cognitive, and materially embodied responses in order to live a life worthy the calling of Christ (Rom 6–8; see also 8:23 and Eph 1:13).

Throughout the gospels and Acts, Spirit-prompted utterances serve not just to encourage or inspire, but to articulate a new worldview which in turn was expected to shape the community's ethos. Matthias Wenk argues that prophetic ministry and charismatic manifestations had a socio-ethical dimension in the New Testament churches.[32] The ethical implications and transformative experiences directly resulted in changed praxis.[33] The idea at play here is that the origin and life of the church as a renewed community within the social order is another manifestation of the Spirit's work. Wenk describes the Spirit's role in these ethical manifestations of the church's eschatological identity:

> The plea for the coming of the kingdom with its "this-worldly" manifestations, expressed in mutual forgiveness as well as deliverance from temptation, is somehow related to the heavenly Father's giving of the Holy Spirit. These structural observations are supported by evidence in the Lukan writings where charismatic manifestations are the means by which the prayer for the manifestations of God's saving benefits is answered. Thus, the Spirit is related to the life of the people of God in its entirety: daily provision of food, forgiveness of sins by God and by each

---

31. Yong, *Spirit-Word-Community*, 30.
32. Wenk, *Community-Forming Power*, 308.
33. Ibid., 147, 189.

other, protection from apostasy and deliverance from demonic enslavement.[34]

According to Wenk, the pneumatic experience at Pentecost and its interpretation given by Peter (Acts 2:42–47) forced the prophetic community to articulate a new self-understanding. They were a congregation of the Holy Spirit through their commonly held goods, communal meals, and adherence to the teachings and to the presence of the Spirit within their midst. The Spirit's transformative work was at the heart of the renewed community's life. The Pentecost experience provided the Lukan church with a hermeneutical key. From this day forward, they understood their role in accordance with the anointed servant of the LORD.

Furthermore, Lukan pneumatology envisions the salvific benefits of Christ's ministry in much broader categories than the individualized conversion-initiation paradigm. The role of the Spirit is better grasped through a restoration motif and as the fulfilment of the eschatological hope. This restoration is described as a renewal of social orders (Luke 1:51–53).[35] The common categories of young and old, male and female, and so on, are no longer crucial.

The Value of Broad Partnership

But how are the New Testament ideals of participation, local leadership, and ordination to be perceived? I chiefly agree with Miroslav Volf in his statement that the presence of Christ and the life of the church are mediated not simply through ordained ministers but through the whole congregation, as *mater ecclesia* to the children engendered by the Spirit.[36] In the search for culturally appropriate social embodiments of the gospel, Volf's ideal is the congregational model. He advocates for the gathered community, which is both voluntary and egalitarian. As the anticipation of the eschatological gathering of the entire people of God, the nature of the church must be understood as a participation in the communion of the Triune God as a present experience (1 John 1:1–4).[37] Wherever the Spirit of Christ is present in its ecclesially constitutive activity, there is the church.[38]

---

34. Ibid., 231.
35. Ibid., 315.
36. Volf, "Community Formation," 213.
37. For a more detailed presentation, see his Volf, *After our Likeness*. Volf refers to Ignatius of Antioch who, in his reference to the presence of Christ, said that wherever Jesus Christ is, there is the universal church.
38. Volf, "Community Formation," 215.

In this respect, the church represents a Spirit-mediated relationship with the Godhead. Against a traditional Catholic position where the church is exclusively the universal reality gathered around the bishop standing in apostolic succession, and against an equally exclusive Eastern Orthodox position of a episcopocentric and eucharistic church which leave no room for alternative church models, Volf prefers the Free Church model. For him, Matt 18:20 plays a key role in his systematic-ecclesiological understanding: "For where two or three are gathered in my name. . . ."[39] What constitutes the ecclesiality of a community is not the acts or the programs, but the people, gathered in the name of God for the sake of worship, listening and participating in the sacrament, all animated by the Spirit (Acts 2:38-39). Volf writes:

> The church nowhere exists *above* the locally assembled congregation, but exists *in, with,* and *beneath* it. A congregation *is* the body of Christ in the particular locale in which it gathers together (cf. Rom 12:5; 1 Cor 12:12-13). Despite the fundamental differences that exist between Free Church and Eastern Orthodox ecclesiologies, they agree on this important point: that the church in the real sense of the word is exclusively the concrete assembly.[40]

There are preconditions for the presence of Christ. The premise, according to Matt 28:20, is to be gathered in the name of Christ. To believe and to confess represents doctrinal specifications. The same can be said about the administration of the sacraments, since there is no church without these signs of his presence. However, there is neither any sacrament without the confession of faith. It is the confession of faith and the presence of the Spirit which unite the churches in all times and places, not the external structures. Professing faith in Christ implies an attitude of unity and openness to all other churches. Based on the constitutive presence of Christ and guided by the ongoing counsel of the Spirit, the nature of the church can be defined as follows:

> Every congregation that assembles around the one Jesus Christ as Savior and LORD in order to profess faith in him publicly in pluriform fashion, including through baptism and the LORD's Supper, which is open for all churches of God and to all human

---

39. The same point of departure is given by the Norwegian Lutheran theologian, Harald Hegstad, in his ecclesiology. Hegstad, *Real Church*. By the way, according to Volf, it was the understanding of Matt 18:20 which shaped the entire Free Church tradition. Volf, "Community Formation," 217.

40. Ibid.

beings, is a church in the full sense of the word, since Christ promised to be present of God in the eschatological reign of God. Such a congregation is a holy, catholic, and apostolic church.[41]

Regarding the relation between the believer and the church, Free Church circles and Protestantism more broadly have advocated a rather individualistic understanding. However, according to Matt 18:20, the presence of Christ is promised to the entire congregation and then to the individual. No one can live in faith quite alone.[42] This perspective implies that the transmission of faith normally occurs through interpersonal ecclesial interaction. No one becomes baptized by themselves. No one serves themselves alone at the Lord's Table. There is always a communal dimension of the mediation of faith and of receiving the sacrament. The experience of faith requires that each person become an ecclesial being.

An Invitation to Participate

In light of the concrete, communal nature of ecclesial identity, it is not appropriate to talk about ecclesial structures and ecclesial offices apart from the issue of participation in church life. The church lives through the participation of her members, regardless of whether they are laity or officeholders. Together with Volf, I allege that the church is a communion of interdependent subjects, that salvation is not exclusively mediated through officeholders, and that the church is instituted by Christ (1 Cor 3:11). She is sustained by the Spirit and through the communal confession of the believing community. The church is thus not a monocentric-bipolar community but a polycentric-participative community (1 Cor 14:26; 1 Pet 4:10).[43] Because she is born by the Spirit (Acts 2) the church is charismatically endowed and sacramentally construed.

Among the most important features by which the charismata may be assessed are confession of Christ as Lord (1 Cor 12:3), universal distribution of the gifts (v. 7; Acts 2:17-21; 2:38-39), common responsibility for the life of the church (1 Thess 5:19-22), mutual submission (1 Thess 5:13: 1 Cor 16:15-16), and the interdependence of the different charismata (Rom 12:6). The charismata of office are here integrated in the church's self-understanding as Spirit-driven. Through the different charismata, the Spirit

41. Ibid., 219.
42. Ibid., 220.
43. Ibid., 231. To varying degrees, this polycentric-participative model has been undertaken by the Baptists, Congregationalist, Quakers, Pentecostal, and by innumerable independent church networks.

is the structuring organizer of the church's pneumatological nature. The distinction between the general and the particular priesthood (ordained ministries) does not divide her into two sections, but rather constitutes two dimensions of the service of every member. On the basis of common baptism, all believers have become priests. They have an independent obligation to realize their charismata so that the church may be edified (1 Cor 14:5).[44]

Founded on his understanding of the narratives of Acts, Luke T. Johnson claims that the stories do not present specific qualifications for members of house congregations who administered, taught, preached, prophesied, baptized, or led the eucharistic meals. The only precondition we observe is that they were full of God's grace and power (Acts 6:3-8). Stephen and the other seven men who were responsible for the daily distribution of food were expected to be "full of the Spirit and of wisdom" (v. 3) and "full of faith and the Holy Spirit" (v. 5). There were no priestly functions as such. As the churches began to consolidate their position, Luke uses the general term "elder" as a collective term for a group of leaders acting representatively as overseers (*episkopoi*), a call given and enabled by the Holy Spirit (Acts 20:28).[45]

The apostolic church had a plurality of leaders. In the Pastoral Epistles, prospective elders/overseers are expected to be people with good reputations both within and outside the congregation. Probably the intention behind the leader's function as role model was that the gospel could be promoted by the quality of the lives of believers (2 Tim 3:10-11). The young church chose people with gifts of leadership and with the capacity to guide others, and the ability to teach and to set goals.[46] The same Epistles validate specific Christian qualities such as the duty of providing hospitality and to give appropriate care. These qualifications are chiefly directed toward overseers and deacons (1 Tim 3:1-13; Tit 1:5-9; Tit 3:14). But all individuals were expected to use their generous resources to help other people in need

---

44. Volf states that every church needs the vivifying presence of the Spirit. Without this presence, even a church with a decentralized structure and culture will become sterile. Extensive participation must be sustained by deep spirituality. Ibid., 235.

45. According to the Pastoral Epistles, the appointment of leaders seems to be done at meetings of the congregation and included the laying on of hands (1 Tim 4:14; 2 Tim 1:6). The role of women was defined in the same letters (1 Tim 5:10; Tit 2:4). They played a significant role in prophecy and teaching, despite the admonition to be silent (1 Tim 2:12-14), which in all likelihood was provoked because of some particular problematic practices in the congregation of Ephesus, compared to other New Testament situations which indicate the public role of the women in the upbuilding of the churches. Fee, *Gospel and Spirit*, 52-65.

46. These lists of leadership qualities were common in the ancient world. Marshall, "Congregation and Ministry," 117.

and to be involved in far-reaching programs of social care (1 Tim 6:18–19; 1 Tim 2:1–2; Tit 3:14).[47]

According to I. Howard Marshall, elders were probably an inclusive term for all leaders, including female deacons (1 Tim 3:1–13; cf. 1 Tim 5:17 and 1 Pet 5:1–4).[48] A clear distinction between clergy and laity did not exist in the apostolic church; neither is there indication of any church task that required what we call ordination. However, there were occasions and tasks for which the imposition of hands was appropriate (1 Tim 1:6). By this intercession Timothy became gifted, commissioned and equipped by the Spirit (1 Tim 4:14).[49]

However, because of opposition which threatened to subvert the gospel, the Pastoral Epistles opt for an orderly form of leadership and ministry. It is no surprise that the congregations developed structures in the interest of greater stability. This basic need for organization found its expression in a corresponding human system consisting of people who demonstrated qualities of Christian character, capacities for leadership, and a fundamental loyalty to the gospel.[50] The term *charisma* was not necessary identical to that of office. However, those who were recognized as spiritually gifted had to express these in particular duties. They were not some sort of spiritual freelancers.

When searching for a balance between charisma and order, both Käsemann, Schweizer, and Dunn state that charisma implied office and office expressed charisma. The latter recognizes the nature of charisma as the particular action of God in a given situation.[51] For Paul, the question of order in the church is not static, resting on offices, ranks, or institutions.[52] Instead, Paul recognized early on the importance of regular ministries within the charismatic community, specifically the ministries of the word, prophecy, and teaching. The main qualification for the variety of services he encouraged during his years as apostle, was obedience to the inspiration of the

---

47. Ibid., 110.

48. Ibid., 119.

49. This perspective has shaped the ordination liturgy, for instance in the Lutheran context. The ceremony includes an epiclesis and a reading of Scripture about the Spirit (ex. John 20:19–23), the laying on of hands, and an invocation where congregants pray that God would sanctify and equip the candidate with the Spirit and charismata. *Gudstjenestebok for Den norske kirke, del 2*, 162–73.

50. Marshall, "Congregation and Ministry," 123.

51. Dunn, *Jesus and the Spirit*, 272.

52. Also the profiled Catholic ecclesiologist, Hans Küng, emphasizes the charismatic structure of the church. Küng, *The Church*, 179.

Spirit. As Schweizer puts it, "the church becomes church, not by tradition itself, but by repeated action of the Spirit."[53]

In the New Testament churches, the body of Christ grew through regular ministries as well as *ad hoc* ministries established because of specific demands. However, all offices had a more or less charismatic character and all could in principle be appointed on the basis of charismatic acts of service manifested beforehand.

The Role of Wonders and Signs

According to different passages of the New Testament, church identity as Spirit-driven emerged from the expectation that she is a channel for mighty deeds and wonders. From the perspective of the groundbreaking work of Gerhard Lohfink, the coming of the Spirit is God's gift to the eschatological community.[54] The presence of the Spirit, symbolized by the link between preaching and healing (Luke 9:1-2), displayed that the rule of God, communicated by the church, came not only in word but also in deed, just as in the ministry of Jesus (Acts 2:43; 3:1-10). The same emphasis is given by the author of Hebrews (Heb 2:3-4; cf. Mark 16:20). The wonders accompanying the gospel served to make salvation a tangible reality and give a taste of the powers of the age to come (Heb 6:5). In other words, they were a constitutive part of preaching the gospel (1 Thess 1:5; cf. Rom 15:17-19).

To the churches in Galatia, Paul declares that salvation is present among them through the Spirit that they have received and through the wonders that take place in their midst. The gift of healing seems to be quite a normal expression of a Spirit-driven church (Gal 3:1-5). As Lohfink describes, these insights from Paul indicate that miracles in the communities were not to be described only as accompanying legitimating signs of the preaching of the gospel, but also as signs of the presence of the Spirit.[55] Faith in the gospel was conferred by the Spirit, just as the basic elements of Jesus' public activity were carried on by the early church.

Read in this way, the Day of Pentecost signified for the earliest Christian communities the eschatological outpouring of the Spirit. The eschatological events are not solely located in the future but are already breaking in

---

53. Schweizer, *Church Order*, 99.

54. Lohfink, *Jesus and Community*, 83. Lohfink holds that the apostle Paul presupposed that wherever a Christian community lives on the basis of the gospel, miraculous powers exist. Ibid., 84. In the days to come I suppose that will imply a more positive attitude to different healing practices.

55. Ibid., 85.

and present for those who grasp the signs of the times. However, the early church rarely spoke of the reign of God as such. According to Lohfink, the decisive experience by which they grasped the reality of the gift of salvation was through the experience of the Spirit. As promised by Joel, the Spirit was poured out on all people (Joel 2:28). Whereas Jesus spoke of the presence of the reign of God (Mark 1:15), the early church spoke of the presence of the Spirit in the communities through a multiplicity of charisms. Signs and wonders were at the essence of the New Testament communities. The future eschatological salvation had already begun.

Another scholarly perspective on the book of Acts, given by S. Scott Bartchy, is to read its main thesis as God's desire to be worshipped through practices of justice and mercy on behalf of those who were poor, whether economically or socially (Acts 4:32–35; cf. Deut 15:7–8).[56] According to this reading, radical compassion is the principal fruit of the apostle's preaching of the resurrection of Jesus. Their sharing with each other and with those in physical needs made plausible their claim to be a church made by the Spirit. Behind this reflection is the notion that God cannot be closed up in pure theological conceptions. Sharing was foundational for the establishing of the church.

In his commentary to the Acts, also Luke T. Johnson states that the gift of the Spirit brought about a community which realized the highest aspirations of human longing; unity, peace, joy, and the praise of God.[57] The gift of the Spirit was made manifest through shared life in a new community. In Acts, the same Spirit gives authority to a number of leaders based on character and commitment, without acts of ordination or any other kind of appointment by the Jerusalem apostles.[58] These lay people were appointed and anointed by the Spirit alone. In the Book of Acts, none of the Twelve are considered indispensable as ongoing guarantors of the traditions concerning "all that Jesus did and taught" (Acts 1:1).

S. Scott Bartchy notes that Luke does not mention the Twelve after Acts 6:2, from which he understands that the apostles did not necessarily represent the beginning of the church offices or prototypes of later church leaders. There is no obvious clergy status in the Book of Acts. Luke describes the ongoing leadership among the early Christians as equipped by the Spirit

---

56. Bartchy, "Power, Community, and Leadership," 91.

57. Johnson, *The Acts*, 62.

58. Among these leaders were Joseph Barnabas (9:27; 11:22–30; 13:1–3; 14:12–20), Ananias of Damascus (9:10–19; 22:12–16), Simeon, Lucius, and Manaen (13:1), Timothy (16:1; 17:14–15; 20:4), Lydia (16:14), Priscillas and Aquila (18:2), Apollos (18:24; 19:1), Crispus (18:8), and the elders and overseers of Ephesus (20:17–28). Bartchy, "Power, Community, and Leadership," 96–97.

THE GIFTED CHURCH OF THE NEW TESTAMENT 71

for necessary tasks. They did not occupy an office as a controlling position. In that light, the alleged importance of the absence of women from this symbolic group (the Twelve) in some church traditions has been exaggerated far beyond the group's significance (Acts 2:17-19; 21:8-9; cf. 1 Cor 11:5; Ro, 16:7). The significance of the Twelve was tied to their roles as founders and preachers, not as a ruling council of decision makers in concrete congregations or as a "sanctified paradigm of exclusively male leadership for the rest of the church history" (cf. Acts 15).[59]

Spiritual Gifts

The Pauline theology of the church has experiential dimensions, not least the experience of grace.[60] Spirit and grace are keywords in his theology (Rom 5:5; 8:9, 14; 6:11; 12:13; Gal 3:1-5; 1 Thess 1:4-6). The power of the Spirit makes faith in God existentially real (Gal 4:6). We simply live by the Spirit (Gal 5:25; 2 Cor 1:21-22), actualized by grace as a generous act of God (Eph 1:6-10; Rom 3:24; 5:15; Eph 2:8). The Spirit is a tangible and verifiable reality (2 Cor 8:1), a gracious power, existentially moving in and upon the life of the believers, both as individuals (1 Cor 3:10) and as communities (Rom 5:2).[61] For Paul, grace is the dynamic experience of being taken hold of and used by God (1 Cor 15:10). The whole life is thus an expression of grace (2 Cor 12:9). That implies a position of seeing faith as the apprehended experience of a world loved by God, and the church as the theo-dramatic practice in which I admit that, were it not for God, I would be without the divine impulse by which my life is supplied with hope.

Charisma derives from grace, understood as gift (*charis*). The difference between those words is insignificant, as both express something given by God, which is distinct from person to person (1 Cor 7:7). The most frequent usage of *charisma* has to do with the different manifestations of grace

---

59. Bartchy, "Power, Community, and Leadership," 100-101.

60. Paul's use of church is primarily oriented around concrete communities, located on specific places as a result of his missionary activities (1 Cor 1:2; Gal 1:1; 1 Thess 1:1). However, when he wrote the letter to the Philippians and applied to "all God's holy people in Christ Jesus at Philippi, together with the overseers and deacons" (Phlm 1:1), he certainly had a sense of the spiritual connectedness of all the churches, though his principal concern was directed to the local communities. A more universal vision of the church in general can be traced in the Deutero-Pauline letters to the Colossians and the Ephesians (Col 1:6; 18; Eph 5:25-32). The Pastoral Letters are more concerned with the need of stable leadership structures, though without precluding the presence of the charismatic gifts which otherwise is emphasized in the letters of Paul (1 Cor 1:7; 2:13; 7:7; 12-14; Rom 12:11; Gal 3:5; Eph 6:18).

61. Dunn, *Jesus and the Spirit*, 203.

coming forth within the context of the fellowship of believers (1 Cor 1:7). These spiritual gifts are all acts of service, all wrought by God, all for the common good, and all manifestations of the Spirit (1 Cor 12: 4–7; Eph 4:12). According to Paul, some of these gifts were utterances which demonstrated the Spirit's presence and activities because of their revelatory character.[62] Charisma was an event, not a possession or an office.[63] Hence, the particular act of service as it is performed, whether it is a miracle, experience of faith, or word of wisdom or prophecy, is not the charisma of an individual but a manifestation of grace by which God chooses to act through one member of Christ's body for the blessing and guidance of others.

Thus the gift of a charisma is given not to the one who manifests it but to the ones whom the charisma serves. It is not a human response to grace but simply God's grace, visible expressed. It is simply given, unachieved, and uncontrived. There is no immediate causal connection between the bestowal of charisma and sanctification, nor is it a sign of maturity. However, the case of Corinth clearly displays the possibilities of having too high regard for gifts and too low amount of love and holiness (1 Cor 2–4). Charismata are different experiences of grace and gracious power, in order to heal, to trust, to believe, to teach, and to be edified through the receiving of words in prayer, praise and prophecy (Rom 12:6–7).[64] There is a wide range of charismatic manifestations and phenomena; they are not at all completely mapped out in the writings of Paul. In line with God's abundance of grace, there is a great multitude of gifts, and their use is determined by the particular situations and needs of the community of faith (Col 3: 16; Rom 12: 1–18). As Dunn describes:

> Not simply worship, but all life is to be lived in conscious dependence on God, open to that charismata, that manifestation of grace which at any time may transform attitudes, relationships, and situations in the direction of God's good, acceptable and perfect will. The grace of God does not recognize human distinctions between sacred and secular. It also follows that the experience of grace in Paul may not be narrowed or confined within some sacramental system or channeled through some priestly hierarchy. Paul indeed knows nothing of sacramental grace as such.[65]

---

62. Ibid., 209, 212.
63. Ibid., 254.
64. Dunn, *Jesus and the Spirit*, 255.
65. Ibid., 257.

Dunn defends his position by positing the primacy of the connection between Spirit and faith over Spirit and sacrament (Gal 3:2). Baptism and the Eucharist as sacraments do give concrete expression to the grace of God by grounding faith in Christ's suffering, death, burial, and resurrection. But grace is not exclusively mediated by a ritual act; in fact, the term is rarely used when describing these. The experience of grace is manifold and varied, and frequently given in direct and unmediated forms.

Surprisingly, Paul also designates rational charismatic experiences, which take place on the level of the mind.[66] The gift of prophecy is connected to what he calls "some revelation or knowledge . . . or teaching" (1 Cor 14:6). Consequently, it is more valuable than the non-rationality of glossolalia, unless the latter becomes interpreted (vv. 7–25). The Spirit talks to humans' understanding *and* spirit. The charismata of knowledge and wisdom (1 Cor 12:8) appear as an alternative way to get insight, compared to the opponents of Paul in Corinth and their use of exclusive knowledge and wisdom through *gnosis* and *sophia*. For the Corinthians, *gnosis* was their charismatic and scriptural insight into the nature of reality, both spiritual and material. The church has received the Spirit, so that we may understand the gifts bestowed on us by God (1 Cor 2:12). Against the wisdom of this world (1 Cor 1:20) God has raised a cross, and against the wisdom of words (1 Cor 2:5; Rom 11: 33; cf. Luke 21:15), the power of God is to be experienced through the gospel of the cross. For Paul, *gnosis* and *sophia* were not only philosophical Greek terms but also represented the Jewish understanding that God was known by his work through the salvation history of the crucified Christ (Eph 3:19; cf. 2 Cor 8:2). That included not only a rational acknowledgement but an experimental participation in that very history, made accessible through the Spirit of God (1 Cor 2:12; Rom 1:16). God's word of wisdom was an inspired proclamation with saving power, often recognized through different kinds of church ministries (Eph 4:11–13).

Inspired Speeches

More often than not, charismata came to expression through inspired speech and utterances, which Paul defined as explaining spiritual realities with Spirit-thought words (1 Cor 2:13). Through these the church is given insight into the deep things of God (v. 10).[67] Paul was firmly convinced that his own preaching was charismatic (1 Cor 2:4–5). The gospel came to the churches with the Holy Spirit and deep conviction (1 Thess 1:5). The

66. Ibid., 217.
67. Ibid., 226.

feeling of being addressed by God and grasped by the power of God made his preaching a demonstration of the Spirit's power (1 Cor 2:4), quite apart from any considerations of reason and logic. This demonstration had nothing to do with his rhetorical skills, arguments, proofs, or intellectual persuasion. Quite to the contrary, it came into view in weakness "with great fear and trembling" (v. 3). However, his fear and trembling did not influence his boldness on behalf of the gospel (Rom 1:16–17).

While the utterance of the gospel was fundamental in creating the community of faith (Rom 10:17; cf. Matt 16:18), the utterance of prophecy aimed to equip God's people for works of service, so that the body of Christ may be built up (Eph 4:11–12; cf. Acts 9:31; 16:5; 1 Cor 14:4–5, 12, 26; Rom 12:6–8; 1 Cor 12:8–10; 28–30). When classifying the spiritual gifts in terms of importance, prophecy was given a clear preference (1 Cor 14:1; Eph 2:20; 1 Cor 12:28). However, prophesying was not only to be regarded as a mouthpiece for divine utterance. Rather it included the ability to give interpretations along with rational discernment, distinct from the role of glossolalia or ecstatic inexpressible utterance (2 Cor 12:4). Prophesying meant speaking intelligible words with the mind (1 Cor 14:19). It was not a skill to be learned but a revelation of words given for comfort and encouragement (1 Cor 14:3). Paul did contrast prophecy and glossolalia, but only with respect to intelligibility, not inspiration (1 Cor 14:18–19). Prophecy was given priority as intelligible speaking forth of words given by the Spirit for particular situations of need in the church. Its edifying role was associated with guidance, comfort, sympathy, encouragement, worship, and humility, in order to shed new light on the salvation of Christ (1 Cor 11:23). However, according to Frank D. Macchia, all of the gifts, including prophecy, are relativized by Paul in subordination to the love of God. Desiring the "best gifts" (1 Cor 12:31) depends on the context in which they are exercised and not on judgment concerning which among the gifts are the least or most important.[68]

Contrary to those in Corinth who misconstrued glossolalia as a sign of superior spirituality and a proof of pneumatic authority, Paul declared the reverse. Glossolalia is a sign for the unbelievers as a sign of divine judgment, and they edify no one but themselves (1 Cor 14:4). Prophecy, on the other hand, is a sign for the believers by its edifying significance in a broad sense (1 Cor 14:22). It reveals God's presence in the midst of the assembly, so that even the unbeliever declares that "God is really among you" (v. 25). Within the framework of the worshipping assembly, prophetic words can bring conviction, a deeper humility and commitment to a believer or groups of

---

68. Macchia, "Groans too Deep," 15.

believers, or unexpected and unintended relevance to particular individuals.[69] With regards to 1 Cor 14:24–25, Dunn writes:

> Prophecy prevents a man pretending to be other than he is – prevents the believer hiding behind a mask of pretended righteousness, of apparent spirituality. At any time the prophetic word may expose him for what he is. He dares not take refuge in the image he portrays to the world, in his reputation, in arguments of self-justification. Where the prophetic Spirit is present honesty with oneself and about oneself is indispensable (1 Thess 2:4). In short, prophecy edifies because it does not exalt man but humbles him, making him aware that he stands before God in all his vulnerability.[70]

The faith community is compelled to reflect upon their own values, priorities, and attitudes on the level of the mind. In addition, by opening the community to a wider dimension of reality, prophecy does not permit the community to construe faith as a matter of purely rational thoughts. Rather, it points to our deep dependence on the life of God as the source of the community's health and well-being (Phil 1:9).

Charismatic Hymnology

Paul describes the phenomenon of singing with his Spirit as well as with his mind (1 Cor 14:15). Dunn recognizes in this a kind of charismatic hymnology: spontaneous and inspired utterance which includes both singing in tongues and with intelligible words (v. 26). The hymnology of Paul included psalms, hymns, and spiritual songs (Eph 5:19), as well as "songs from the Spirit" (Col 3:16). These acts of worship—spontaneous or liturgical—were direct outcomes of Paul's spiritual admonition to be filled with the Spirit (Eph 5:18), "singing and making melody to the LORD in your heart" (v. 19). All songs, psalms, and hymns were embraced by the adjective "spiritual." The distinctions were not whether they were spontaneous or not, but presumably whether they were songs of intelligible words or not. Though we do not have any direct examples of glossolalic hymnody in the New Testament, we do find different forms of worship such as doxologies (1 Tim 3:16; Rom 11:33–36; Phlm 4:20) and expressions of deep feelings (Rom 8:26–27). These different kinds of hymnology shared a common purpose of instruction and

---

69. Dunn, *Jesus and the Spirit*, 232.
70. Ibid.

edification within the community. They were not vehicles only for inward and vertical oriented praise (Eph 5:19; Col 3:16).

In the Pauline material, praying and prophesying are closely related (1 Cor 11:4). Paul gives a clear admonition to the Ephesians: "Pray in the Spirit at all times in every prayer and supplication" (Eph 6:18).[71] Prayer in tongues and rational prayer were recommended to the Corinthians, all in a fitting and orderly way (1 Cor 14:14–17, 40). Prayer was an expression— silent or audible—of the inner confidence of sonship, of belonging to God (Rom 8:15–17). It was something given and brought to utterance through their lips by the Spirit (Gal 4:6), a conscious cooperation with God.[72] When Paul was talking about a sigh too deep for words or wordless groans (Rom 8:26), Dunn takes a different interpretation than Käsemann or Macchia.[73] While the latter two, together with Gunkel and Stendahl, understand the Pauline phrase as a reference to glossolalic cries involved in our yearnings for redemption, Dunn asserts it as the only form of prayer left to the believer who comes "to the end of himself." In these Pauline passages we observe two sides of charismatic consciousness: that of human impotence and that of divine power in and through weakness.[74]

The ecstatic character of glossolalia in Corinth resulted in disorder, confusion, competition, and immorality, as criticized by Paul (1 Cor 1–6, 12–14). However, his assessment of glossolalia on the whole was positive because of its inspired character (1 Cor 14:5). The great European researcher on Pentecostalism, Walter J. Hollenweger, repudiates the idea that speaking in tongues is ecstatic by nature. There may be hot speaking in tongues, though the person is never outside their own control. And there is cool speaking in tongues, sometimes mystical and sometimes sounding like an incomprehensible foreign language.[75] As a legitimate charismatic gift, glossolalia has a role to play in the assembly. However, Paul preferred speaking intelligible words (v. 9). Glossolalia had to be restrained when the utterance was inappropriate (vv. 28, 32–33). Because Paul considered tongues not to be different languages, glossolalia had to be accompanied with the gift of interpretation (1 Cor 12: 10; 14: 5, 27–28). Paul seems to have regarded the glossolalist as holding secret conversation with God (1 Cor 14:2). Speech in tongues "of mortals and of angels" (1 Cor 13:1) for Paul probably meant that

---

71. Ibid., 239.
72. Ibid., 241.
73. Käsemann, *Romans*, 230–44. Macchia, "Sigh too Deep," 59.
74. Dunn, *Jesus and the Spirit*, 242.
75. Hollenweger, *Pentecostals*, 344.

glossolalia was a heavenly language rather than a worldly.[76] However, when it came to presentation in public, he favored the more controlled speaking in tongues over ecstatic glossolalia (1 Cor 14:26–28). Those who experienced glossolalia apprehended the phenomenon as effective communication with God (Rom 8:26).[77] All in all, Pauline teaching on glossolalia can be summed up like this: it was permitted and perceived as a gift, but it was not to be encouraged in the assembly unless it became interpreted. First and foremost, it functioned to edify the individual, while the one who prophesies edifies the church (1 Cor 14:5).

Presupposing that glossolalia stands in the service of the church and is a manifestation of the Spirit for the common good (1 Cor 12:7), the demand for the gift of interpretation seems to be obvious. This is not an independent gift of its own right, but serves to give tongues their edifying significance. You may ask why speaking in tongues is a charisma at all, if the overarching aim of the charismata is the mindful edifying of the congregation. Why this form of an apparently selfish expression of spiritual enthusiasm? Dunn's answer lies in the interpretation of tongues. The glossolalic utterance had to be balanced by an inspired utterance in the vernacular. Thus, the gift of interpretation to some extent can be considered as the assembly's control over glossolalia and a safeguard against possible abuse.

A Drive for Love and Service

The charismatic activities also included spiritual guidance and discernment of God's will in matters of ethical conduct and decision making (2 Cor 2: 14; cf. Ps 119:125). The capacity of the believer for ethical decision depends on the renewal of his or her mind (Rom 12:2), which in turn is ascribed to the Word and the Spirit (Eph 6:17; 1 Thess 2:13; Heb 4:12). The gift of testing and distinguishing between spirits (1 Cor 12:10) and the spiritual fruit of gentleness and self-control (Gal 5:23) are concrete expressions of love combined with a spontaneous awareness of how God's standard of righteousness sheds light on particular ethical dilemmas (Phlm 1:9).[78]

Serving ministries are also charismatic gifts and need to be observed and evaluated as such. Paul initially describes the Spirit-driven services of deacons as giving, caring, helping, leading, and guiding (1 Cor 12:7–10,

---

76. Dunn, *Jesus and the Spirit*, 244. Possible allusions to glossolalia, though not explicitly mentioned, include passages as Rom 8:23, 26; Eph 5:19; 6:18; Col 3:16, and 1 Thess 5:19.

77. Ibid., 245.

78. Ibid., 225.

28). These may not include manifestations of inspired speech, revelation and miracles. But they are no less spiritual for that reason. Paul even defines his own ministry as an act of service (2 Cor 11:8; Rom 11:13; 2 Cor 5:18). Giving to the poor was a charisma because it reflected God's unmerited generosity of Christ, freely and cheerfully carried through. All three gifts in Rom 12:8 (to give, to lead, and to show mercy) covered the whole range of the early church's welfare service that cared for vulnerable members of the community such as widows, orphans, slaves and strangers.[79] As such, these gifts were an expression of the vitality and the ethical quality of the community. It was within the frame of the common life that the Spirit-driven church expressed herself in a loving and vigorous concern for the less fortunate (1 Cor 12:25–27).

Thus the charismata designated themselves by verbs; they manifested in action and were not dependent upon an official position. They were undertaken at the urging of love and acknowledged by the community as gifts and ministries (1 Thess 5:12). This includes gifts of helping and of giving guidance, which gradually became linked to established positions of deacon and overseer (Phlm 1:1; 1 Tim 3:1–10). All in all, in Scripture we observe a combination of both ordered ministries and spontaneous, Spirit inspired actions. Together these fulfilled important functions within the community. Those who were channels for gifts possessed them only to the extent they were involved in the actual deeds. The prophecy was always more important than the prophet.

For Paul, the shared experience of Spirit and grace was fundamental to the living reality of the community. While some, like Dunn, holds that the most important common denominator in Acts is the testimony of the conversion-initiation event (see Gal 3:2; 2 Cor 2:21–22), it can be stated that the decisive moment of Pentecost claimed that participation in the church meant communion with the Holy Spirit who gives the church her unique and holy character (2 Cor 13:13; cf. 1 John 1:3). The unity which was received as a result of that common sharing of the Spirit, was the source for the oneness of the spiritual experience of the new life in Christ (1 Cor 12:13; Eph 4:3).

Normally, the words of 1 Cor 12:13 (that we were all baptized by one Spirit so as to form one body) has been connected to the understanding of baptism.[80] However, the debate continues whether that passage rather may refer to the Spirit or to Spirit baptism. Dunn argues that the primary reference in this passage, grounded in the specific context of the letter, is

79. Ibid., 251.
80. Beasley-Murray, *Baptism*, 167–71.

that Paul does not say "one baptism, therefore one body," but "one *Spirit*, therefore one body."[81] According to Gordon Fee, the reception of the Spirit is for Paul the *sine qua non* for the Christian life. The Spirit is what makes a person a child of God (Rom 8:14–17). Paul's concern in this chapter is not how the Corinthians became believers, which should point in favor of water baptism, but how the many of them, diverse as they were, are in fact one body.[82] Since the unity of the church derives from the unity in the Spirit, it seems to be something given and not something created by help of confessional declarations alone. It is not a goal but the point of departure (cf. John 17:21).

So also in Corinth, the local church was designated as the body of Christ (1 Cor 12: 14–27), but she was also part of all churches (Rom 16:16b). Each member of the local church had received their gifts in accordance with the grace given to them (Rom 12:6). No one lacked a manifestation of grace and power, and each contributed in worship by letting that grace come to expression.[83] In the light of this, membership became a question of having a function. It was the many who formed the body (1 Cor 12:14). As a living organism, the church was characterized by relationships of mutual reliance, and charismatic expressions did not exist for themselves but for the community. Any idolizing of individuals became an antithesis of the community (1 Cor 14:2), because individually "we are members one of another" (Rom 12:5). This corporate dimension of Christian life united in the Spirit of God clarified the identity of the church. The result was a mutual interdependence which created unity in the midst of a variety of ministries and charismata. It is important to remember that Paul did not conceive of two kinds of Christians: those with the Spirit and those without. You are a Christian since you have the Spirit. To be a Christian is to be charismatic; one cannot be a member of the body without sharing the charismatic Spirit.[84]

In the case of Corinth, however, the charismata appeared to be a threat to the community. Self-styled and gnostic oriented spiritual men caused confusion by their words of knowledge (1 Cor 3:18–23; 8:4). Their eagerness for experiences of inspiration and ecstasy, the lack of order in worship, impatience, jealousy, boastfulness, and selfishness, where far from any expression of unity in the Spirit.[85] Their problems centered largely on the importance attributed to charismatic phenomenon. The church of Rome

81. Dunn, *Jesus and the Spirit*, 261.
82. Fee, *Empowering Presence*, 178–79.
83. Dunn, *Jesus and the Spirit*, 263.
84. Ibid., 264.
85. Ibid., 266.

had a similar problem with the charismata disrupting rather than unifying the body (Rom 12:3). Nevertheless, Paul's guidance in 1 and 2 Corinthians and in Romans 12 was of great importance for churches who sought to combine openness toward the dynamic elements in the churches with the clear regulations of the charismata (Rom 12:3–8) and an appreciation of sincerely love and hospitality (vv. 9–13).

One of the arguments against the rather pessimistic approach regarding the healthiness of charismatic fellowship is that charismata are by definition a manifestation of grace, a Spirit-given function in order to strengthen and edifying the church in general. Anything that threatens the community—though it poses as charismata—has to be unveiled for what it is: powers that display themselves as false imitation of genuine charismata. The charisma of distinguishing between spirits is given specifically for exposing such impostors (1 Cor 12:10).

Manifestations of Grace

So charismata were perceived as integrated elements in the body of Christ, understood as manifestations of grace. In the ecclesiology of Paul, the body of Christ was synonymous with the charismatic community. Without church, charisma is fruitless. Without graceful manifestations, the church is lifeless.[86] The overall motif of Paul was to follow the way of love and eagerly desire gifts of the Spirit (1 Cor 14:1). However, 1 Cor 12–14 teaches that the more extraordinary the gift, the less valuable it becomes. What counts is not flying high but building up. Though not everyone speaks in tongues (1 Cor 12:30), all are charismatics because all have a ministry. There are no ministries that exist apart from the Spirit. Though some ministries may seem to be more important than others, the health and function of the whole body relies upon interdependence of the different parts (1 Cor 12:12–26). From God's point of view, human hierarchical structures are turned upside down (vv. 24–25).

This is the ground-breaking message of the Spirit-driven church: All have immediate access to grace, and all may presume being an instrument of grace to others. After Pentecost, each church is part of the body of Christ through the grace of God and the gifts of the Spirit. Although the narrative of Corinth exposes the dangers of misusing charismata, they are fundamental to the functioning of a healthy church when understood rightly.[87]

---

86. Dunn, *Jesus and the Spirit*, 297.
87. Ibid., 298.

Passages in the letters of Paul sketch out how the exercise of the charismata includes their own safeguards: they have to serve to whole community (1 Cor 14:12), and they must be used according to the measure of the given faith (Rom 12:3). Healing seems to be dependent on faith or at least a positive expectation, prophecy has to be tested, and tongues must be interpreted. All the gifts must be evaluated in light of the apostolic-kerygmatic tradition, the authority of the whole community, and the criteria of love (1 Cor 12:8–10; 13:1–13). Only a responsible charismatic community can adequately express the same grace that was manifested by Christ in his mighty deeds and graceful message.

The combination and interdependence of both the charismatic and sacramental dimensions of the church helps secure this healthy balance. Despite of our propensity to systematize, there is a dimension of the Spirit as the unexpected guest who refrains from being tailored to our boundaries (John 3:8). That is why the church does not have to close the mouth of the prophets. According to the NT, her inner life is both sacramental and charismatic in character (Acts 2:38–39). When faith, baptism and the Spirit find each other like a burning focal point in an ecclesiological ellipsis, then the church can brightly reflect the presence of God's salvation in the midst of the world.

Constructive Reflections

During the life and ministry of Christ, the plenitude of the power and presence of the Spirit was understood as a key characteristic of the kingdom, now already present but still not yet in its fullness. The interaction of sonship and Spirit shaped the distinctive character of Jesus' ministry as a manifestation of grace. These charismatic and ethical elements were carried on by the believers in the early church, insights that gave birth to Christianity and shaped the establishing of the church. Easter and Pentecost thus ran together. The outburst of the Spirit on the Day of Pentecost created continuity between Jesus and his followers, establishing a line back to the Jewish tradition and forward toward the young Christian church.[88] In the first stories of Christian communal life, pneumatology and Christology are woven together. Christ had to be recognized in the works of the Spirit, functioning as a regulatory element in corporate spirituality. Thus the Pentecost had epochal significance in the linking together of Christology and pneumatology.

Christians from the earliest parts of church history had the feeling of being a community made by the Spirit, in the midst of an otherwise fluid

---

88. See McDonnell, "A Trinitarian Theology," 191–227.

order and structure. Their sense of community stemmed from a common experience of having received the eschatological Spirit on the Day of Pentecost. Then the resurrection of Christ authorized them to act in the name of Jesus. The sharing of the table fellowship and the practice of baptism found its roots in the life and ministry of Jesus.

The coming of the Spirit on the first Christ-believers signified the creation of the Spirit-endowed, Spirit-empowered, Spirit-led community. The reality of the Spirit embraced all believers and formed God's people to be one fellowship. By grace, all things were being made new in a resurrection of the dead through the baptism in the Holy Spirit. This was the witness carried by the community of Christians around the world. Pentecost was the foretaste of the kingdom, inspiring the Spirit bearers to proclaim forgiveness and life in the name of Jesus. Thus, the Spirit enabled mission and became a source of prophetic activity.

The ethical implications of prophetic ministry and charismatic manifestations within the New Testament churches were not merely side effects. The Spirit became related to the life of the people of God in its entirety: the daily provision of food, forgiveness of sins by God and by each other, protection from apostasy and deliverance from demonic enslavement. The Spirit was located at the heart of the renewed community's life. The Pentecost experience provided the Lukan church with a hermeneutical key which shaped a vision of both personal and social renewal. By sharing with each other and with those in physical need, the apostles made plausible their claim to be a church made by the Spirit. The shared life of this new community was itself a gift of the Spirit. Even the Twelve played the roles of founders and preachers, not a ruling council of decision makers.

The presence of Christ and the life of the church were mediated not simply through ordained ministers but through the whole congregation. Signs and wonders belonged to the essence of the New Testament communities, indicating that the future eschatological salvation had already begun.[89] What constituted the church's ecclesiality was not her structures or programs, but the people gathered in the name of God for the sake of worship, listening, and participation in the sacrament, all animated by the Spirit. In that regard, the ideals coming from the Lukan corpus indicates a church with a charismatic identity as well as a sacramental self-understanding.

The apostolic church had a plurality of leaders. Individuals, overseers, and deacons were expected to use their resources generously to help other people in need and to be involved in far-reaching programs of social care. These ministries were understood as inspired by the Spirit of God. Thus,

---

89. For a broader presentation, see Lohfink, *Jesus and Community*.

charisma implied office and office expressed charisma. Such charismata built up the body as visible manifestations and concrete realizations of grace, rather than claiming special merit for themselves. Throughout human history, the church exhibits cracked greatness, so we will never be able to determine the full reach of the Spirit's multifaceted impact. Though the Spirit works on the level of individuals, the New Testament writers remind us that the true nature of the Spirit's work is that of corporate transformation.[90] The church is the world's hope within the present and the world's future for the age to come.

In the following chapter we will search for an understanding of the gift of the Spirit or the baptism of the Spirit. Drawing from interlocutors of various traditions, I identify the outpouring of the Spirit on the Day of Pentecost as the key to understanding the church's character as both charismatic and sacramental. Broadening the concept of the Spirit will enable us to build a bridge between a Pentecostal and a more classical understanding of the gift of the Spirit.

---

90. A recent work, based upon empirical studies of three contemporary churches, discusses the conditions for individual commitments in a postmodern context, see Tangen, *Ecclesial Identification*.

4

The Gift of the Spirit

> *The Holy Spirit may be the last article of the Creed but in the New Testament it is the first fact of experience.*[1]

Introduction

ACCORDING TO PAUL, SOME of the spiritual gifts *build up the church* (1 Cor 14:12; Rom 1:11). So to what extent does the term "the gift of the Spirit" function as an organizing principle when talking about the church? What does it mean that early Christianity did not adjust itself in accordance with a cultic act, but in accordance with the act of God revealed in the giving of the Spirit?[2] In this chapter, our discussion of these questions will be guided by four theologians who have concerned themselves with such topics since the 1970s.

James D. G. Dunn: The Experiential Nature of the Spirit

Among the most central findings attributed to James D. G. Dunn, is that the New Testament understands the gift of the Spirit in thoroughly experiential terms. Becoming a Christian is essentially a matter of receiving the Spirit (Gal 3:1–5, 14), and the reception of the Spirit is what constitutes the individual as Christian and as a member of the church.[3] The term refers

---

1. Newbigin, *The Household of God*, 89.
2. Preisker, "Apollos und die Johannesjünger," 304.
3. Dunn, *Baptism in Spirit*, 123. Though 45 years or so since this early classic was first published, probably no other book about this specific issue has been subjected to such a comprehensive debate among Pentecostal scholars. The main position of the book still deserves to be summarized. Regarding my own reflections of the relation between faith and water baptism, see the chapter called *Graceful Gifts*.

to the various experiences and actions of the Spirit in the life of individuals and Christian communities. With the exception of the phrase "filled with the Spirit," the different terms that describe the experience of the Spirit in the narratives of Luke refer mainly to the first coming of the Spirit upon a person or group.[4] Luke evidently did not think of anybody in his narratives as having the Spirit prior to the Spirit coming upon him or her, or prior to being baptized in the Spirit. Thus, the New Testament does not know a distinctively second experience of the Spirit, according to Dunn.[5] In contrast, the gift of the Spirit is the most fundamental aspect of becoming a Christian. It is the breath of divine life and the bond between the human and the divine, without which no one can belong to Christ (Rom 8:9, 14; Gal 3:2-3, John 4:14; 7:37-39; 20:22). However, this position has been opposed in various ways by theologians from the Pentecostal tradition, which will be reflected later in this chapter.

The initiatory character of Spirit baptism is defined in 1 Cor 12:13. Being "baptized in one Spirit into one body" expresses, according to Dunn, what baptism in the Spirit accomplishes. It refers to the beginning of the Christian experience, the action by which God draws the individual into the sphere of the Spirit, into the community of those being saved, and thus makes a decisive beginning of the work of saving grace in the individual.[6] To Paul, the Spirit is the substantial sign of God's acceptance. God's instruments of saving grace are the gospel and the Spirit. The gift of the Spirit is God's decisive act of grace, grasped by faith and expressed in baptism.[7] Debates about the relationship between Spirit and baptism often focus on Acts 2:38-39. Dunn argues that the clearest reading of this text is to interpret the actions of repentance and baptism for the forgiveness of sins as a response to the gift of the Spirit.

In the Cornelius episode, the audience heard Peter's sermon, believed, and received the Spirit. It was a saving action (Acts 11:18). Then the Spirit

---

4. Dunn, "Baptism in Spirit—Once More," 33. The stories within the Acts contain different formulations: the Spirit came upon them (1:8; 19:6), the Spirit was poured out on them (2:17, 18, 33; 10:45), they received the Holy Spirit (5:32, 8:18; 11:17; 15:8), and the Holy Spirit fell upon them (8:16; 10:44; 11:15). However, while there were many events of being filled with the Spirit (2:4; 4:8, 31; 9:17; 13:9, 52), the term of being baptized in the Spirit seems to be connected to a particular promise from God's side throughout the New Testament (Matt 3:11; Mark 1:8; Luke 3:16; Acts 1:5; 3:38; 11:16).

5. Dunn, "Reponse to Pentecostal Scholarship," 5. See also Dunn, *Baptism in Spirit*. For an introduction to the debate among Pentecostal Scholars, see Atkinson, *Spirit Baptism and the Dunn Debate*. See also Cheung, "Spirit-Baptism." Turner, "Appreciation and Response." And Dunn, "Baptism in Spirit—Once More."

6. Dunn, "Reponse to Pentecostal Scholarship," 6.

7. Dunn, *Baptism in Spirit*, 172.

came as a sign and transmitter of forgiveness (11:14-15, 17). As a result of their reception of the Spirit, Peter deduced that they should not be refused baptism (10:47). The gift of the Spirit is the definitive sign of the new life bestowed. When Peter later on recalls what happened (15:7-9), he states that the preaching and the call for a response opened up the opportunity for divine action, described in terms of the gift of the Spirit and the cleansing of the heart by means of faith (vv. 8-9). As Dunn puts it, the descent of the Spirit at Jordan and on Pentecost day inaugurated a decisive new stage in God's purpose in the world. The ministry of Jesus commissioned at Jordan (Luke 3: 18-21) brought the eschatological kingdom into the present as a significant new stage in the salvation story. But Jesus' anointing for witness was only part of the story.

Pentecost has a similarly epochal character because it inaugurated a new stage in God's saving purpose for all, Gentiles and Jews. That is why Luke draws a parallel between the Day of Pentecost and the Cornelius event (10:47; 11:15-17; 15:8), as well as between Jordan and Jerusalem. The key phrase in these episodes in Luke-Acts is simply "baptized in the Holy Spirit" (Luke 3:16; Acts 1:5; 11:16). The symbol of baptism in the time of Luke included not only immersion in water but also a new relationship with Christ as LORD and the beginning of a process of transformation of one's status and character. The Pentecostal outpouring is bound up with salvation as the fulfillment of the promise of the Father with all its soteriological, empowering, and prophecy-inspiring force.[8]

Furthermore, Luke-Acts closely links the gift of the Spirit with faith (Acts 2:44; 38-39; 6:5; 10:43-44; 11:17, 24; 15:7-9; 19:2). As Dunn describes, the fact that God gave the same gift to them (Cornelius and his house) as he gave to the disciples who believed in the LORD Jesus Christ (11:17), implies that faith was the human side of the divine-human transaction in which the Spirit was bestowed. As with Cornelius, Peter and the others entered into this new era of God's gracious openness to both Gentiles and Jews by being baptized in the Holy Spirit. To Luke, the act of believing and the gift of the Spirit are two sides of the same event. This still leaves us with the peculiar problem of the Samaritan episode in Acts 8:12-16, where the people believed, were baptized, but still had not received the Holy Spirit.

---

8. Anthony C. Thiselton reflects a position often repeated within the Lutheran tradition, that the different occasions of charismatic eruptions in the Acts of the Apostle were decisive boundary-crossing moments in the successive stages of the expansion of the gospel. Thiselton, *The Holy Spirit*, 491. However, such an approach may lead to a weakening of the fact that spiritual experiences in principle may be multiple, renewable and repeatable and applied to all committed Christians, not only the elite of "spiritual people" as in Corinth, which Paul rebuked (1 Cor 1-3).

Only the laying on of hands by Peter and John solved the problem. Dunn's point is as follows: where the pattern of the Jerusalem narrative cannot be found, for whatever reason, the concern is precisely not to affirm Christian identity despite the absence of the Spirit, but to emphasize the necessity of the Spirit in order that Christian identity might be clearly established.[9]

For Luke, the gift of the Spirit was regarded as the decisive determinant, the *sine qua non* in the making of a Christian. Surely, the conversion-initiation is also a commissioning for witness, ministry, and mission (Luke 3:16; Acts 1:5, 8; 9:15–18; 22:15–16; 26: 12–18). On these points, Dunn states, Luke and Paul are not as far apart in their pneumatological understanding as is often assumed. They both assume that the Spirit has a soteriological function. But in the living body of Christ, the Spirit has a clearly dynamic character. In Paul's teaching, the same picture appears. He consistently refers to the gift of the Spirit when reminding his readers of the beginning of their Christian experience and their life within the church's fellowship.[10] The reception of the Spirit is the beginning of the Christian life, its major constitutive element, and the only indispensable resource for ministry. For Paul, the best way to define a Christian is to talk of someone having received the Spirit and having a continuing experience of the Spirit (Rom 8:9; cf. Gal 3:1–5, 14; and Eph 5:18). According to Dunn, the statement of Paul in 1 Cor 12:13 that "we were all baptized by one Spirit so as to form one body—whether Jews or Gentiles, slave or free—and we were all given the one Spirit to drink," does refer to the Spirit and not to the baptismal rite. Being baptized into one Spirit is the means by which individuals become members of the one body of Christ. To Dunn, this passage is the only explicit reference in Paul to being baptized in the Spirit. The passage is important since it makes clear that participation in Christ and membership in the church is made possible by being baptized in the Spirit. This passage does not envisage an equipping for ministry distinct from and subsequent to becoming a member of the church of Christ. For Dunn, to be baptized into membership of the body is closely connected to being graced with the

---

9. Dunn, "Reponse to Pentecostal Scholarship," 25.

10. The Spirit is referred to as the life-giving Spirit (2 Cor 3:3, 6); the love of God is poured out into our hearts (Rom 5:5); we are given the Spirit to drink (1 Cor 12:13), a deep conviction and joy (1 Thess 1:5–6); our sonship is also presented us by the Spirit (Rom 8:15); we have the seal of the Spirit and the anointing, the Spirit is given us as a deposit (Eph 1:13–14; 2 Cor 1: 21–22) and as a blessing of Abraham (Gal 3:14). The descriptions have, on the whole, clear soteriological connotations. Dunn, "Baptism in Spirit—Once More," 36. See also the statement of Friedrich Schleiermacher: "For being taken up into living fellowship with Christ includes at the same time being conscious both of our sonship with God and of the Lordship of Christ; and both in Scripture are described to the indwelling of the Holy Spirit." Schleiermacher, *Christian Faith*, §124.1.

charism that is each member's particular function within the body (1 Cor 12:11–27; 14:26; Rom 12:3–8). The gift of the Spirit is dynamic, an initiation into ministry as well as discipleship.[11]

Furthermore, Dunn sees the Pentecost event as inaugurating the age of the church and constituting the disciples as the new covenant people of God. The Spirit was the reality on which the church was founded. It was given to all members of the New Testament community, not only a few as in the Old Testament.[12] In the Lukan depiction of the epoch of the church, prophets are no longer isolated individuals. All members of the eschatological community are prophets.

Spirit Baptism Related to Water Baptism

Dunn places his understanding of baptism directly between a Pentecostal view (Spirit baptism as a second blessing) and a more sacramental position (water baptism as a baptism in water and Spirit). Thus he offers a unique perspective on the relation between Spirit baptism and water baptism. Dunn considers the experience of Jesus at Jordan as a unique moment in salvation history: "It was not so much that Jesus became what he was not before, but the history became what it was not before."[13] This decisive change was effected by the Spirit coming upon Jesus (Luke 3:22; cf. Is 11:2; 61:1). For him, the anointing with the Spirit was essentially an initiatory experience that marked the end time by which Christ became empowered for service. Only with the descent of the Spirit does the new covenant begin. The anointing of Jesus at Jordan also equips him for his messianic ministry of healing and teaching (Acts 10:38). Likewise for the church: through the gift of the Spirit she is initiated into the new age and anointed for life and service in the world.

In Luke, the descent of the Spirit coincides with Jesus' prayer and is a response to his prayer, rather than to the water baptism alone (Luke 3:21b). According to Dunn, water baptism is a pure rite of immersion, connected to conversion.[14] For him, the coalescence of water baptism and Spirit baptism

---

11. Dunn, "Baptism in Spirit—Once More," 39.

12. Schweizer, "Pneuma," 410.

13. Dunn, *Baptism in Spirit*, 21.

14. Ibid., 33. With reference to Acts 2:38, Eduard Schweizer states that water baptism was a natural part of the much more important issue, that of conversion. Hence Luke was not concerned by the fact that the Spirit was poured out on the 120 on the Day of Pentecost without any baptism (see also the Cornelius narrative, Acts 10). To Luke, baptism was not an essential means of obtaining the Spirit. Prayer was far more important as a preparation for the reception of the Spirit. Faith—not baptism—purifies

has distorted the church's understanding of the Holy Spirit. The emphasis in any theologizing about the relation between baptism and Spirit should be on the advantage of the Spirit, in line with the significance John gave the coming of the Spirit, compared to the rite of baptism. For Dunn, the rite of baptism plays a role, but not the decisive role:

> Baptism leads to and results in the bestowal of the Spirit, though not because of any virtue or sacramental efficacy in the rite itself, but rather because of the submission and commitment it expresses. As a type of Christian conversion-initiation, we see that entry into the new age and covenant is a single complex event, involving distinct actions of man (baptism) and God (gift of Spirit), bound together by the repentance and commitment which is expressed in the former and results in the latter.[15]

Regarding the miracle of Pentecost (Acts 2), Dunn's position is that it represents a watershed in the salvation history, much like the Jordan text. In Luke's understanding of the history of salvation, the 120 gathered before Pentecost were in a position analogous to that of Jesus before Jordan. What Jordan was to Jesus, Pentecost was to the disciples. Indeed, Jesus had already breathed his Spirit upon the disciples on the day of the resurrection, weeks before (John 20:22). Yet the climax of Jesus' ministry for the disciples was the event of Pentecost, the day when the prophecy of Joel was fulfilled (Joel 2:28–30). For the gift of Jesus in his death and resurrection is ineffective without the gift of the Spirit. While the gospel of Luke closes with the story of the ascension of Jesus, the Book of Acts starts with both the ascension of Jesus and the story of the descending of the Spirit (Acts 1–2). While the former ends the story of Jesus, the latter begins the story of the church. Historically, the age of the incarnated Jesus ends at the same time as another story begins, the age of the Spirit and the story of the church (Acts 2:33).

Luke understands the church as being a missionary and confessional body, composed of witnesses of Christ and built upon the certainty of his lordship and exaltation (Acts 1:8; Acts 10:26; cf. 1 Cor 12:3). The invitation to fellowship, repentance, and baptism in the name of Christ was based on the promise of the Spirit and conducted in the name of Jesus (Acts 2:21; 2:38). These characteristics, including the apostolic teaching, the establishment of the LORD's Supper, the use of the spiritual gifts, prophetic speech,

---

for the reception of the Spirit (Acts 15:8–9). Thus, Luke is interested in the free operation of the Spirit within the church. As such the Spirit is not in an exclusive way tied to baptism. Nevertheless, the Spirit is connected to baptism because both are central elements in the conversion-initiation process. Schweizer, "Pneuma," 413–14.

15. Dunn, *Baptism in Spirit*, 37.

healing activities, and diaconal ministries, were not present in their fullness until after Pentecost (Acts 2:38–47). The gradual establishment of the Pauline concept of a fellowship (*koinonia*) makes it reasonable to state that the church, properly conceived, did not come into existence until Pentecost, nor can we talk about an existence of Christians in the New Testament sense of the word.

A whole new understanding followed Pentecost. Being a disciple meant entering into a relationship with God based on the death, resurrection, and exaltation of Jesus and the descending of the Spirit. Before that day they were in a kind of pre-Christian existence.[16] From Dunn's position, Pentecost can never be repeated, but the *content* of Pentecost must be repeated in the experience of those who would become Christians. Peter's concluding remark was that one becomes a Christian simply by receiving the same Spirit as the disciples did at Pentecost (Acts 2:38). That is a promise, not a question of fortune. Dunn confirms the approach of the Pentecostals: they are quite right to emphasize that Pentecost was an experience of empowering for witness (Luke 24:49; Acts 1:8; 2:4; 4:8, 31; 9:17; 13:9, cf. Eph 5:18). However, the Pentecost event was not primarily an experience of empowering. The Spirit is primarily initiatory and secondarily equipping.

Tormod Engelsviken: The Gift of the Spirit in Light of Ecclesiology

In his work "The Gift of the Spirit," Lutheran theologian Tormod Engelsviken describes his attempt to delineate a common fundamental theology of Charismatic Christianity that transcends the ecclesial context in which it appears.[17] His research reveals variety but also a great number of common presuppositions, motifs, and tenets.[18] Regarding the question of compatibility between the Pentecostal doctrine of Spirit baptism and a Lutheran position, Engelsviken suggests a way around the lack of shared doctrine in this area. A common presuppositional framework or common motifs could make the charismatic experience feasible even within a Lutheran theology.[19]

---

16. Ibid., 53. Or as D. R. Forrester says, cited in Dunn: "There is no genuine Christianity on the wrong side of Pentecost." Ibid.

17. Engelsviken, "The Gift of the Spirit," 21. Engelsviken's long standing influence in Scandinavia regarding the relation between Spirit and church makes him a natural figure within the frame of this work.

18. Ibid., 300–19.

19. In his documentation of the charismatic movement, the catholic-charismatic writer Kilian McDonnell defines charismatic spirituality in terms of the three main phrases, "presence, power, and praise;" indicating the intrinsic kinship between these

The charismatic movement emphasized the gifts of the Spirit as operative in the lives of individuals and Christian communities without requiring any initial evidence. This led to a more flexible understanding of the charismatic experiences than what was the case in the decades after the onset of the Pentecostal movement.[20]

In his investigation, Engelsviken establishes a biblically based interpretation of the charismatic experience. He holds that the charismatic experience within Pentecostalism and the Charismatic Movement respectively has similar structures, even if they differ on doctrinal particularities.[21] The pneumatological experience is not a merely human phenomenon. It is a real, present, and personal encounter with the trinitarian God. A religious experience within the context of the Christian community is more than emotional responses to God's intervention in the life of an individual or a community. It is also a comprehensive term for all aspects of God's work that create within a person an awareness of God's tangible presence and reality, in order to renew their life in Christ and to equip them for ministry.

Accordingly, the abundance of charismatic testimonies from all parts of the global church can no longer be ascribed to theological naivety or a lack of academic sophistication. The variety they represent is both biblically valid and personally desirable. They serve to rehabilitate the parts of Christianity which during the last century often were discredited because of their firm approval of the charismatic elements in the life of the church. The basic communal character of Christianity welcomes a broad comprehension of charismatic experiences, and it points to the need for an approving church environment, in which the social-charismatic dimension can be confirmed.[22] Without a doubt, the proper place for the experiences of the Spirit is the believing community, though no one can restrict the free acts of the Spirit (John 3:8).

As to its significance, setting, content, and effects, the Charismatic experience indicates a conscious encounter with God that has empirical

---

concepts in the theological appraisal of experiential Christianity. For more, see McDonnell, *Presence, Power, Praise*.

20. Engelsviken, "The Gift of the Spirit," 30.

21. Ibid., 37.

22. Concerning the significance of a Charismatic experience, the phenomenological identity between contemporary experiences and analogous experiences recorded in the biblical narratives, is taken for granted. This is based on the general assumption of the continuity of the Spirit's operation in the era of the church from Pentecost to the end time, though the cultural and religious contexts of these epochs are different. Various features of the Spirit's work may correspondingly be different. Ibid., 303.

ramifications in the lives of individuals and churches.[23] It involves an initiatory crisis experience and fosters a fresh spirituality. The setting is communal as far as the sustenance of the experience is concerned within the framework of the actual church and her willingness to provide a constructive environment for the acknowledgment of charismatic experiences.[24] According to Engelsviken, the value of having a supportive-critical fellowship is unquestionable. The church plays an interpretive role in making sense of these experiences and may function as a maturation arena for their concrete expressions. The effects of a charismatic experience are linked to the content of the experience, Engelsviken contends. He rightly admits that unless the distinction between the objectivity of the experienced God and the subjectivity of the modus of the experience and its effects is maintained, one cannot understand the nature of the spiritual experiences. On the contrary, it may result in serious misunderstandings.[25] The power of the Spirit is directed towards a renewal of the interest in mission and ministry, shown by a growing courage in witnessing, endurance in persecution, and boldness in the face of opposition. The charismatic gifts, as listed in 1 Cor 12, may be regarded as signs of the reality of the presence of the Spirit and as vehicles for different manifestations of God's power in the midst of the believing community.

Concerning the gift of tongues, Engelsviken describes this as a normal gift functioning primarily as a personal gift of prayer, initiating people into the wider dimension of charismatic ministry, and providing a sign and evidence of the reality of the Spirit's presence in individuals. Likewise, prophecy and healing are considered gifts of the Spirit in the midst of the Christian community, and they function as direct interventions of God, based on the Godhead's concern for the whole person.

Experience and Ethics

Another important observation made by Engelsviken is the fact that a charismatic experience in most cases seems to have a notable ethical effect (Gal 5:24–25; cf.1 Cor 6:9–11). This is evidenced by a renewed love of

---

23. Ibid., 81–85, 306.

24. Lutheran charismatics prefer to state that the possibility of an experience of God (baptism in the Spirit) makes one's Christian heritage (water baptism) come alive in new modalities of Christian growth (sanctification). Opsahl, *Holy Spirit in the Life of the Church*, 232.

25. Engelsviken, "The Gift of the Spirit," 83–84, 53. This is particularly relevant within experiential Christianity, where the need for discernment is incontestable.

God and of one's neighbor, more deeply committed relationships between people within the congregation, the feeling of unity among Christians from other denominations, and by involvement in new, social actions. J. Rodman Williams, a prominent representative of the charismatic stream of the Presbyterian Church, makes a more radical statement, saying that "baptism in the Holy Spirit as such has nothing to do with holiness of character, but with penetration of life. The effect is not a certain quality of existence but a way of life in which one is open to the Spirit's activity."[26] But, as Engelsviken points out, "it would have been remarkable if the encounter with God that is at the heart of the Charismatic experience should not have had any ethical implications. In that case one would have had good reason to doubt whether it was an encounter with God at all."[27]

Even if the gifts of the Spirit are not in any way dependent on the fruit of the Spirit (Gal 5:22-23), the encounter with the Spirit should yield a natural growth in mature ethical attitudes.[28] Consequently, the fruit of the Spirit would accompany the charism as an expression of an encounter with the trinitarian God, corresponding with what the ecclesiastic purpose of the charisms to build up the church. The gift of the Spirit results in an inner transformation of both religious and ethical attitudes, giving the believer a new heart that reflects the nature of the believing people. This substantial new relationship to God manifests in the relations and attitudes that characterize a reconciled, transformed, and resurrected community. The accompanying word of God, functioning as a critical norm for all kinds of religious experiences as they occur in the framework of Christian fellowships, both recognizes and qualifies the church as a lived reality. The close connection between the word of God and the experience of the Spirit of God deserves proper attention in the circles of Charismatic Christianity. Indeed, there has to be a correlation between gifts and fruits.[29]

The Scriptures understand and validate charismatic experience in the framework of graceful fellowship of God's people. The Old Testament in particular displays the Spirit in charismatic terms as an expression of God's relatedness to the world and as an endowment for specific tasks (Exod 31:1-4; Num 11:16-30; Judg 3:10; 1 Sam 10:6; 16:13; 1 Kings 18; Ezek 11:5). The exilic and post-exilic prophets referred to the Spirit of God as a

---

26. Williams, *Pentecostal Reality*, 13.

27. Engelsviken, "The Gift of the Spirit," 77.

28. Connected to the questions of growth in ethical reflection as a result of the Spirit are the wisdom literature and the wisdom tradition of Israel (Prov 1:1-7; 16:3; 13; 22:29; 22:11). As divine power, the Spirit grants mental abilities (Gen 41:38-40). Ibid., 359.

29. Ibid., 181, 375.

mediator of divine revelation and inspiration, including prophetic ministry (2 Chr 24:20; Sec 7:12; cf. Neh 9:20; 30). This includes charismatically equipped leaders, and a promise of a coming eschatological reality where all God's people would receive the Spirit as a permanent possession with direct access to the LORD, (Joel 2:28–32), resulting in a renewal of their ethical consciousness.

In a strict historical sense, the Day of Pentecost represents something unique and unrepeatable. In a more dogmatic sense, the uniqueness is found in the establishment of the visible church, but the filling of the Spirit for renewal is a perpetual event (Acts 4:31; 7:55; 11:24; 13:9; 52). This initial inauguration opened something quite new: the presence of the Spirit in the midst of the church. After Pentecost there is no need to pray for a new Pentecost, but rather for a renewed filling of the Spirit already at work by its dynamic existence within the believers.

The Understanding of Charismatic Experiences

The orientation of Engelsviken coincides, to a considerable extent, with the more Pentecostal wing of Christian tradition. He understands baptism in the Spirit to be a unique gift of the Spirit that identifies with the experience of the disciples on the Day of Pentecost. At the same time, there is an obvious association between faith, forgiveness, and giving of the Spirit, evidenced in the narratives of Pentecost (Acts 2), the conversion of Paul (Acts 9), and the story of Cornelius (Acts 10). In the case of the conversion of Paul, it seems clear that the encounter with Jesus on the road to Damascus led him to repentance and faith. In baptism he received forgiveness of sins and he was given the gift of the Spirit (Acts 9:17–19; 22:16).

However, in the Samaritan's Pentecost (Acts 8:4–25) there is a time interval between baptism and the reception of the Spirit, which has served the Pentecostals as support for their understanding of Spirit-baptism as a separate experience subsequent to the initiation rite. You *can* have a real faith and become baptized without being filled with the Spirit in the bestowing sense of the word.[30] The phrase "for as yet the Spirit had not come upon any of them" (v. 16), echoes the description of the Pentecost event in Jerusalem (Acts 1:8) but also the giving of charismatic gifts for missional purposes (9:31). And clearly the Book of Acts talks about repeated fillings of the Spirit. Engelsviken distinguishes between those narratives which describe the fundamental bestowal of the Spirit as the initial process and those referring to the endowment of the Spirit as ongoing charismatic equipment

30. Atkinson, "Pentecostal Responses to Dunn," 118.

for ministry.³¹ In the Pentecostal tradition, the former is seen in the light of salvific regeneration while the latter is understood as a falling upon-experience, giving the church the power to make the Great Commission come true (Matt 28:18-20). In a similar way, the Ephesus narrative (Acts 19:1-7) describes how the Spirit came upon them and they spoke in tongues and prophesied (v. 6). Here the time interval between the endowment and the bestowal of the Spirit disappears, resulting in the Spirit's joint salvific and empowering act. Interestingly for the Pentecostals, these events were indeed an integrated part of the baptismal rite administered by Paul. However, the clear differentiation between Pentecostal and Lutheran theologies of the charismatic experience which Engelsviken describes has been toned down over the years. The idea that the charismatic gifts only include the nine mentioned in 1 Cor 12:7-10, the exaggerated distinction between the supernatural and natural functions of the gifts, and the view of glossolalia as exclusive evidence of Spirit baptism, are under serious debate in the Pentecostal movement worldwide. This has consequences with regard to the disagreements mentioned by Engelsviken, for the question of ecumenism, and for hermeneutical reflections.³²

Engelsviken is right to present Christian initiation as more than participation in eschatological salvation and membership to the Christian church. Charismatic endowment is also an active ingredient throughout the narratives of Luke, equipping Christians for ministry and proclaiming God's action in Christ through the church.

Frank D. Macchia: Expanding the Boundaries and Broadening the Horizon

Unlike earlier Pentecostal contributions, Pentecostal theologian Frank D. Macchia uses "baptism in the Holy Spirit" as a key interpretational term and a gateway to his dogmatic approach in general. By developing a broader understanding of the term, he construes Spirit baptism as an organizing principle in his theological construction. This brings him closer to the position of both Dunn and Engelsviken, though he does not differentiate passages in NT using the same conversion-initiation schema as Dunn. There are still distinctives to the Pentecostal approach which Macchia defends.

---

31. Engelsviken, "The Gift of the Spirit," 466. See also Dunn, *Baptism in Spirit*, 58-60.

32. As I can see, Engelsviken's considerations of the Pentecostal approach to hermeneutics, characterized by him as an interpretation of Scripture "according to the norm of personal revelations and guidance," is not an appropriate description today.

One of these is the instrumental aspect, which perceives the work of the Spirit primarily as a power that equips for witness and ministry.

Another distinctly Pentecostal category for the reading of Luke/Acts involves a certain quality of communal life that is reconciling and rich in praise and acts of self-giving.[33] Thus Macchia speaks of a theology of the Spirit that is soteriologically, charismatically, and sacramentally defined. It is a result of the divine act in redemption and the conversion-initiation that involves faith and baptismal sealing, but it also functions as empowerment for Christian life and ministry. Like Dunn, Macchia talks about the gift of the Spirit as an experientially defined theological distinctive, essential to the church:

> I would never say that Luke's depiction of the winds of the Spirit that set the church aflame with the love of God and propelled them outward are a *super additum* or a luxury item with regard to the church. The church without this clothing, without this enrichment of life in the Spirit that enhances the living witness of the church to the kingdom of God, is somewhat defective.[34]

In this light, the Spirit of God in an active agent searching for a deepening of personal relationships with humans. The relational depiction of God is a pneumatological concept. The kingdom's reign of divine love is inaugurated and fulfilled as Spirit baptism. Pentecost may thus be characterized as an outpouring of divine love (Rom 5:5).[35] I *am* insofar as I am loved, even if I am in emotional darkness. Love is the primary manifestation of Spirit baptism.[36] As an eschatological gift, this love integrates both soteriological and charismatic dimensions.[37]

---

33. Macchia, *Baptized in the Spirit*, 16. The following is a presentation of some aspects of his book.

34. Ibid.

35. Ibid., 17.

36. William Seymour from the first, famous Azusa Street revival in Los Angeles in 1906, regarded love as the main sign of Spirit baptism, assording to Nelson, "For Such a Time as This," 7–15.

37. However, Pentecostal theologians such as Roger Stronstad and Robert Menzies underscore that in the context of Pauline pneumatology, Spirit baptism is recognized as integral to salvation and thus initiatory, while for Luke the Spirit is the spirit of empowerment. The main position in: Menzies, *Empowered for Witness*, and Stronstad, *Charismatic Theology of Luke*. Dunn, on his side, argues against the alleged split between Luke and Paul and holds that Luke and Paul differ only in accentuations and motifs. Dunn, "Baptism in Spirit—Once More." The problem in classical Pentecostal theology seems to be an inability to embrace Luke except at the expense of Paul. As I see, Pentecostal theology has to work toward an integrated pattern in order to achieve a balanced doctrine of the gift of the Spirit. By considering the gift of the Spirit in light

Furthermore, providing satisfactory biblical support for a fragmented twofold initiation into the life of the Spirit is a demanding task. Characterizing Spirit baptism as charismatic empowerment only and advocating for a separate initiatory reception of the Spirit seems to be a too narrow definition. From a presupposition that the Spirit is the very substance of the Christian life, it follows that an integration of Luke's and Paul's seemingly different and compartmentalized pneumatologies ought to be integrated in a more comprehensive way than what has been the case within Pentecostal theology so far. Thus Macchia aims to provide a broader horizon and a more inclusive context for the understanding of the Spirit. The purely experimental and revival aspects are not well adapted to contemporary ecclesiological challenges. Furthermore, an understanding of the work of the Spirit that is primarily connected to dramatic moments of regeneration and sanctification may prove to be problematic in pastoral care and counseling. Without neglecting the positive aspects of a soteriology that in some way stresses personal experience and the need for moments of spiritual renewal, a separation of Spirit baptism from God's redemptive work in Christ runs the risk of being an otherworldly spirituality combined with a this-worldly pragmatism. Moreover, a higher-life experience can lead to the misunderstanding that someone occupies a superior position in the body of Christ.[38]

On the other hand, Spirit baptism may indicate a participatory metaphor of significant value for our relationship with God. According to Macchia, the gift of the Spirit says something about the diverse ways the Spirit makes Christ present in the church. There is both a vocational and charismatic dimension to the Christian life that is relevant to the shaping of a globally diverse pneumatology.[39]

The Church and the Life-transforming Presence of the Spirit

By widening the power for ministry-category in the Pentecostal understanding of Spirit baptism, Macchia's more expansive definition implies a participation in the life-transforming presence of God.[40] Spirit baptism metaphorically reflects the believer's *koinonia* fellowship in relation to God and the church. Macchia describes this as "baptism into Christ and into God, a participation in the divine life by which we place on God our

---

of the kingdom and by employing the writings of Matthew and John, the contribution of Macchia is obviously a step in promising direction.

38. Macchia, *Baptized in the Spirit*, 32.
39. Ibid.
40. Ibid., 42.

death, sin, suffering, and isolation in order to partake of his life everlasting, righteousness, healing, and fellowship."[41] Consequently, the aspects of initiation into the life of the Spirit are integrated as one work of the same Spirit within the framework of the church. Macchia writes:

> One enters Spirit-baptized existence at Christian initiation. But the experience of Spirit baptism connected to and following from initiation is meant to bring to conscious participation the justice of the kingdom, the growth in sanctifying grace, and the charismatic openness to bless others and to glorify God that begins in Christian initiation. These experiences are to be ongoing. (. . .) Spirit baptism has decisive roots in Christian initiation, but it has also to be reaffirmed in the daily walk in the Spirit as well as in definitive moments of the Spirit-filling. Ultimately, it is realized in cosmic transformation.[42]

This life-transforming presence is the conceptual framework in which to understand the concept of Spirit baptism as it relates to the church's communally gifted life. Seen as such, Spirit baptism gave rise to the global church and can be understood as the substance of her life, including the initiatory elements (her sacramental identity) but also her charismatic orientation and missional obligation.[43] The Spirit is uniquely ecclesial in nature.[44] Stating that the church has her being in the ecclesial Spirit implies that the natural outcome of the Pentecost event is first and foremost the communion of believers. Communion implies participation in God's love and graced relationship in her weakness (2 Cor 12:9–10, cf. Rom 8:26).

The implicit connection between the gift of the Spirit and the life and mission of the church can be construed in this way: in Spirit baptism there is a relational dynamic at play which gives birth to the church as a diverse charismatic body in which the Spirit's presence embraces the whole fellowship. This results in a reflex movement of worship and witness, attested by the fact that the most forceful expression of the outpouring of the Spirit at Pentecost was the emergence of a visible community (Acts 2:42). The Spirit bridges the link between the proclaimed kingdom and the church in her concrete reality (1 Pet 1:2; Eph 1:4–14). Thus Spirit baptism appears as a profoundly personal yet not individualistic experience. The different tongues on the Day of Pentecost symbolize the disciples' reconciliation with people of other cultures (Acts 2:4–11). Macchia calls Spirit baptism an initiation

---

41. Ibid., 46, 49.
42. Ibid., 154.
43. Ibid., 155.
44. Chan, "Mother Church," 198.

into a reconciled communion of persons across cultural boundaries. This presence for the other is at the heart of a Spirit-driven ecclesiology.[45]

This communal life of sharing lies at the heart of Macchia's interpretation of the gift of the Spirit. As a growing and empathetic fellowship in which members are bearing one another's burdens in the love of Christ (Gal 6:2), her dynamic characterizing of the Spirit must be cultivated and given a diverse range of expressions. This dynamic speaks to a longing within humanity and all creation to be renewed through graced relations. As a community of wounded healers, the Spirit of God is active in the gracious transformation of persons through relationships.[46] Miroslav Volf writes: "The Spirit enters into the citadel of the self, de-centers the self by fashioning it in the image of the self-giving Christ, and frees its will so it can resist the power of exclusion in the power of the Spirit of embrace."[47] In other words, the goal is not self-reference but dedication to God and to what Macchia defines as a prophetic empathy for others in the Spirit.[48] That is why the church is more than an institution; she is a way of being and a mode of existing.

When characterizing the church as a humble servant to Christ, Macchia understands her role as both witness and sign.[49] The church holds her treasure as in a vessel of clay, and in this weakness she bears a limited witness of the Spirit. As such, being a Spirit-driven church does not entail an unqualified possession of the Spirit but represents a dynamic dialectic between what is given her as a sign of her ecclesiality—the very core of her essence as a dwelling place of the Spirit—and her functioning as a "not yet" manifestation of God's eschatological reign. Hence, the church has to oppose the temptation of pretending to have a total perspective (1 Cor 13:12). Her kerygmatic, sacramental, and charismatic life does not give license to triumphalism, but rather requires an eschatological humility with regard to any kind of unqualified identification between the kingdom to come and the church in her concrete reality.

The church is not the final word but a place for the Spirit to talk and act, and for us to listen, believe, and obey in modesty and humility. Otherwise we may be accused of spiritual snobbery. As a divine infilling, Spirit baptism implies a love and communion that must be cultivated, a mutual indwelling

---

45. Macchia, *Baptized in the Spirit*, 167.

46. Remark a jewel of a book, written by Henri J. M. Nouwen, *The Wounded Healer*. The book states that in our own woundedness, we can become a source of life for others, 99–100.

47. Volf, *Exclusion and Embrace*, 91.

48. Macchia, *Baptized in the Spirit*, 174.

49. Ibid., 191.

that cannot be taken for granted. It implies both grace and fallenness.[50] For the church, Spirit baptism is an event that has happened but is also ongoing and yet to be fulfilled.

Living out the Book of Acts

Macchia explains why many Pentecostals are uncomfortable with the term "sacrament." The term represents an institutionalization of the Spirit and an apparently formalistic liturgical tradition, associations they inherited from the Zwinglian critique of sacramentalism. On the other hand, glossolalia represents an unmediated, direct, and audible manifestation of God's presence, which has sacramental significance yet bypasses liturgical forms of mediation. Among Pentecostals, the sign of speaking in tongues is explained as a linguistic symbol of the sacred,[51] or a cathedral of the poor, signifying the majestic presence of God among people who cannot afford to worship in a gothic church settings.[52] As Macchia describes:

> Glossolalia accents the free, dramatic, and unpredictable move of the Spirit of God, while the liturgical traditions stress an ordered and predictable encounter with the Spirit. The allergic response of Pentecostals to liturgical worship may be one-sided but reveals a valuable accent on the spontaneity and freedom of the Spirit in worship.[53]

However, Rahner and Schillebeeckx do not locate sacramental efficacy in some kind of material causation, necessitated by the elements as elements. They rather see them as a personal encounter between God and the believer as a Word-event; not unlike the way God is perceived among Pentecostals as uniquely present in glossolalic manifestation.[54]

For most Pentecostals, glossolalia traditionally has served as evidence of Spirit baptism and a sign of being in line with the Book of Acts. This understanding is not so much an inductive method of scholarly hermeneutics as it is a creative interaction with Acts. In their effort to "live" this book, Pentecostals have discovered a pattern by which to justify certain expectations in worship when the Spirit moves in freedom and power.[55] Macchia

---

50. Ibid., 193.
51. Samarin, *Tongues*, 232.
52. Macchia, "Tongues as a Sign," 61.
53. Ibid., 63.
54. Rahner, "What Is a Sacrament?," 276.
55. Macchia, "Tongues as a Sign," 65.

understands tongues as a free and transcendent response to the free and transcendent move of the Spirit.⁵⁶ Despite the need to be wary of spiritual sensualism, such spiritual practices seem to be an embodiment of grace and a sort of incarnated hope, going beyond the established categories of Word and sacraments.⁵⁷

However, it is reasonable to ask whether a visible and audible phenomenon does qualify as sacramental, since a sacrament represents an implied and integral connection between the sign and the divine action signified therein. Tongues give the worship practices of Pentecostals a sacramental dimension. Thus, it is not legitimate to characterize Pentecostal spirituality as purely subjective. Macchia states that in their reading of Acts they are probably more impressed by the mediation of an empowered church than with the *ordo salutis* (order of salvation) of individual souls which has become so central in other Protestant circles. The physical dimension of worship and healing represents a sacramental spirituality which has the character of a sign more than a proof of God's empowering presence.

Donald G. Bloesch: The Deifying Work of the Spirit

When it comes to the question of Spirit baptism, Evangelical theologian Donald G. Bloesch seeks to discern the role of the Spirit within water baptism without separating the two elements or confusing them.⁵⁸ While water baptism is a more fluid metaphor indicating immersion, initiation, and purification, Spirit baptism is related to the notion of being submersed in and inundated by the Spirit. The latter is a more progressive and dynamic conception, including charismatic endowments. The former is ordinarily synchronous but not synonymous with the latter, while the latter is an experience that fulfills and confirms the former. Baptism in the Spirit is equivalent as to be sealed with the Spirit. One cannot be a Christian without the work of the Spirit (Rom 8:9).

In his analysis of the gift of the Spirit to the church, Bloesch focuses on the deifying work of the Spirit.⁵⁹ We can never possess the power of divinity, but we can reflect its power, because the Spirit enables us to do works that

---

56. Macchia, "Sigh too Deep." Another Pentecostal scholar, Murray Dempster, views tongues as a new language, signifying the creation of new integrated communities that witness to the transforming power of God in history. Dempster, "Moral Witness," 1–7.

57. Macchia, "Question of Tongues," 127.

58. Bloesch, *The Holy Spirit*, 288.

59. Ibid.

exceed our human capacity. The Spirit equips the church to speak and act in ministries of healing and deliverance as well as in more regular ministries. Through the Spirit, she becomes a messenger of God's grace and a bearer of God's glory (2 Thess 2:14; 2 Pet 1:4). Bloesch writes:

> To be adopted into the family of God as his sons and daughters means to be baptized into the service of this glory. Such a baptism will cause us to radiate his glory if we truly draw near to him in repentance and faith. Yet even though submersed in his glory we remain mortals vulnerable to temptation and subject to all kinds of infirmities. The closer we grow toward God the more keenly we are aware of the infinite gulf that separates us from God, the more conscious we become that we are only sinners saved by grace.[60]

Regarding Pentecost, Donald G. Bloesch challenges both the classic Catholic position as well as the Pentecostal approach. While mainline churches tend to see the receiving of the Spirit in connection with the rite of the sacraments (usually with the laying on of hands), and the Pentecostal adherents consider it an empowering grace received by a second blessing after conversion, Bloesch stakes out a third course. He does not consider the disciples to be believers until after Pentecost, a position which corresponds with Dunn. Their confidence in Christ was Jewish more than Christian; they were seekers rather than believers (John 13:19; 14:29; Acts 1:6; Heb 3:5-6).

But after Pentecost, when their hearts were purified by faith, they received the gift of the Spirit (Acts 15:9). Bloesch understands repentance and baptism not as conditions for receiving the Spirit but the correlatives of the Spirit (Acts 2:37-38).[61] The Spirit is the great creator of faith. It is when we believe in Christ that we receive the power of the Spirit. In its deepest sense, the charismatic empowering belongs to that same new birth.

By the power of the Spirit, a Christian is enabled to believe.[62] And the church is continually in need of the regenerative and transforming activity of the Spirit. Bloesch is afraid that when Pentecostals consider faith only as preparation for the gift of the Spirit which in turn equips for ministry, this diminishes the significance of faith. But faith is already a kind of empowerment, an inner renewal. Reflecting the position of Catholic theologian Karl Adam, Bloesch says that it is not *we* who believe, but the Holy Ghost within

---

60. Ibid., 289-90.

61. Ibid., 298.

62. Bloesch quotes Luther, saying: "To him who has the Holy Ghost is the power given; to him, that is, who is a Christian. But who is a Christian? Whosoever believes has the Holy Ghost." Ibid., 298.

us: "The experience of Pentecost is continually repeated, and our faith is in its essence nothing else than the Pentecostal faith of the apostles."[63] Every believer is in need of the Spirit in order to believe, though not all believers have the gifts of the Spirit manifesting in their daily life.

According to Bloesch, the filling of the Spirit includes various dimensions of the work and blessing of the Spirit. The concepts of filling, anointing, outpouring, and empowering cannot be reduced to only one kind of experience. One must therefore be wary of stereotyping encounters with the Spirit. To Bloesch, the hallmarks and constituent elements in receiving the Spirit are repentance of sin, initiation into the community of faith, endowment of power for ministry, and loving concern for people in need. The fact that the gift of the Spirit is for those who struggle in faith and want to serve in love, is indeed the message of Pentecost.[64]

When it comes to concrete experiences of the Spirit, theologian Tak-Ming Cheung defers to a Catholic position: the rhythm of spiritual growth differs from person to person. It may be dramatic, or it may be slow and hardly perceptible. For one who is already under the influence of the Spirit, a new filling may happen at any time. Thus the one who was baptized at infancy can release the Spirit through prayer or confirmation. Periods of renewal of the original grace of the Spirit is possible, and the Spirit can be manifested in answer to seeking prayer, according to 1 Cor 14:1.[65] The goal is to preserve the integrity of the Spirit in our understanding of these experiences, while at the same time accounting for the various possibilities which may emerge in Christian life and church ministry. By rooting all blessings and manifestations in the endowment of the Spirit at initiation, Bloesch evades the temptation to divide Christian believers into different classes of spiritual maturity.

Constructive Reflections

A key concept regarding a mature understanding of the term the gift of the Spirit is the Pauline definition of spirituality, which includes both "living

---

63. Cited in ibid., 299.

64. While the experiences of the Spirit may have their distinctive features and constituent elements, it is necessary to underline that it is the *fruit of the Spirit* which represent evidence of whether we talk about genuine spiritual breakthroughs or not. The appearance of fruits (love, joy, peace, patience, kindness, generosity, faithfulness, gentleness, and self-control, as listed in Gal 5:22–26) confirms a life touched by the Spirit. Not without reason Jesus warned against building one's identity upon signs and wonders (Matt 24:24; 7:22). Ibid., 303.

65. Cheung, "Spirit-Baptism," 121.

and walking in the Spirit" (Gal 5:25). As Paul writes in the letter to Titus, "He saved us through the washing of rebirth and renewal by the Holy Spirit" (Tit 3:5). The Spirit enlivens theology to breathe in a new way and to approach the Christian life as simultaneously christocentric, trinitarian, and ecclesial. In fact, it is legitimate to attribute to the Holy Spirit a constitutive role in identifying and actualizing the person and work of Christ. Adoration and praise then arise as fruits of this graced encounter with God and form the existential participation of the Christian in the trinitarian life of God. The salvation of Christ has a substantial pneumatological orientation (Gal 3:1–5). Charismatic experiences reveal the trinitarian structure of Christian faith and ecclesiology. We can hardly distinguish between our experience of the exalted Christ and our experience of the Spirit of God. The salvific presence of God is simply known as the risen Christ in the Holy Spirit (1 Cor 12:3; 15:45).[66]

In the New Testament, there are diverse interpretations of the phrase "baptized in/with" the Spirit.[67] The somewhat one-sided emphasis on Spirit baptism as empowerment in ministry, found among Pentecostals, is too limited and needs to be supplemented with a broader perspective which includes soteriological dimensions. On the other hand, the charismatic and prophetic dimensions, particularly in Luke's account, seem to be well grounded. Spirit baptism is obviously more than regeneration. In Luke, there is a separate endowment of the Spirit after conversion (Luke 24:49; Acts 1:5, 8; 2: 4; cf. John 7:37–39) and subsequent to the Day of Pentecost (Acts 4:31).[68] After Pentecost you do not need to wait for something already given.

Charismatic empowerment is not the only connotation of Spirit baptism or the gift of the Spirit. The more initiatory significance of Spirit baptism has scriptural support as well.[69] It seems clear that in the New Testament, Spirit baptism or its equivalent phrases have both an initiatory foundation and a charismatic feature.[70] It is connected to Christian baptism,

---

66. Del Colle, *Christ and Spirit*, 96.

67. The phrase is used by John the Baptist (Mark 1:8; Matt 3:11; Luke 3:16; John 1:33), Jesus (Acts 1:5; 11, 16), and is probably alluded to in 1 Cor 12:13 and in Tit 3:5.

68. See the following passages: Luke 4:18; Acts 2:17–18; 10:44–46; 19:6; cf. Luke 1:41–45, 67–69; 10:21; 12:12; 24:48–49; Acts 1:2, 16; 13:2; 20:23; 21:4,11. For an introduction to the topic, see Cheung, "Spirit-Baptism."

69. The phrase is presupposed, though not always mentioned explicitly, in John 3:5; Acts 2:38; 10:47; 11:7–18; 15:8–9; Rom 6:2–11; 1 Cor 2:12; 6:11; 12:13–14; Gal 3:1–4; Eph 4:4–5; Heb 6:2–4; Tit 3:5–7. The fact that the Spirit also causes regeneration is self-evident. You cannot believe without being exposed to the Spirit (1 Cor 2:14–15; Rom 3:11–24; 8:13–14, 16; 1 John 4:2). Paul is clear on the issue, see Rom 8:9.

70. Norbert Baumert, "Charism and Spirit-baptism," 149.

in contrast to that of John the Baptist (Matt 3:11), modelled on the event at Jordan (Luke 3:21–22) which foreshadowed the passion of Christ (Matt 3:16–17; Rom 6:3–4). The Spirit is released and given to the church by the reconciled work of Christ (John 7:39; Acts 2:33). It is normally granted in connection with the conversion-initiation, which includes repentance and baptism (Acts 2:38–39, 41; 9:18; 10:47–48; 19:1–7), as well as the laying on of hands (Acts 8:14–17; 9:10–19). Moreover, the effect of this gift upon the church is a Spirit-sensitive mission marked by power and various manifestations of charisms (Luke 24:49; Acts 1:8; 4:31; 1 Cor 12:4–11; Heb 4:8; cf. Mark 16:15–20).

Notwithstanding, we cannot place the Spirit's actions within the barriers of a closed system (John 3:8). To allow space for the variability and multiplicity of utterances of the Spirit is a ongoing challenge for all kinds of churches. The different narratives of the New Testament reveal that the filling of the Spirit can operate independently of all of the sacraments. Whether the gift of the Spirit refers to an initiation or to a charismatic experience is not conceptually clear. In Acts 2, the breaking of bread is placed side by side with dramatic signs such as tongues without any theological explanation (Acts 2:4, 42). Nevertheless, for the understanding of the dynamic life in a church, whether of classical or a charismatic persuasion, Spirit baptism is the most comprehensive expression of being given the Spirit for both life and ministry. Rebirth and renewal are not mutually exclusive terms (Tit 3:5). In this regard, repentance and water baptism are the normal prerequisites for reception of the Spirit, which is promised to every believer as a result of the Pentecost event.

Further, we are allowed to understand Spirit baptism metaphorically rather than literally. It is not a technical term. In its verbal form it expresses a surplus of life.[71] Metaphorically, it describes both the initiation-conversion process and the experience of spiritual empowerment. Their interchangeability prevents an either/or choice. Luke and Paul have a broad and inclusive analysis of how Spirit baptism can be perceived: an abundant endowment of gifts for salvation, renewal, and ethical formation.

The broad range of images and metaphors hardly supports the position that water baptism and Spirit baptism are quite identical terms. Otherwise,

---

71. NT uses a whole range of metaphors, images, and terms for the same event, the coming of the Holy Spirit. In Luke the terms are even used interchangeable. In the Pentecost narrative (Acts 2): baptize, come, fill, and pour. In the Samaria account (Acts 8): receive, and fall upon. In the Cornelius' passage (Acts 10–11): pour, receive, fall upon, give, baptize, purify, and grace. And the Ephesus account (Acts 19): come, and receive. Cheung, "Spirit-Baptism," 123.

why are they described as two different events in the New Testament?[72] Accordingly, J. David Pawson writes that the two baptisms (water and Spirit) are never so closely identified in the New Testament that either mediates the other. Though they often happen very closely together, there is no recorded case of them happening simultaneously.[73]

However, the Spirit does not create a special upper class of spiritual-gifted Christians over against others. All are included in the establishing of the Spirit-driven church. The outpouring of the gift of the Spirit shatters the barriers of individual blessing and points to a new historical, corporative, and relational-communal reality. The results are purification (Matt 3:12), remission of sins (John 20:21–23), confirmation of salvation (Eph 1:13; Rom 8:16), union with Christ (1 Cor 10:2–4, 12:13), renewal of heart (Tit 3:5), abundance of life (John 7:37–38), empowerment for ministry (Luke 24:49, Acts 1:8), and gifts for ministry (Eph 4:4–13).

All these are blessings placed in the church (1 Cor 12:28), tailored to the inner life of the faith community (Acts 13:1; Eph 3:8–12). The all-embracing work of the Spirit must not be over-simplified and identified with just one part of the Spirit's field of operation. If the reality of the coming of the Spirit is to function as a key concept, all parts of the work of the Spirit need to be acknowledged and admired. Baptism in the Spirit represents a baptism into the ecclesial dynamic of the Spirit. The demand and calling to believe is always directed to the human, but the ability to believe comes from God. Faith is never a human work but a fruit of the Spirit.[74]

According to the gospel of John, God gives the Spirit without any limits or restrictions (3:34). The Spirit of prophecy is the charismatic dimension of all parts of Christian life, worship, and service. This has eschatological dimensions also: the Spirit is the pledge of our own future resurrection from death.[75] But in the meantime, the Spirit pours into our hearts the gift of salvation and the strength to be disciples of Christ who practice graceful attitudes of friendship and hospitality. In a gesture of ecumenical inclusivity, we may define the gift or baptism of the Spirit as the only reason for a life shaped by faith, hope and love, and our source of power for embodying God's reconciliation with the Other.

72. Baumert, "Charism and Spirit-baptism," 161.

73. Pawson, *Christian Birth*, 165.

74. Rom 3:20–24, 27–31; cf. Matt 21:22; Mark 5:34; John 3:18; Acts 15:8–9; 1 John 5:12, 24. According to the latest WCC text about the church, faith is evoked by the Word of God, inspired by the grace of the Holy Spirit, attested in Scripture and transmitted through the living tradition of the Church. It is confessed in worship, life, service and mission. World Council of Churches, "The Church," §38.

75. Pannenberg, *Systematic Theology*, vol 3, 11.

In the coming chapter I give voice to a few more theologians and their understanding of the relation between church and Spirit. These scholars represent different traditions and approaches to the topics discussed in this work. As the reader will observe, there is considerable agreement between them, more than we normally could expect. This is a promising sign, by which important ground is gained for an understanding of the relation between Spirit and church across confessional borders.

5

God's New Reality

> *The true church is to be found where Christ is present. (. . .) We cannot start from the concept of the church in order to discover the happening of Christ's presence; we have to start from the event of Christ's presence in order to find the church.*[1]

Introduction

WITH THE TERM "A relational ecclesiology," German Reformed theologian Jürgen Moltmann seeks to identify the church by simply pointing to her living nature. Everything exists in relationships. The church does not live for herself but exists in relation to God and the world by her service and missionary acts. Well situated among the great Protestant theologians of his time, Lutheran Wolfhart Pannenberg introduced a re-emphasis on the doctrines of the Holy Spirit and the church. Remembering that the church and her institutions function as a sign pointing to God's kingdom, he presupposed that the doctrine of the Spirit might help oppose attempts of hierarchical domination when describing the life of the church.

A third writer, the Orthodox John Zizioulas, holds that knowledge of God is experiential rather than theological, because the Son and the Spirit—the two hands of God—are present within the church.[2] The outward construction of the church is secondary in significance to her sacramental life. She lives by virtue of the ongoing Pentecost. In a similar way, Catholic theologian Yves Congar states that the Spirit is the principle of unity and life. God acts salvifically in history through the particular and concrete church.[3]

---

1. Moltmann, *Church in the Power of the Spirit*, 122.
2. Breck, "The Two Hands of God," 231.
3. Congar, *Mystery*, 153. For the scriptural support of considering the church as a

The Spirit creates a desire for prayer and sensitivity for the generous love of God. Through that, the formation of a doxological church identity takes place. It is widely acknowledged that theologians like Yves Congar and Karl Rahner were pointing to the church as the charismatic body of Christ long before the charismatic renewal began in the Catholic Church in the 1960s.

In this chapter, I present pneumatological perspectives of several church traditions as they are explained by these prominent theologians. The positions of Moltmann, Pannenberg, Congar, and Zizioulas deserve particular attention for their innovative understanding of the spiritual life of the church, expressed both as charismatic and sacramental gifts.

A New Reality Has Come

Christianity is a religion of the future. That is why the church has to look forward in order to be part of the hope for the world and for the coming kingdom of God. But in order to safeguard a Christian identity and serve the people of the present, the church also looks to her apostolic past and her long ecclesial tradition. The theological legacy of the Orthodox Church is based on two sources: the divine Eucharist and the experience of Christian life.[4] The church is fundamentally connected to God by her participation in worship and by the grace-enabled mystery of the communion. Consequently, as *koinonia*, the church has ontological priority over the individual believer. Christology is essentially conditioned by the Holy Spirit who has filled the gap between Christ and the church by making the Christ-event real in history. Hence, the church is pneumatological constituted. The body of Christ is literally composed of the charismata of the Spirit.

Therefore, it is reasonable to declare Christ as existing pneumatologically in his actual presence within the physical world. Accordingly, the foundation of the church is a result of a pneumatologically constituted Christology. The question of truth cannot be considered on its own; rather, truth is realized in the Spirit, much like at Pentecost. As the power and giver of life, the Spirit transforms our life into a dynamic life of communion (2 Cor 13:13).

In his three-volume *I believe in the Holy Spirit*, Congar clarifies and highlights the crucial role of the Spirit in the constitution of the church.[5]

---

temple of the Holy Spirit, see 1 Cor 3:16–17; 6:19; 2 Cor 6:16, Rom 8:9 and Eph 2:19–22.

4. Zizioulas, *Lectures*, 121.

5. For the following outline, see Douglas M. Koskela and his presentation of Congar's pneumatological ecclesiology. Koskela, *Ecclesiality and Ecumenism*, 123–63. See also Groppe, "Contribution of Yves Congar," 451–78.

The Son and the Spirit co-instituted the church. The charisms of the Spirit are dynamic elements given to all believers for the up-building of the church and for the carrying out of the Great Commission (Matt 28:18–20; see also Luke 24:49).[6] This is also strongly emphasized by Brazilian liberation theologian Leonardo Boff, who states that the church ought to give rise to new initiatives, to continuously carry out its mission to make Christ and the Spirit present in the world, and to make his message of liberation, grace, forgiveness, and boundless love heard.

Or to put it differently, Christ is the founder of the church and the Spirit is the sustainer of her life. Given the recognition that the church is established in the world as a result of the Day of Pentecost (Acts 2:1–11), the church's universality and missional profile is incontestable. On the Day of Pentecost, everyone expressed the wonders of God in their own language. It is to be noted that the church became universal not through uniformity but through diversity.[7] The Book of Acts displays the way Pentecost intertwined multiplicity, plurality, otherness, openness, and unity. The Spirit paved the way for new perspectives and shaped the distinctive character of the church, different from any other fellowship in human society. The christological constitution of the church becomes visible as a concrete event, taking place by the proclamation of the Word, the celebration of the sacraments, and the empowerment by the gifts of the Spirit.[8]

Given his view of a social, embodied, Spirit-driven church identity, Congar warns against an idealistic and grandiose ecclesiology distanced from the daily life of ordinary men and women: "The mystical communion of which the Holy Spirit is the sovereign principle, calls for a concrete, human and personal relationship."[9] This is a fellowship that displays its character in the concrete, everyday life of believers. The treasure of the church is contained in an earthly vessel (2 Cor 4:17) made visible as charity and love, the most unique expressions of the work of the Spirit (1 Cor 13:4–5).[10]

These reflections are visible in the official catholic documents of Vatican II, such as *Lumen Gentium*, The Dogmatic Constitution on the Church,

---

6. Boff, *The Base Community*, 87.

7. Congar, *I Believe in the Holy Spirit*, 25.

8. The so-called ecclesiality of the church—what makes the church a church and what constitutes the material elements of the church's identity, under the guidance of the Spirit)—is, according to Congar, recognized by 1) the material principle as the deposit of faith, sacraments, and apostolic powers; 2) the exercise and transmission of faith through the governmental and sacramental functions; and 3) the extension of the laity. Koskela, *Ecclesiality and Ecumenism*, 99.

9. Congar, *I Believe in the Holy Spirit*, 21.

10. Ibid., 156–57.

§ 2. The opening chapter reflects the relation between the intrinsic being of the Triune God and the life of the church. Instead of beginning with standard notions about the church as a perfect society and a hierarchical institution, the document identifies a people brought into communion by the unity of the Trinity. Hence the church is a mystery, a sign, an instrument, and a sacrament.

The definition corresponds with the utterance of Mgr Ignatius Hazim: "the newness of creation cannot be explained by the past, only by the future. The activity of the living God can only be creative."[11] No ministerial office can be efficacious without the contribution of the Spirit, who works through the ecclesial body as a whole. The Spirit did not come simply to give life to an institution already developed in all its structures. Rather there is the co-instituting principle of all kinds of church development processes, showing that the church is not finished or fully designed once and for all from the start.

The Affirming of Life

For Moltmann, the true church is to be found where Christ is present. We cannot start from the concept of the church in order to discover the presence of Christ. We have to go the other way around. In light of this, the church needs to maintain an attitude of openness to God, to humans, and to the future. Thus, the writings of this theologian contribute to expanding the space of the church and broadening the operating area of the Spirit. It is not the church that "administers" the Spirit. It is the Spirit who administers the church by those elements that mark the church as church. Because the church participates in Christ's messianic mission and in the creative mission of the Spirit, we cannot say *what* the church is in all her varieties. But we can tell *where* the church happens. The church is present wherever the Spirit manifests (1 Cor 12:7).[12]

---

11. These words are from the opening address of the Fourth Assembly of the WCC in Uppsala, August 1968. In the same assembly, Hazim gave this outstanding message: "The Holy Spirit is himself Newness, at work in the world. (. . .) Without him, God is distant, Christ is in the past and the gospel is a dead letter, the Church is no more than an organization, authority is domination, our mission is propaganda, worship is mere calling to mind, and Christian action is a slave morality. In him, however, (. . .) the Christ is present, the gospel is the force of life, the Church is the fellowship of the Trinity, authority is a service that sets free, our mission is a Pentecost, the liturgy a commemoration and an anticipation, and human activity is defied. (. . .) We need a prophetic theology which is able to detect the coming of the LORD in history." Ibid., 34.

12. Moltmann, *Church in the Power of the Spirit*, 65.

Moltmann refers to the formulation of the Augsburg Confession (VII) that "the Church is the congregation of saints, in which the Gospel is rightly taught and the Sacraments are rightly administered." For him, this is obviously correct but yet he church is more than this in that the distinctive work of the Spirit extends beyond the bounds of the sacraments. Therefore, it is reasonable to describe Christ as existing pneumatologically in his actual presence within human's world.

For Moltmann, pneumatology must be understood in a holistic way since the Holy Spirit can be defined as the universal affirmation of the spirit of life.[13] Wherever there is a passion for life, the Spirit of God is engaged in opposition to death, oppression, violence, and injustice. Accordingly, the Spirit is more than the Spirit of redemption, and its place is not only the church. If the Spirit is only the Spirit of redemption then the Spirit is cut off from bodily life, which leads people to turn away from this world in their longing for a better world beyond. The future is here, by the power of the Spirit as the energy of life, connected to body and nature. The work of the Spirit is far too comprehensive to be confined to the Christian version of reality. He thus welcomes the appearance of new theological approaches to the doctrine of the Spirit, which leads the understanding of the Spirit beyond the limits of the church. God's *ruach* is the life force immanent in all the living, in body, sexuality, ecology, and politics.[14]

The Spirit really is the unrestricted presence of God. We may feel, taste, touch, and see our life in God and God in our life.[15] The imagery of the wellspring of life (John 4:14) is used as a way of explaining the effects of the Spirit in the life of the believer (John 7:37–38). The Spirit, considered as the shining face of God, is the expression of God's life and love, recorded in the Aaronitic blessing. Since God has made his light shine in our hearts to give us the light of the knowledge of God's glory displayed in the face of Christ (2 Cor 4:6), the Holy Spirit is the source of that light. Indeed, the sending of the Spirit on the Day of Pentecost was the revelation of God's indestructible and joyous affirmation of life.

Rather than defending a Christian civilization, Moltmann asserts that the church should speak up for a universal culture of life or mission of life, rendered by Joel as a promise: "I will pour out my Spirit on all people" (Joel 2:28). If a person is seized by the Spirit of life, then the whole personal life

---

13. In line with Moltmann's own book from 2001, *The Spirit of Life, a Universal Affirmation*.

14. Ibid., 2. Observe also Kärkkäinen, *Pneumatology*, 128.

15. Moltmann, *Source of Life*, 10.

becomes a charismatic experience.[16] No sector is excluded. The Pauline teaching in Rom 12 displays the everyday charismata of the life lived in God's Spirit. To Moltmann, this began on the Day of Pentecost:

> The Pentecost story is not a new sociological doctrine. It is talking about an experience of God. It is the Spirit who descends on men and women, permeates them through and through, soul and body, and brings them to a new community and fellowship with one another. In this experience people feel that they have been filled with new energies which they had never imagined to exist, and find the courage for a new lifestyle.[17]

This experience of the Spirit is a life which honors diversity. The acceptance of other people, in the midst of their particularity, is part of the freedom of community. This leads to a holistic doctrine of God the Holy Spirit, seeing him as life's vitalizing energy.[18] The experience of God deepens our quality of everyday life as it comes to us in all its beauty and complexity. The feeling of God's presence awakens the unconditional yes to life. The life in the Spirit asks for a spacious place free from restriction (Job 36:16).

According to Moltmann, the church lives with a paradoxical identity as both the church as she is believed and as she is experienced.[19] A church down the road is also a church from above. Statements about the church's unity, holiness, and catholicity are not to be considered as analytical judgment about her characteristics, but rather as synthetic judgment about her standing between hope and reality.

---

16. It is, however, a demanding task to adjust a universal position within a historical folk church tradition. These churches face a double challenge: The majority position give them a responsibility which call for a broad, open, and inclusive approach, in line with the theological position of God's love for all humanity. At the same time, these churches are spiritual homes also for those among their members who are personally committed by their devotional faith and desires. They have expectations of a more vivid church who gratifies their spiritual needs. For a Nordic perspective of this, see Hagman, *Efter Folkkyrkan*, 54, 176.

17. Moltmann, *Source of Life*, 104.

18. Moltmann is here inspired by the Old Testament term *ruach*, meaning something that simply lives and moves, over against what is rigid and petrified. It is the force of the Creator's power, both his wrath and his life-giving mercy (Ezek 13:13; 36:26, cf. Ps 51:10; 31:5). The Spirit is the divine presence from which everything that has life lives (Ps 139:7.) As the power to live, and as the confronting event of the personal presence of God, *ruach* may be interpreted pneumatologically as an experience of the Holy Spirit, giving humans "a spacious place" (Ps 31:8).

19. Moltmann, *Church in the Power of the Spirit*, 22.

A Place for the Spirit

In a similar way, Pannenberg understands the Spirit as the particular source of the new life given through the resurrection of Christ. As a spiritual person, every Christian is dependent on the Spirit as her/his divine source (1 Cor 15:44–45).[20] In line with the position of Cheung,[21] Pannenberg understands *pneuma* as an eschatological gift that operates within the church in accordance with the salvation event. Like Moltmann, Pannenberg broadens the scope of the endowment of God's Spirit, stating that the breath of life is already given to all in creation (Gen 2:7).[22] The different manifestations of the Spirit are simply intensive forms of an earlier given endowment, handed to a person as a special capacity for insight, leadership, prophetic inspiration, artistic gift, and so on. To Pannenberg, the Spirit is an all-pervasive breath that animates all life, just as truth is rationally discernible for everyone and history is accessible for all. Every creature is dependent on God's life-giving Spirit. He regards the Holy Spirit as the power that determines everything. Through the Spirit, God's presence is manifested in the creatures' ability to transcend themselves and move beyond their immediate environments. The Spirit moves them to the coming future when God will become all in all (1 Cor 15:28).

In other words, we can conceive of the gift of the Spirit as a lasting and persistent endowment that makes the church a dwelling place for the Spirit to rest upon his children because of their sonship and anointing (Isa 11:2; 42:1; 61:1).[23] Through this gift, the Spirit binds himself to the lives of the recipients. Death cannot separate us from his creative power (Rom 8:38–39). In Pannenberg's words:

> The imparting of the Spirit as gift thus characterizes the distinctiveness of the soteriological phase of his work in the event of reconciliation. The form of the gift does not mean that the Spirit comes under control of creatures but that he comes into them and thus makes possible our independent and spontaneous entry into God's action of reconciling the world and our participation in the movement of his reconciling love toward the world.[24]

---

20. Pannenberg, *Systematic Theology*, vol 3, 6.
21. Cheung, "Spirit-Baptism," 125.
22. See also Rybarczyk, *The Spirit Unfettered*, 99.
23. Pannenberg's approach reflects Johannine thought regarding the promise of the Spirit (John 14:16–17; cf. 1 Sam 16:13).
24. Pannenberg, *Systematic Theology*, vol 3, 12.

Through his indwelling and movement within believers, the Spirit lifts them above their own particularity. That makes the Spirit more than a gift. He becomes the quintessence of the ecstatic movement of the divine life (Rom 8:9–11). The theophanic character of the outpouring of the Spirit on the Day of Pentecost led to a deep feeling of collective enthusiasm among the apostles, expressed in ecstatic speech (Acts 2:1–4). However, the Spirit came to build the church, not only to deliver individual experiences. In the account of the coming of the Spirit on the Day of Pentecost, Luke's perspective is pointedly inclusive.[25]

For Pannenberg, it seems clear that the narrative of Luke emerges as a theological statement about the church as the end-time people, established by the outpouring of the prophetic Spirit on all who were given the promise (Acts 1:8). Pentecost is the story of how the dynamic of Christian missionary proclamation for the life of the church was unleashed. Here Pannenberg comes close to those younger church traditions which interpret the Lukan corpus as an account of the disciples' experience of being liberated from the boundaries of fear and equipped by the Spirit, in order to receive power for witness, ministry, and missionary activities (Acts 2:43–47).[26]

A viable ecclesiological concept based upon the Pauline and Lukan accounts calls for an intrinsically unifying view that the church is instituted by Christ and sustained by the work of the Spirit. By grace and by the free movement of the Spirit, Christ dwells in the believer (John 3:8; Rom 8:9–11). According to the variety of gifts and utterances within the pneumatologically oriented church environment, the believer finds his or her expression in harmony with all the others in order to bear witness to the mighty acts of God (Acts 2:4, 11).

This also corresponds with Paul, who opted for no single form of authentic spirituality but rather preferred to describe a variety of spontaneous workings of the Spirit. He urged the believers to tolerate these different manifestations alongside those spiritual gifts and fruits he considered most important: love, faith, and caritative involvement, given to everyone equally.

---

25. They were "all together in one place," the Spirit came to rest "on each of them," and "all of them" were filled with the Holy Spirit (Acts 2: 1–4). The use of "all" is connected to the salvation history, to the outpouring of the Spirit, and to the proclamation of the gospel (Joel 2:28; Matt 28:19; John 1:12; 12:32; Acts 2:39; 4:31; 10:43; Rom 3:22; 6:3; 8:32).

26. Menzies, *Empowered for Witness*. See also Wenk, *Community-Forming Power*.

Christ Is in the World as *Communio*

Within the Orthodox tradition, a theological construction of the church states that through Pentecost Christ's historical existence is communal, not individualistic. People belonging to this fellowship are transformed by the Spirit from individual beings into beings-in-relation within the community, incorporated by the baptismal act. In the resurrection aspect of baptism, the believer is raised from a privatized existence into an identity established by the Spirit (John 3:5–8). This is rendered visible by the church's sacramental life. Through the vertical dimension of the Eucharist and its anamnetic and epicletic character, history is transformed into future-oriented and charismatic-pentecostal events.

For Zizioulas, truth does not arrive solely through linear successional developments, but rather as a Pentecostal breakthrough, turning linear history into a "charismatic present-moment."[27] He suggests that a strong dose of pneumatology has to be injected into ecclesiology.[28] That is why Vladimir Lossky advocates describing the Spirit as the subjective aspect of the church, while the more objective and sacramental dimensions of church life may be ascribed to Christology. In any case, both are necessary components to ecclesiological considerations.[29]

However, the question of how charismatic activity relates to the institutional aspects of the church seems to be unsolved in Orthodox theology. Zizioulas argues that, according to New Testament writings, the Spirit is given by Christ (John 7, 39). On the other hand, the presence of Christ presupposes the Spirit at work. It was the Spirit that constituted Christ's very identity in connection to his biological conception (Matt 1:18 and Luke 2:35) and his baptism (Mark 1:10). Throughout most of the early church period, baptism and confirmation were considered a liturgical unity. Thus the Spirit was involved in the entire process of Christian initiation as well as in the chrismation of those who were baptized. Accordingly, pneumatology will always occupy an important place in the eastern theological ethos

---

27. Zizioulas uses this perspective to explain the church's infallibility and the notion of bishops possessing a certain *charisma veritatis* (gift of truth). In Orthodox theology, the bishop in office is the apostles' successor only inasmuch as he is the image of Christ within the community. This is, of course, a disputed position in other parts of Christianity. Zizioulas, *Being as Communion*, 116.

28. Zizioulas, *Eucharist, Bishop, Church*, 124.

29. Lossky, *Mystical Theology*, 135. Catholic writer Johannes Möhler has the same approach as Lossky in his work *Die Einheit in der Kirche, oder das Prinzip des Katholizismus* from 1825, as does Russian Orthodox A. S. Khomiakov in *Russia and the English Church during the Last Fifty Years* from 1910.

because of its liturgical meta-historical approach to Christian existence.[30] In the mystical tradition of Eastern Christendom, the presence of the Holy Spirit marks the commencement of the spiritual life of each believer and thereby also of the church. In the baptismal liturgy of the early church, those who were baptized also received the laying on of hands in order to open them up for the descending of the Spirit, made visible by the manifestation of spiritual gifts.

According to Zizioulas, no spiritual gift derives from a natural or ethical quality of man. It comes from above or outside history: Every gift is every time a new event.[31] The church is built up through a multitude of new events, not through a transmission of historical realities alone. As opposed to the catholic notion that local churches are based on the existence of the universal church, Zizioulas argues that the Pentecostal event is an ecclesiologically constitutive event, presenting the body of Christ as an intrinsically local church. The local is just as primary as the universal.

With regard to the church as a pneumatological reality, the local and the universal dimensions operate simultaneously. There is only one church as there is only one God. But the proper expression of the one universal church is the communion of many local churches. In that sense oneness and communion coincide, just as unity and diversity are both integrated parts of her reality. The core value for the church is not the achievement of consensus in all respects but being a place where God's unbounded grace may be experienced. By the way, there seems to be an interesting unanimity between the Orthodox emphasis on the distinctive local aspect of the church and different kinds of congregationalist church models within the Free Church tradition.[32]

Among the Orthodox, the theological principle of oneness is displayed in their view of the canonical institution of synods. The presence of church requires an institution that safeguards her oneness as well as her multiplicity. This is expressed through the twofold ministry and the twofold structure of the church: the bishops as the head of the local churches and the presbyterium of other ministries. The one—the bishop—cannot exist without the many, the community. And the many cannot exist without the one. For the Orthodox, the headship of the bishop is a condition for the existence

---

30. Zizioulas, *Being as Communion*, 129.

31. Zizioulas, *Communion & Otherness*, 295.

32. However, while the former has secured a close link between the local and the universal by at the same time emphasizing the hierarchical structure, the latter has preferred to claim the value of self-governance and independence without having established any unifying supervision.

of the community and its charismatic life.[33] There is a mutual interdependence between the one and the many. There is no church without the community and no Christ in the world without the one body, representing the many.[34] Within this tradition, ecclesiology and liturgy are the most essential theological elements. Any theological reflection presupposes that there is a celebrating and discerning fellowship.

Furthermore, because of the ontological nature of the church, Zizioulas gives pneumatology a constitutive and qualifying role. It is the Spirit that makes the church to be church. That is why pneumatology not only refers to her well-being but to her being itself. It is the very essence of the church.[35]

In the Image of God

The idea that we all are baptized into the oneness of the church (1 Cor 12:13) is a statement with deep significance. However, the communal dimension is also deeply personal. On the Day of Pentecost tongues of fire separated and came to rest on each of them (Acts 2:3), with the result that all were filled with the Holy Spirit (v. 4). Every "you" in John 14 and 16 points to the whole of the community and to the individual persons as well.[36] What Congar designates as a pneumatological anthropology—a precondition for his understanding of Spirit-driven and sacramentally oriented ecclesiology—builds upon the conviction that the human being is created in the divine image of God. Humans are relationally oriented to God and to others. To Congar, it is important to understand the church from a human perspective, as a social and corporeal society existing under general human conditions.[37]

Under such conditions, women and men enjoy the freedom of truly mutual relationships despite their propensity toward conflict and separation. Through the Spirit they are invited to partake in a divine life that can even exceed the human capacity for love and creative activity. A panoply of spiritual fruits and gifts may come to the fore as the believers cooperate

---

33. Zizioulas, *Being as Communion*, 137.

34. Zizioulas argues against the catholic notion that the one Church precedes and "subsists" in each local church. In her structure and ministry, the church has to express and realize the freedom of otherness. On the other side, Zizioulas does not give the same attention to how his alleged freedom of otherness can be harmonized with the doctrinal exclusiveness which otherwise distinguishes Orthodox ecclesiology. Zizioulas, *Communion & Otherness*, 38–39.

35. Zizioulas, *Being as Communion*, 132.

36. Congar, *I Believe in the Holy Spirit*, 16.

37. Koskela, *Ecclesiality and Ecumenism*, 74.

in a disciplined synergy with the grace of God (Gal 5:22–23). Implied in this pneumatological anthropology is the thought that persons exist in a being-toward one another. Hence the personal indwelling of the Holy Spirit can be explained as an interpersonal and ecclesial mystery.[38] The Holy Spirit indwells all of the faithful and this personal indwelling has implications for the life, structure, and mission of the church.[39]

In this respect we see an impressive interdependence between the four gospel accounts. Strikingly, all four Gospels render the sending of the apostles, the outpouring of the Spirit, and the dynamic character of the post-Pentecost church in quite a consistent way (Matt 28:18–20; Mark 16:15; Luke 24:47–49; John 17:18; 20:21–23; cf. Acts 1:8). The Spirit gave Christ to the world through a church that is global, empowered, missional, and contextual, and the church understands her own actions and character as subject to the gifts and activities of the Spirit.[40]

But all theology is marked by its conceptual restrictions. When talking about God, the Spirit, and the church, we cannot help but rely upon analogies, parables, images, and stories. The great symbols of the Spirit—water, fire, air, and wind—call to mind the idea of being invaded by a presence and a deep and irresistible expansion.[41] But the Spirit might as well come as an inner whispering and silence (cf. 1 Kgs 19:12). For Congar, the highest form of theology is doxological engagement, for worship is actually an interpretation of life. A doxological attitude rescues us from conceptualizing and objectifying theology as pure theoretical formulations. When talking about God through doxology, theology becomes visible in dynamic events. This is what Congar defines as the transcendental condition of being a Christian and having the Spirit of God, based on the firm belief of being shaped in the image of God.

And finally, while the connection between Christ and the church is a mystery, the church in its visible rendering is incomplete and therefore perpetually in need of continuous renewal. That means that the foundation of the church does not have to be understood in an exclusively historical and chronological sense.[42] Because of his persuasive pneumatological ori-

---

38. Groppe, "Contribution of Yves Congar," 465.

39. Or as articulated by Groppe: "An adequate theology of the Holy Spirit demands precisely the ecclesiological dimension that had been lacking in the turn-of-the-century Roman Catholic theology." Ibid., 460.

40. Congar, *I Believe in the Holy Spirit*, 65. Likewise, Justin Martyr declared that charismatic gifts would accompany the church throughout its history until the end. *Dial.* 39, 2–5; 88, 1.

41. Congar, *I Believe in the Holy Spirit*, 3, 4.

42. Congar, "The Council as an Assembly," 65.

entation, Congar states that every generation establishes the church in new contexts, in new times, and, to some degree also in new forms, by ministries characterized by an attitude of faithfulness to the original testimony.

Joseph Ratzinger considers that the birth story of the church in the Book of Acts ought to be read as a narrative ecclesiology, because of its departing point on the Day of Pentecost. From the narrative of wind and fire he deduces the systematic-theological reflection that the Spirit was church-constitutive. In fact, the Spirit created—and still creates—the church. She is not a result of human decision.[43] A Spirit-driven and sacramentally founded church is not an establishment in which past forms are preserved. It is part of a tradition broad enough to accommodate both healthy critique and well-grounded creativity.[44]

The Catholic tradition has characterized the Spirit as an indwelling resource of power. This tradition has been conducive to the increasing interest in spirituality and charity. But when the doctrine of the Spirit is discussed within the framework of the church, the focus traditionally has been on the institution and its magisterium. That is why Congar insists that the church belongs to the domain of pneumatology as an essential theological statement. In her global variety, the church has an abundance of charisms. Consequently, she cannot be a ready-made object, sustained and effectual only by virtue of her legal structures. The church exists because of the influence and work of the Spirit (Rom 1:6; 1 Cor 1:1; 3:6; 12:4–11; Eph 4:11–16).

A Presence Called Friendship

In the eyes of Moltmann, the sacramental and liturgical life of the church is not less than a representation and actualization of the history of Christ. Remembrance and hope of glory pave the way for liberation and grace. His sacramental orientation fuses together the objective and subjective dimensions of faith and experience as co-inherent with each other.[45] Moltmann leans on the reflection of Hans Küng, saying that the church is expressed in historical form, while her eschatological future already has begun in the present existence of the church. This cannot be expressed more clearly than in the sacramental event.

---

43. Ratzinger, *Called to Communion*, 41.

44. Movements like Pietism, Methodism, and Pentecostalism are by Congar recognized as genuine movements of the Holy Spirit, having a significant spiritual value. Congar, *Word and Spirit*, 49–52.

45. Moltmann, *Church in the Power of the Spirit*, 27. See also Küng, *The Church*, 5.

This does not stand over and against a more charismatic orientation. Our mystical encounter with God comes to the fore in both dimensions. By also pointing to the pneumatological nature of the church, Moltmann tries to resolve the tension between faith as tradition and faith as experience. Paradoxes, dialectics, and diversities lose their partial character in the history of the Spirit's presence in the church. By the Spirit, the believer receives the ability to face the teleological questions of meaning and intention. The ultimate purpose of the work of Christ is the universal glorification of God through Christ (1 Cor 15:28; Phlm 2:10). Because the church is the eschatological creation of the Spirit, the historical community of Christ comes about through a common sharing in the Spirit (Col 1:8; Phlm 2:1) in anticipation of the divine future.[46] Moltmann writes:

> The church is the concrete form in which men experience the history of Christ. In the longer-range history of the Spirit the church is a way of transition to the kingdom of God. It lives in the experience and practice of the Spirit from the eschatological anticipation of the kingdom. As the fellowship of Christ it is hope lived in fellowship. The experiences and powers of the Spirit mediate the presence of the history of Christ and the future of the new creation. What is called "the church" is this mediation. As the church of Christ it is the church of the Holy Spirit. As the fellowship of believers it is creative hope in the world.[47]

This mediation role of the church is for Moltmann realized as friendship,[48] based upon the inner relationship which exists between the divine and the human. Being a friend—not a servant—is a personal designation. We experience ourselves as respected and accepted by God, and we relate to others in the light of this same acceptance. Reciprocal friendship combines affection with loyalty. It proves itself in sorrow, it reflects its happiness in delight, and it is the foundational passion undergirding any truly human fellowship. The first reason we are given for seeing the church in light of friendship is Jesus' relation to tax collectors and sinners and the messianic feast they celebrated together as a proleptic sign of the coming age. By his friendships, he modelled a hospitality that signals his desire to share and welcome by the law of grace (Luke 7:34–50).

---

46. Moltmann, *Church in the Power of the Spirit*, 33.

47. Ibid., 35. Moltmann gives credits to Orthodox theology and its pneumatological understanding of the life and work of Christ. Consequently, a pneumatological Christology leads to a charismatic ecclesiology. However, this Christology is beneficial only when it is developed within the trinitarian theology of the cross. Ibid., 37.

48. Ibid., 115.

The feast was an expression of the righteousness of the kingdom by which men and women were no longer identified by their sins, diseases, and earthly positions. The unlovable became God's free friends. The fact that Jesus declared himself the friend of his disciples became symbolic for the nature of the church (John 15:13-15, cf. Luke 11:5-10) and for her confident life in prayer to and worship of the LORD (John 15:16). The highest form of human liberty and of irreplaceable dignity is realized in this dialogue between heaven and earth. God's friends pray out of trust and freedom when they talk to God as friend to friend. Practicing this openness in friendship with God in the context of a worshipping community prepares the ground for a friendly world. Behind this reflection lies the fact that friendship in the Christian tradition has been translated as love. From Ambrose to Augustine to Aquinas, love is the friendship which captures the very essence of the church and releases diaconal resources.[49]

The Constitutional Basis of the Church

To Pannenberg, it is essential to clarify the constitutional basis of the church. Saying that she derives from the outpouring of the Spirit at Pentecost does not mean that the church's existence is based on an act of collective enthusiasm, but instead on the proclamation of the resurrection of the crucified LORD and his position as Son of God and Kyrios (cf. Matt 16:18).[50] In that sense, the church is not yet the kingdom of God but is a sign preceding the fellowship to come under God's reign. In order to communicate that reality, the symbolic significance of her liturgical life, particularly the Eucharist, will always be more important than other parts of the church, i.e., her structure and activities. Even in its weakness as a sign pointing beyond itself to the thing signified, the church's liturgical life nevertheless bears the presence of the future salvation.[51]

In this way, the church is prevented from arrogating to herself the glory of the kingdom. Only in spiritual poverty and humility can the power of the Spirit manifest as a unique sign of the universality of the kingdom of God (2 Cor 12:9-10). The church consists of a pilgrim people rather than ruling conquerors. Thus she grows by fostering attentiveness to the Spirit and an identity of being committed to Christ as LORD together with the worldwide church (Rom 10:9-13). As a divine witness to the gospel and steward of the liturgical life, the church is the mother of believers across all denomination

---

49. Ibid., 121.
50. Pannenberg, *Systematic Theology*, vol 3, 27.
51. Ibid., 31.

lines. We are in touch with holy things; we participate in Jesus himself as he is present in Word and sacraments. Saying that the church is the body of Christ is not only a metaphor with illustrative power but a depiction of the nature of the church (1 Cor 12:27).

For Pannenberg, no confession or sacramental act has of itself the power to unite with Christ. Irrespective of how much the confession may involve the personal commitment of individuals, they need to join in the proclamation, praise, prayer, and confession of the church as a whole.[52] But part of the Spirit's work is to release and reconcile the tension between the fellowship and the individual:

> The work of the Holy Spirit lifts individuals ecstatically above their own particularity not only to participation in the sonship of Christ but at the same time also to experience of the fellowship in the body of Christ that unites individual Christians to all other Christians. (. . .) Not just the individual but the church, too, in its liturgical life has its existence outside itself in Christ. In this way it shows to be a fellowship of the Spirit.[53]

To Pannenberg, unity in the Spirit means that all members are responsible for cultivating the pneumatological well-being of the church.[54] Drawing upon the symbolic and sacramental definition of the fellowship, the church has her essence not within but outside of herself. She appears as a signifying prefiguration of the eschatological fellowship of the new humanity, in which her uttermost destiny will be reached in the coming kingdom of God. However, the church as a fellowship still shares the brokenness of earthly life. Consequently, the broken form of the Spirit's dwelling in the church leaves room for a legitimate critical function of individual believers relative to the church's provisional nature.

Baptism, a Door to Go Thorough

For Congar, the rite of baptism cannot legitimately be regarded as the instrumental cause of the reception of the Holy Spirit, because baptism and the reception of the Spirit are fused together in the same conversion-initiation process. To him, all sacraments are invisible operations of the Holy

---

52. Ibid., 122.

53. Ibid., 130. Pannenberg holds that we have to recognize the church as a fellowship of the Spirit precisely in her historical reality. This is said in opposition to Tillich (and Brunner), who set the New Testament title *ekklēsia* in opposition to the historical form of churches. Tillich, *Systematic Theology*, 3, part IV, 150.

54. Pannenberg, *Systematic Theology*, vol 3, 133.

Spirit and need a liturgical, celebrative commemoration. They have the function of being both signs and effective means for bringing the members of the church into direct contact with Christ. They constitute a symbolic-real celebration and connect the participants to the historical act of Christ's redemption as a unified body. John the Baptist's witness to the one who "baptizes with the Holy Spirit" (John 1:33) is a textual reference important for the church's pentecostal identity.[55] With the in-breaking of the kingdom of God, baptism could no longer be identified with just a rite. Instead, the messianic era was inaugurated by a specific sign: the anointing of the Spirit at the time of Jesus' baptism (Luke 3:21–22).[56] Without the presence of the Spirit, the sacraments are just religious rites.

As liturgical acts made in the Spirit, sacraments extend their gifts and responsibilities to both the worshipping community and the individual.[57] First and foremost they are given to the fellowship, but they are pronounced to the individual: I baptize *you*; I declare *you* the forgiveness of your sins; I anoint *you*. Then this personal announcement leads back to the communal level, where the church behaves in accordance with what is given to the individual. There is no doubt whether Congar regards baptism as a reality that includes repentance, conversion, and faith in order to become effectual. Also for James Dunn, a close relation between baptism and faith is unquestionable within the frame of the New Testament.[58] The

---

55. Isaacs, *The Concept of Spirit*, 114–15.

56. An interesting position in the writings of Congar is his understanding of the Johannine formulation "unless they are born of water and the Spirit" (John 3:5). He states that this phrase probably does not refer to water as such, since it would have made Nicodemus think of the baptism administered by John the Baptist. More likely the text simply contains "unless they are born of Spirit." According to Congar, the Spirit is not given as the effect of the water alone. The section seems to deal with two principles, Spirit and water, yielding the result of a rebirth from above. The dialogue involves also the dimension of faith. John regards the new birth of the Christian as the effect of faith in Christ and of the act of conversion. In the context of John, faith is the act of God, given as a baptism from on high. The text in John 3 is about Jesus who baptizes with water (3:22, 26; 4:2), but who also enables humans to be born again from above by faith in the name of the Lord Christ (3:15–18), from whom the gift of the Spirit is given. Congar, *I Believe in the Holy Spirit*, 108.

57. In the light of this, Congar holds that the practice of infant baptism is also catechetically problematic because the instruction in faith normally precedes the time of baptism as a celebration of personal commitments in the believing community. Ibid., 106.

58. Dunn, *Baptism in Spirit*, 99. Congar reserves himself from using the phrase "baptism in the Holy Spirit" as distinct from, and opposed to, the water baptism. A middle road is to include both baptisms by pointing to the inner interdependence between them and by underlining the role of the Spirit in both in initiation-conversion process *and* in the empowering of the church for different ministries.

Spirit is given in response to faith. The intrinsic connection between faith and baptism clearly comes into view in the narratives of Acts and the letters of Paul. It makes sense to declare that baptism is both a sacrament of faith and a gift of the Spirit.[59]

According to Zizioulas, entrance into the ecclesial communion takes place through baptism. The Pauline formula of being baptized into Christ (Gal 3:27) implies an ontological event and a condition for union with Christ. Individual human beings are united with Christ in the Spirit by the transferal of the Christ event into those being baptized (Rom 6:3–5). The baptismal death becomes the death of an individual, and the baptismal resurrection becomes their resurrection. Zizioulas stakes his claim on an understanding of Christ and the church as a communion realized in the Spirit, in which past, present, and future coexist through the Holy Spirit's presence in the life of the church. The one baptized is reconciled into a network of relationships.

For Pannenberg, coming to faith and coming to baptism cannot be separated. Being baptized in the Triune name of God is an act of transfer, a change of ownership.[60] To believe and to be baptized enacts a sign through which God sets his people free, leading them in the direction of the kingdom to which the sign points. Thus baptism is more than just an expression of faith. It makes a claim on the baptized and demands conduct in accordance with a life worthy of the LORD (Phlm 1:27; Col 1:14). This covenantal aspect of being a Christian thus unites the sign of water baptism (cf. Rom 11:27, Col 2: 11–12) and the gift of the Spirit (Eph 1:13).

But Pannenberg acknowledges that in the early church, faith always preceded baptism.[61] For him, baptism certainly does not bring salvation without faith. On the other hand, faith does not cause baptism but receives it. By baptism, those who already confess Jesus Christ receive the seal as a sacramental sign of the event of justification that links their lives to the death and resurrection of Christ. Baptism is the actual reconstitution of the person in the form of a sacramental sign. Hence, for the churches practicing infant baptism, there is an additional need of a later personal faith acceptance, through instruction in the faith. To Pannenberg, this is a work of the Spirit, who constantly reminds Christians of the work of Jesus (John 14:26; 16:13–14) and of their new identity on the basis of what baptism communicates (Rom 6:4). Baptism brings us into harmony with our natural destiny.[62]

---

59. Congar, *I Believe in the Holy Spirit*, 194.
60. Pannenberg, *Systematic Theology*, vol 3, 239.
61. Ibid., 257.
62. The ecumenical attitude of Pannenberg comes to the fore in his correcting of

Moltmann links his understanding of sacrament to the sending of the Spirit. Fellowship, proclamation, worship, and every sacramental speech-act and exercise of spiritual gifts and diaconal practices take place in the power of the Spirit.[63] Together, Word and sacrament, ministries and charismata all provisionally reveal the mystery of Christ, until the day he is universally made known (1 Cor 2:6–16). Sacraments are important as emblematic expressions of the saving work of God to humans. For Moltmann, the story-telling community is a fellowship of more than words of proclamation. She is a liberated, open, reconciled community of charitable actions of hope for those condemned to silence. Following his reflection, baptism becomes a personal and public sign of the life in the Spirit, uniting believers with Christ and bringing about a new generation of people raised from the dead through the glory of the Father to live a new life (Rom 6:4). What is objectively obtained through Christ is subjectively appropriated through the Holy Spirit.[64] Baptisms are framed by words of promise and subject to an expressively stated divine intention.

Moltmann argues that only children of Christian parents should be baptized, because faith precedes baptism. He sees infant baptism not as a token of prevenient grace, but rather a sign of the prevenient faith of the parents. The child gradually grows into the responsibility to believe for herself. Accordingly, infant baptism does not cogently represent prevenient grace and the unconditional justification of a sinner. These are rather aspects of the process of coming to belief. They are not tied to baptism in an exclusive sense.[65]

Since there is a link between baptism and faith, Moltmann calls into question the role of infant baptism as a basic pillar of the the Christian society *(corpus christianum)* and as one of the main propositions of a national church. Though the folk church thus regenerates itself from one generation to another and though both faith and baptism can serve in the social structure of life and function as a public sign of hope, social structures are

---

the historical condemnation of the opponents of infant baptism, as recorded in the *Augsburg Confession* of 1530. The references to Matt 18:14 in the Latin version of §9 are out of place, since these passages do not refer to the baptism of infants but to an act of blessing. Pannenberg states that both baptismal forms should be practiced alongside one another. Rebaptizing those already baptized is the one thing that does cause division. Ibid., 264–65.

63. Moltmann, *Church in the Power of the Spirit*, 205.

64. Ibid., 227.

65. Moltmann talks about the parents' messianic function towards their children. Ibid., 229. He thus differentiates between the parents' role of being committed to this representative service on behalf of Christ and being representative for the faith of another person or being a temporary substitute for that faith. Ibid., 230.

not sufficient to pass along faith. The freedom of faith takes form in the freedom to be baptized, and can only be practiced in accordance with that proper meaning.[66]

Moltmann concludes his reflection by stating that as representation and recognition of the reconciliation brought about by Christ, baptism manifests the creative power of the Spirit and belongs to the spirit of resurrection. Baptism is a call to faith, and it demonstrates the believer's new fellowship with Christ and with one another. There can be no talk about the efficacy of baptism *ex opere operato*.[67] For baptism is, above all, a call to obedience, freedom, and hope.

Then Moltmann points to the need for a new baptismal orientation, a process leading from infancy toward adult baptism for those who believe and confess their faith. As a first step, Moltmann recommends making baptism a matter of free decision, left to the parents. Infant baptism should eventually be replaced by a blessing for children in the congregational service of worship and by an act of ordination where both parents and congregation are commissioned for their messianic service to the children.[68]

Moltmann understands parenthood to be a living charisma in faith, by which parents realize their missionary service to their children. Confirmation classes can then be directed towards baptism as a missionary sign, understood as a call to discipleship and liberty. This requires the church to move past an identity as a welfare institution. She must take the step from being a church of ministers, functioning on behalf of laymen, toward becoming a charismatic fellowship in which everyone recognizes her/his ministry and takes hold of her/his charisma. People then become subjects rather than objects with respect to the work of the church. By the Spirit, the church is an open, missional, diaconal, supportive, and prophetic society in the midst of public society.

The Eucharist: A Repeatable Sign of Hope

Zizioulas perceives the Eucharist as the supreme expression of the body of Christ and the central element of the holy liturgy. As a meal, it highlights the

---

66. Ibid., 232. On the other hand, Moltmann fears that baptism of adults on the basis of personal confession probably will lead to a life in an exclusive circle of the converted.

67. Ibid., 240. The term *ex opere operato* is a phrase particularly used within Catholic sacramental doctrines to declare that the efficacy of the sacraments does not lie in the merits of either the priest or the participant, but is based upon God's grace alone.

68. Ibid., 241.

church's relation to the Trinity and its place between history and the coming aeon. As a liturgical act, it brings fresh life into the congregation through the Spirit. The result is a community—a network of relations—in which every communicant is the whole Christ and the whole Church.[69] As the center of the church's liturgical life, the Eucharist represents a progressive movement, guided by the Spirit and attentive to the needs of the people. The divine gathering around the LORD's Table liberates participants from individualism and egocentricity.[70] The body of the one: Christ, and the body of many: the church, are closely related to each other. Accordingly, the Eucharist is regarded as an all-inclusive expression of the mystery of the church.[71] The Holy Spirit personalizes Christ in the framework of the church and brings him to life in a very concrete, but spiritual, way.

Steeped in the Orthodox tradition, Zizioulas conceives of the Eucharist as the mystical experience *par excellence*. By participating in the eucharistic body, the assembly enters a new aeon, crying at the end of the liturgy, "we have seen the true light; we have received the heavenly Spirit." The celebration thus embodies the eschatological dimension of the life of the church. In the early church, prophetic words were also part of the eucharistic mystical experience. Prophets were allowed to speak at the Eucharist meal.[72] The sacraments are declarations and proclamations of the kingdom present and the kingdom to come. They are eschatological realities visiting us in history. Thus they accompany prophetic utterances *within* the kingdom, not only *about* the kingdom. That is why the aspect of sacramental presence is fundamental in the Orthodox tradition. Because of the Spirit's abiding presence and constant activity in the church, the will of God is no longer external to the worshipping community. It is among us.

A view of the church as pneumatologically constituted is based on some presuppositions: By the act of baptism, humans become personalized.[73] Consequently, only in communion with the Triune God can human beings be regarded as really free persons. The church is founded upon an asymmetrically reciprocal relationship between human beings and Christ. Through his relationship with his father, Christ is an incarnate person who incorporates the many into himself.[74] The Eastern tradition understands this as the pneumatic de-individualization of Christ, giving the identity

---

69. Zizioulas, *Being as Communion*, 60.
70. Ibid., 64.
71. Volf, *After our Likeness*, 99.
72. Zizioulas and Knight, *Communion & Otherness*, 299.
73. Volf, *After our Likeness*, 83.
74. Zizioulas, *Being as Communion*, 145.

of Christ an ecclesial character. Through the incarnation, he introduced his body into his eternal relation to his Father: "We ourselves as the other, the many, the church".[75] This incorporation of the many into himself is constituted by the Spirit through the incarnation and made visible in the Eucharist event.

While baptism is a burial and a confession and thus a sign of the grace, the LORD's Supper is the repeatable sign of hope, according to Moltmann. For him, it is the prefiguration of Christ's redeeming future glory. Both past and future are simultaneously present in a coincidence of remembrance and hope, of history and eschatology, of liberty and fellowship.[76] The Eucharist is not celebrated secretly or even privately. It is a public and open meal of fellowship, worship, praise, and thanksgiving. And because it is the Supper of the *Lord*, it cannot be the church's Supper, organized and owned by a specific denomination. Thus it follows that the Godhead's graceful gifts always transcend confessional borders. No church traditions ought to limit Christ's invitation on their own account. It is the open table that most clearly demonstrates the catholicity of the community. The meal is a sign of fellowship and not of line of demarcation. It is the place where the liberating presence of the crucified LORD is celebrated as a prevenient invitation to Christ's salvific reality.

Thus, the meal is an invitation to reconciliation and inclusivity, as open as the outstretched arms of Christ on the cross. It is the table of grace, not of reward. Through the prayer for the presence of the Spirit, the church becomes aware of her charismatic commission and her call to welcome all churches to the feast in hospitality and friendship. When we consider the sacrament, we do not see the Spirit in the sacrament but the sacrament in the Spirit.

For Pannenberg, the Eucharist meal is a sign of God's presence and a continuation of the table fellowship of Jesus directed toward tax collectors and sinners of different kinds (Luke 7:33–50; Mark 2:17). Christ's fellowship represented an acceptance of other participants into the future community of salvation.[77] The good news came to everyone in the inclusive fashion of a banquet, issued by God the Father (Luke 15:11–31; 14:15–23). Originally, the worship of the church was worship around the table. The promise of Christ's presence in the sign of the elements, distributed and received, encouraged the disciples to continue the table fellowship with the confidence

---

75. Or as said here by Volf in his interpretation of Zizioulas: "Without the church, one only has the eternal Son, not the incarnate Christ." Volf, *After our Likeness*, 85.

76. Moltmann, *Church in the Power of the Spirit*, 243.

77. Pannenberg, *Systematic Theology*, vol 3, 285.

that the LORD himself was present. The church was invited to an event greater than her members could imagine, to fellowship with Christ himself as host.[78]

However, the eucharistic remembrance of Christ's sacrifice is more than an act of human remembering.[79] It is a re-presentation of the paschal mystery of the death and resurrection of Christ, and an anticipation of the future kingdom. This sense of transformation is not built upon human consciousness but upon what we may define as a worship revelation, caused by the Spirit according to the promise of Christ (John 14:26; cf. 1 Cor 10:16–17). The Eucharist expresses itself as an ecstatic elevation.[80] The participants, when recalling the passion, are outside of themselves and within Christ. The prayer for the LORD's coming by the Spirit (the *epiclesis*) is a part of this remembrance process. It does not imply a transfiguration of the presence of Christ, but actualizes the resurrection of the crucified as it comes to the fore in the eucharistic worship and as an anticipation of his future return (Rom 8:11). As such the epiclesis is not a magical trick for speedy experiences but an expression of a substantial openness to the eucharistic reality and for our adoption into sonship, received by the Spirit. As regards the role of the Spirit, Pannenberg writes:

> It is always by the Spirit alone that the spiritual reality of the risen LORD is present to the believers, and it is only in this way that it can be a living reality in the church's worship.
>
> (. . .) As recollection of the LORD's death in the church always take place in the light of the Easter message, so Eucharistic anamnesis as a whole is sustained by the work of the Spirit and the prayer of his assistance.[81]

BEM states that through the Holy Spirit the crucified and risen LORD becomes present.[82] No priest has power to effect the change of bread and wine, nor can our prayer by itself do so, Pannenberg states. We can only pray with confidence that the Spirit will bring about the presence of Christ. The Eucharist meal has a truly unique role in visualizing the church's pneumatological identity. The practice of the LORD's Supper shows that the unity of the body of Christ is not grounded in uniform perceptions, common

---

78. Ibid., 304.

79. According to Peter Brunner, the eucharistic anamnesis is a work of the Holy Spirit within believers. Brunner talks about a Spirit-effected presence of the one-for-all saving event. Brunner, *Worship*, 145.

80. Pannenberg, *Systematic Theology*, vol 3, 307.

81. Ibid., 321.

82. World Council of Churches, *BEM*, 10.

performance, and structured jurisdiction. God has joined the members of Christ's body together around the LORD's Table, and it is God who has defined what their values are (1 Cor 12:12–31; Eph 5:22–25).[83]

Accordingly, the Supper belongs to the LORD of the church. The word of institution is in Jesus' stead, accessible for all who belong to his name. Any restriction of admission of baptized members of the body of Christ, on the basis of historical circumstances, seems to break the intentional hospitality Jesus practices in his own table fellowship (Luke 7:34).[84] Only an open Eucharist table reflects Jesus' open invitation.

Spiritual Gifts, Diaconal Power to Serve

To Zizioulas, mysticism best reflects the charismatic character of all ministries in the church. Ministry is always relational, since the Spirit realizes the body of Christ here and now as a complex of interdependent ministries. The mystical, the relational, and the charismatic inform each other. Thus, from the standpoint of Zizioulas, the concept of mystical experience is not based upon individual consciousness. Rather, the center of spirituality is what happens between the other and me. Mystical experience in the tradition of orthodoxy does not lead one to ask, what is in it for me? It turns the attention in another direction: towards the communion. A ministry is not conditioned upon human competence. On the contrary, participation in ministries requires a prophetic environment of anticipation in the midst of the church. It demands an understanding of ministries as mystical events that take place on behalf of the believing community.

For Congar, the extremes of individualism or authoritarianism can only be tempered when the gifts are in general use and not something extraneous. If the Spirit's freedom is downplayed, the function of the hierarchy in mediating divine guidance tends to be overstated and the fellowship becomes relegated to a role of passive obedience. Thus Congar perceives the charismatic gifts of the Spirit as gifts of grace in order to edify the church (1 Cor 14:5 and 12:7). They affirm her identity as being gifted. All members are called to use their charisms, whether they are of the more exceptional kinds (1 Cor 12:8–10) or gifts of helping, administration, exhortation, and acts of mercy (Rom 12:8).[85]

---

83. Pannenberg, *Systematic Theology*, vol 3, 326.

84. Observe the formulation in *Didache* 9.5: "But let no one eat or drink of your Eucharist, except those baptized into the name of the LORD." Milavec, *Didache*, 23.

85. Congar believed there was a charism of prayer, even though Paul does not mention it. The lists of charismatic gifts (1 Cor 12–14) do not claim to be understood

Thus, it is quite possible for a charismatically gifted person to act without presuming a spiritual monopoly and without perceiving others as less qualified to receive abundantly from the Spirit. The gifts are to be manifested in a broad range of expressions. In their deepest sense, all the charisms exist for charity, which is their summit and criterion. Where there is charity expressed among God's people, there the Spirit's gifts are at work.[86]

Congar recognizes that God intervenes in the local congregation by means of the Spirit.[87] Believers give words of encouragement, edification, and exhortation in the believing community according to the gifts they have received. Congar emphasizes the role of prophecy in particular, placing it is as the second after that of being an apostle (Eph 4:11, cf. the accounts of Luke in Acts 11:27; 15:32; 21:10). For Congar, the prophet has a function that operates both occasionally and permanently. Thus, the opposition between charismatic and institutional ministries is clearly artificial. All the ministries are charismatic and there is no group of ministries that is not institutional.[88]

According to New Testament passages, prophecy sometimes seems to be integrated into the charismatic liturgy and sometimes serve to support the inner structure of the church (1 Cor 12:28; Rom 12:6). Prophets continuously question the role of the church in society and confront unjust structures. Congar admires those prophets who are workers for liberation and committed to the poor, the disappointed, the voiceless, and those who speak out against every manifestation of oppression and racism. It is reasonable to state that persons who confront the status quo point towards the future by opening up a path for essential changes. They are prophets in their time, despite the opposition they meet. [89]

Likewise, Congar is eager to emphasize the special charism of discernment, closely connected to the gift of prophecy (1 Cor 14:29) and equivalent to the role played by the interpretation of tongues.[90] The universal principle of spiritual prudence is at the same time unique and complex, human and divine, personal and ecclesial. The task is to consider whether charismatic activities are authentic and in correspondence with the fruit of the

---

exhaustively. The series remains open, in accordance with the abundance of grace. Congar, *I Believe in the Holy Spirit*, 165.

86. Sr Jeanne d'Arch in the Pentecostal Conference in Rome in 1975, referred to by Congar. Ibid., 164. The writings of Congar aim to affirm different healthy renewals of the Spirit as they fit into the life of the church worldwide.

87. Congar, *Word and Spirit*, 63.

88. Ibid.

89. Congar, "The Council as an Assembly," 68.

90. Congar, *I Believe in the Holy Spirit*, 180.

Spirit as described in Gal 5:22–23. Other criteria are the Word of God, the observation of the commandments (1 John 2:3–5), and the christological approach as condition for the soundness for any pneumatology. Any church environment needs looking to those acts and practices which have acquired consensus, not only in the local community, but in a wider context of churches throughout centuries.

As a way of gradually getting in touch with the pneumatological nature of the church, Moltmann places spiritual gifts alongside the administration of sacraments, prayers, and acts of blessings:

> As the mediations and powers of the Holy Spirit, they (the charisms) lead the church beyond itself, out into the suffering of the world and into the divine future. It is precisely in its character as a fellowship in word and sacrament, and as a charismatic fellowship, that the church will understand itself as a messianic fellowship of service for the kingdom of God.[91]

All ecclesiastical characteristics are brought forth by the Holy Spirit. They communicate the message that this *is* the church, neither more nor less. Through the Spirit, the meaning of the history of Christ is revealed to all people. This purpose encompasses the charismatic dimension of the church as much as the sacramental. The church is both joy in the Spirit and a reality under the cross, both a song of thanksgiving and a cry for freedom (Rom 8:18–27). Since the New Testament presents the church as Spirit-driven, Moltmann holds that every person is a charismatic.[92] Every human potentiality and capacity can become charismatic through a person's call, as they are used and sanctified by Christ.[93]

If we do not see the whole community as Spirit-gifted, but only those within ministries, then charisma becomes a cult of religious genius. Moltmann depicts the church as the place where the Spirit manifests in an overflowing wealth of spiritual gifts (1 Cor 14 and its OT equivalent in Isa 44:3; Ezek 36:27, and Joel 2:28). According to him, the church members should not be afraid to give the Spirit room in our bodies too, since the bodies are supposed to be a temple of the Holy Spirit (1 Cor 6:19).[94] The charismata

---

91. Moltmann, *Church in the Power of the Spirit*, 198.
92. Moltmann, *Spirit of Life*, 180.
93. Moltmann contends that it is not the facticity, but the modality that defines a charisma. What is important is not the gift in itself but its quality and manner of use. The universality of the eschatological outpouring of the Spirit on all flesh comes to the fore when the charismata in the local church is baptized into love (1 Cor 13), and when the gifts are translated through the catalogue of virtues for Christians living in the world (Rom 12). Moltmann, *Church in the Power of the Spirit*, 297.
94. Regarding the gift of speaking in tongues, Moltmann sees this charisma as to

should also be visible in everyday life, because they are not given to anyone in order to flee from this world into a world of religious dreams. The charismatic gifts need to be "secularized" to witness to the liberating lordship of Christ amidst the world's conflict: in peace and ecology movements, and in the movements of liberation.[95]

However, the gifts of grace are expressed first and foremost as diaconal ministries. All the gifts of the Spirit are—rightly understood—diaconal power to serve (1 Cor 12:5). The result hopefully will be a loving acceptance of the other in friendly relationships, in solidarity with the poor as modelled by Jesus. Like Moltmann, my principle position is that the church is to be understood primarily from below. She is an exodus church and thus a provisional reality, turned towards the future, but at the same time rooted in history and committed to a liberating praxis within the life of ordinary people. The church finds her identity in the crucified Christ. Thus she is bound to the world by her corresponding identification with those with whom the crucified Christ identified. She is spiritual only in the sense that she reflects the Spirit's acts in the world.

Constructive Reflections

The dynamic-subjective and sacramental-objective essence of the Christian church is emphasized by prominent theologians such as Yves Congar, John Zizioulas, Jürgen Moltmann, and Wolfhart Pannenberg, each of whom represents a different theological tradition. To some extent they underscore these characteristics differently, but they all agree about the close link that exists between Spirit and church. There is a "soundtrack," so to speak, of the inner life of the faith community that emerges from the balance of experiential and sacramental dimensions. It constitutes the church as Spirit-driven and attentive to the fruit of the Spirit (Gal 5:22–23). As a dwelling place in which God lives by his Spirit (Eph 2:22), the church fosters a fellowship of both humility and boldness. The theologians presented in this chapter insist that theology is always more than verbal expressions and dogmatic statements. Faith has to be embodied in an honest search for a responsive belief,

---

be an inward possession by the Spirit so strong that the person can no longer find adequate expression in comprehensible language. It takes utterance as glossolalia, which can be expressed by unrestrained weeping, extreme joy, jumping and dancing. It is a body language and an expression of faith that is experienced in a distinct personal way. Moltmann, *Spirit of Life*, 185.

95. Ibid., 186.

nourished by both affective confirmation and sacramental verification of what is received from above.

The strength of Orthodox ecclesiology is its emphasis on the trinitarian, christological, and pneumatological identity of the church. Since Christ is present in the church through the Spirit, a pneumatologically sensitive Christology leads to a charismatic ecclesiology, made visible through the liturgy. Thus, the Church is portrayed in sacramental, pneumatological and mystical terms. Because of the wide array of human diversity, the Spirit cannot be captured in uniform patterns. Instead, the Spirit flows freely through the distinct personality of each human being.

However, the Orthodox tradition gives a clear prerequisite for access to the gifts of the Spirit: only in and through the Orthodox Church can one receive from the fount of the Holy Spirit. This rather exclusive Orthodox claim about the church represents a huge ecumenical challenge. Many people outside the Orthodox Church are seeking to recover the theological treasures they detect among the Orthodox, especially as regards the way in which Scripture has been experienced through the ages. The renewed connection between east and west, stimulated by ecumenical dialogue on different levels, is bringing awareness to the significance of this theological tradition as a living and liturgical source.

One key contribution from John Zizioulas and Vladimir Lossky is that through baptism a person becomes a being-in-relation, released from a privatized existence and included in the sacramental life of the Spirit-responsive church. The church is built up by the individual and corporate succession of charismata and spiritual encounters. Thus the gap between sanctification in the Western protestant tradition and the Eastern conception of deification is not unbridgeable. The strength of the Eastern tradition is that faith is given an embodied expression through lights, art, icons, aroma, and taste. The sending of the Spirit at Pentecost is understood as the proper aim of the incarnation.[96]

However, higher standards of scholarship, increased contact with western Christians, and involvement in the ecumenical movement has led some Orthodox believers to confront their own uncritical attitudes to the past. Working and studying across lines of Christian tradition has enabled

---

96. The Orthodox position goes like this: "The Spirit comes in order to found the church in time. Without Pentecost, there is no church and no presence of Christ possessing any historical reality. Only after Pentecost were the apostles able to begin their apostolic office or commission, and only then they found the visible, organically organized, charismatic and universal communion (. . .) The Spirit acts with Christ together and is present through him among the apostles and through them among all who believe in the kerygma." Nissiotis, *Die Theologie der Ostkirche*, 74f. Cited in Hütter, *Suffering Divine Things*, 114.

them to more seriously distinguish between Tradition and traditions in order to avoid extreme conservatism, to clarify what is indispensable in their own inheritance, and to avoid the transmission of a theology of repetition.

For Congar, the ecclesial life is first and foremost life in the Spirit. The Son and the Spirit co-instituted the church, and the charisms of the Spirit are ongoing dynamic elements given to all believers in order to build up the church and carry out of the Great Commission. One valuable contribution from Congar's position is his insistence that the nature of the church is not either to be charismatic or institutional; it must be both. The foremost example of this is the charismatic renewal in the Catholic Church, which infused that tradition with new life without being restricted by its extensive institutional apparatus.

Congar's ecclesiology essentially states that the church is built up by the life of the Spirit, the sacraments, and the free gifts of God, as well as by ordained ministries. This is a controversial position, since many of the significant ecclesial elements and endowments exist outside the visible boundaries of the Roman Catholic Church. The written word of God, the life of grace, faith, hope, charity, and the gifts of the Holy Spirit come from Christ and lead back to Christ. These elements belong by right to the global Church in her great diversity. Only a robust doctrine of the Spirit can achieve a balanced relationship between the charismatic and institutional dimensions of the church. A theology that is both ecclesiologically sophisticated and spiritually rich expands the view of the sacraments to include an experiential logic that acknowledges the presence of the Spirit through a variety of utterances which glorify Christ.

Moltmann's remark that we cannot always state what the church is, only where she happens to be, is a demanding yet important statement. Indeed, the borderline between the church and the world is not for us to draw, and the manifestations of the Spirit are in no way restricted to the frame of the concrete church (Joel 2:28–29). However, the church is realized in the concrete experience of the presence of the Holy Spirit through dynamic gifts, and in the identification of the church's sacramental nature. Moltmnn's appeal that the church's first word is not church but Christ, is a call to all church leaders to listen to the cry coming from the outside. The church will always be a humble community of justified sinners, liberated by the salvation of Christ. With her eyes fixed on Christ, the church lives in the Holy Spirit.

For both Pannenberg and Moltmann, liturgical living is a gateway to the transformational energy of life given by the Triune God. In that sense, the sacraments function as representations and recognitions of the reconciliation brought about by Christ. As visible actions, the sacraments are linked metaphorically to the invisible reality of God's gift. Our lives are sanctified by sacramental-liturgical actions and practices. Baptism is a call to faith. It demonstrates the identity of the believer's new fellowship in Christ and with fellow believers. By virtue of the process of remembrance and of the epiclesis of the Spirit in the Eucharist, we recall the passion, receive its effects, and are pointed to the future salvation. In this sense, the sacraments have a sign structure, and yet they effect what they signify.

In the following chapter, *Shaped by Pentecost*, some core aspects of Pentecostal ecclesiology are presented, though this theology is still in the making. However, different voices contribute to highlight the distinct vantage point of this particular pneumatic ecclesiology.

6

Shaped by Pentecost

> *The community of the Spirit and Word functions as a worshipping, witnessing, forming, and reflective whole; but at the heart of all this is the liturgical life of the community.*[1]

Introduction

THE PENTECOSTALS ARE THE new theologians of experience. Their spirituality is particularly concerned with the relationship between church and Spirit and thus thematizes many of the issues raised in this book. Despite the fact that Pentecostalism is a diverse movement, this group of believers has traditionally regarded the shared experience of the Holy Spirit within their community as a core of their mutual identity. A Pentecostal ecclesiology identifies the church primarily as a charismatic fellowship of the Spirit. However, the movement has different polities, it appeals to a broad range of subcultures, it emphasizes different aspects of the gospel and it celebrates worship in very different ways. No single group of Pentecostals can speak authoritatively on behalf of all the others.

Nevertheless, there are several contributions which the rise of Pentecostalism has bestowed upon contemporary Christianity: a) the rediscovery of the central role of the Holy Spirit, b) the request of conversion to Jesus Christ in an explicit and continuing manner throughout the life of every single Christian, c) the emphasis placed upon prayer and the power of prayer, and d) the rediscovery of charisms and spiritual gifts as realities, effective and necessary, in the life of the believer. The movement is young, has grown rapidly, and has no clear historical or theological self-understanding.[2]

---

1. Steven J. Land is a Pentecostal theologian. Land, *Pentecostal Spirituality*, 34.
2. Robeck Jr. and Sandidge, "The Ecclesiology of *Koinonia* and Baptism," 509. Observers have dubbed Pentecostalism "Catholicism without priests," meaning an

Thus, I hold that Pentecostalism appeared as a movement inside—not outside—existing churches in the beginning of the 20th Century. If we consider that the roots of Pentecostalism can be traced back to a broad range of Christian traditions, as Walter J. Hollenweger argues, then it seems appropriate to observe and evaluate the fruits of that movement within Christianity as a whole.[3] The Pentecostal churches have no copyright on a pneumatologically oriented spirituality. Pentecostalism is a phenomenon existing within different ecclesial bodies more than it is a church in a strict sense. However, through its particular focus on the work of the Spirit, the Pentecostal world has made substantial contributions to trinitarian theology, offering an approach to life that is open towards both Word-anchored and democratic experiences of the Spirit. This tradition underscores the church as a charismatic community of ordinary people.

In this chapter, we will listen to several different Pentecostal voices that address the relationship between church and Spirit. In particular, we attend to the possibilities for using a sacramental approach to engage Pentecostal experiences.

Key Components

Community and worship are key components in Pentecostal Christian formation. The Holy Spirit works effectually through the interpersonal relationships of community. "As the community joins together in worship, the elements of the worship facilitate a divine-human encounter between God's Spirit and the worshipper. The outcome of pristine Pentecostal community and worship is a lived Christian faith," R. Jerome Bonne writes.[4] Steven Land reflects upon the distinctiveness of Pentecostalism in a similar way. The powerful, sensed presence of the Spirit leads to a clear testimony focused on Christ as Savior, Sanctifier, Baptizer in the Spirit, Healer and coming King. Within this scheme, the church can be understood as a redeemed, sanctified, empowered, healing and eschatological community.[5] On the whole, the distinctive beliefs and practices of the Pentecostal tra-

---

expression of folk spirituality without the Roman juridical system or complicated scholastic theology. See Cox, *Fire From Heaven*.

3. Regarding the search for a Pentecostal identity, researchers expose a complexity of both theological profiles and multicultural and heterogeneous historical origins. Hollenweger talks about four different roots regarding the originin of the pentcostal movement: the black oral root, the catholic root, the evangelical root, and the ecumenical root. *Pentecostalism*, 18–384.

4. Boone, "Community and Worship," 142.

5. Yong, *Renewing Christian Thology*, 165.

dition are rooted in the affections which essentially characterize believers. Beliefs normed, shaped and altered these affections, while practices grew out of and fed them. Without this intertwined relation of beliefs, affections, and practices, there would be no continuing Pentecostal identity and presence in the twentieth century.[6]

Historically, it can be said that Pentecostal ecclesiology was not so much a specified theology as a lived reality.[7] The ideal was to search for models that could stimulate a spiritually committed congregation. But simply insisting on the spiritual nature of the church did not solve the challenges raised by their own unavoidable denominational process. Today, an increasing number of Pentecostals seems to admit that theological reflection on the essence of the church is integral to a viable Christian spirituality. On the other hand, they still maintain that any self-aggrandizing image of the church might give the impression that the Spirit serves the church, not the other way around.

When it comes to the question of identity, we normally consider that a religious body cannot exist as a recognizable collective unless it has some beliefs which can be identified as indispensable. But instead of seeking one's identity in contradistinction to other Christian churches, the Pentecostals tend to concentrate on characteristics that define the general marks of the church, a quest which mirrors the ideals held by many ecumenical circles today.[8] Rather than a strict focus on discursive doctrinal formulations, spirituality plays a defining role as local living fellowships search for a sustainable identity. Through deeper ecumenical involvement and engagement in trustful dialogues, the Pentecostals are receiving access to resources available in the church tradition which helps to clarify an identity of being an organic part of the worldwide church. Veli-Matti Kärkkäinen holds that Pentecostal ecclesiology is of an ad hoc nature which leaves much room for improvisation; it is often practical rather than systematic in nature, and is

---

6. Land, *Pentecostal Spirituality*, 120–21. Regarding Pentecostal theology, there are several reasons for the lack of extensive theological reflection. One reason has been the fervent eschatological expectation of the coming kingdom of God, which has made Pentecostals better missionaries than theologians. Macchia, "Struggle for Global Witness," 9–13.

7. Lee, "Pneumatologcial Ecclesiology," 16.

8. The question is whether perceived differences are obstacles to unity or whether they are complementary. The latter seem to be the prevailing position in recent ecumenical reflections, which describe unity and in diversity as a Christian mosaic. For more of these reflection, see Yong, *Renewing Christian Thology*, 171. See also Kärkkäinen, *Pneumatological Theology*, 53.

strongly restorationist. Pentecostals exhibit all forms of church structures from congregational to episcopal to all kinds of independent models.[9]

However, materials from ecumenical talks with the Roman Catholic Church during the period from 1977–1982 reveal an excellent attempt to define the fundamental ecclesiological identity of Pentecostalism and show that Pentecostals understand themselves on the basis of their spirituality:

> It is the personal and direct awareness and experiencing of the indwelling of the Holy Spirit by which the risen and glorified Christ is revealed and the believer is empowered to witness and worship with the abundance of life as described in Acts and the Epistles. The Pentecostal experience is not a goal to be reached, not a place to stand, but a door through which to go into a greater fullness of the Spirit. It is an event which becomes a way of life in which often charismatic manifestations have a place. Characteristic of this way of life is the love of the word of God, fervency in prayer and witness in the world and to the world, and a concern to live by the power of the Holy Spirit.[10]

The approach above displays what Hollenweger calls a new confession, an identity formed by orality of liturgy, narrativity of witness, participation of a reconciled community, inclusion of dreams and visions, and a correspondence between body and mind. It was brought into existence by the Spirit, and a moment became a movement.[11]

Worldview and Practice

Is there a specific worldview latent in Pentecostal practice? Are there some implicit theological and philosophical assumptions embedded within Pentecostal rituals? I agree with James K. A. Smith that insofar as the Pentecostal and charismatic renewal has reminded the church of her Pentecostal heritage, Pentecostal spirituality is a catholic spirituality with an ecumenical potential. Smith underlines that traditional Pentecostalism is not mainly a doctrinal or intellectual tradition, but an affective constellation of embodied rituals, a form of life that emphasizes the narrativity and orality of spirituality.[12] In contrast to the Enlightenment ideal of an abstract knower, Pentecostalism affirms an affective, confessing knower, based on

---

9. Kärkkäinen, "Pentecostal Ecclesiology," 251.
10. Sandidge, *Roman Catholic/Pentecostal Dialogue*, 141.
11. Hollenweger, "Twenty Years of Research," 6.
12. Smith, *Thinking in Tongues*, xx.

his own personal faith story. This makes her able to communicate to others her relationship with God.

According to Smith, there are five key elements or assumptions in a Pentecostal worldview. Firstly, a position of radical openness to God and to otherness, understood as openness to the continuing operation of the Spirit in the church and in the world through charismatic gifts. Secondly, a theology of creation and culture that perceives material creation as charged with the presence of the Spirit. Thirdly, a non-dualistic and holistic affirmation of embodiment and materiality, expressed as an emphasis on physical healing. Fourthly, an affective, narrative epistemology that makes use of an experience-oriented, theological approach. And fifthly, an eschatological orientation regarding the urgent need of mission and justice.[13] Altogether, this represents an approach to spirituality and the world that transcends the sacred-secular divide.[14]

For Smith, Pentecostalism is not just about speaking in tongues, but also thinking in tongues.[15] The Pentecostal commitment is not a specific way of worshipping, but rather a distinct way of thinking. This includes a liturgically shaped theology, not formulated within academia but emerging from the kerygmatic matrix of worship, testimony, and sermons. It contains serious theological reflection on the work of the Spirit, with an emphasis on affective understanding on a level prior to propositional articulations. Thinking in tongues may be interpreted as a passional orientation or a pneumatological imagination that includes customs and practices, being and doing; a theoretical understanding implicit in practice.

A Community of Reconciled People

According to Jerome Boone, the key components of Pentecostal formation can be summarized in terms of its community and its worship. Pentecostal worship has a playful style of passionate praise, emotional release, and exercise of spiritual gifts. The tone emphasizes experience and expectation of a vibrant, transformative relationship with God and an in-breaking of the Kingdom.[16] While the Spirit supplies the freedom for unscripted expression,

---

13. Ibid., 12.
14. Ibid., 25.
15. Ibid., xviii.
16. Boone, "Community and Worship," 130. See also Land, *Pentecostal Spirituality*, 59–60. The anti-structural nature of early Pentecostal worship was so consistent that Grant Wacker calls it "planned" spontaneity. Wacker, *Heaven Below*, 99.

the community gives the structure for the worship tradition.[17] Reconciliation with God brings humans into community with the reconciled people of God. In that regard, the church is a spiritually formative community. Pentecostal formation depends upon the environment of the faith community being a place called and instituted by the Spirit who illuminates the knowledge of God revealed in Scripture. The self that emerges from the life of the community is formed by the fellowship experienced there, which is understood as a work of the Spirit. In this way, Pentecostal ecclesiology leaves room for the Wesleyan concern for sanctification and holiness as an integral part of Pentecostal formation.[18]

There is also an issue of intentionality in the reciprocal relationship between ethos and liturgy, which comes to the fore within a Spirit-driven community. Without compromising freedom of expression, the community must develop rituals that deepen and honor the combination of affections, beliefs, and practices. This enculturation is a call to be responsible for the ways members live and act in a tradition-bearing community. The community functions as a social-spiritual matrix which is permeated by the ideals, values and ethics of the kingdom of God and characterized by love, justice, reconciliation, and compassion.[19] Pentecostals especially emphasize the ideal of egalitarian as well as complementarian relationships as modeled by the early church. The brother and sister metaphors point to a leveling of hierarchy, transcending the social structures determined by roles and offices (Gal 3:28). The experience of being known, accepted, and affirmed by the congregation, regardless of social status, is a key condition for spiritual growth.[20]

The Spirit-driven church is an environment for both confirmation and contradiction. One painful result of the influence of the Spirit is confrontation with inner resistance to the will of God, such as prejudice, ignorance, and self-interest. These contradictions can only be resolved within an atmosphere of hospitality and within a climate of a mutual confession. Given that the community has the required amount of communicative competence, in

---

17. Alvarado, "Worship in the Spirit," 140.
18. Land, *Pentecostal Spirituality*, 23.
19. Boone, "Community and Worship," 132.
20. Boone refers to the writings of Gerhard Lohfink, who describes the unique welfare system of the early church. Care was provided not only for widows, orphans, the elderly, and the sick, but also for those incapable of working, the unemployed, prisoners, and exiles. The fraternity reflected in the early church, permeated with love and egalitarian relationships, can be regarded as the key component in the formative Christian environment. Ibid., 133. See also Lohfink, *Jesus and Community*, 75–114.

truthful dialogue participants discover shared values, similar viewpoints, areas of concern, histories and goals. These elements create community.[21]

A Worshipping Approach to Life

The Pentecostal service functions as a worshipping, witnessing, forming, and reflective whole with the liturgical life as the heart of the community, according to Daniel E. Albrecht, Jerome Boone, and Steven J. Land.[22] The liturgical rites of the Pentecostal faith community actualize and dramatize the theological ethos of the worshipping community.[23] They nourish imaginative visions, facilitate order, and interpret reality. By their transformative effects and potential to shape human lives, they demonstrate the significance of Pentecostal worship. Based on the insights of Tom Driver, Boone contends that human beings are formed more by actions performed with the body than by ideas communicated to the mind. Thus, the manifestation of spirituals gifts has been regarded as an important element in the shape of Pentecostal worship, specifically because of their significance in signaling the presence of the Spirit. Traditionally, they have had a theophanic value, attesting the presence of God in an immediate and experiential way which includes both body and mind.

Today, more and more Pentecostals realize that the Spirit's movement within the church environment does not contradict the importance of the celebration of the sacraments. On the contrary, a longing for encounters with the Spirit is in fact the perfect setting for services centered on the Eucharist meal.[24] Spirit-sensitive rituals express the power inherent in the connection to the supernatural. As intermediaries, these rituals elicit confession, adoration, and conscious prayer from worshippers. And they convey the presence of God which can be grasped by faith alone. This attitude of receptivity leads to a process of reflection and a deeper cognitive understanding of what it means to be carried on the wings of God's grace.

However, these two approaches to attending to the Spirit are rarely considered complementary. Instead, liturgical forms that seek the spontaneity of the Spirit tend to dismiss formal liturgical rites as objectifications

---

21. Boone, "Community and Worship," 134–35.

22. See Land, *Pentecostal Spirituality*, 34.

23. Boone, "Community and Worship," 136. See also Albrecht, "Pentecostal Spirituality," 108.

24. For a wider reflection on the sacramental potential of Pentecostalism, see Hegertun, "Bridge over Troubled Water," 244. See also Biddy, "Pentecostal Understanding of the Eucharist," 228–52.

of the Spirit.[25] The emphasis on singing and worshipping, often in a mode of celebration or deep receptivity, is given an importance that verges on sacramental value. Worship is experienced as a manifestation of the Spirit's presence and functions as a transition from the mundane to the sacred.[26] Although Pentecostals may not be aware of it, the formative elements of Pentecostal theology imply that they do in fact live a sacramental life in a sacramental universe.

According to Evangelical theologian Donald G. Bloesch, Pentecostalism has also drawn attention to the empowering work of the Holy Spirit. God is not only the loving heavenly Father who forgives, but also the power of creative transformation.[27] For Bloesch, a community shaped by Pentecost is broadly understood as a missional fellowship, centered on Word and means of grace. One reason why Pentecostalism has experienced such spectacular growth is that people are drawn into a fellowship of love that manifests itself among its adherents and appears as a poignant expression of the priesthood of all believers.[28] This contemporary pneumatological scene is marked by a continuing tension between revelational and experimental theology. Bloesch admits that revelation itself contains a mystical dimension, otherwise revelation would be reduced to the communication of concepts that affect the mind but not the whole human being.[29] It is important to notice the complementarity of Logos and Spirit while still maintaining the subordination of Spirit to Logos.

---

25. Pentecostals have a tendency to characterize historical churches in an inappropriate and insensitive way, accusing them of being representatives of dead religiosity and dry doctrinism. The so-called "man-made creeds" were not rejected for what they affirmed but rather for the sovereign initiatives of the Spirit they seemed to exclude.

26. Boone, "Community and Worship," 139.

27. Bloesch, *The Holy Spirit*, 204–7.

28. The Catholic Church has also provided the Pentecostals with statements of appreciation. In a text from 1992, Pope John Paul II wrote that as a vibrant spiritual movement, Pentecostalism provides the Catholic Church with a fresh challenge and an opportunity to rethink its own identity and mission as church. The evangelical success and tremendous growth of the Pentecostal movement should be a reminder to the Catholic Church of the need to continue reviewing its own self-understanding. The challenge from the same Pope was clear: "Be open to Christ, welcome the Spirit, so that a new Pentecost may take place in every community!" On July 21, 2014, Pope Francis visited a Pentecostal gathering in the Evangelical Church of Reconciliation in Caserta in southern Italy. Here he asked for forgiveness for the words and actions of Catholics who have persecuted Pentecostals in the past. In his speech he stated that diversity is reconciled to unity through the action of the Holy Spirit. Source: Vatican Radio, http://www.news.va/en/news/pope-in-caserta-asks-pardon-for-persecution-of-pen.

29. Bloesch, *The Holy Spirit*, 223.

The Primary Locus of the Work of the Spirit

A traditional view in Pentecostal circles is that we cannot conceive of fellowship with God apart from fellowship in God through the Spirit. The church thus becomes the primary locus of the work of the Spirit. This is the position of Pentecostal theologian Simon Chan. He states that the church gives birth to believers and grants them their specific identity. The church is the new creation in Christ. As a body, she is invigorated by the Spirit of the life who raised Jesus from the dead.[30] Chan critiques the Protestant tendency to see the church as essentially a service provider, established to fix the needs of individual Christians:

> Rarely are individuals thought of as existing for the church. When the church is seen as existing for the individual, then the focus of ministry is on individuals: how individual needs can be met by the church. But when individuals are seen as existing for the church the focus shifts from the individual needs to our common life in Christ.[31]

According to Chan, the practice of giving priority to individuals over the ecclesial life has led to an interpretation of the Pentecost event as primarily a personal experience of the vivifying power of God's Spirit. An assumed sociological understanding of the church sees the church as a community brought about by people united for a common purpose, not primarily as a creation of the Spirit. Thus it is the people who make the church. The alternative to this individualistic approach is to think in terms of an *ecclesial* pneumatology. Then the primary locus of the work of the Spirit becomes the church. To be baptized into Christ is to be incorporated into a Spirit-empowered entity. Thus the term Spirit baptism becomes an event of the church prior to any personal Spirit baptism as normally perceived within the Pentecostal tradition. When the primary focus of Spirit-baptism is to actualize the communal fellowship in Christ, then relationships with others and the needs of others become of the highest concern.[32] Together with their personal experience, Pentecostals may begin to talk about the corporate Pentecostal reality which all members share within the frame of the believing community.[33]

---

30. Chan, "Mother Church," 177–78.
31. Ibid.
32. Ibid., 180.
33. The new postmodern openness to various religious experiences seems to represent both an opportunity and challenge to Pentecostal spirituality. According to Rebecca Jaichandran and B. D. Madhav, although Pentecostal spirituality shares similarities

In general, Christian spirituality has its centre of gravity in a personal relationship with Jesus Christ. Daniel E. Albrecht holds that Pentecostal ecclesiology understands worship as having three main connotations: 1) worship as a way of Christian life, especially outside of the church services and activities; 2) worship as the entire liturgy, the whole of the Pentecostal service; and 3) worship as a specific portion, an aspect or rite within the overall liturgy.[34] Ecclesial worship refers to the encounter with the divine as mediated and manifested by God's divine presence. The heightened awareness of this presence often occurs within an environment of worship where forms of musical expression, including symbolic worship, choruses and verbal praise serve to trigger a close sense of God's presence.[35] There is obviously a connection here to the sacramental practices of traditional churches. Whereas sacramental churches consider sacraments to be the preferred way of securing the divine presence along with the preached word, for Pentecostals the emphasis has been on the gifts of the Spirit.

However, some Pentecostal theologians have attempted to find commonalities between Pentecostal spirituality, especially its emphasis on glossolalia, and Christian spirituality in general, seeing the sacraments as signs of God's divine presence.[36] Pentecostals are delighted to speak of the church in the language of fellowship, because fellowship focuses on the personal rather than structural, sacramental, or ecumenical aspects of *koinonia*. In the present century, the Pentecostal tradition has taken *koinonia* with the Holy Spirit out of the cloistered mystical tradition of the church and made it the common experience of the whole people of God.[37]

This is inspired by New Testament teachings which describe worship and mutual sharing as fundamental characteristics of fellowship. By referring to Lesslie Newbigin, Kärkkäinen states that a real congregational life, wherein each member has an opportunity to contribute to the life of the whole body through gifts of the Spirit, is as much a part of the essence of the church as ministries and sacraments. The experience of worship and

---

with postmodern spirituality, there is also some dissimilarity. While the emphasis of postmodern spirituality is on the deconstruction of language, Pentecostal spiritual experience centers on the language of God-experience. While postmodern spirituality emphasizes silence, Pentecostal spirituality emphasizes audibility. Jaichandran and Madhav, "Pentecostal Spirituality," 57. See also Robeck Jr., "Nature of Pentecostal Spirituality," 103.

34. For a broad presentation, see Albrecht, "Pentecostal Spirituality: Ecumenical Potential."

35. Jaichandran and Madhav, "Pentecostal Spirituality," 58.

36. Kärkkäinen, "Pentecostal Ecclesiology," 253.

37. Ibid., 252.

adoration, with a deep desire to meet with the LORD, stands at the heart of Pentecostal church life.

The Sacraments as Signs of God's Presence

As already mentioned, Pentecostals have been ambivalent regarding the question of sacraments. They struggle with whether these means of grace are signs of God's presence in an exclusive way, or just variations of human acts and testimonies of faith. To what extent can a distinctly Pentecostal characteristic, such as speaking in tongues, be considered to have sacramental value, even if Pentecostals are not conscious of it as such? Pentecostals cherish the notion of the unmediated presence of God, conveyed by the Spirit and often bypassing liturgical structures. However, this distinction between freedom and mediation may prove to be unwarrantable as long as the sacramental efficacy can be perceived in the context of sign. The reality signified is experienced through visible (read: sacramental) signs in the process of signification, realized by the presence of God in the midst of the believing community.

According to Frank D. Macchia, glossolalia simply signifies the presence of the Spirit in an audible and identifiable way. Tongues can be designated as a linguistic symbol of the sacred.[38] Therefore, as a point of departure, we may define the fundamental essence of the sacraments as manifested words related to the secondary function of the elements, the clarifying of the Word.[39] It should be clear that without the word of God proclaiming and surrounding the sacramental events, there is no means of grace at all, regardless of liturgical tradition. This is said not to question the mandatory prescription of the elements but rather to underline the word- and grace-event character of the sacraments in line with Pentecostal beliefs. When understood as an expression of the manifested, eventful word of grace and as a congregational proclamation of the LORD's death and resurrection, the doctrine of sacraments can become meaningful also for those who are not familiar with the deep liturgical traditions of the historical churches.

In fact, even within Pentecostal circles the word of God has a manifestive character. It effects what it signifies. The kerygmatic and ecclesial word is realized and becomes an event in a mode effective for salvation and

---

38. Macchia, "Tongues as a Sign," 61. Se also Samarin, *Tongues*, 152. Macchia observes the irony that even if Pentecostalism represents a kind of protest sacramentality and is critical of sacramental traditions, they bear significant similarities with the sacramental tradition. Macchia, "Tongues as a Sign," 73.

39. Rahner, "What Is a Sacrament?," 276.

the forgiveness of sins. Analogously, Macchia contends that it is possible to consider the glossolalic signification as a sacramentally significant medium imparting the presence of God and empowering believers for service. He mentions one differentiation: while glossolalia accentuates an unpredictable move of the Spirit, liturgical traditions emphasize a predictable encounter.[40] But freedom in the Spirit should not be ignored or dismissed as chaotic, just as the more organized liturgical forms need not be rejected as empty traditions or as an objectification of the Spirit.

Here emerges the tension between classical and Free Church traditions: The catholic sacramental identity is developed in the context of the church as the institutional embodiment of the risen Christ, making the church vulnerable to the danger of restricting the free movement of the Spirit into institutionalized forms. However, Free Church environments represent the opposite inclination, a theophanic approach of God's self-disclosure through the gifts of the Spirit, developing a culture characterized by a demand for signs and wonders. The latter finds its christological determination in the pneumatic Christ. It sees the church as an event that must continually be renewed in accordance with God's redemptive activity in the world, rather than a permanent embodiment of the incarnate Word as such.[41]

The sacramental dimension in the free manifestation of tongues is obvious. Along with Pentecostal theologian Gary McGee, I hold glossolalia to be an initial sign, linking together the early Jewish and Gentile community of Christ-believers in a common understanding of the reality of the Spirit, bringing forth new life and empowerment for ministry. These manifestations were not random coincidences but a pattern, made visible in the Book of Acts (Acts 2, 8, 10 and 19).[42] By being informed of the life of the ancient church and by including into their own contemporary traditions what they regarded to be manifested elements within the apostolic story, Pentecostals want to be connected to these ancient communities.

In this way, they continue the book of Acts by creative interaction more than by an inductive method of biblical interpretation.[43] As initial evidence, the many tongues of Pentecost represented the continuity between biblical stories of the Spirit's anointing of different groups of believers, as recorded by Luke and Paul. However, with respect to the sovereignty and freedom of the Spirit, we cannot make as normative a closed interpretation limited to

---

40. Macchia, "Tongues as a Sign," 63.
41. Ibid., 73.
42. McGee, "Early Pentecostal Hermeneutics."
43. Macchia, "Tongues as a Sign," 65.

quite specific modes of practices that demand a certain uttered experience of the Spirit.

The Spirit, Not a Possession of the Church

The founder of the form criticism, Hermann Gunkel, observed how the term "Spirit" became interpreted during the age of the apostles. He stated that the Spirit is the supernatural power of God which works miracles in and through the person."[44] The Holy Spirit is neither begotten nor transmitted by human beings and must not be conceived as a product or a possession of the church community.[45] The Spirit is God's free gift who descends only upon believers who are converted through the instrumentality of the community. Every outpouring of the Spirit is nonetheless a new and independent act of God. The overall perspective of Gunkel seems to be that every kingdom exists so long as there is power to preserve it. So the kingdom of God is in a quite special sense inconceivable apart from the power of God. Wherever his transcendent power is manifest, there is the kingdom of God.[46] The coming of the kingdom is thus an act of God's supernatural power. For Gunkel, the activities of the Spirit by his power of word and deed are the legitimation of the gospel. Gunkel also ascertains that Paul—without hesitation—acknowledged glossolalic utterance. He used it alongside other witnesses.

The Spirit's "sighs too deep for words" (Rom 8:26) are uttered by Christians when they are in a condition in which the Spirit has no way to express the feelings which powerfully seize them other than in sighs, whose meaning words cannot express. Because they are expressed by the Spirit himself, the pneumatic, glossolalic-ecstatic outbursts are used by the great apostle

---

44. Gunkel, *Influence of the Spirit*, 35. According to him, the New Testament sources give no specific doctrinal statements regarding the Spirit, though we find a host of descriptions of the Spirit's activities. Ibid., 14. Gunkel is close to an early Pentecostal position in stating that being a believer and being seized by the Spirit are separate events. Faith comes through preaching, and the Spirit descends usually by the laying on of hands as an event following baptism (Acts 8:17; 19:6) or by the laying on of hands prior to (Acts 9:17) or during baptism (Acts 2:38). The reception of the Holy Spirit is God's witness to the existence of faith (Acts 15:8ff; 11:17). Gunkel holds that the first disciples had long been believers and had witnessed the appearances of the risen LORD when they first shared the outpouring of the Spirit. Gunkel underscores, in line with a traditional Pentecostal view, that it was the glossolalia at Pentecost that first revealed the Spirit's descent upon the believers, as revealed in the narrative of Cornelius' conversion. Ibid., 25.

45. Ibid., 42.

46. Ibid., 72.

as valid proof for the reality of the blessing of salvation. Thus, the presence and the activity of the Spirit in the world function as a divine guarantee for the Christian faith and for the divine origin of the churches of the apostolic age.[47] Gunkel's position is clear. Only the person who is able to think himself into the supernatural worldview can understand the Pauline teaching about the Spirit as *pneuma*. Accordingly, only the person who approves of this worldview can teach concerning the Spirit, in the full New Testament sense of the term.

In a similar way, Pentecostals interpreting Acts have been concerned with the role tongues may play as a visible sign of the Spirit in experience and worship. To a large extent these spiritual encounters shape a common liturgical practice that can be considered as sacramental experiences of the Spirit. Macchia portrays tongues as a free and transcendent response to the free and transcendent move of the Spirit.[48] Glossolalia can also be regarded as a new language, signifying the creation of a new community and its witness to the transforming power of God in history and in the age to come. However, the wider connections between tongues and the anointing of the Spirit with "initial tongues" (a classical Pentecostal position) should not be described as a rule of thumb to know if someone has been anointed by the Spirit. Instead, tongues can be regarded as an integral dimension of a broad understanding of the encounter of the Spirit and of a wider theology of Spirit baptism. The tongues debate also calls into question the relevance of using the term "evidence." Such a term tends to corresponds to a scientific and simplistic approach, hardly suitable for the theological complexity and nuances involved.

As I observe, utilizing a more sacramental approach when interpreting the integral connection between the sign and the divine self-disclosure of the Spirit, may lead to a more suitable arrangement.[49]

Guided by an emphasis on the spiritual presence of Christ in the celebration of the Eucharist, Pentecostals are closer to a broad, sacramental understanding of the means of grace than a Zwinglian memorial approach.

47. Ibid., 81.

48. Macchia, "Tongues as a Sign," 68.

49. By referring to Paul Tillich, Macchia attempts to avoid an idolatrous objectification of the Spirit in visible forms and to prevent one-sided, radical emphasis on the freedom of the Spirit. Tillich talks about "a kairos event" that seeks to detach the divine self-disclosure from a visible form, as well as an objectification of the divine action in the form itself. It leads to an understanding of sacramental signification consistent with the notion of sign as an instrument of making something present. Tillich, *Protestant Era*, 94–112. In a similar way—though more intuitive—Pentecostals may understand tongues as an event that signifies the divine presence and abundance of life, given by the Spirit. Macchia, "Tongues as a Sign," 68–69.

Discussing tongues as sign rather than evidence serves to underscore divine freedom in a context in which the visible experience of God is acknowledged and manifested. Charismatic gifts are both free and sacramental.[50] Furthermore, the physical dimension of tongues as a sign disproves the denouncement of the classical churches in their characterization of Pentecostal spirituality as radical subjectivism. God's desire to empower his church in order to spread the gospel to all nations can hardly be designated as subjective or individualistic. The same holds true for the Pentecostal focus on healing and empathetic worship, which involve both body and mind. These are best understood as a signal of a kissing act between earth and heaven, where intellectual reflections, rational observations and affective involvement are all at play. Thus Macchia's use of the word sacrament regarding the function of glossolalia as sign of the presence of God is a well-qualified and relevant approach.[51] In order to steer clear of a metaphysical understanding of the sacraments within a liturgical context of the church service, the means of grace may be viewed simply as a dynamic and personal encounter between humans and the divine.

Glossolalia as Part of Liturgical Worship

Is it plausible to place glossolalia within a sacramental understanding which may be acknowledged by Pentecostals? Richard Baer minimizes the difference between glossolalia and liturgical worship by saying that strangeness has blinded interpreters from observing the fundamental, functional similarity between speaking in tongues and other widespread religious practices such as Quaker silent worship and Roman Catholic or Episcopal liturgical worship.[52] All these practices permit the analytical mind, the focused, objectifying dimension of human intellect, to rest, thus freeing other dimensions of the person, what we might loosely refer to as spirit, for a deeper openness of divine reality.[53] The intent of the many tongues of Pentecost (Acts 2) is not religious hysteria, Spirit possession, or uncontrolled expression of emotion in contrast to intellectual consciousness, but rather to free believers in the depths of their spirit to respond to the immediate reality of the living God.

---

50. Ibid., 70.

51. Ibid., 71.

52. Baer states that from time immemorial, saints and mystics have witnessed to the fact that a certain letting go, a being open to, is a necessary requirement for deeper experiences of the presence and power of God. Baer Jr., "Moods and Modes," 220.

53. Ibid.

This includes expressions of deep anguish, inner sorrow, intercession and petition, as well as spiritual joy or release into the flow as the Spirit leads in the worship event. Praying in tongues may well be the most satisfying religious response available (Rom 8, 26–27), because of it involves a kind of letting go.[54] There are also elements of playfulness in glossolalia, a sheer childlike delight in praising God, and sometimes also a sympathetic and joyful laughter that may appear liberating. To Baer, those phenomena reflect a welcome lack of pomposity in the midst of an often super-serious church environment. By referring to the Quaker tradition, Baer reminds his readers that it is almost universally felt in those circles that rational analysis and argument over what is spoken out of silence is inappropriate. Participants are not there to analyze or judge or to rouse emotions, but to listen and obey and to be confronted in their inner depths. Something similar could be said about the phenomenon of glossolalia in the Pentecostal tradition.[55]

Perhaps surprisingly, the same can be said about more traditional sacramental worship and written liturgy. The repetition of prayers, responses, and creeds frees the worshippers from needing to focus purely consciously on what is being said. Both mind and heart become stimulated by the theological content and aesthetic movement of the liturgy and mass. The impact of the church environment, Christian symbols, organ music, and even incense produce a sense of awe and mystery. Baer admits that in these traditions also the analytical mind is permitted to rest, and the human spirit is free to experience the reality of God on another level in the particular playfulness of the liturgy. At the same time, there is no conscious attempt to manipulate the emotions to achieve some desired affects.[56]

Nevertheless, the occurrence of countercultural sacramental worship within the Free Church tradition emerges to some extent as a corrective to the fixed and planned liturgies in traditional churches. But, while the latter tradition can be used to insulate from real changes, the first may be

---

54. As in the case of glossolalia, the process of speaking out of the silence and listening in the silence (as in Quaker circles) involves a resting of the analytical mind, a refusal to let the deliberative reflection dominate the act of worship. Ibid., 222.

55. Here someone may well point to the Pauline prescription that in public worship one should not speak in tongues unless there is someone present to interpret (1 Cor 14:28). But significantly, the actual interpretation usually appears to be less a word for word translation than a kind of paraphrase of the tongues with particular emphasis on reproducing its spiritual tone and general direction.

56. In his reflection about a more sacramental understanding of Pentecostal experiences, Macchia admits that the proliferation of charismatic signs and gifts in mainline liturgical traditions and the rise of formal liturgies in the Free Church movements complicate the picture. Thinkers of both traditions are involved in the complex issue of the relation between charisms and institution. Macchia, "Tongues as a Sign," 72.

employed to escape from a more reflective approach to the question of God's will and God's leading. In the Spirit-driven church, neither feelings nor the analytical mind is the dominant or controlling factor in the liturgy. Instead, a real encounter with the Spirit directs worship, in which different types of liturgical practices are addressed to the human spirit. At the same time as the sacraments in the context of the divine/human encounter have objective significance, the freedom of the Spirit forces us to maintain that all means of grace, in its deepest sense can be described as experienced realities. By admitting this and by defining sacrament carefully and broadly, new spaces may be opened for liturgical renewals which break the framework of our own limited traditions and restricted experiences. Macchia concludes in this way:

> If tongues call our church institutions and formalized liturgies into question and accent a free and unpredictable encounter with the Spirit of God, the ecclesial sacraments refer us to the fact that our ecclesiastical routines, structures, and programs may also be vehicles of God's liberating and healing grace. Similarly, if tongues point to spontaneous and unforeseen turns toward liberation and healing in the midst of the Church's witness in the world, the ecclesial sacraments may put us in touch with the liberating grace of God as it emerges through programed and structured attempts at interpersonal and social transformation.[57]

This indicates that different theological accents are more complementary than contradictory. Together they have a critical function against the non-articulated, self-complacent attitudes so prevalent within circles satisfied with their own brilliance. A giant of Pentecostal research, Walter J. Hollenweger, writes about the therapeutic and sacramental value of speaking in tongues in the twentieth-century Pentecostalism. As he describes, a member,

> afraid to express himself in public, experiences a feeling of dramatic tension which is resolved when the psychological blockage is overcome in speaking in tongue – which is analogous with to the practice of free association in the group-dynamic process, (. . .) helping to overcome loneliness, anxiety and fear, releases emotional blockages in cathartic sessions and makes it possible for the individual to integrate himself into a community by

---

57. Ibid., 75.

passing through and leaving behind him a shared experience of
guilt for the past.[58]

With that background, it is legitimate to emphasize that power, as used in the New Testament, is first of all the power of the cross, of the resurrection and of the coming age, by which Christ was raised from the death (Rom 1:4; 8:11; 1 Cor 1:17; 6:14). It is later described as a personal equipping given by the Spirit (Luke 24:49; Acts 1:8), but even so, this power is made perfect in weakness (2 Cor 12:9). From this perspective, Spirit baptism is the beginning of a miraculous transformation in the individual which will reach its final goal in the coming resurrection of the body (2 Cor 4:16–18; 5:1–5). Healing, manifestations and effectiveness in witness are concrete manifestations of the resurrection power of the Spirit, powers of the age to come.

A Relational Impulse Towards Intimacy with God

Pentecostalism may essentially be seen as the spiritual impulse driving the Christians towards personal intimacy with God.[59] In terms of practical liturgical living, it operationalizes a type of spirituality and theological formation which corresponds with an interpretation of the Pentecost event which sees the Spirit as the personal indwelling of the church. Simon Chan states that long before Pentecostals heard about the term, they have been practicing *epiclesis*, the praying for the coming of the Spirit in the Eucharist liturgy. This spirituality not only worked behind the scenes but was spoken of as the subject of primary activities and personal devotion for individuals, as described in Acts 11:12; 13:4; 16:6–7; 20:22. The experience of the Holy Spirit as personally present is a common denominator in Pentecostal spirituality. Interestingly, this does not necessarily lead to pneumatocentrism, since Christ traditionally has been placed at the center of a pneumatologically reconstructed ecclesiology, based on a fundamental insight in Johannine pneumatology that the Spirit shall glorify Christ (John 16:14).

Within the context of personal intimacy, it is possible to understand the role of glossolalia as an inward, wordless groan (Rom 8:23–27), a kind of spiritual language which is received as an expression of deep gratitude, longing, and hope. This is a reality nearly impossible to explain satisfactorily. Intimacy is also a key component to understanding Pentecostal worship practices and the way this kind of passionate spirituality gives energy

---

58. Hollenweger, *Pentecostals*, 203.
59. Chan, "Jesus as Spirit Baptizer," 149.

to large-scale mission activities and the desire to bring people into a similar personal relationship with Christ.[60]

However, in order to give satisfactory attention to the Father as the integrating factor within the Godhead and to prevent both egalitarianism and authoritarianism which is perceptible throughout the history of Pentecostalism, Chan proposes to focus on the *differentiated communion*. This trinitarian focus helps to stabilize the more fluid nature of Pentecostal spirituality. Differentiated communion presupposes the development of a liturgy in which the story of the Triune God culminates at the Lord's Table, as a communion with the Father, through the Son, and in the Spirit. A spiritual-corporate understanding of the church means that the church is governed by spiritual resources, primarily words and sacraments, "with which Mother Church nourishes her children."[61] Given his position, Chan's robust Pentecostal ecclesiology requires a pronounced sacramental theology by which its own identity can be deepened.[62]

Radical Congregationalism: A Nordic Perspective

I finalize this chapter with a perspective from the Nordic Pentecostal tradition. In his reflection on the distinctive features of the ecclesiology of Swedish Pentecostal leader Lewi Pethrus, Torbjörn Aronson points to elements from Pietism, Holiness and Baptist theology as well as from historiography to explain the strong restorationist traces found in traditional Pentecostal churches.[63] According to this view, classical denominational structures cannot contain the liberating work of the Spirit. The church is made out of individuals who by faith have become new creations in Christ (2 Cor 5:17).[64] God's assembly consists of believers in one local area and in the universal assembly of believers of all times. The role of the Spirit is to bring restoration and liberty to the church through a new understanding of Scripture, and through the baptism of the Spirit which unites people as the one

---

60. For an overview, see Dempster et al., *Called and Empowered*, 2–5.

61. Chan, "Jesus as Spirit Baptizer," 155.

62. To get rid of an occasionally excessive individualism within Pentecostalism, Pentecostal theology needs to appreciate the nature of the Christian as an intrinsically *ecclesial* being who has God as Father and the church as mother. At its deepest level, the Pentecostal instinct would probably not oppose this perspective, according to Chan. Ibid., 156.

63. According to Ulrik Josefsson, the Pentecostal movement in Sweden in the 1920s combined radical congregationalism with charismatic episcopalism because of the strong position of the pastors. Josefsson, *Liv och Överflod*, 100.

64. Aronson, "Spirit and Church," 196.

body of Christ.[65] A challenging characteristic of this church model is the conviction that part of the Spirit's work is found in the confrontation of hierarchical structures of other denominations, causing tensions which in next turn lead to splits and more confrontations. Pethrus argued that radical congregationalism was the only biblical model, through which the Spirit had the freedom to build fellowship between Christians without regard to church affiliation.

This assessment of church denominational structures *can* be relevant, but the situation has instead become quite the opposite. No church bodies have provoked such divisions and subdivisions worldwide than Pentecostals. On the other hand, no single church denomination—perhaps together with the Catholic church—has caused such renewal and fresh initiative as the Pentecostal movement worldwide.[66] The picture is contradictory, to put it mildly. The essence of Pethrus' teaching on "the bridal church waiting for the rapture" was, according to Aronson, a focus on sanctification and purification, which led to strict church discipline that included a disputed practice of excommunicating of members and resulted in various leadership conflicts.[67] A paradox became more and more evident:

> The Swedish Pentecostal movement, which did not have a formal denominational structure and proudly denounced all of such a character, showed an internal discipline and conformity that was stronger than the actual Free Church denominations. The ideology of radical congregationalism had been turned upside down. Lewi Pethrus continued teaching about present-day apostles, but never initiated or accepted any formal or public apostleship or any other kind of denominational leadership. The effect of this was that the wide difference between the informal apostolic and hierarchical structure of leadership in the Pentecostal movement, and the formal emphasis on the independence of local congregations, became obvious. (. . .) Pethrus did not hesitate to isolate or excommunicate whole congregations and groups of preachers who challenged his policies, irrespective of his cherished thesis about the sovereignty of local congregations. This was further complicated by the fact that these measures seldom were accomplished through formal decisions but mostly through informal but very effective processes. (. . .) The

---

65. Ibid., 197.

66. Maas and Burgess, *Dictionary of Pentecostal and Charismatic Movements* gives a broad overview.

67. Aronson, "Spirit and Church," 203.

point here is to show the problems arising from an ecclesiology with strong built-in tension.[68]

The restorationist ecclesiology, with its strong congregationalist structure and emphasis on the completely autonomous leadership so decisive within early Nordic Pentecostalism, became partially revised by Pethrus later in life.[69] As assumed by Aronson, Pethrus emphasized the sovereign move of the Spirit in restoring the body of Christ worldwide to such a degree that it took precedence over the emphasis of the independence of the local congregation.[70] In that regard, Pethrus became a voice for the future and a sign of the move of renewal within this specific church environment.

A concluding perspective from Singaporean Pentecostalist Tan-Chow May Ling is appropriate before closing this chapter. She warned against the temptation for Pentecostals to disconnect the experiential dimension of church life from the life, death and resurrection of Christ, creating the facile alternative of either *theologia cruces* or *theologia gloriae*. However, passion and Pentecost are not antithetical realities. Instead of a sequence of disconnected events, the cross and Pentecost are in fact deeply interwoven, as narrated in Luke, John and Paul's writing.[71] The result is an integrated *theologia pneuma*, which balances the persons of the Godhead within the doctrine of the Trinity. A consistent Pentecostal theology of the Spirit is not a journey away from the cross. It is an intensification of the gospel of the life, death and resurrection of Christ. Easter and Pentecost are inseparably interwoven, just as the salvific and prophetic dimensions

---

68. Ibid., 207–8.

69. During his lifetime, Pethrus declared his belief in the independence of local congregations, but warned against what he perceived as an unbiblical over-emphasis on the sovereignty of the local congregations. In the 1970s, Pethrus welcomed the charismatic renewal, interpreting that particular revival as a fulfilment of the prophecy of Joel 2. He regarded the charismatic presence within the historical churches as the major solution to the question of Christian unity. Ibid., 209. See also Pethrus, *Times of Changes*, 206.

70. Joel Halldorf writes about Pethrus and his activities of creating a Christian counterculture in Sweden through the establishing of a daily newspaper, a temperance movement, and a political party. Halldorf points to the fact that these institutions exist today, while the radical congregationalism within the Swedish Pentecostalism was practically abandoned in 2001 when the Pentecostal national denomination (Pingst) was established. The present teachings and practices of the baptism in the Holy Spirit and speaking in tongues have also changed, compared to the times of Pethrus. Joel Halldorf writes that it is thought-provoking that while these aspects of his fading heritage are all but vital, a thriving legacy emerges if we turn to the institutions he created. Halldorf, "Christian Counterculture," 368.

71. Tan-Chow, *Theology for the Twenty-First Centur*, 103. See also Macchia, "Struggle for Global Witness," 15.

are coordinated in a mature ecclesiology. The Spirit of both initiation and liberation is a distinctive mark of the contemporary church, coherent with the narrative of Christ: The gospel shaped church of the resurrected LORD (Matt 28:1–10) is the empowered church of the charismatic Christ, Christus Victor (Acts 2:33).[72]

Constructive Reflections

Jürgen Moltmann observes Pentecostal spirituality as a third article theology in this way: "Orthodoxy in the Spirit and orthopraxis in action is followed by an orthopathy in the feelings and motivations."[73] This new branch of Christianity is part of the greater worldwide movement of the Spirit. The experience of God's presence does not predominantly consist of events that come and go, but rather the permanent indwelling of the Spirit which points to the transforming eschatology of the coming kingdom. At the same time, the Pentecostal movement presupposes that God is already among his people as an abundant, graceful presence, calling humans to respond in faith and trustful surrendering. Pentecostal theologians today consider how to constitute the church in ways that take seriously the trinitarian view of God and the defining marks of a faith community. In this tradition, the church is a living community that emphasizes the narrativity and orality of her spiritual life.

This is not only a question of worshipping, but also a distinct way of thinking. A liturgically shaped theology is not formulated first from within academia. Instead, it is visible as a kerygmatic matrix of worship, testimony, and ministries that gives the congregation an affective understanding on a level prior to propositional articulations. It is a vision for everyday life, a fundamental orientation through which humans are able to interpret their being-in-the-world as ordinary people. However, exposure to the influence of the Spirit also entails pain as a result of our resistance to the will of God and involves the confrontation of prejudice, ignorance and self-interest.

As already said, from the beginning of its modern emergence, Pentecostal ecclesiology was not so much a thematized theology as a lived reality. Despite the fact that Pentecostalism is still a diverse movement, traditionally these believers have regarded their shared experience of the Holy Spirit

---

72. Or as said by Miroslav Volf: the church is not a club of self-sufficient charismatics, but a community of those whom the Spirit of God has "endowed for service to each other and to the world in anticipation of God's new creation." Volf, "Community Formation," 233.

73. In the preface of Kärkkäinen, *Emerging Pentecostal Theologies*, ix.

within community as a core of their mutual identity. A Pentecostal ecclesiology identifies the church primarily as a charismatic fellowship of the Spirit. That is why community and worship are key components in Pentecostal Christian formation. The powerful, sensed presence of the Spirit leads to a clear testimony focused on Christ as Savior, Sanctifier, Baptizer in the Spirit, Healer, and coming King. So the church can be understood as a community where the redeemed, sanctified, empowered, healing and eschatological aspects of living in the presence of God are emphasized.

Today, many Pentecostals realize that the expectation of the Spirit within the church environment does not contradict the importance of celebrating the sacraments. Since the word of God has a manifested character, the sacraments also may be seen as signs of God's divine presence in Pentecostal environments. Perhaps without being aware of it, Pentecostals live a sacramental life in a sacramental universe. In order to emphasize the character of the sacraments as both word- and grace-event, speaking in tongues can be designated as a linguistic symbol of God's sacred presence. Pentecostal churches aim to continue the book of Acts by fostering a creative interaction with the biblical texts, applied to their own contemporary context.

Spirit baptism renews and releases sanctified life through the love of God and by a deeper sensitivity for the will of God. Pentecostals see Spirit baptism as exposing a transformative baptism of divine love (Rom 5:5).[74] With all its charismatic, diaconal and ministerial gifts, Spirit baptism is the way Christ equips his church with his life and presence, regardless of ecclesial differences or how this experience is perceived emotionally. While other ecclesiologies tend to connect the doctrine of Spirit baptism to regeneration and to the process of initiation, the Pentecostal tradition sees Spirit baptism also as empowering for gifted and prophetic service in the world. This results in an ecclesiology shaped in light of the third article of the Creed. The Spirit is the unforeseen guest who transcends our ecclesial patterns and forms a community through which the gospel is communicated within a context of changing landscapes: by words, deeds and charismatic-sacramental life.[75] Without being a sacramentalist, a Pentecostal can still make peace with the

---

74. Frank Macchia regards the relation between Spirit baptism and sanctification as a consecration unto God (2 Cor 3:18). A separation between Spirit baptism and sanctification "can be sustained only through a reductionistic understanding of sanctification as an outward cleansing and of Spirit baptism as an outward empowerment for a holy task," Macchia warns. Spirit baptism ought to be seen as vocational sanctification. Macchia, "Kingdom and Power," 122.

75. For an introduction to Pentecostal ecclesiology, see Hegertun, "Church in Light of the 3. Article," 165–86.

sacramental elements of the church service in ways that represent an expanding of the Pentecostal identity.

Ecclesiology is not an activity of abstraction. Thus, the last section of this work points to different aspects which result from the gifts given to operationalize a pneumatologically sensitive church. These aspects reflect some fundamental convictions about spiritual practices and attend to how certain perspectives are to be lived out within the church fellowship and its wider context. My conviction is that the faith community serves the world just by being a church with a Spirit-responsive identity.

The next section of this book starts with a chapter focusing on how all of life is an act of worship. It continues by bringing to the table a discussion about the role of the sacraments—here mainly defined as graceful gifts—in order to foster a liturgical living. The penultimate chapter is concerned about hospitality as an expression of graceful relationship. I close this work by focusing on the church as ecumenically advised and missionally enlightened; a church who is one in the Spirit, despite her manifold diversity.

7

A Life of Worship

> *Because the worship of the church takes place in the Pneuma, it takes place in Christ. Consequently, the worship of the church is a participation in the one world-redeeming, never ending worship of the crucified and exalted Christ before God's throne.*[1]

Introduction

THE CHURCH IS ALWAYS more than she seems to be from the outside. Rather than being a church of doctrines, she is a church of worship. The presence and dynamics of the Spirit in the worshipping community are indisputable. Worship is the heart and pulse of the living faith community. This chapter aims to reflect on some of the fruits that result from the further consideration of the church as a sign of God's graceful presence. One of these fruits is to apprehend one's life through the lens of worship. The relationship between the formative power of Christian worship and the pivotal role of Christian ethics is made concrete in the local assemblies of believers. Thus, the facilitation of the church's practices, theology and program needs to be in accordance with the insight that the believing community desires something different than what is offered by the liturgies of the prevailing surroundings, culture and mass media. To engage in the church is to transform our imagination rather than to saturate our intellect. It is not about what we know, but rather about what we love as a result of the formation of our desire. Since God is the source for our living, the church makes our stories come to life.

This chapter deals with the church from the perspective of love and graceful practices. As a pneumatologically shaped liturgy, the worship

1. Brunner, *Worship*, 78–83.

service can be regarded as a sacrament of the Spirit.² Insofar as the doctrine of the church is determined from the perspective of the exposition of Christian faith (*doctrina evangelii*), the doxological and eschatological essence of her character will be exhibited throughout her visible reality.³

The Liturgy, a Dance on the Wings of Faith

The liturgy of worship is a dance on the wings of faith, a hidden bodily wisdom pointing to the relation between nature and grace by which a person is invited to partake in the divine life given by the Spirit in the midst of an otherwise complicated reality. The mission of the church is concerned with shaping hopes and passions (Rom 8:24–25) and with forming the vision for good life (Gal 6:9; 1 Thess 5:21). Every week, churches plan for worship services that mediate the presence of God through religious disciplines and rituals. There is a firm belief that just the mediated presence of God in the services has a transforming effect.⁴ What is a service other than an event where the Triune God, through the Holy Spirit, breathes life, grace and virtues into the believing community, while also giving the church access to the resurrection power of Christ? Every service and mass is a liturgical event where words of worship are directed to God, the good news is heralded, the Lord's Table is open and the grace of God is received in an atmosphere of hospitality, reconciliation and humility (John 4:23–24; cf. Rev 4:1–11). The people of God realize their fallenness, confess their sins and proclaim the glory of God. In sum, this is indeed an expression of the work of the Spirit.

In the ancient church, the worship and glorification of the Triune God was a witness to the understanding of the Spirit within the divine economy before a more conceptual understanding became enunciated in the Creeds. The worship life of the church informed the church's theology, not the other way around. Later on, that insight came to be expressed in the liturgical tradition by the term *lex orandi, lex credendi* (the rule of prayer expresses the rule of faith).⁵ Marva J. Dawn contends that the church as community is at stake in how the fellowship worships. Dawn warns against

---

2. This is a formulation presented in Yong, *The Spirit Poured Out on All Flesh*, 160.

3. Hütter, *Suffering Divine Things*, 116.

4. Cf. Emil Brunner's well known claim that the Spirit is (or, better yet, has been) the stepchild of theology since theologians are accustomed to using the logic of faith to the neglect of its dynamism. For a presentation of his thoughts, see Brunner, *The Misunderstanding*, 48. It is reasonable to make doctrine determinative for worship and worship determinative for doctrine. See also Wainwright, *Doxology*, 218.

5. Elowsky, *Believe in the Spirit*, 246.

seeking the good feelings rather than worship in a public way. Good worshipers welcome the stranger.[6] That is the point behind the whole liturgical tradition, which even means "the work of the people." They offer their praise, whether it is the cantor in a cathedral or the worship leader in a Free Church congregation. Liturgy denotes the idea of ministering on behalf of a community. It is a work performed for the benefit of others. Dawn warns the churches of ending up with a kind of worship war between traditional and more contemporary forms of worship. She refers to the sensible position of David Heim, saying as follows:

> Most church members don't align themselves with either of [two opposing] camps. They are ready to listen and learn (. . .) to test what they hear against the witness of Scripture, tradition, and Christian experience. This approach will not appeal to those who would banish imagination from theological thought, or who think tradition is fixed and settled (. . .). This approach does promise to treat Christian witness with critical faithfulness and wise openness (. . .). Honest and charitable debate and criticism are necessary if Christians are to understand, judge and act on matters that demand the church's attention.[7]

However, worship involves an even deeper level. In his book, *Desiring the Kingdom*, James K. A. Smith states that the human heart is primarily oriented toward what it loves, and those desires are shaped and molded by habit-forming practices, or a pedagogy of the heart.[8] Both sacred and secular liturgies make us certain kinds of people, because what defines us is what we love. What is at stake is not primarily ideas on the informative level, but rather love: a dimension of life which is of formative value. The fact that the Spirit-driven church is a formative institution makes love a matter of ultimate concern. This kind of approach to the church's being and living in the world is for Smith a pedagogy that understands different kinds of learning as an issue of formation. You see people as more than thinking things and cognitive machines,[9] giving voice to an philosophical anthro-

---

6. Dawn, *Reaching Out*, 140. In her book, she mentions seven elements which pervade all forms of public worship: it is beautiful, thought-stirring, edifying, and gives a common note of humility, awe, thanksgiving, and petition.

7. Heim, "Sophia's Choice," 339–40.

8. Smith, *Desiring the Kingdom*, 18–26. In this book, Smith is first and foremost concerned with Christian education, but in principle his reflections are relevant for other related topics within ecclesiology as well. In the following presentation, I am indebted to some of his reflections and his depiction of a pedagogy of desire. See also Wolterstorff, *Educating for Shalom*.

9. Smith, *Desiring the Kingdom*, 28.

pology that takes into account feelings, emotions, and affections in both the personal and corporate learning and formation processes, not only the rational head.[10] A precognitive and pre-rational orientation to the world is shaped by embodied practices and attuned to the formative role of rituals. Without this very consciousness, the believing community will tend to communicate Christian ideas rather than be involved in the formation of a peculiar people, the followers of Christ.

In fact, a Christian is a *homo liturgicus*, because we are what we love. Bodily training shapes our hearts and gives us an implicit understanding of the world. Often a Christian worldview is identified primarily as a set of doctrines, propositions, claims or a system of beliefs constructed around a set of implicit ideas and correct thinking. However, is it possible to imagine the concept of worldview as something that generates an identity located more in the body than in the mind?[11] A person or church oriented to the world by the primacies of love and desire seeks to be immersed in different practices of worship and liturgies as part of their daily lifestyle. This may be realized without forgetting the need for cognitive reflection and discernment. Following Smith, what the church prays is what the church believes. A reassertion of this classical axiom goes like this:

> Before we articulate a worldview, we worship. Before we put into words the lineaments of an epistemology we pray for God's healing and illumination. Before we theorize the nature of God we sing his praises. Before we express moral principles we receive forgiveness. Before we codify the doctrine of Christ's two natures we receive the body of Christ in the Eucharist. Before we think we pray. That's the kind of animals (metaphorically understood) we are, first and foremost: loving, desiring, affective, liturgical animals who, for the most part, don't inhabit the world as thinkers or cognitive machines.[12]

---

10. This is not to say that there is no room for regarding rational reflection, which seeks the coherence of the truth, to be just as much evidence for the work of the Spirit as sudden affective illumination or momentary revelation. The Spirit is the Spirit of order as well as of surprise, assessment and desire. See Doctrine Commission of Church of England, *We Believe in the Holy Spirit*, 14.

11. Smith, *Desiring the Kingdom*, 32.

12. Ibid., 34. In his writing about worldwide Pentecostalism, Walter J. Hollenweger has a similar approach when he characterizes specific non-white indigenous churches. He states that the medium of communication is, just as in biblical times, not the definition but the description, not the statement but the story, not the doctrine but the testimony, not the book but the parable, not a systematic theology but a song, not the articulation of concepts but the celebration of banquets. Hollenweger, "Twenty Years of Research," 10.

The substantial understanding put forth here is that human persons are actors who realize their Christian identity by being involved in embodied practices that precede the pursuit of conceptual ideas. In general, Christian worship can be described as the realization of an alternative cultural body, making its members into agents of love, desire, and discernment. This holistic endeavor opposes a notion that characterizes theology as a heady affair organized as messages that disseminate Christian ideas and abstract values.[13]

The Formative Power of Christian Worship

One may go a step further and argue that there is no compelling reason to state that worship is a purely religious activity confined to a physical location or to a fixed cultural sphere. Worship involves the activity of ascribing worth and honor to serve something or someone, because every human life is bent toward whom or what is worthy of allegiance and sacrifice. In that manner, every human life and many aspects of life are acts of worship and thus doxological.[14] Here the ethical perspective comes into view. Human judgment involves the worthiness of certain actions, projects, dispositions, values, principles and ideas. The social interaction and dynamic in which most people are formed and shaped involves different human gatherings. These gatherings have inevitably formative power since they shape an imaginative landscape which is determinative for reflections, virtues, habits, actions, desires and dispositions. They are prescriptive for the ordinary way of life and become a form of ascribing worth: a form of worship. According to Philip Kenneson, the social imagination, which in no sense stands in opposition to practical reason, is something individuals simply receive: "Human persons are always the recipients of an imaginative world within which they are called to live and through which they are encouraged to understand themselves and their place within that world."[15] We are not offered a value-free or commitment-free rendering of the world, but rather a particular kind of inhabitable space in which meaningful human action is allowed to take place.

Among the manifold of formative gatherings which exist in a human's life, the church renders a complex web of stories, practices, passions and dispositions which contributes to a formation system for those who participate.

---

13. For the more relational construal of Christianity, see also Smith, *Who's Afraid of Postmodernism?*, 140–41.

14. Kenneson, "Worship, Imagination, and Formation," 54.

15. Ibid., 56.

It offers a partial answer to what it means to be a human being and to live a good life. Thus it has a transformative potential. Through the church's life, liturgy and various practices, the disciples of Christ are initiated into a comprehensive vision, a social imagination that animates the Christian life. A liturgical life of worship seems to be paradigmatic for all other actions, in that the manner of life lived outside the liturgy is itself an external expression of worship and adoration. If our worship does not involve courses of action in everyday life, the liturgical involvement is more or less inconsequential.[16] The relationship between the formative power of Christian worship and the pivotal role of Christian ethics is, according to Kenneson, visualized in local assemblies. Within the communal form of life, skills, convictions and dispositions shape life and are learned in order to be lived out as embodied signs of God's reconciliation and healing of the world.

However, this is based on a conviction which goes even deeper. God's church, his *ekklēsia*, which is called to be a light for the nations (cf. Luke 2:32), has the glory and honor of the Triune God as her horizon. According to Kenneson, God's work of bringing wholeness, healing and reconciliation to the entire cosmos does not happen by means of magic, but rather by means of a people who have been formed and animated by the Spirit of God in Christian worship to serve as agents of God's reconciling work in the world.[17] As a reflection of this ultimate concern, the gathering—which itself is an act of worship—forms people in ways that edify the church for further service and embodied witness. The doctrine of the Spirit also allows for an understanding of the history of salvation as the successive spiritualization of the Scripture's meaning, enabling the emancipatory core of Christianity to expand itself even beyond the sacral and clerical sphere. In a fragmented age of distraction, those engaged in worship learn to pay attention to the right things rightly. As part of the communion across time and space and as a response to God's call on their lives, they are drawn out of their private and narcissistic world in order to enter the area of God's reconciling purposes. They learn to go to God in prayer and intercession, to uncover gods made

---

16. This issue is demonstrated in the Pauline teaching about the Eucharist meal (1 Cor 11:17–22). How they were gathered was of the greatest importance. The LORD's Supper became dishonored because the congregation maintained the divisions between rich and poor and forgot the demand of hospitality and reconciliation. Their gathering violated the purpose of the meal. The warning of Paul stands as a sobering reminder to attend to the Spirit that animates certain liturgical practices. Ibid., 59.

17. Ibid., 60. By referring to the Italian philosopher Giovanni Vattimo, Jayne Svenungsson holds that the outpouring of the Spirit marks the continuation of God's revelation to mankind and thus implies that the history of salvation is still in progress. Svenungsson, "Transcending Tradition," 68.

by their own hands, and to speak truthfully about God, the world and their own faithlessness (Isa 44:9–20).

Worship cultivates a posture of dependence and acknowledges that human life has a transcendent purpose that is not self-created but affirms the need for God, for his word and sacraments, and for the guidance of other people.[18] In turn, it fosters a posture of humility, trust and hope as the worshipping community waits for the reign of God and for Godhead's coming righteousness in a kind of disciplined inactivity (Matt 6:10).

The church's reference to God unites history and liturgy, story and worship. In other words, a church does not only talk *about* God. She first and foremost directs her speech *to* God. This act, as it is expressed in the sacraments and in praise and worship, represents a reconstruction of the pure rational ideals of the language categories. We recapitulate or summarize history, not only by means of traditional words and explanations, but also by speech-actions in worship. These perspectives may have implications for how we understand theology. It is not just an ordinary scientific activity concerned with explanations and clarifications. Its self-understanding is most clearly demonstrated by the association with prayer and shows that religious language does not require a total perspective: "For now we see in part, as in a mirror" (1 Cor 13:12). You do not need to know everything in order to trust God. Perhaps we should say the opposite: we believe, we confess, and we pray precisely because we do not have the complete picture. Our understanding is limited. We are like children, expressing our human incompleteness before God (Phlm 4:7; 1 Cor 13: 9–12).[19]

Based on these perspectives, we may talk about the recognition of a new silence which leads us in the direction of prayer and worship rather than to discussions, debates, theological battles and conflicts.[20] Prayer takes religious practice seriously. And if theology is, as it were, the grammar for religious practice, it is directed towards the worshipping people in their praying and worshipping and by reflecting God's face in society and by doing his will in the world. Against this horizon, the church community may appear more clearly. Theology can be no more and no less systematic than the processes of faith to which it is answerable.

---

18. Kenneson, "Worship, Imagination, and Formation," 63.
19. Williams, *On Christian Theology*, 6.
20. Williams, *Silence and Honey Cakes*, 41–60.

The Life-interpretive Function of Worship

Where are the enemies of such an approach to a life of praise and worship? Secularism may be defined above all as a negation of man as a worshipping being, *homo adorans*, one for whom worship is the essential act which fulfills his or her humanity. According to Alexander Schmemann, this threat cannot be resolved and defeated by isolating the church from the world.[21] Quite the contrary, worship implies a specific idea of humanity's relationship not only to God but to the world, one determined by observing the sacramental character of the world and of human existence in the same world. God's revelation, presence and power are accessible as an epiphany of God through creation (Rom 1:18–20). Thus humans are essentially worshipping beings *in*—not outside—the world. If the world is a "sacrament," then being in community with God is the only true communion with the world. Within an ecclesiological context, Christ becomes the fulfilment of worship as adoration and prayer, thanksgiving and sacrifice, communion and knowledge on behalf of the world.[22] Accordingly, the basis for all Christian worship is Christ incarnated and made visible, such that people are without excuse (Rom 1:20). Its content and theme are the cross and the resurrection. Worship functions as a remembrance of Christ's work at the same time that it is an expectation and an anticipation of the Kingdom to come (Rom 8:18–30). By definition, worship is neither activities nor Christian projects. It is a reality with cosmic, historical, and eschatological dimensions, the expression not merely of piety, but of an all-embracing world-view.[23]

Furthermore, worship seems to have a life-interpretive function. Oswald Bayer writes that "being interpreted by the biblical text is something that takes place only in the church itself, in the community of those who first hear and believe, and only then speak, "I believed, therefore I have spoken" (2 Cor 4:13). Hermeneutical and theoretical questions are essentially pneumatological-ecclesiological. Only from the perspective of worship does an appropriate concept of theology emerge.[24] Reinhard Hütter remarks:

> Being interpreted by Scripture is not some sort of magic inherent to the Bible, but the implicate of the engagement of central church (and especially worship-related) practices in those context we learn to love the Bible. Only an explicitly developed reference to worship as a specific church practice that itself is

---

21. Schmemann, *Sacraments and Orthodoxy*, 117–34.
22. Ibid., 121–22.
23. Ibid., 123.
24. Bayer, *Autorität und Kritik*, 7.

developed ecclesiologically establishes the context in which specific pathos of being interpreted by Scripture can be actualized in the different individual practices.[25]

Inherent in both Bayer's and Hütter's reflections is the thought that Christian freedom is spoken to the believer through their engagement in the worship life of the church, which is itself animated by the Spirit. It is not a product of one's own effort. A person is in need of someone who promises freedom to them in the name of Jesus in concrete situations and in a particular form. The church is the place where this distinct language act takes place: in the proclaimed word, in baptism, in the Eucharist and in pastoral care. The created faith, prayer, worship and hymn are responses to that given message. This is a theological activity. The word of God became an object to reflect upon retrospectively as past events occurred, but it can also be used proleptically for future events.[26]

Consequently, a static person-as-thinker model and a person-as-believer model needs to be supplied with a more Augustinian anthropology of a person-as-*lover* model. A person who understands herself as an embodied agent of desire and love articulates a more dynamic sense of human identity. She or he gets an identity that is characterized by its temporal and intentional nature, and involved in the world as a tradition actor.[27] According to the phenomenological tradition, there are different modes of intentionality. We may *think* about an object, but we may also let it be encircled by our memory, care, hope, longing, desire and love.[28] Our discussion of the mode of love ultimately involves our being-in-the-world, which shapes our positions, animates our desires and marks our actions. Put differently, love is what we *worship*. In the vocabulary of Smith, worship signifies a form of life that is primordially shaped by an orientation to the world which is formed prior to conceptual reflections and sophisticated articulations.[29]

Further, the teleological aspect of ultimate love orients our imagination towards what governs and shapes our life in the best way, affecting our decisions and actions. Transferred to the reality of the church, these imaginative and affective pictures are communicated in testimonies and

---

25. Hütter, *Suffering Divine Things*, 90.

26. See Bayer, *Autorität und Kritik*, 149.

27. Worship is more than "routinized" charisma. Liturgies of worship shape human experience and behavior and have the capacity to organize theology around worship. Stated by Hardy, *God's Way*, 5–6.

28. Heidegger, *Being and Time*, 38–42. For Smith's own discussion, see Smith, "Confessions of an Existentialist."

29. Smith, *Desiring the Kingdom*, 51.

stories, in liturgical texts and hymns, and in down to earth speeches rather than in monographs and dissertations. The result is a holistic portrait of human persons as essentially embodied. Through bodily practices and the repetition of rituals, the believer is pictured in a way that forms her routines, habits, behavior and precognitive dispositions. To Smith, the senses are portals to the heart, and thus the body is a channel to our core disposition and identity.[30] Seeing one's life in the church as worship has an intentionally formative function. At best, it can be understood as the restoration of a creational desire for God and of a counter-formation to the dis-formation of secular liturgies into which we all are infused.[31]

Smith is concerned about what kind of understanding of the world is carried in liturgical practices and what kind of vision of the kingdom is embedded in Christian worship. Does Christian liturgy envision a flourishing human community? Is it possible to describe the particular form of life of the Christian faith by examining what persons *do* when they come together as a community, not only by what they *think*, in order to shape a distinctly Christian social imagination? Smith problematizes the traditional model of pointing to Scripture, the shaping of doctrines and the forming of liturgical practices when considering the outcome of biblical studies and theological reflections. In the time of the New Testament, churches were communities of worship long before the doctrines were composed as elements in the Christian worldview and long before the biblical canon was solidified.[32] Worship preceded the formation of the biblical canon.

In his letters to the congregation of Corinth, Paul gives concrete advice regarding good order in worship by referring to practices they had already established. He challenged their theologically loaded reflection by pointing to what they really did during their gatherings (1 Cor 14:26). Then he writes about hymns, words of instruction, revelations, tongues and interpretation of tongues. All these elements have to be esteemed and evaluated in accordance with their ultimate purpose: "let all things be done for building up" (1 Cor 14:26). In the New Testament we find other traces of early Christian

---

30. Ibid., 58. Smith distinguishes between so-called thin habits (our daily, trivial routines) and thick habits or practices, involving those *telos*-laden habits which play a significant role in the forming of one's identity, core values, and most significant desires. These include religious routines like going to church and being involved in daily prayers. The habits express something about our commitment to the believing community and our relationship with other people. In this way Smith distinguishes between *rituals* and *liturgies* (the latter understood as rituals of ultimate concern). Ibid., 82–86.

31. Ibid., 88.

32. Ibid., 135. This statement is in accordance with the writings of Eduard Schweizer, stating that long before the Spirit was a theme of doctrine, He was a fact in the experience of the community. Schweizer, "Pneuma," 396.

worship practices, hymns, doxologies and references to sacramental acts (Rom 16:25–26; 1 Cor 15:3–7; 11:23–25; Gal 3:26, 28; Col 1:15–20; 1 Pet 3:18–19). Through worship, prayer and song, these texts were read and received as expressions of divine events, as a means of grace and as a conduit of the transformative power of the Holy Spirit, which in our time may lead to a pedagogy of desire in accordance with being a contemporary Spirit-driven church in a secular age.

The Education of the Heart

If it is correct that before the Christians had a fixed worldview they were marked by their desire for God's Kingdom when they were singing their psalms, celebrating their Eucharist, and sharing their property, what does it say about the people who frequented the church? It points to the possibility of having an inner world of worship, desire and prayer. This formative aspect of the Spirit's work within the church can be refined within different church traditions. Pentecostal theologian Amos Yong states that Protestants must learn from the Catholic and Orthodox traditions, especially with regard to how human knowing of God is mediated through formation, imitation, affectivity, intuition, imagination, interiorization, and symbolic engagement.[33]

James K. A. Smith argues for a similar position when he writes that lived worship is "the fount from which worldview springs, rather than being the expression or application of some cognitive set of beliefs already in place."[34] Christian discipleship as a formation in Christ is fundamentally a matter of the precognitive education of the heart. There are good reasons for connecting these processes to the work of the Spirit within the frame of the faith community (John 14:26). By opening oneself to the transformative power of the Spirit, liturgy is given priority over a purely cognitive doctrinal engagement. The life of the gathered people precedes the formulas that emerge from theoretical reflection. These formulas have been considered important to the church's well-being, and they really are. But they can never replace the spirituality that is given by the more dynamic presence of the Spirit through the church's worshipping activities.

---

33. Yong, *Theology and Down Syndrome*, 208.

34. Smith, *Desiring the Kingdom*, 136. Smith is concerned with those who are disinclined to engage in theological abstractions. He argues in favour of children and the mentally handicapped. Their cognitive ability to access theological abstractions is limited. Nevertheless, they achieve their fullness in Christ. Christian worship touches and transforms even those who cannot grasp sophisticated didactic disquisitions but need to proceed with the formation of the heart first and the mind second.

Kyongsuk Min says that our age, with all its divisions and hostilities, is in special need of the Holy Spirit as the Spirit of fellowship and solidarity. The very cry of oppression, alienation, and loneliness is a silent invocation of the Holy Spirit, an *epiclesis* to the Spirit of fellowship to come and connect us once more.[35] He thus serves our reflection with a foundational understanding of the Spirit:

> As the Spirit proceeds from the Father and the Son precisely as their mutual love, so it is the function of the Spirit to create, empower, inspire and liberate finite beings precisely for solidarity and communion with God and with one another through the exemplary mediation of the Son whose life is the definitive embodiment of solidarity of Others.[36]

Consequently, if the personhood of the Spirit lies in the Spirit's ability to relate, to reconcile and to create communion and solidarity, the consequences for the doctrine of the church are obvious according to Amos Yong. One of the youngest and fastest growing denominations, worldwide Pentecostalism, normally reads the outpouring of the Spirit on all flesh (Acts 2) as part of its own self-understanding as a catalyst for the renewal of the church worldwide. Moreover, the many tongues on the Day of Pentecost may be considered as an expression of the biblical claim that the Spirit leads into all truth, and the outpouring of the Spirit on all flesh is seen to represent a catalyst for the renewal of ecclesiological practices and of the world in general (Joel 2:28–29). The charismatic movement in the 1960s and 1970s seemed to consolidate and strengthen the understanding of the coming of a theology of the third article (of the Creed) and a focus on pneumatology which would gradually penetrate world Christianity as well as parts of the theological academy.

According to Yong, what emerged over the course of the twentieth century was a distinctively charismatic ecclesiology which understands the church to be constituted first and foremost not by apostolic succession (ecclesial structure) or apostolic teaching (ecclesial doctrine)—even if these are not at all to be neglected—but by apostolic practices (ecclesial charisms). The Pentecostal contribution to the church worldwide can be seen as restoring to centrality the role of the charisms in the life of the church "by bringing to the fore just the agency of the Spirit in the church."[37]

35. Min, "Solidarity of Others," 417–18.

36. Ibid., 418.

37. Yong, "Poured Out on All Flesh," 17. The Pentecostal contribution to the church worldwide can be described as restoring the role of the charisms in the life of the church by bringing to the fore just the agency of the Spirit in the church. Ibid., 18.

Furthermore, within the frame of an egalitarian Pentecostalism, many churches worldwide have been churches of women, of resistance against discrimination and oppression, of the poor, of the vulnerable and of persons with disabilities. Those who acknowledge the potential of the prophecy of Joel and a theology of the Spirit also have visions of its distinctive power to shape a postpatriarchal, postcolonial and postmodern world. These local churches presuppose an attitude of inclusiveness and of humility in the midst of a broken world. Without an environment for the cultivation of the fruit of Spirit (Gal 5:22–23), a Pentecostal church risks being the antithesis of otherwise dignified theological positions.

Seeing life as worship and the church as Spirit-driven come, to a certain extent, from the influence of Eastern Christianity. The content of the orthodox faith is provided not only by the biblical witness but by its living experience, primarily in the church's worship, i.e., its liturgy.[38] As an expression of God's self-revelation, the act of worship serves to interpret and re-actualize the witness of Scripture. The constitutive principle is that the law of worship determines the law of faith.[39] This tradition begins with the experience of God in worship, particularly in the Eucharist celebration, and then seeks to judge and confirm these experiences not only with reference to Scripture, but also with what this particular church defines as the Holy Tradition, described as the life of the Holy Spirit within the Church.[40] While God's mighty acts are grounded in the past and in Christ's death and resurrection, the tradition of orthodox liturgical worship gives shape to the present, actualized in distinctive elements: sacraments, creeds, hymnography, iconography and the reading of biblical passages. The emphasis on the worship gives the orthodox ecclesiology its own particular pneumatological character, which has lent worship as term a deeper dimension in other church traditions as well.

This view of worship as the substantial expression of the church is based on the gospel tradition of the double sending of the Spirit by the Son (Luke 24:49; Acts 1:5–9; John 15:26; 16:7) and of the Son by the Spirit (Luke 1:35; 4:18; Mark 1:12; Matt 4:1; 12, 17, 18). Jesus' baptism and transfiguration both appeared as theophanies of the Holy Trinity: the Son baptized, the voice of the Father and the descending of the Spirit upon the Son (Luke 3:21–22). The outpouring of the Spirit on the Day of Pentecost was accomplished by the exalted and glorified Christ. Thus the sending of the Spirit

---

38. Breck, "The Two Hands of God," 231.

39. This term refers to the old Latin maxim *Lex Orandi, lex Credendi* which addresses the centrality of worship in the understanding of the Church. From that, we perhaps could state that the law of worship is the law of life.

40. Breck, "The Two Hands of God," 232.

by the Son served to inaugurate a new age in the history of salvation: the age of the church.[41] Seeing life as worship also has theological support in the Nicene-Constantinopolitan Creed.[42] Here the Spirit is clearly expressed as being worthy of equal honor and adoration as the Father and the Son. There is a reciprocal indwelling of the Son and the Spirit within the immanent Trinity as well as in the divine economy.[43] The trinitarian formula of three persons in one divine essence lays particular emphasis on the role of the Spirit in the consecration of the Lord's Supper and in the deification of the faithful.[44] The same Spirit, who eternally proceeds from the Father and indwells in the Son, is poured out by the Father through the Son upon the body of the faithful, making the church Spirit-driven. Her members are bearers of the Holy Spirit and they are defined by Christ as true worshippers (John 4:23-24).

In order to transform the life of the believer, Eastern inspired theology talks about a complementary economy of the Holy Spirit through which baptism and chrismation are celebrated as one single sacrament in order to incorporate a person into the body of Christ and to give them the seal of the gift of the Spirit (2 Cor 1:22; Eph 4:30). Baptism thus corresponds to Easter while chrismation corresponds to Pentecost. The work of salvation represents the restoring of human nature, while the indwelling of the Spirit points to the lifelong process of the sanctification of the human person (Rom 8:11; 2 Cor 3:18).

Ethical Consciousness through the Lens of Worship

When Paul instructed the Galatians to walk by the Spirit (Gal 5:16) when dealing with conflicts between Spirit and flesh, he was preoccupied with how to use their given freedom to serve one another humbly in love (v. 14).

---

41. Ibid., 237.

42. The text goes like this: "And we believe in the Holy Spirit, the Lord, and Giver of Life, Who proceeds from the Father, Who with the Father and the Son together is worshipped and glorified."

43. Breck, "The Two Hands of God," 239.

44. The Orthodox tradition has a theology which begins with the affirmation that God is one essence in three persons *(hypostasis)*. It is an apophatic approach to the mystery of divine life where the Spirit is seen as the source of mutual love, uniting the three divine Persons. Said in another way, the Spirit is communicated reciprocally between Father and Son and by the Father and the Son to the world, as the effulgence of divine love. Regarding the *filioque* dispute, Breck's approach is as follows: while the Spirit proceeds from the Father alone, he is communicated by the Father and the Son together. One does not think of the Father without the Son, and one does not conceive of the Son without the Holy Spirit (Eph 2:18). Ibid., 242-43.

Those who live by the Spirit have to keep in step with the same Spirit. Paul then presents what he defines as fruit of the Spirit (vv. 22–23), which can be defined as the manifestations of the Spirit's work in the believer and the ethical virtues of dignity and grace.[45] It is important to note, as Ronald Y. K. Fung asserts, that the phrase directly ascribes the power of fructification not to the believer but to the Spirit and to the ethical characteristics produced by the Spirit as the believer's life-transforming power.[46] When the Galatians lived in the Spirit-driven church, they were given the roots out of which different fruits were able to grow. The singular fruit was different facets of the same jewel. Thanks to the fruit of the Spirit, incomprehensible love became the controlling force of the Christian life (2 Cor 5:14). Ethical grace, more than spiritual gifts, represented Paul's distinctive understanding of the Spirit. He forced a shift in emphasis from the more outwardly focused spiritual gifts to the inner qualities which controlled conduct. Remark the Pauline utterance, "I will show you a still more excellent way." (cf. 1 Cor 12:31), pointing to the following chapter of love.

The pivotal connection between Christian ethics and the formative power of Christian worship, as actualized in the local assemblies, is underscored by Stanley Hauerwas and Samuel Wells.[47] According to them, the discipline of Christian ethics can be perceived through the lens of worship, particularly the act of Eucharist. The assertion that the field of ethics may be informed by the practice of worship is based on the expectation that God will make himself known through deliberations, investigations and discernment. The point is that the convictions and assumptions by which one aspect of life is shaped interact with key dynamics of another aspect. If it were not possible to bring different parts of life together, the inability to do so would cause considerable bewilderment. Normally ethics and worship have been held at a clear distance from each other because of the supposition that the former is tangible and connected to the real world, while the latter is spiritual and aspires to the ideal world. Worship is about beauty, ethics about the good. Worship is subjective, ethics objective. Worship talks

---

45. Catalogues of virtues and vices were common in Paul's day. They can be traced back to Plato and to his ideal society being "wise, brave, sober, and just," and to Aristotle and his cardinal virtues. These kind of lists appear frequently elsewhere in the New Testament, both in the Gospels and in the Pauline Letters (Mark 7:21–22; Rom 1:29–31; 13:13; 1 Cor 5:9–11; Eph 4:31–32; Col 3:5–8; 1 Tim 1:9–10). The list of virtues confronts that of vices. The former is made visible as serving in love and as living in the Spirit. Ethical lists were popular and important among early Christians. They were included in the catechetical teaching and probably used in connection to the baptismal act and church liturgies. See Longenecker, *Galatians*, 41, 249.

46. Fung, *The Galatians*, 262.

47. Hauerwas and Wells, "Christian Ethics," 3.

to the heart, ethics to the head. Worship is about the internal, ethics about the external. Worship is about words, ethics about actions. Worship is about stories from the past, ethics about life in the present, and so forth. While ethics is supposed to be judgment of right and wrong, worship is assumed to be a question of what is fitting for me. Worship is a practice for only some, while ethics is a discipline with a bearing on everyone. While worship is a kind of play, ethics is not. According to the Kantian approach, the immanent world of experiences should not be mixed with the transcendent world of religion.

Wells and Hauerwas challenge these assumptions by stating that all of life is a rehearsal of worship in which different kinds of rules are at play. The distinction between the subjective and objective is not quite clear, and goodness, truth and beauty are perhaps not as detachable as is often supposed. In worship, a person seeks the God who combines these aspects of life without downplaying any of them. Worship communicates that in God there is no shortage of goodness, truth, and beauty; no competition of scarce resources; and no deliberation over their distribution. This approach aspires to a politics that discerns the best use of the unlimited gifts of God, rather than the just distribution of the limited resources of the world.[48] A strict division between public and private seems to be drawn when a person, through baptism, is called to give up any sense of owning her or his body (Rom 6:3–4; cf. Gal 2:20). All are included in the church as the new body, something quite different than a mass of discrete individuals.

To be included in that body means to aspire to be a manifestation of a reality which is not detached from ethical, political and social concerns. Worship is about both words and actions. Words constitute the life of worship and amplify what is done. However, the mass of words must not obscure the fact that worship is shaped by habits of action and of biblical instruction (Matt 28:18–20; 1 Cor 11:23–26; Matt 18:20). Worship commemorates the past and anticipates the future, particularly through the LORD's Supper, which itself appears as an embodied configuration of a communal eschatological promise. Thus a regular practice of liturgy informs and shapes the common life:

> The liturgy offers ethics a series of ordered practices that shape the character and assumption of Christians, and suggest habits and models that inform every aspect of corporate life—meeting people, acknowledging fault and failure, celebrating, thanking, reading, speaking with authority, reflecting on wisdom, naming

---

48. Ibid., 5–7.

truth, registering need, bringing about reconciliation, sharing food, renewing purpose.[49]

These insights provide reasons for arguing that the Eucharist is not a magic act, achieved by saying a few words in the right order. Both in the Eucharist and in worship, we are at the heart of the unchanging gospel in order to build up the church and for carrying out what is the good for our common life.[50] In a broad sense, the performance of worship is an ordered series of specific practices. An attention to these practices shapes the character of Christians and the ethical mind of the church as a whole.

Shaped by the Praise of God's Name

The fact that worship is something the church *does* implies that these practices carry their own understanding. In turn, these practice shape imaginations, which paves the way for intellectual reflections to deepen the doing. According to James K. A. Smith, the action of the gathering contains a visceral training of the imagination that shapes how the believer thinks about her identity and her calling as human, both in her relation to God and to others.[51] In that regard, a person's imagination, shaped by the commitment to church practices, contributes to the way one construes the world.

The gathered congregation gets a distinct feeling of being welcomed by God. All elements are part of a common agenda to let the communion be embraced by God's blessing and grace. People simply open their hands, mouth and heart in prayer and worship. They take part in the liturgy by joining in the creeds and by receiving the means of grace as an expression of God's abundant love (2 Cor 12:9; Gal 6:18; Eph 1:1–14). Through worship, God's blessing is experienced as affirmation, as empowerment and as the renewal of the community's creational mandate. Using the terminology of Smith, Christian worship is dialogical and relational in nature. God is calling people and by God's grace they respond by their gathering. They invoke God's grace and mercy; God in turn responds to their cry. This is part of the true human nature: when a person looks beyond her own selfishness, an instinct of self-preservation and self-sufficiency, to consider the richness of her dependence on God and existence as *imago Dei* (Acts 17:28). When a person is welcomed by God's grace, she welcomes others into the same relation with a feeling of being sons and daughters of the same community

---

49. Ibid., 7.
50. Ibid., 9.
51. Smith, *Desiring the Kingdom*, 167.

of God. This activity is not something external but rather a response to the relationship of trust in which one is placed in order to flourish as a people who bear God's image in humility. These open rooms of worship are not an expression of self-satisfaction but of hospitality, an integrated aspect of a Christian worldview.

In Ps 18:49 the church is encouraged to sing the praises of God's name. In song, there is a performative affirmation of our embodiment, a physical longing to express the great deeds of God (Ps 40:4; 96:1-2; Isa 12:4-6; Col 3:16; Rev 5:9). Music and song seem to be privileged channels to the process of imagination. They function as an aesthetic expression of interdependence and intersubjectivity. They seem to stand as a packed microcosmos of what it means to be human, implanted as they are in the believer as a mode of bodily memory.[52] A song evokes the remembrance of time, place and even smells and tastes. According to the teaching of Paul, the act of singing and playing is closely related to the filling of the Spirit (Eph 5:18-19; Col 3:16). The song texts that have been used and remembered, such as hymns, express beliefs; they lend words to the expression of trust, sadness, joy and hope. Such texts have become essential as integral parts of the theology by which the congregation lives,[53] and by which the spiritual heritage is received and handed over to the next generation. Smith sees songs as fused into the very core of our being.

That is why worship and music are an important constitutive element of our identity: they affect how we imagine ourselves.[54] While only a few persons within a congregation are preachers, all the gathered take part in worship, a practice which makes them speech communicators about our faithful God, our identity and about our hopes. Worshipping God with heart and mind is to speak out the language of the Kingdom, which acts as an incubator for the Christian faith in the formation of the Christian

---

52. Ibid., 170. Against this background, it is possible to understand the tensions which sometimes surface within multi-generational fellowships when discussing music styles and other controversial issues. If these, as Smith contends, function as primary means of reordering people in the context of Christian worship, then the tension needs to be taken seriously and discussed with the intention of offering creative solutions and curative compromises. See Arjona, "Time to Sing," 781-90. This article focuses on the role of songs and dance as significant tools for pastoral care with older adults.

53. Don Saliers writes that "this knitting of an embodied theology happens whenever Christian congregation sing, even though they do so in a great variety of ways from one culture to another (. . .) The Trinitarian character of faith was sung long before it was put into the language of doctrinal theology. Indeed, the church's theology was embodied in its liturgical and singing practices before more formal theology developed." Saliers, "Singing our Lives," 185-86. See also Saliers and Saliers, *A Song to Sing*, 169-81.

54. Smith, *Desiring the Kingdom*, 172.

worldview.[55] What we sing says something about who we are. Worship has a broader signification than just being a religious rite. It is a reminiscence of the core elements forming an identity that continuously seeks the face of God; it acts as the most normal ingredient of being a loving, human self. Accordingly, a worshipping community fits the characteristics of the church as a Spirit-filled fellowship and the main purpose of the church.[56] The church is a community of persons who are both called out and called together as the people of the LORD. The way a congregation worships reveals her understanding of God and contributes to her spiritual formation.[57] Johnathan E. Alvarado sums up these reflections as follows:

> The biblical text seems to be communicating a message that it is at least two-fold in its essence. In one sense, Spirit-filled worship is a very divine exercise initiated by God through the Spirit. It is this understanding of worship that embraces the Spirit's trans-local nature, his fluidity and dynamism, and the "otherworldliness" of his character. On the other hand, worship seems to be a human response to the greatness and goodness of God. This response seems to be volitional and purposeful, formal and ritualistic, both planned and orchestrated. It is the appropriate response to a worthy God. Spirit-filled worship necessitates the recognition of and appreciation for the transcendence and immanence of God.[58]

Worship, understood as "seeing the glory of the LORD as though reflected in a mirror" (2 Cor 3:18), is a transformational and spiritually formative event given by the Spirit which displays the nexus between ecclesiology and liturgical spirituality. However, in order to find the delicate balance in worship between order and ardor, there is a need for some liturgical structures to house and sustain an authentic move of God in worship.[59]

Song and worship contribute to the expression and formation of the identity of the church in ways that correspond with the identity of one's individual life. Worship and joy are vowed together but so too are worship and pain (observe the difference between Ps 98 and 88). A multifaceted language about the rhythms of life includes light and dark sounds. The wholeness of a complicated life must, in one way or another, be reflected in what

---

55. Richard Mouw states that a hymn impresses the theological point on your consciousness as no scholarly treatise can do. Mouw and Noll, *Words of Life*, xiv.

56. Alvarado, "Worship in the Spirit," 137.

57. Ibid., 135.

58. Ibid., 145.

59. Ibid., 136.

is communicated in worship. If not, only parts of the human reality are mirrored through the liturgy, a practice not sustainable over time. The message of worship must communicate the completeness and variety of Christian faith, in line with the kinds of expectations about sermons. Is the whole gospel to be heard in the texts, including the call for conversion and the demand to a life in holiness and discipleship? What about the image of God and the message of grace? Is there a healthy balance between the manifestations of God's grace as gift and as responsibility? Is worship able to challenge the temptation of self-expression that comes as a result of self-exposure? Where are the songs reminding the church about the protection of creation, about migration, about natural disasters and about the dignity of humans? And what about music composed against the persecution of Christians and other religiously discriminated groups?[60]

When I take part in worship and liturgy, I presume that in these holy actions my whole life is included, not just the joyful aspects of it.

Constructive Reflections

As already stated in this work, the transformation of the world is not possible without a people transformed by worship. Being engaged in the church means transforming our imaginations rather than saturating our intellects. It is not about what we know, but rather about what we love within the framework of the formation of our desire. What is a service other than an event where the Triune God, through the Holy Spirit, breathes life, grace and virtues into the believing community and thus gives the church access to the resurrection power of Christ? Every service or mass is a liturgical event where words of worship are directed to God, the good news is proclaimed, the LORD's Table is opened and the grace of God is received in an atmosphere of hospitality, reconciliation and humility.

The existence of the church as a community is at stake in how the fellowship worships. Liturgy denotes the idea of ministering on behalf of a community. It is a work performed for the benefit of others. The church renders a complex web of stories, practices, passions and dispositions, all of which contribute to a formation system for those who participate. It offers a partial answer to what it means to be a human being and to live a good life, and thus it has transformative potential. Through the church's life, liturgy and practices, together initiated into a comprehensive vision, the disciples of Christ are given a social imagination that animates the Christian life.

---

60. An interesting study of how worship traditions have changed the church, see Ward, *Selling Worship*, 165–210.

Worship cultivates a posture of dependence and acknowledges that human life has a transcendent purpose that is not self-created. It affirms the need for God, his word and sacraments.

In turn, worship fosters a posture of humility, trust, hope and patience—in a kind of disciplined inactivity—for the reign of God and his coming righteousness. Our talking about the mode of love involves ultimately our being-in-the-world, which shapes our positions, brings to life our desires and marks our actions. Or, put differently, love is what we *worship*. Worship signifies a form of life that is primordially shaped by an orientation to the world prior to conceptual reflections and sophisticated articulations. The result is a holistic portrait of human persons which is essentially embodied and down-to-earth. Through bodily practices and repetitions of rituals, the believer is pictured in a way that forms her routines, habits, behavior and precognitive dispositions.

Worship communicates that, in God, there are no shortage of goodness, truth, and beauty. During the church service, the gathered congregation gets a distinct feeling of being welcomed by God. All elements are part of the same agenda: to let the communion be embraced by God's blessing and grace. People simply take part in the liturgy by joining in the creeds and by receiving the means of grace, which is everything given as an expression of God's abundant love. Rational coldness has to step aside, since the mystery of the deeds of God is grasped through contemplation and partaking more than by common-sense understanding. Human life is stamped with the image of God. Thus, life becomes something given which needs to be received with confidence.

A Word-anchored spiritual fellowship is not preoccupied with words but rather wants to communicate—and be communicated to by God—through graceful gifts, something that can be recognized and qualified within a lived, concrete and visible reality. The relationship between the Spirit and the church becomes visible in the sacraments. They are highly pneumatic in their essence because they affect the deepest relationship between human and God. What makes a sacrament a graceful gift is not any inherent magical essence. Their impact depends alone on the work of the Holy Spirit. The sacraments as graceful gifts are the subject of the coming chapter.

8

Graceful Gifts

> *The Scriptures do not seem concerned about which comes first: our personal union with Christ or our membership in the Church. (. . .) To belong to Christ means to belong to his Church. (. . .) Faith and baptism lead us into the Church.*[1]

Introduction

THE CHURCH IS BOTH something given and something received. Many would say that the church is never more church than when she, in worship, baptism, the LORD's Supper and the passing on of the gospel, celebrates her faith through a liturgical living. Classical theology's position, in its confessional breadth, is that God has chosen to reveal himself through these visible realities and that the church is an instrument through which the salvific action is mediated by graceful gifts, whether they are charismatic or sacramental.[2] Both baptism and the LORD's Supper belong to a category of practices that define the church's identity and remind her that she exists primarily by the grace of God.[3]

Though the New Testament text contains no direct references to the word sacrament, this post-Testament term describes an ecclesial reality well grounded in Scripture.[4] Moreover, the sacraments were liturgically defined

---

1. Boersma, *Violence, Hospitality, and the Cross*, 212–13.
2. Yong, *Renewing Christian Thology*, 141.
3. Ibid., 136.
4. J. N. D. Kelly holds that we should note that, while the technical terms for sacrament were *mysterion* in Greek and *sacramentum* in Latin, there is no absolute certainty about the instances of their use before the Alexandrian fathers and Tertullian respectively. From the beginning, baptism was the universally accepted rite of admission into the Church. "Only those who have been baptized in the LORD's name may partake of the Eucharist." Kelly, *Early Christian Doctrines*, 193.

as holy long before they were explored theologically.[5] However, the possibility to conceptualize and schematize the means by which the Holy Spirit is given is, from the New Testament's perspectives, confined because of the mixed order of the initiation elements as recorded in the narratives of the Acts (Acts 2; 8; 10; 11). Luke seems to be concerned with showing that the Spirit is not subject to human control.[6]

In this chapter, I assess the church through the lenses of the sacraments, described as graceful gifts. Through these gifts and imaginative acts, the community is provided with spiritual properties outside of what humans can contribute through their own efforts. The aim of this chapter is to give some reflections on baptism and Eucharist and to explore the relationship between sacraments and faith.

The Sacraments, Actualization of a Mystery

From the beginning, the church was seen as the place in which faith became concrete and through which the means of grace—the ordinances—became visible. In a deep sense, you cannot belong to Christ without at the same time being a part of the body of Christ, the church. Thus, the sacrament of baptism was the universally accepted rite of admission into the church.[7] Wolfhart Pannenberg describes baptism as an act of ecstatic placing outside themselves done by implanting themselves into Christ.[8] Because of this anamnestic participation in the one saving mystery of Christ, the sacraments do not have power only as signs, but as their actualization of the mystery of the salvation present and at work in the church. The sacraments integrate in a concrete way what the recipients have been given by faith and through the gift of the Spirit (Acts 2:38–39). In other words, what we may

---

5. For a comprehensive introduction of ancient understandings of the Spirit and spiritual gifts, see Elowsky, *Believe in the Spirit*.

6. Barrett, *Church, Ministry and Sacraments*, 59. For an extensive introduction and key readings of the history and theology of Christian worship and sacramental rites from the New Testament to the present, see Johnson, *Sacraments and Worship*.

7. According to Hermas' view of baptism, we descend into the water as dead and come out again alive; we receive a white robe which symbolizes the Spirit—who is God dwelling in the believer—and the resulting life is a result of re-creation. In the third century, however, we observe a tendency to limit the effect of baptism itself to the remission of sins and regeneration and to link the gift of the Spirit with chrismation and the laying on of hands (Acts 8:17). Kelly, *Early Christian Doctrines*, 194, 207.

8. Pannenberg, *Systematic Theology*, vol 3, 345, footnote no. 760. Drawing upon the liturgical character of the church, he states that the sacrament is first a sign commemorating the past event of Christ's passion. Second, it is a sign of the working grace in us. Third, it is a prognostic sign of future glory. Ibid., 354.

refer to as a sacramental presence is conditioned by the pronouncement of the gospel and by the fact that we are part of the nature and under the influence of the Spirit.

To the Romans, Paul declares that those who live according to the Spirit and through the law of the Spirit have been set free from the law of sin and death through the new life of Christ (Rom 8:2, 4). This specific life in the Spirit is not an isolated existence, just as faith is not an activity on distance from a fellowship. Those who belong to Christ through the Spirit are prepared to share in the feast together with those who have accepted the same invitation and those who enjoy the same blessings. In fact, there is no place for God's exception; God does not show favoritism (Rom 2:11).

Simon Chan opines that the church is the special place where the Spirit is present to and on behalf of the world. This has been the confessional standard of the church, to which Scripture bears unequivocal testimony (1 Tim 3:16; John 16:8–11). So it is not only the Spirit that constitutes the church and gives her a unique identity as a Spirit-filled body. The church, thus construed, gives the Spirit a distinctive role in the world as the church-establishing Spirit and forms an ecclesiological pneumatology.[9] According to Douglas Farrow, the ascension of Christ demarcates a special period of redemptive history in which Christ is bodily absent and yet spiritually present by his Spirit.[10] He is neither totally absent nor totally present, but rather he is present eucharistically and pneumatologically. Communion is as much the celebration of Christ's presence ("this is my body") as it is a reminder of his absence ("until he comes"). It is because of the Spirit that we are able to hold together the tension of the already and the not yet. During the act of the LORD's Supper, we celebrate the spiritual presence of Christ. At the same time, we are reminded that salvation history and world history have not yet converged.[11] The embodied Christ is no longer present in the world, but the church still is. In the Upper Room discourse, Jesus assured the disciples that the descent of the Spirit would correlate with his ascension (John 16:7). The Spirit takes the place of Christ's physical absence in the church, thus making the church the temple of the Spirit (1 Cor 6:19), i.e., the special locus of the Spirit's presence. However, the Kingdom of God is still in the future. What we have now is only a foretaste of the age to come. In the meantime, we are given some graceful gifts.

These graceful gifts are expressed when God speaks through material substance, the mundane world and the earthly body. This appears to be a

---

9. Chan, "Mother Church," 198.
10. Farrow, *Ascension and Ecclesia*, 42.
11. Chan, "Mother Church," 199.

performance of the affirmation of God regarding the materiality of his own creation. Implicit in Christian worship and in our receiving of the means of grace, there is a performative sanctioning of the incarnation. This action is not only concurrent with the coming of Christ in flesh, but also acts as a reminder that the church, in its worship and liturgies, reflects that the Triune God of creation "traffics in ashes and dust, in blood and bodies, fish and bread," as said by Orthodox writer Alexander Schmemann (Ps 24:1; Acts 17:28).[12] To figure out the concept of the sacraments within Evangelical traditions which contain divergent positions, one might say that the means of grace offer a window into the transcendent reality, presuming that God structured creation in such a way that this is possible.

James K. A. Smith describes a particular intensification of God's general sacramental presence within the framework of the theology of creation. The alternative is falling into a condition of disembodied abstraction in which spirituality is disconnected from visible realities, materiality and the very stuff that we touch and taste. According to Schumann, sacrament signifies that for the world to be a means of worship and a means of grace is not accidental but the revelation of its meaning, the restoration of its essence, the fulfilment of its destiny.[13] This implies that elements like bread and water are not made magical by a transformation as such. Rather, their natural sacramentality is completed when they are blessed and delivered in the hands of the worshipping community. The elements have become subject to a reordering of their ultimately God-created materiality. The natural world is always more than just nature; it is charged with the presence and glory of God.[14] Through that sacramental dynamic of the substance, the presence of the Spirit can be regarded as intensified in particular places, things and actions. Not surprisingly, declaring that the material is nothing more than just material, as is postulated in some Evangelical/Pentecostal traditions, seems to be a kind of naturalism which does not take into consideration the dynamic nature of the theology of creation. Using the elements of the sacraments for their sacramental purpose is a form of material movement, a removal by which the substance becomes more than just particles and atoms since they have become part of my life story in an exalted way.

Like worship, the means of grace are infused in an action of art and aesthetics. More than being accessible by the science of logic, the means of grace have a formative ability to nurture an identity of being looked after by

---

12. Cited in Smith, *Desiring the Kingdom*, 141.
13. Schmemann, *Sacraments and Orthodoxy*, 121.
14. Smith, *Desiring the Kingdom*, 143.

the LORD. Resting in an atmosphere of worship, adoration and communion, they represent an invitation to partake in everyday liturgical living.

Seeing the Spirit as the one who acts in and through the church is a question of material and daily life practices. Honoring the incarnational nature of God's dealing with humanity has been considered as essential for the gathered body of Christ through the ages. Within an atmosphere of worship and adoration, the means of grace have been channels for the Spirit's work and have acted as crucial parts of the Christian service. Since it is the work of people to offer their praise, different kinds of liturgies give the whole congregation an unmistakable feeling of being part of the voice declaring God's wisdom in the midst of the present world. The call to worship in a material way is an invitation to be human.[15] As Smith has already pointed out, the comprehensiveness of elements in worship is important because we otherwise might lose those practices that function as counter-formations to the liturgies of the mall and of secular culture.[16] The church is a people of memory that is gathered in response to a call to worship and that is formed by old traditions. She is a people of expectation and of eschatological hope, looking forward to a coming Kingdom. That makes the church a stretched people, inhabitants of a realm both older and newer than anything offered by the contemporary time.

Perceived and Made Effective by Faith

Nowhere in the New Testament is Christianity presented as a cult or a religion. In a profound sense, Christianity is the end of all religion. As stated by Schmemann, Christ has broken down the wall between humans and God. He offers a new life, not a new religion.[17] In the time of the early church, pagans accused Christians of atheism because of their break with sacred geography (John 4:21) and because of their lack of need for temples built with stone (John 2:19). Instead, the new people of the Spirit made up the Body of Christ as the only real temple. Christ's continued presence in the

---

15. Dawn, *Reaching Out*.
16. Smith, *Desiring the Kingdom*, 153.
17. The position of the Orthodox theologian Alexander Schmemann is that all theology ought to be liturgical. The main point of reference within theology is to the faith of the church as it manifests and communicates itself in liturgy and practice. As such, the living reality of the church is the hermeneutical foundation and ontological condition for a more theoretically oriented theological work. A dynamic relation needs to be established between theological reflection and liturgical experience. In its deepest sense, theology is a gift of grace and a witness. Its exercise is a ministry. Schmemann, *Sacraments and Orthodoxy*, 19.

church through the Spirit was far more significant than any of the places where he had lived. In him, his followers found the end of religion since he was the answer to all religion and to all hunger and desire for God. From the time of Pentecost, when Jesus returned to earth by virtue of the presence of the Spirit, the understanding of the church surpassed the notion of being simply an administrator of given sacramental activities.

The Church herself became the "sacrament" of Christ's presence and action in the world. Before discussing her programs, projects, and techniques, the church is called to have an intermediary role and to enter into the joy of the gospel (Luke 2:10). This is both the beginning and the end of the gospel of Luke (Luke 24:52).

Accordingly, Pentecostal theologian Simon Chan underscores that the action of the Spirit in the church as ongoing and dynamic is characteristic of ecclesial pneumatology. The word "catholic" means that the church is constituted as whole by the Spirit when the whole church gathers together in the name of Jesus Christ to celebrate communion.[18] Catholicity was a concept that was first applied to the local congregation before it was used as a universal concept. As a eucharistic community sharing one bread and one cup, the church transcends all social and racial boundaries and fuses together the charismatic and sacramental character of the church:

> To believe in the Spirit-filled church means that the charismata operate freely within the life of the church, especially in the eucharistic event when the action of the Spirit is particularized. In short, the Holy Communion should be the best occasion for prayers of reconciliation and healing to take place.[19]

However, when talking about the richness of the inner life of the church, the role of faith is crucial. During the whole of church tradition, baptism has been regarded as the sacrament of faith. This fact indicates a prerequisite in two respects: 1) the close connection to the catechumenate and 2) the presupposition for the entrance into the community with the confession of faith and the receiving of the gift of the Spirit.[20] James D. G. Dunn holds that all of the rich metaphorical images in the New Testament that express salvation, the forgiveness of sins, justification, and sanctification are all elements which include and presuppose the existence of faith in one or another way. There is an intrinsic link between faith and baptism in salvation (Mark 16:16).

18. Chan, "Mother Church," 184.
19. Ibid., 189.
20. For a broad introduction to the emphasis of the gift of the Spirit related to water baptism, see Dunn, *Baptism in Spirit*.

Pauline theology also outlines the role of the Spirit in the conversion-initiation process. According to Paul, "in the one Spirit we were all baptized into one body—Jews or Greeks, slaves or free—and we were all made to drink of one Spirit" (1 Cor 12:13). This is a key passage for understanding the Spirit as at work both in the regeneration and the empowerment of ministry. According to this passage, baptism has a clear ecclesial dimension. It is the church which celebrates baptism and it is also the faith of the whole church which is expressed within the testimony of the baptized and of the godparents. In the view of Catholic Walter Kasper, it seems clear that the liturgical celebration of baptism is not the end of the matter.[21] Rather, the New Testament is concerned with the element of *paraclesis* and the reminder to live in the spiritual reality of what baptism confers (Rom 6: 3–14; Col 3:1–7; 1 Pet 1:3–25). It is not the baptism as such which is to be repeated, but instead the content of what baptism declares which is to be continuously realized afresh in daily life, according to the nature of baptism as both initiation and mission.[22] In a wider sense, there is a pneumatological dimension of baptism specifically emphasized in the Orthodox Church, where the sacrament has been described in terms of a mystery: a symbolic representation of the salvation in which the Holy Spirit works and imparts his gifts through the chrismation. The Augsburg Confession says that through the Word and Sacrament, as through instruments, the Holy Ghost is given, who works faith; where and when it pleases God. For the heirs of the Reformation, the proper use of the sacraments consists in assessing them to be signs and testimonies of the will of God toward us, which are instituted to awaken and confirm faith in those who use them.[23]

---

21. Kasper, "Ecumenical Implications," 530.

22. This perspective is clearly stated by Luther in his formulation, "by daily sorrow and repentance," *The Small Catechism*, (§IV, The Sacrament of Holy Baptism). Here Luther declares, "it is not the water that produces these effects, but the word of God connected with the water, and our faith which relies on the word of God connected with the water." Observe the following statement: "For without the word of God the water is merely water and no baptism. But when connected with the word of God it is a Baptism, that is, a gracious water of life and a washing of regeneration in the Holy Spirit, which he poured upon us richly through Jesus Christ our savior, so that we might be justified by his grace and become heirs in hope of eternal life". Tappert, *Book of Concord*, 349. Likewise, Augustine of Hippo refers to John 15:3 and the declaration of Jesus that his disciples were clean because of the word he had spoken to them, not because any baptismal rite: "Take away the word, and the water is neither more nor less than water. The word is added to the element and there results the sacrament, as if itself also a kind of visible word." *Tractate on the Gospel of John*, 80, 3, cited in Kelly, "Ecumenical Endeavour," 161.

23. Tappert, *Book of Concord*, 31.

A similar perspective comes from Stanley Hauerwas. According to him, the sacraments enact the story of Jesus by which a community in Christ's image is shaped.[24] Without them, there would be no sustainable church. By these, the story is not only told but practiced. Baptism is a demonstration of the story of the death and resurrection of Jesus. Those baptized become part of that story. Religious rites are not just things Christians do. Through them, they learn who they are. Thus, sacramental living really is effective as social work and witness.[25] Furthermore, a wider notion of the teaching of Paul in Romans 6 points to a significant theological insight: a deep sense of unity flowing from the fellowship shaped by the fact that all baptized Christian have been buried with him in the same tomb as Christ through a baptism into death. Thus, because of the resurrection, we all share the same new life "so we too might walk in newness of life" (Rom 6:4). From its innermost nature, baptism has an importance that goes beyond any one local or confessional church, Kasper declares.[26] By sharing one baptism, we have become members of the ecclesial body of Christ (Eph 4:5).[27] This is, however, an expression of pneumatological nature. It points to the relation between the recognition of baptism and a fundamental understanding of the sacraments within their ecclesiological context. Without such a common understanding of what is going on when the faith community is gathered, the ecumenical dialogue cannot be much more than friendly gestures and interchurch diplomacy, devoid of real theological substance and commitment.

Linked to the Outpouring of the Spirit

A common denominator of this reflection is that all sacramental acts are linked to the outpouring of the Spirit on the Day of Pentecost. They all stand

---

24. Hauerwas, *Peaceable Kingdom*, 107.

25. Notice the ethical-moral context in which the baptismal text is placed by Paul in his letter to the Romans (Rom 6:1–12). By including dogmatic statements when discussing public moral behaviors of the members of the church and the relation to their earlier identity as Gentiles (vv. 1–2), Paul gives these statements an ethical weight that is applicable to the social life of the church (vv. 13–14).

26. Kasper, "Ecumenical Implications," 531.

27. The question of membership normally has been understood in light of the baptism, which acts as the entrance into the body of Christ (Acts 2:41). Through baptism, a person is drawn into the mystery of life in Christ. This challenges some more contemporary understandings of membership and underlines that the church is not merely a human institution, but rather the *koinonia* of believers in communion with the Triune God and in communion with one another. World Council of Churches: "One Baptism," §65.

in the great context of the salvation-history. The Holy Spirit has been given to all as an eschatological gift, by which the person and work of Jesus Christ has become present. The power to effect salvation must not be regarded in the light of a ritual working by magic but rather in the light of the *epiclesis* (the invocation of the Spirit) and of the authoritative promise of salvation given in the trinitarian confession, which is the sum and substance of the entire Christian faith.[28] The promise is received by faith, which constitutes the *sine qua non* for the existence of the living church worldwide.[29]

The Evangelical/Reformed scholar Donald G. Bloesch writes that while the outward sign, understood as a sacrament, has an important role in confirming and deepening the faith, it must never be confounded with the thing signified, the gift of the Spirit. "The sign is not extraneous to the reality that it represents, but it is always distinct from this reality."[30] The sacraments become vehicles of the Spirit who communicates to us the real presence of Christ as long as we have faith in his work of redemption. This problematizes the doctrine of the efficacy of the sacraments *ex opera operato* (from the work performed). The notion that the sacraments confer grace through the mere act of being performed lacks sufficient scriptural support. However, according to the more contemporary understanding of the Catholic Church, ex opera operato seems to require a disposition of faith, while the validity of a sacrament does not rest not upon the merits of the individual administering it but rather upon the merits of the one who instituted them in the first place: Christ. It is not faith that makes the sacrament to be a sacrament, but the promises of God upon which the sacrament is built. Therefore, we may consider the sacraments to be elements coming from the outside.

On the other hand, when the recipient is properly disposed, then the sufficient grace of the sacrament is efficacious. In themselves, the sacraments do not contain the Word; it must be proclaimed as part of every sacramental act.[31] However, when receiving the means of grace alongside

---

28. Kasper, "Ecumenical Implications," 528.

29. David S. Dockery holds that it is extremely difficult—if not impossible—to believe that the examples of household baptisms (Acts 11:14; 16:15, 31; 18:8) mean that the faith of the head of the household was sufficient for the children, relatives, or household slaves. The household references most likely designate only those of mature age who confessed their faith in Christ. Baptism served as an initiatory rite, incorporating the followers of Christ into the new community and identifying them with their LORD and his people. Dockery, "Thology of Acts," 53. See also Ladd, *Theology of New Testament*, 350. See also the more sacramental oriented baptismal reflections given by Pannenberg, *Systematic Theology*, vol 3, 258–83.

30. Bloesch, *The Holy Spirit*, 33.

31. Tappert, *Book of Concord*, 35.

the announcement of the Word, the Spirit is integrated and the whole act points to the saving event described in the Bible. Without this proclamation, the sacraments as such become an act without theological foundation and without life-giving substance.[32] In the proper sense, the Spirit of God does not subsist in the means of grace except when he decides to manifest himself through these means. The Spirit communicates to us through Scripture, through spiritual gifts and through visible means of grace, but all these graceful gifts are based on the sovereignty of God's mercy and faithfulness alone. The church is not master of either the written Word or the sacramental elements.

The contextual background of 1 Corinthians is that Paul had to deal with a situation in which baptism and the Supper were getting out of control, because the people supposed that the Supper worked independent of how they lived, guaranteeing them complete security against the consequences of sin. Baptism admitted them into a community in which all things were lawful. The Supper maintained the social structure of the community by turning the fellowship meal into an occasion of rioting for the wealthy and giving hunger and shame to the poor, creating parties and division within the congregation (1 Cor 1:10–17; 5:2.). In that situation, Paul made use of the corrective he knew: he proclaimed Christ crucified and insisted that Christian rites had to proclaim the same to have theological legitimacy (1 Cor 10:31; 11:26–34).

This is confirmed by the French Roman Catholic theologian, Louis-Marie Chauvet, who writes that although every sacrament is a rite, the rite becomes a sacrament only if it is converted by the Word and the Spirit.[33] This implies that every sacrament is a sacrament of the Word, or rather, a sacrament is the Word itself, albeit mediated under the ritual mode and by help of the visible elements. It is as the Word that Christ gives himself in the Eucharist. To receive communion, you have to "eat the book" (Ezek 3:3) and ruminate on the Word. According to Augustine, we eat and drink in order to participate in the Spirit.[34] Another representative of the Catholic Church, Yves Congar, penned that water baptism and the baptism of the Spirit were two associated and combined realities, not separate ones. Water cannot be interpreted as the instrumental cause of the gift of the Spirit. That would eventually lead to mysticism and a kind of sacramentality foreign to the concept of a Spirit-driven church.[35]

---

32. Barrett, *Church, Ministry and Sacraments*, 68.
33. Chauvet, *The Sacraments*, 47–48.
34. Referred to in Johnson, *Sacraments and Worship*, 41.
35. In the story of the disciples of Ephesus, they were baptized by Paul and then

In general, the Reformers related the work of the Spirit to the visible word of baptism and Eucharist. However, they did not tie the grace of God exclusively to the sacraments. Through the Spirit, the means of grace can function in interaction and accordance with Scripture.[36] Luther made the important observation that the Spirit is not immanent in either Scripture or the sacraments, but the Word as Spirit works by and through the sacramental signs.[37]

According to the gospel of John, the Spirit does not glorify himself but Jesus (John 16:14). The Spirit receives from Christ what he will make known to his disciples. The Spirit carries the word and operates in the sacraments, but the latter cannot by itself guarantee the Spirit. The close connection between Word and Spirit is a relation not of cause and effect but of promise and fulfilment. While it is proper to declare that the Spirit of God works through the witness of Christians (the preaching of the gospel) and through different loving services and ministries, Paul Tillich taught that the freedom of the Spirit was part of what he termed "the Protestant principle." According to that theology, the Spirit's operations could not be bound exclusively to the sacraments as such. Like the wind, the Spirit is free to do what he wants, where he wants. Neither is he bound to reveal himself only within the church and through specific appointed means like church officials and sacramental rituals.[38]

Voices from the Church Tradition and the New Testament Witnesses

The relationship between the terms sacrament, faith and Spirit mentioned so far reflects our indebtedness to a longer church tradition. Tertullian

---

had hands laid on them. The Holy Spirit came on them, and they spoke in tongues and prophesied (Acts 19:1–6). The Spirit did not seem to come through the rite of baptism as such, but as a result of the interactive reciprocity between baptism and the act of intercession, released by their faith in Jesus as LORD.

36. According to James Dunn, "where the sacraments are valued within the New Testament it is because they embody in a strikingly symbolical way the heart of the Christian belief in Jesus." Dunn, *Unity and Diversity*, 188.

37. In this regard, Luther clearly states that it is not the sacrament "but faith in the sacrament that justifies (. . .) Indeed, any sacrament requires a completely pure heart. Otherwise the recipient will be guilty of the sacrament and will incur judgment upon himself (cf. 1 Cor 11:27)." Here, Luther refers to a wording of Augustine, "It (the sacrament) justifies not because it is performed, but because it is believed." And further Luther declares: "The heart is not purified except through faith, as Acts 15:9 says. Therefore, the person who is baptized 'does not attain grace because it is baptized, but because it believes.'" Luther, *Lectures*, 29, 172.

38. For a broader insight, see Tillich, *Protestant Era*.

appears to regard the Spirit as being given after the baptized has come out of the waters and received the anointing: "Not that in the waters we obtain the Holy Spirit; but in the water (. . .) we are prepared for the Holy Spirit," Tertullian wrote.[39] According to church historian Robert L. Wilken, in the early church there was no Christianity without an altar. But there was also no Christianity without a bath, without passing through the waters of baptism. [40] Baptism was a moral, as well as spiritual, experience. As observed from early Christian liturgies, baptism was not a private affair but rather a celebration with the entire community. Following the Didache, the instruction was clear:

> As for baptism, baptize in this way: Having said all this beforehand, baptize in the name of the Father and the Son and the Holy Spirit, in running water. If you do not have running water, however, baptize in another kind of water; if you cannot [do so] in cold [water], then [do so] in warm [water]. But if you have neither, pour water on the head trice in the name of the Father and Son and Holy Spirit. Before the baptism, let the person baptizing and the person being baptized—and others who are able—fast; tell the one being baptized to fast one or two [days] before.[41]

In his commentary on the Didache, Kurt Niederwimmer presumes that parts of this text must be the work of a redactor. The phrase "in running water" most likely means in "living" water. However, the point in *Did.* 7.2–3 is that one should use the most appropriate water available for baptism, and that the effect of baptism is unquestioned even if the water is less suitable and even if baptism consists solely of pouring water on the head.[42] As Kelly puts it, the early view seems to be like the Pauline one that baptism is the

---

39. Tertullian, *On Baptism*, chapter 6.
40. Wilken, *Early Christian Thought*, 37, 39.
41. Didache, 11.7, 1–4, in Niederwimmer and Attridge, *The Didache*, 125.
42. Here, we may observe the influence of the Jewish-Christian tradition in *The Apostolic Tradition* of Hippolytos, 21.2–3 (Sahidic version): "Let there be flowing water in the font, but flowing water from above. Let it be done in this fashion, unless there be other need. If, however, there is some continuing and pressing need, use whatever water you find." Observe the formulation in 21.4: "And first baptize the small children. And each one who is able to speak for themselves [sic], let them speak. But those not able to speak for themselves, let their parents or another one belonging to their family speak." Bradshaw et al., *Apostolic Tradition*, 112. The practice of infant baptism is attested to in the third century by Tertullian (*De bapt.* 18), Cyprian (*Ep.* 64) and Origen (*Hom. on Lev.* 8.3). In his comment to 21.4, Bradshaw notes that those "who cannot answer for themselves" here are not necessarily just infants but any child from infancy all the way to the age of seven years, i.e., the ancient Roman interpretation of *infantes*. Ibid., 130.

vehicle for conveying the Spirit to believers.[43] In the writings of the second-century church fathers, there are no references to the existence of a separate rite, such as the unction or the laying on of hands. Rather, the model in which the believers were anticipated to be filled with the Spirit seems to be derived from the descent of the Spirit upon Jesus at his baptism in the Jordan. Tertullian thus insists that the Church is the unique home of the Spirit, because it is the sole repository of the apostolic vision.

Insights from biblical theology point in the same direction. According to the eschatological vision of the Revelation, an angel says to John, "I will give water as a gift from the spring of the water of life" (Rev 21:6, see also 22:1). Because of the many biblical allusions to water as the agent of spiritual cleansing and renewal, the mysterious relation between water and Spirit has been the subject of extensive reflection.[44] A sacramental view considers a close association between the two but exactly how this has to be understood is disputed.[45] Does the rite of baptism convey grace by the very fact of being performed? Is the gift of the Spirit related to the laying on of hands, or is the work of the Spirit quite autonomous and thus independent of any outward sign? Do the various references to water in the New Testament texts refer to the inner cleansing work of the Spirit or to an outward rite that symbolizes interior renewal? What is the living water referenced by Jesus and recorded in John (John 4:10-15; 7:37-39)? And finally, what about the words of Jesus to Nicodemus about the requirement for entrance into the Kingdom, "no one can enter the kingdom of God unless they are born of water and the Spirit" (John 3: 5-8)?

The epistle to Titus also contains an unmistakable allusion to water baptism, where salvation, mercy, the washing of rebirth and renewal of the Spirit all are connected together (Tit 3:5). Several of these questions are, as Bloesch observes, connected to a normal development within religious lives of various kinds. Normally, initial experiences pave the way for ritual performances in order to preserve continuity.[46] Thus, mainline church traditions regard water baptism as the outward and visible sign of an inward

---

43. Kelly, *Early Christian Doctrines*, 195.

44. See passages as: Ex 29:4; 40:12-13; Isa 55:1; Ezek 36:25-26; Zeck 13:1; Mark 1:4; Luke 3:1-22; Heb 10:22.

45. Richard A. Jensen gives an account of a classic Lutheran position. He writes that water baptism is concurrent with Spirit baptism: "The giving of the Spirit stands in the closest possible relationship to baptism in water. To be baptized with Christian baptism is to receive the gift of the Holy Spirit." Jensen: *Touch by the Spirit*, 123. For the classical Pentecostal position, see other parts of this work, or Wyckoff, "Baptism in the Holy Spirit," 423-55. For an ecumenical inspired approach to the issue of rebaptism, see Hegertun, "Bridge over Troubled Water."

46. Bloesch, *The Holy Spirit*, 280.

and spiritual grace. However, the Pauline reference to the Spirit as a seal (Eph 1:13; 4:30; 2 Cor 1:22) by which Christians are marked opens interpretations as to whether it alludes to the sacrament of baptism or to an inward regeneration and renewal caused by the Spirit and received "by believing what you heard" (Gal 3:2), even outside any sacramental frame.[47]

As far as I understand, being sealed with the Spirit most likely indicates the inward experience of which baptism is the effective symbol without being the real content of the spiritual regeneration performed by the Spirit. The event of sealing may be considered as the confirming work of the Spirit, as Calvin understood it.[48] The whole collection of biblical passages draws in the direction of the interplay between faith and the Word. There is a need to warn against concepts which obscure the Reformation jewel: that we are saved by grace through faith alone (Eph 2:8). Ascribing the means of grace to the work of the Spirit is well suited to making visible the close relationship which exists between performing sacramental acts and receiving what these act proclaim through faith (Acts 2:38-40).

James D. G. Dunn strongly emphasizes that John's use of the word water (John 3:5-8) symbolizes the activities of the Spirit and is not tied to a sacramental rite alone.[49] He acknowledges that Jesus' speaking to Nicodemus probably includes, in close connection, two baptisms, that of water and that of the Spirit.[50] Obviously, there is a sacramental dimension in coming to faith, being a committed follower of Christ and being a limb on the body of Christ.[51]

But all in all, water baptism seems to be a vehicle of faith more than a vehicle of the Spirit. This position preserves God's freedom in imparting God's grace. In addition, this position is more in line with the overall experience of what it is that promotes growth within the global church today,

---

47. According to the example of Apollos in Acts 18, it is possible to have the gift of the Spirit without being baptized ("he spoke with great favor and thought about Jesus accurately," v. 25). However, this is among the exceptional passages within Scripture. In the next chapter, a more normal structure is referred to when some disciples from Ephesus were baptized by Paul in the name of the LORD Jesus: "When he placed his hands on them (after having baptized them), the Holy Spirit came on them, and they spoke in tongues and prophesied" (Acts 19:1-7).

48. Referred to by Bloesch, *The Holy Spirit*, 281.

49. Dunn, *Baptism in Spirit*, 101.

50. I agree with Bloesch's contention that the New Testament is actually talking about four baptisms: the baptism of John the Baptist (John 1:26), Christian baptism (Matt 28:19; Mark 16:16; Acts 2:38; 22:16), Spirit baptism (Luke 3:16; 24:49; John 1:33; Acts 1:5), and the baptism with blood (Mark 10:39), Bloesch, *The Holy Spirit*, 282. For an opposite position, see Bruner, *A Theology of the Holy Spirit*, 170.

51. Bloesch, *The Holy Spirit*, 302.

and it seems reasonable in light of the personal appropriation of grace by faith alone as it is expressed as one of the Protestant distinctives. Studies of Luther display his deep concern for the relationship between Spirit and baptism. He would say that baptism is not a sign but a garment. As one of the Great Reformers, he was opposed to any automatic imparting of grace through ritual performances alone. A sacrament has no efficacy unless it is connected to the proclaimed Word and, even more, is received by faith as result of the animating work of the Spirit.[52]

The sacraments carry the promise of new life, but they do not assure this new life as such. Rather, they remind the believer of one's utter dependence on God's grace. Churches have to find a balanced pathway between, on the one hand, a personalism in which the believer is related to God through personal encounter (Matt 3:2; Mark 1:15; Acts 2:38; Rev 3:3), and, on the other hand, a more sacramental approach which in some way limits the Spirit to being conveyed by certain prescribed ritual acts.[53]

A widely recognized ecumenical understanding can be described like this: although the ministry of baptism is carried out by human agents and the baptizands submit voluntarily to baptism, it is a divine work linked to the process of conversion-initiation (Acts 2:38-39).[54] Consequently, the divine action does not exclude but rather presupposes the individual's personal response through repentance and faith. That is why baptism *also* can be described as a confession of faith and as the gateway into the church. By using the phrase "in the name of Jesus Christ" (v. 38), the baptizand is aware of what is going on: a shift of identity and a deep feeling of belonging to the ruling of the LORD Christ and to the church.[55]

According to Engelsviken, a Lutheran theologian, baptism is an act which has to operate both within a surrounding of faith in home and church and also as a proclamation of the gospel. Consequently, it is only when the message is received in faith and when baptism is placed where it belongs, as an integrated element in the process of Christian conversion-initiation,

---

52. Luther, *Large Catechism*, 83. That a sacramental understanding of baptism does not imply a magical understanding of the act is clearly emphasized by Edmund Schlink, a Lutheran theologian. Schlink, *Doctrine of Baptism*, 44.

53. Bloesch states that while faith has need of ritual support, it does not gain its vitality from ritual observance. Without faith, sacramental observance may promote a false sense of assurance and, in the worst cases, an idolatrous fixation. Bloesch, *The Holy Spirit*, 284.

54. Engelsviken, "The Gift of the Spirit," 442.

55. Ibid., 444. The most renowned ecumenical document of WCC, *BEM*, underscores the significance of faith connected to the baptismal rites: "The personal faith of the recipient of baptism and faithful participation in the life of the Church are essential for the full fruit of baptism." World Council of Churches, *BEM*, 5.

that it is possible to give real meaning when talking about baptism in terms of forgiveness. Engelsviken takes into account that the gift of the Spirit cannot be equated with baptism as such, but it may appears as its result.[56] The gift of the Spirit is only granted to those who repent (and believe) and are being baptized.

The Book of Acts reflects a temporal association between the act of baptism and the reception of the Spirit (for a look at the varied practice, see Acts 2:38-39; 4:31; 8:17; 10:44-47; cf. 11:15-17; 18:25; 19:1-6). However, among those accounts, the pericope in Acts 2 seems to have played a major role for mirroring its pattern for conversion-initiation, which is reflected in Christian experience throughout the centuries. Here all elements are addressed: the proclamation of the gospel, the call to conversion and faith, baptism and the forgiveness of sins, and the impartment of the Spirit (vv. 38-39). In the narrative of Cornelius (Acts 10:44-48), the corpus shows that forgiveness and the gift of the Spirit are not exclusively tied to baptism, but rather that the preceding events, as a matter of fact, called for the baptismal act.[57]

Edmund Schlink remarks that none of the relevant passages of Acts ought to be regarded independently of each other.[58] It was because Cornelius and his household received the Holy Spirit, spoke in tongues and praised God, that they were to be baptized. And because the new believers in Samaria were baptized, Peter and John prayed that the new believers might receive the Holy Spirit. Also, the account of the disciples in Ephesus (Acts 19:1-6) supports the idea of a connection between baptism and reception of the Spirit. Even though the act of baptism and the gift of the Spirit do not always coincide in time, they are still intimately related. The Spirit is not given to the believer through baptism alone (Acts 8:14-17; 19:1-7), but is given in association with baptism. This fact underscores the necessity of seeing baptism as a sacrament or an ordinance which has to operate within a surrounding of faith in home and church, connected to different kinds of faith learning programs within churches.

Baptized by Water and Spirit

James D. G. Dunn holds that in Acts repentance and/or faith is normally closely linked to water baptism (Acts 2:38, 41; 8:12; 8:37; 16:14-15, 31-33;

---

56. Engelsviken, "The Gift of the Spirit," 450.
57. Ibid., 462.
58. Schlink, *Doctrine of Baptism*, 64-65.

18:8; 19:1-7).[59] The idea of an unbaptized Christian is simply not attested to in the NT. Baptism was the natural expression of commitment to Christ (Acts 2:21; 22:16).[60] Repentance and faith shaped one's readiness to be baptized. In light of the Cornelius narrative (Acts 10), it is problematic to state that baptism as such conveys, confers or affects the forgiveness of sins.[61] The argument of the apostle to let Cornelius and his house be baptized was connected to their experience of the Holy Spirit and their belief in Christ (11:17). In Luke, the sacrament acts on faith and faith acts on God. Here it is beneficial to refer to the Jordan narrative of the baptism of Jesus. The anointing with the Spirit took place after the baptism was completed and while he was praying (Luke 3:21-22).

The same pattern can be observed in Acts 19:4-6 (see also 8:15-17). In a sense, the preparatory nature of the Johannine baptism (John 1:31) was carried over into Christian baptism.[62] However, unlike John, it is preparatory in a dialectic way in that baptism after Pentecost became part of the conversion-initiation process and pointed to the messianic baptism in the Spirit, which alone effected entrance into the kingdom of God (John 1:32-33; Acts 2:38-39). In the NT, baptism continues in the Christian area both as a fulfilment of John's baptism and as a contrast to the latter (Acts 1:5; 11:16).

Thus, the contrast element is not between two different rites of water baptism, but between the baptism of John and the new (metaphorically used) baptism of Jesus: the baptism of the Spirit. It is *this* baptism that operates both as the main element of the conversion-initiation process and as the equipment for ministry, the inspiration for prophetic speech, the giver of spiritual gifts and so on. If we should talk about what really mattered for Luke, it obviously would not be water baptism but Spirit baptism. While water baptism is a natural expression of faith, God gives the Spirit unmediated though still on the basis of faith, as is clearly indicated in the narrative of Jerusalem and that of Cornelius (Acts 2 and 10).[63] Water bap-

---

59. Ibid., 98. Dunn refers to words saying that water baptism confers, imparts, brings, bestows, or gives the Spirit. See also Schlink, *Doctrine of Baptism*, 58.

60. Dunn, *Baptism in Spirit*, 97.

61. However, there are a number of occasions where Luke writes about repentance and faith as prerequisites for receiving forgiveness as well: Luke 5:20; 24:47; Acts 3:19; 5:31; 10:43; 13:38; 26:18. See also: 4:4; 9:35, 42; 11:21; 13:48; 14:1; 17:12, 34.

62. Dunn, *Baptism in Spirit*, 99. The Spirit is the element used in the Messiah's baptism that contrasts with the water used in John's baptism (Matt 3:11; Mark 1:8; Luke 3:16; John 1:33 and Acts 1:5; 11:16). Ibid., 128.

63. Dunn refers to "the highly critical audience" when Peter gave his report to the leaders in Jerusalem in Acts 11:15-18. They were not concerned about the issue of water baptism in the house of Cornelius but did take interest in a more important issue: the experience of the Spirit. Dunn says that only one baptism is mentioned—Spirit baptism. That was all that mattered. Ibid., 100.

tism is a vehicle of faith more than it is the channel or means of the giving of the Spirit. Faith reaches out to God in and through water baptism, while God reaches out to people and corresponds with faith as received by them through the Holy Spirit.

Just as Luke could not conceive of a Christian without having the Spirit (Acts 8:14–17; 9:17; 19:1–7), so it is also the case with the local church. She was an assembly of those who had received the Spirit and acted in the Spirit (Acts 2:42–47; 4: 32–35; cf. 6:8; 12:5, 12; 13:1–3). For Luke it was self-evident that Spirit-filled men and women attended to and served communities as a result of their life in the Spirit. The church became the sphere of Spirit and grace in which the believers were invited to belong to and act through different ministries by taking part in the church's sacramental life. Water baptism and Spirit baptism appear as distinct entities, yet the gift of the Spirit remained as the nerve-centre of the initiation process in which the sacraments played a crucial role. The Spirit became the burning heart of the identity of the church. Early Christianity did not adjust itself in accordance with a cultic act, but in accordance with the act of God revealed in the giving of the Spirit.[64]

The letter to the Galatians (2:1–5, 14) clearly connects the receiving of the Spirit to the beginning of the Christian life, not to a specific event many years later. The blessing of Abraham and the gift of the Spirit is fulfilled in Christ and is received by faith (v. 14), making the believer a child of the promise (4:28). According to Gal 3:26f, a Christian is baptized into Christ, a metaphor describing the spiritual relationship given in the process of conversion-initiation. The phrase of having clothed yourselves with Christ (v. 27) is likely a metaphor meant to describe more expressively what already is communicated in this particular letter: the spiritual transformation by the Spirit by which a person has become a Christian through faith (3:5). Paul does not point to a rite but to the cross and resurrection, to faith and to the Spirit (2:19–20).[65] In light of Paul's letter to the Corinthians (1 Cor 1: 10–17), baptism is a change of ownership, a transaction into the hands of a new Master and a commitment to Christ, who is the source and centre of the fellowship.

---

64. Ibid., 102.

65. Another central passage is 1 Cor is 12:13. Dunn understands this verse neither to refer to water baptism nor to the baptism in the Spirit. Instead, it may have a third meaning: Baptism *by* the Spirit, which has an initiatory and incorporative significance. Here Paul is speaking of spiritual realities and spiritual relationships in metaphorical language of water and irrigation. Ibid., 128–31.

Following these letters, the preaching of the gospel is the most vital means of grace.[66] The New Testament writers rejected any separation of the decisive moment of faith from baptism, whether by putting the act of faith prior to baptism, thus reducing baptism to a mere symbol, or by putting faith after baptism, thus exalting baptism to something that operates on a person without his or her contribution. The purposive approach in the New Testament seems to be that while the Spirit was the vehicle of saving grace, baptism was the vehicle of saving faith.

Spirit baptism and water baptism remain distinct, with the latter being a preparation for the former and the means by which the believer in faith receives the former. According to Dunn, the rite of water baptism cannot be given the most central role in the process of conversion-initiation, because it symbolizes the spiritual cleansing effected by the Spirit. Faith demands baptism as its expression. Baptism demands faith for its validity. The gift of the Spirit presupposes faith as its condition. And faith is shown to be genuine only by the gift of the Spirit, is the conclusion of Dunn.[67]

A Covenant Ritual of Initiation

As far as water baptism is concerned, James K. A. Smith reflects that baptism can be regarded as situated in the context of gathered worship, because it announces a social and political reality.[68] By dying and being raised with Christ, a Christian becomes a new person with a new identity in her belonging to the risen LORD. Not only does it have illustrative and imaginary value, baptism does what it promises to do according to Rom 6:4. By virtue of the salvation story, baptism shapes a new people. As such, baptism represents a profound social reality in which the priesthood is open to all. Marginalized people get their new status regardless of birth or class. All are called and equipped to take up humanity's creational vocation of being priests for the world.[69] The church—or the baptismal city—has constituted a people marked by baptism.

---

66. Ibid., 119.
67. Ibid., 228.
68. Smith, *Desiring the Kingdom*, 183.
69. Ibid. Regarding another central NT passage, the Nicodemus text in John 3:1–21, it seems clear that the Spirit is the constitutive element, not water baptism. Most likely, John is talking about both water baptism and Spirit baptism, and that "the birth from above" involves both baptisms while emphasizing the new birth as Spirit-given. Water, on its side, is a fitting Old Testament symbol of God's activity in quickening men to life (Jer 2:13; Ezek 47:9). Dunn, *Baptism in Spirit*, 190.

Paul declares that this is a different religio-political reality than that of the Jewish and Roman/Greek environment. The social and gender classes are obliterated (Gal 3:27–28). An upside-down kingdom is established (1 Cor 1:27–28), entrusted with the honorable mission of being a bearer of the new life given by Christ's resurrection. The baptized are situated in the context of the worshipping fellowship. They are linked together in a covenant, tied together as a *koinonia* and configured as a family, the household of God (Eph 2:19). In light of the church and her signs of God's graceful presence, baptism is both a challenge and a blessing. According to Smith, the promises of baptism counter the configuration of a family being a private, closed home: Love and its obligation traverse the boundaries of private residences and nuclear families because they initiate us into a household that is bigger than what is under the roof of our house.[70]

Baptism represents another layer in the theology of the family, in the sense that its social role is designed by its dependence upon a larger social body, the church. While regeneration is to be dedicated to Christ and a genuine work of the Spirit (Tit 3:4–8), baptism is a fundamental sign of that very dedication (Col 2:11–13; Rom. 2:29; cf. Gen 17:10–14). Baptism can be considered a covenant ritual of initiation into the relational fellowship of the New Testament church, inspired by the model of the circumcision ceremony in the Jewish law.[71]

Faith and baptism are related to each other in such a way that the effect of baptism is conditioned by its connection to the repentance, conversion and faith of the individual person. In that sense, baptism indicates the process of surrender of individuals and symbolizes the fellowship established between God and the church (Col 2:12–13). In his commentary on the confessions of the Danish National Church, Peder Nørgaard-Højen declares that if you break the relationship between baptism and faith, you cause a factual abandonment of the doctrine of justification (Rom 1:17).[72] In his opinion, the New Testament narratives of personal faith complicate the notion of vicarious faith (*fides vicaria*) applied to infant baptism. Sooner or later the baptismal fruits have to be acquired personally.

Though the baptismal act can still be regarded as valid, the baptism is not effective without faith. Human beings receive the gift of God not on the basis of understanding or cognitive ability, but only through the grace of Christ (Rom 3:24; 1 Cor 1:26–31), which also includes disabled persons. In the early centuries of the church's life, the term "I believe" found its

---

70. Smith, *Desiring the Kingdom*, 186.
71. S. Green, "Församling och medlemskap," 17–37.
72. Nørgaard-Højen, *The Confessions of the Danish National Church*, 301–21.

expression in various ways, especially in baptismal confession, the creeds, and worship. Christian communities shared baptismal creeds, the trinitarian professions, hymns, vows, and prayers as signs of their deep unity.

Towards an Ecumenical Approach

In a joint statement all the way back in 1974, a dialogue group from the Pentecostal movement and the Roman Catholic Church states that sacraments are in no sense magical but must be appropriated by faith. As such, where infant baptism is practiced, it gains meaning only within the context of faith community.[73] However, it is possible to suggest that the baptism of infants may be considered a baptism of corporate faith, and that believers' baptism is a baptism of personal confession. In this way, it is conceivable to preserve the values of infant baptism and the values of believers' baptism without the one cancelling out the other. The obvious implication is that what has found acceptance and usefulness in one set of churches might also be useful to other churches, as they explore legitimate and equivalent alternatives in reciprocal relationships.[74] The parallels that exist between the Pentecostal practice of infant dedication (or blessing) and the Roman Catholic or Lutheran practice of infant baptism hold considerable promise for mutual understanding and appreciation, presupposing that the intention is clear: both practices must lead to living faith and committed discipleship within the framework of the Spirit-driven church.

Concurring with Amos Yong, I contend that the claims of baptismal regeneration must be rejected if they are understood to be referring to a magical ability of the water to wash away sins (1 Pet 3:21). But they can be accepted if baptism is understood pneumatically as an action of the Spirit (Tit 3:5) responding to the faith of believers, as is presupposed in New Testament writings and practices (Acts 2:38-39; Rom 6:1-6; Col 2:12).[75] In addition, according to *BEM*, the celebration of baptism as a Christian rite should include the invocation of the Holy Spirit. In this way, the location of the sacramentality of baptism would not be tied to the materiality of

---

73. Robeck and Sandidge, "The Ecclesiology of *Koinonia* and Baptism," 507. This perspective is displayed in *BEM*. Regarding those churches that embrace the both forms of these practices, the commentary goes like this: "It has been possible to regard as equivalent alternatives for entry into the Church both a pattern whereby baptism in infancy is followed by later profession of faith and a pattern whereby believers' baptism follows upon a presentation and blessing in infancy." World Council of Churches, *BEM*, 5.

74. Robeck and Sandidge, "The Ecclesiology of *Koinonia* and Baptism," 529.

75. Yong, *The Spirit Poured Out on All Flesh*, 157.

consecrated water but to the living acts of the Spirit.[76] In line with Pauline teaching in Rom 6, baptism is a concrete experience of the death and life of Christ. It is an actualization of, an incorporation into and an identification with his body on earth. Every baptism is in one sense a re-enactment of Christ's death, burial and resurrection, and, as such, it must be assessed as representing the initiation work of the Spirit.

According to same document (§5), the Holy Spirit is at work in the lives of people before, in and after their baptism. With respect to the question of what happens in baptism, the document states that it is the same Spirit who revealed Jesus as the Son (Mark 1:10–11) and who empowered and united the disciples at Pentecost (Acts 2) that is at work during the act of baptism. Since we talk of a real—though spiritual—resurrection and not a dead ritual, baptism can be defined as a work of the Spirit, just as the Spirit was involved in the resurrection of Christ (Rom 1:4; 8:11). The new life in Christ is a life in the Spirit. It comes either as a result of a crisis experience and/or as an intensifying of the conversion.

Consequently, the dynamic initial movement and graceful gift called baptism must be attributed to the Spirit's transformative impact. If not this, what else? From the particular perspective of the given relationship between baptism and Spirit, it should be clear that baptism is much more than just a naming ceremony or a confession of obedience. Therefore, the Pentecostal and Baptist traditions should seek to include elements of prayer for the fullness of the Spirit to overwhelm the newly baptized, in accordance with models from the early church.[77] Ambrose of Milan said that after the rite of baptism there follows the spiritual seal. For after the font, it remains for the "perfection" to take place, when, at the invocation of the priest, the Holy Spirit is bestowed."[78]

The new study document, "One Baptism: Towards Mutual Recognition," from the Faith & Order Commission, also explores the close relation between baptism and the believer's life-long growth into Christ as a basis for a greater mutual recognition of baptism.[79] The aim of the document is to offer fresh perspectives in order to clarify the meaning of this mutual recognition, to consider the consequences for church practice and to clarify con-

---

76. World Council of Churches, *BEM*, 6. In some baptismal traditions, baptism looks to completion but before having reached the final goal. The demand on the baptized is to seek to grow in faith and to become what they are: the children of God (John 1:12; 1 John 3:1–3). At any rate, the reality of baptism needs to be lived out as a daily experience. Again and again the baptized will need to repent and turn to Christ (Rom 6:1–11, Eph 4:21—5:2). That is the theological call for all churches, regardless of baptismal practice. World Council of Churches, "One Baptism," §49.

77. Hegertun, "Bridge over Troubled Water," 251.

78. Strawley, *Ambrose on the Mysteries and the Sacraments*, Books III/8.

79. World Council of Churches, "One Baptism," §1.

troversial issues.[80] *The ecumenical definition of baptism states that baptism is the central event of the initiation process in which a believer is incorporated into the body of Christ.* Thus, it is quite possible to accept each other's baptism as one unified baptism into Christ. An important recognition in the latest baptismal document from WCC is that the term *sacramentum* or *mysterion* is applied to baptism and the Eucharist because, in these events, one presupposes that the work of Christ is effected by the power of the Holy Spirit. Without this pneumatological conviction, these events are confined to a pure religious rite.[81] Only in the light of a pneumatological approach is it possible to presume that an outward and visible sign truly can confer an inward and spiritual grace.

Accordingly, churches tend to emphasize either the spiritual fruits and results of sacramental activities or the concern for the shortage of those outcomes. Churches emphasizing the principle of *sola fide* or *solo spiritu* are less susceptible to being swayed into any kind of magical sacramentalism.[82] With WCC, one may assert that the sacramental events are both instrumental (God uses them to bring about a new reality because of the presence of the Spirit) and expressive (they refer to an already-existing reality). These definitions are not mutually exclusive but provide a wider understanding across churches. After Pentecost, the liturgies of all the sacraments have an element of invocation and sealing of the Holy Spirit, before, during or after the officiating. To answer the question of whether a sacrament is an effective sign or just a symbol is not appropriate without considering an underlying presupposition: what the elements signify must be received in faith, bestowed by the gracious gift of the Holy Spirit and based upon Christ's mighty acts of salvation. You may be immersed in water, but, more importantly, you are anointed by the Spirit (Matt 3:11) and nourished by the Eucharist.

---

80. The fact that churches take practical steps to nurture and express a mutual understanding of the need of the catechumenate for instruction in the faith *prior* to baptism, and a more widespread generous use of water in the baptismal act—including a more frequent use of immersion fonts—are signs of ecumenical progress across denominational lines. Ibid., §8.

81. Ibid., §27.

82. The term is among the lesser known cardinal principles of historic Protestantism, notably in John Calvin's work, which holds that the Holy Spirit suffices for recognizing God's revelation. There is, as such, no need of a hierarchical Church to identify or explain the meaning of the revealed word of God.

Sitting at the Lord's Table

Many of the same preconditions already stated in this chapter affect the jewel of the liturgy and the crown of the graceful gifts: the communion's gathering around the Lord's Table. Worship culminates in the Eucharist; it is the compact microcosm of what worship is all about. As a sanctified salivation, this liturgical practice and holy ordinance reaches not only our ears and eyes but also our mouths.[83] During the Eucharist ceremony, we are situated in the midst of the dramatic story of Maundy Thursday, the breaking of the bread the night before Christ's death (Matt 26:17–30; cf. 1 Cor 11:23–26). The Eucharist is the central liturgical act within the church service, because the meal defines the church as a speech act of the living memory and concrete presence of the Spirit. What happened in the past actualizes in the present and holds a message for the future of inclusiveness across any borders and classifications. It is this sacrament that conveys the presence of the trinitarian God. We are invited to the table by God, who makes the Eucharist a divine *mysterion*.

The meal represents a deeply affecting practice, one which is spelled out like a great performance of the gospel. Smith perceives a hallowing of the everyday in the simple elements of bread and wine, a sanctification of the domestic and a creational affirmation of the stuff of the earth. As a means of grace, the Eucharist intensifies the sacramentality of the world as such. It signifies that the kingdom of God, of which the church is an anticipation (Matt 26:29), is not concerned with a wholly other world but of this world transformed and transfigured. The Eucharist meal adds prestige to our everyday items. It is a blessing of our habits and practices as they come to fore in our being as dependent and finite creatures. As cultivated stuff in our hands, the blessed bread and wine become part of a Christian worship that rehearses the blessing of God in the first creation (Gen 1:28–31). The bread and wine are equally and freely distributed independent of condition, positions, preferences, class or ethnicity. In the Lord's Supper, Christians celebrate the theology of forgiveness and reconciliation. The Eucharist is not only a gracious communion with the forgiving God, but also a meal we share with one another in order to build sustainable fellowship.

As Smith notes, human flourishing cannot take place in isolation.[84] Humans are created for community, and the Eucharist meal is an outstanding expression of a community that is not there because of its structure or technical regulations but because of the sharing of love. The community

---

83. Smith, *Desiring the Kingdom*, 198. I am indebted to James K. A. Smith for some of the reflections in this passage.

84. Ibid., 201.

is not invited to the table of award but to the table of unlimited grace. The chalice is not a cup gained in competition but an utterance of the fact that God always comes first towards us (1 John 4:9–11). The Eucharist represents a reduction of all hidden competition between the members of the fellowship: A kingdom-shaped community cannot be satisfied with private, isolated individuals only reconciled vertically to God, for the manifest witness of such reconciliation will be the love of neighbors.[85]

The table before the face of God constitutes a liturgical practice that reminds participants of the connection between food and fellowship. It has a clear social dimension and functions as a disciplining catalyst for reconciliation on the horizontal level. The Eucharist teaches the Spirit-driven church to embody its purpose as a reconciled community in which forgiveness is a practical outcome of partaking of the meal. During this act the church functions as a school, learning to love people who are our brothers and sisters, chosen by God and given to each other as gifts which expand our own heart. Nonetheless, first and foremost, the Eucharist is an eschatological event. It is the victual for the faith journey on earth, a meal on the way. It is a table in the wilderness (Ps 78:19) and in front of enemies (Ps 23:5). It is an anticipatory meal the church consumes within an eschatological horizon as a foretaste of the feast to come (Rev 19:9). The fellowship recapitulates the salvation story while being formed as a community of hope: the people of the future.

The Eucharist Communion in the Presence of the Spirit

The Christian tradition talks about the Body of Christ in three ways: as the historical body referred to in the Creeds; as the fellowship of believers, the church; and as the eucharistic communion, sharing the bread and wine as the body and blood of Christ. The Roman Catholic theologian and cardinal, Henri de Lubac, talks about the Eucharist by which the church is made visible. The holy Church is the body of Christ, made alive by the one Spirit. Nourished by the LORD's Supper, the people of God drink of the one Spirit, and thereby the church is made real.[86] In the *anaphora* prayer spoken over the bread and wine in the liturgy of both the Eastern and the Catholic tradition, the bishop beseeches the Holy Spirit to descend on the elements: "And we pray that you would send your Holy Spirit upon the offerings of your holy church; that gathering them into one, you would grant to all your saints

---

85. Ibid.
86. Lubac et al., *Corpus Mysticum*, 88.

who partake of them to be filled with the Holy Spirit."[87] Hauerwas and Wells say it this way:

> Celebrating the Eucharist means much more than eating bread. It means gathering, and thus becoming a visible people. It means being reconciled, and thus finding unity in Christ, rather than in "common humanity." It means listening and responding to the scriptural story, and thus sharing a tradition. It means remembering God's action and invoking the Spirit's presence, and thus being redirected to true power and unique sacrifice. It means being sent out to witness and serve, and thus being given a shape for living.[88]

In a similar way, the Church of England acknowledges the extensive work of the Spirit in the celebration of the LORD's Supper.[89] The relationship between the Spirit and the function of liturgy cannot be reduced to a question of language and applicability. The Spirit does use a whole range of tools, non-verbal as well as verbal and invisible as well as visible, to bring us into the presence of God and into a relation with the sacramental Christ. The *epiclesis* in the liturgy of the Holy Communion is a concrete expression of a pneumatological reality and the hope of the community gathered for service. The Spirit conveys the effects of God's presence in manners as manifold as the variety of human beings themselves.[90] Especially among the Orthodox, there is a deep conviction that the Eucharist is the entrance of the Church into the joy of the LORD.[91] In the broadest sense of the word, liturgy is an action by which a group of people become something corporately which they had not been as a mere collection of individuals.[92] The goal of every liturgical action is to be what you see and to receive what you are, just as Augustine said.[93] Or, as it is formulated in the Holy Communion of the Anglican Church in South Africa, "Behold who we are, May we become what we receive."[94]

Schmemann proposes to think of the liturgy of the Eucharist as a journey and an entrance into the presence of Christ. This can be taken quite

---

87. Wilken, *Early Christian Thought*, 32.
88. Hauerwas and Wells, "Gifs of Church," 23.
89. Doctrine Commission of Church of England, *We Believe in the Holy Spirit*, 82.
90. Ibid., 84.
91. Schmemann, *Sacraments and Orthodoxy*, 25.
92. Ibid.
93. According to Augustine, the sacrament comes about "by the invisible operation of the Spirit of God," *De Trinitate* III/4.
94. Cathedral Church of St George, Cape Town, South Africa.

literally. You leave your home in order to come together in one place (Acts 2:1). This coming together as the Body of Christ represents a dimension that transcends the categories of common worship and prayer. The purpose is no less than to fulfill the church's mission of making Christ present, to enter into his joy and to be part of a conversion to another reality. Becoming a temple of the Holy Spirit (1 Cor 6:11; 19–20) for the LORD's glorification is realized only through the mysterious death in the baptismal font, through the anointing of the Holy Spirit. It is known, as Schmemann describes, only in the fullness of the Church, as she gathers to meet the LORD and to share in His risen life.[95]

This leaving and coming is the starting point for living a sacramental life in the world as a follower of Christ—*homo liturgicus*—shaped by doxological praise. As Christ's incarnational presence in the world, the church is given the mandate to participate in culture without partaking in its sins. According to an American Pentecostal thinker with roots in Eastern Europe, Daniela C. Augustine, the church is sent into the world in the power of the Spirit as a countercultural reality of the Kingdom.[96] In the life of the church, culture becomes liturgy. God's divine presence transforms the human project and makes them means of grace as a redemptive pedagogy:

> Thus, art, architecture, poetry, music, rhetoric as 'a second creation' that has found its origin and inspiration in the 'supreme art' and divine creativity (as described in the book of Genesis) participates in the recreation of the world into the Kingdom of God. (. . .) The church of Pentecost, herself a sacrament 'for the life of the world' (John 6:51), living in the 'ancient future' between the first and the second *parousia* of the Lamb, embodies, mediates, articulates, and enacts this process of cosmic renewal in her liturgical life. (. . .) The sacramental life of the church continually brings culture face to face with its need of cleansing and consecration.[97]

Drawing on these insights, the *epiclesis* within the liturgy is considered as the unique location for God's tangible healing presence. The life of the Spirit-driven church is God's sacrament to the world. Within the tradition of the Eastern Church, it is the Holy Spirit who manifests the bread and wine as the body and blood of Christ. The transformation of the elements is performed not by the words of institution but through them by the invocation of the Holy Spirit in the *epiclesis*. It is because of the presence of the

---

95. Schmemann, *Sacraments and Orthodoxy*, 28.
96. Augustine, *Pentecost, Hospitality, and Transfiguration*, 130.
97. Ibid., 130–31.

Spirit that the elements can be perceived as giving communion with Christ. The same Spirit transforms the Church to be the body of Christ and makes the consecration real. Then the time comes to return into the world.

A Pneumatological Celebration

The LORD's Supper is the celebration in which the Christians gathered around his table receive the body and blood of Christ. As worship, it glorifies the Father for everything accomplished in creation, redemption and sanctification. As a memorial, it remembers the death and resurrection of Christ Jesus and what was accomplished once for all on the cross. Pneumatological, it invokes the Holy Spirit to bless the elements and the participants. The sacramental rites thus express both the institutional and charismatic aspects of the Church. They are visible, effective actions instituted by Christ and made effective by the action of the Holy Spirit, who equips those receiving the sacraments with a variety of gifts for the edification of the Church and for her being and ministry in a secular society.[98] The Eucharist shapes our identity as Christians and defines who we are as the church.

While old church traditions hold that the Eucharist mediates the salvific grace of God, in other traditions the sacraments are only ordinances, symbolic activities performed in obedience to the memorial command of Christ. Still, there are discussions of how a spiritual and more realistic view of the Eucharist may be understood in light of different biblical passages. To a large degree, the notion of transubstantiation is based upon an Aristotelian distinction between substance and accidents. Through the consecrated act the elements are thought to bring about a transformation into the body and blood of Christ, while they at the same time retain their accidental texture. Among Catholics, the Eucharist celebration is the constitutive aspect of the church and the burning core of the Mass.

The most contested point of this celebration, seen from other traditions, is that the idea of the transubstantiated presence of Christ in the elements implies that his salvific sacrifice becomes repeated at each enactment of the Eucharist.[99] For the Reformers, the real presence of God accompa-

---

98. World Council of Churches, "The Church," §42. The same reflection applies when it comes to the gift of authority in the ministry of the church. The authority which Jesus Christ, the one head of the Church, shares with those in ministries of leadership is neither only personal nor only delegated by the community. Authority is a gift of the Holy Spirit destined for the service (*diakonia*) of the Church in love, and its exercise includes the participation of the whole community. Ibid., §51. Implied in this perspective is the issue of decision-making in the Church. It seeks and elicits the consensus of all and depends upon the guidance of the Holy Spirit, discerned by attentively listening to God's Word and to one another.

99. Yong, *Renewing Christian Thology*, 141.

nied the elements not because of a process of transubstantiation but because of the proclamation of the gospel and the pronunciation of "this is" (Matt 26:26; cf. 1 Cor 11:24-25). However, Zwingli developed his view because of his understanding of the more memorial aspect of Christ's presence (Luke 22:19).[100] The understanding of a symbolic presence has been balanced by a *via media* (Calvinist) position, seeing the Eucharist as a real—though spiritual—presence of Christ invoked through the Holy Spirit.[101] This is a more pneumatological oriented notion of the presence and reception of the Holy Spirit which is related to the history of Christian initiation, to the Orthodox invocation of the Spirit in the *epiclesis* and to the understanding of the spiritual presence of God within contemporary Pentecostal liturgy.[102]

Across the spectrum of Christian churches, there seems to be a growing agreement of the efficiency of the sacraments given certain preconditions. Pentecostalist Amos Yong brings to the table a significant reflection on the relationship between the notion of the sacrament and the efficacy of intercession. If divine grace can be given and received sacramentally, might it also be possible that a sacramental theology can illuminate a spiritual dimension of the material world, including the workings of spiritual forces that are malign rather than salvific?[103] Yong sets forth that there are reasons to hold to a pneumatologically oriented sacramentality, not only to clarify the way God saves people through the work of Christ in the power of the Spirit, but also to describe how salvation involves deliverance from the destructive powers of human life. The time has come for moving beyond the old debates about sacramentality that depend on dualistic categories of nature and grace. Rather, the sacraments can be understood as interpersonal

---

100. Zwingli claimed that by the Lord's Supper we are showing our mindfulness of Christ's victory and the fact that we are members of his church. We "give proof that we trust in the death of Christ, glad and thankful to be in the company which gives thanks to the Lord for the blessing of redemption which he freely gave us by dying for us." Zwingli, *True and False Religion*, 184.

101. Calvin stated that the Lord offers us mercy and the pledge of his grace in his sacred Word and in his sacraments while also acknowledging that these presuppose faith. However, the efficacy of the Word is brought to light in the sacrament, not because it is spoken, but because it is believed. Further, the power to act rests with the Spirit: "The sacraments properly fulfill their office only when the Spirit (. . .) comes to them, by whose power alone hearts are penetrated and affections moved and our souls opened for the sacraments to enter in. If the Spirit is lacking, the sacraments can accomplish nothing more in our minds than the splendor of the sun shining upon blind eyes, or a voice sounding in the deaf ears." Calvin, *Institutes*, 1277-303.

102. For the Orthodox approach, see Schmemann, *Eucharist*.

103. Yong, *Renewing Christian Theology*, 147.

practices through which the Spirit is at work in a redemptive way, thus becoming windows into the solidarity of ecclesial life.[104]

Furthermore, an ecumenical understanding of the sacraments may lead to the notion that they indeed are holy practices, bearing a christological and pneumatological weight because of their relational and semiotic essence through which divine grace is communicated to undeserving humans. They represent a redemptive encounter by which God reveals Godself through the saving actions of Christ. As pneumatically infused enactments, the gracious effect is always connected to the proclaimed word in an ecclesial environment of faith and hope. Presupposing their ability to communicate the gospel and to portray Christ as crucified (Gal 3:1), these holy practices are iconic signs of the church as the body of Christ in the world. Only the Spirit can make them efficacious. In this regard, I fully agree with the position of Yong that participation in holy practices shapes the identity of the church and thus has social ramifications on Christian confession. They illuminate the missional dimension of the church, and they function as signs of the presence of the Spirit and of the coming reign of the kingdom of God.[105]

In other words, a pneumatological theology of the liturgy focuses on the working of the Spirit during the LORD's Supper. The invocation of the Spirit is fused together with the church's memory of Christ. Together these two aspects of the meal recollect the historical remembering of Jesus and make real the presence of Christ. The congregation becomes the living body of Christ. According to Yong, the transforming of a worshipping community shaped by God's graceful presence has five dimensions. Firstly, the physical act wherein the word of God is consumed by the body of Christ through the working of the Spirit.[106] Secondly, the mysterious presence of Christ, implying that we are mutually present to Christ in an interpersonal encounter. Thirdly, the social act of solidarity, which makes the church open to the world and forms a renewed and reconciled relationship between the

---

104. Yong refers to the gospel of John and to the centrality of the incarnational motif throughout this gospel. The Johannine logic of sacramentality invites us to reflect on the incarnation logic and the touchability of the Word made flesh (John 1), the connection between water and Spirit when talking about the kingdom of God (John 3,4 and 7), and the link between the material nourishment of eating and the spiritual reception of eternal life (John 6). The Johannine incarnational theology presupposes both a christocentric and pneumatologically mediated sacramentality. Ibid., 151–52.

105. Ibid., 159.

106. Yong, *The Spirit Poured Out on All Flesh*, 163–66. In some traditions, like Pentecostalism, this internalization of the body and blood is said to release healing by virtue of Christ's wounds (cf. 1 Pet 2:24; Matt 8:17), in line with the use of other material elements, such as anointing and the laying on of hands. See the presentation in Alexander, *Pentecostal Healing*.

members of the community (1 Cor 11:28; cf. Matt 5:23-24). Fourthly, the political and prophetic act, which provides an alternative way of liberated life in terms of being a public body that transgresses class, gender, ethnic and national boundaries. These members are caught up in a narrative through which the future is imagined in the present. Fifthly, the act of eschatological anticipation gives the church a proleptic vision of the days to come.

The Transcendent Potential of the Graceful Gifts

The sacraments as gifts are not only means of grace, ordinances or whatever terms you may prefer to use. They are tied to a specific way to organize religious words and images with respect to how people experience their social lives. According to the former Archbishop of Canterbury, Rowan Williams, the Christian life describes itself in ways other than what is common in secular or functional arenas. Sacramental living outlines the transition from one reality to another by specific signs and by the means of grace.[107] This is based on some substantial observations: firstly, a pre-sacramental condition implying that we live in a state of loss and need, and secondly, a calling to transcend our own limitations and move towards a state that provides us with another identity shaped by rites instead of rational categories and pure doctrines. Theologically, the sacraments recapitulate aspects of the Easter event. The ritual of baptism is in its structure and nature a reminder of our dependence on God's grace, a demonstration of the work of God in Christ and the incorporation of the church into the kingdom of God. Its ambitious goal is to tie those who become baptized to a coming life of discipleship and faith. Thus the sacraments are acts of gifts, transformative actions indicating that a new belonging is realized.

When this transition takes place, the presence and the power of the sacred is believed to be at work. We are turned in a certain direction, first to God and then to the recognition of our own limitations. We are facing a situation that we cannot negotiate, for the most important decision has already been taken by God on behalf of us and our destiny. Furthermore, the material elements of bread and wine connect the Christian faith to creation theology and to salvation history. By expressing himself as bread and wine, he announces his death by identifying himself as a thing to be broken and consumed. Thus, the new covenant in his blood (Luke 22:20) is a guarantee of hospitality. The Other is the subject of love and trust. It says something important about what should characterize the religious community in a post-Christian era.

---

107. Williams, *On Christian Theology*, 209-21.

Constructive Reflections

In a deep sense, no one can belong to Christ without at the same time being a part of the body of Christ: the church. What we may refer to as a sacramental presence is conditioned by the pronouncement of the gospel. The ascension of Christ demarcates a special period of redemptive history in which Christ is bodily absent and yet present by his Spirit. He is neither totally absent nor totally present but rather present eucharistically and pneumatologically by virtue of his dynamic trinitarian omnipresence. We are given some graceful gifts as a foretaste of the aeon to come. The use of the elements of the sacraments for their sacramental purpose is a form of material movement in which stuff becomes more than just particles and atoms. They are part of the believer's life story in an exalted way. Like worship, the means of grace are infused in an action of art and aesthetics.

Since Pentecost, all liturgies of the sacraments involve invocation and the sealing of the Holy Spirit before, during, or after the officiating. To answer the question of whether a sacrament is an effective sign or just a symbol is not plausible without considering the underlying presupposition that those who partake need to receive by faith that which the elements signify. The sacraments are bestowed by the gracious gift of the Holy Spirit, and they are based upon Christ's mighty acts of salvation. The church is a people of memory and receiving, gathered in response to the call of worship and preserved by sustainable traditions. She is a people of expectation and of eschatological hope, looking forward to the coming of God's reign. As a eucharistic community, the church transcends all social and racial boundaries. Thus, the charismatic and sacramental character of the church is obvious.

However, although every sacrament is a rite, the rite becomes a sacrament only by virtue of the accompanying Word and by the invocation and blessing of the Spirit. Water baptism and Spirit baptism appear as distinct entities, yet the gift of the Spirit remains as the nerve-centre of the initiation process and thereby a primary element of the church's identity. Early Christianity did not adjust itself in accordance with a cultic act but in accordance with the act of God revealed in the giving of the Spirit. Baptism is a means of grace used by God to appropriate to humans the result of Christ's redemptive work.

Consequently, the divine action does not exclude but rather presupposes the individual's personal response through repentance and faith. That is why baptism can be described as a confession of faith and the gateway into the church. Through baptism with water in the name of the Father, the Son and the Holy Spirit, Christians are united with Christ and with each other in the church, across time and place. Baptism is the introduction to and celebration of new life in Christ and of our participation in his life, death and resurrection. Baptismal regeneration must be rejected if it is understood to refer to a magical ability of the water to wash away sins. But it can be accepted if regeneration is understood pneumatically and mystically as an action of the Spirit that includes the faith response of believers presupposed in New Testament writings and practices.

The eucharistic table before the face of God constitutes a liturgical practice that reminds participants of the connection between food and fellowship. It has a clear social dimension and functions as a disciplining catalyst for reconciliation on the horizontal level. The Eucharist teaches the Spirit-driven church to embody her purpose: being a reconciled community in which forgiveness is a practical outcome of the partaking of the meal. The sacramental rites express both the institutional and charismatic aspects of the church. They are visible, effective actions instituted by Christ. The Holy Spirit equips those who receive the sacraments with a variety of gifts. An ecumenical understanding of the sacraments sees them as holy practices which bear a christological and pneumatological weight because of their relational essence, through which divine grace is communicated to undeserving humans.

An observation regarding the profile of some postmodern megachurches today is that many of them seem to downplay sacramental and charismatic elements in their public services because of the efforts to appear fashionable and streamlined. The question is to what extent the search for relevance and "feelgood emotions" affect the sustainability of church life in the long term. The church is not a performer of a program but a perfumer of God's presence. That is why the service needs to live close to those elements that facilitate the gifts of salvation in an audible, visible and incontestable manner.

The next chapter focuses on attitudes and virtues concurrent with being a community with a pronounced pneumatological and sacramental profile. Inspired by the notion of God as the supreme giver and sustainer of life, church practices become an act of hospitality, of giving and receiving in the tone of inclusiveness. This involves an appeal to open the Lord's Table. Being a Christian is to be welcomed home in every sense of that word.

9

The Church Spells Relations

> *Rejoice in hope, be patient in suffering, persevere in prayer. Contribute to the needs of the saints; extend hospitality to stangers.*[1]

Introduction

CHURCH IS FRIENDSHIP. A Spirit-driven community is a fellowship of grace and hospitality. The call is clear for all churches to abandon self-righteousness and elitism and to be radically welcoming as Christ was. A precondition for this is sustainable spirituality and social involvement, combined with a compassionate sensitivity to human vulnerability. My claim is that a church, open for charismatic expressions and conscious of her sacramental foundation, will achieve mature congregational virtues characterized by gracious relations.[2]

Inspired by the notion of God as the supreme giver and sustainer of life, church practices are an act of hospitality and friendship, of giving and receiving gifts in an environment of kindness and generosity. In this chapter, I am searching for the relationship between a pronounced, pneumatologically profiled community and a church inspired by virtues consistent with an inclusive theology of hospitality. Church practices are an act of giving and receiving graceful gifts, infused by the fruit of the Spirit, among which *love* is the most prominent (Gal 5:22–25). Moltmann states that of the many names for the Holy Spirit, the Comforter is the one he prefers.[3] By

---

1. Rom 12:12–13.

2. According to Heb 13:1–2, the believing fellowship shall "keep on loving one another as brothers and sisters." They must "not forget to show hospitality to strangers, for by so doing some people have shown hospitality to angels without knowing it" (cf. 1 Pet 4:9; 1 Tim 5:10).

3. Moltmann, *Source of Life*, 10.

the Spirit, the Triune God and the believing community are united in the pulsating relation of love that is God. This is supposed to be reflected in the world by the church. For many, the way into the church is marked by hospitality (Rom 16:23). Shared table fellowship is an expression of graceful relationships and friendships, presupposed to exist without an expectation that the favor will be returned.

The metaphor of table fellowship is interpreted by some as an inclusive reading of liberation theology's axiom, "option for the poor." But for others, the notion of hospitality is entangled with the hidden language of hierarchy, imperialism, exclusivism and even violence. The problem of the expectation of different kinds of reciprocity can only be solved by unconditional hospitality. The temptation to suppress the otherness of the other must be balanced by an encounter with the other that puts us under the obligation to provide hospitality that is without limit. This unique understanding of hospitality presupposes no invitation, only a surprise of the coming of the guest.

However, no conditions exist such that a purely equal exchange can happen. Veli-Matti Kärkkäinen uses the term gracing relationship as an alternative formulation.[4] According to Jan-Olav Henriksen, a gracing relationship is characterized by virtues where "both parties are recognized by each other as someone not determined by the conditions of one's own horizon, but rather as an Other (. . .) Hence, in such a relationship one is invited into the world of the other by means of an open invitation."[5]

Gracing relationship and cheerful inclusiveness have the theology of love as their fountain and expose that there are many ways to Christ. In its concrete version, love is the ultimate expression of Pentecost and of cross-marked power (Rom 5:5; 2 Cor 13:4). The church's charismatic or missionary nature requires that the empowerment needs the distillation of love to be grasped in an appropriate way. Churches without a comprehensive diaconal heart are in danger of being ignored by the wider society because of their apparent lack of confidence. In the teaching of Paul to the "charismaniac" church of Corinth, he concludes that the charismatic elements and different utterances must be baptized into the doctrine of love, as he so tastefully describes in the chapter of love (1 Cor 13). For him, power is made perfect in weakness. There the strength of the church is hidden (2 Cor 12:9-10). From an ecclesiological point of view, Christian belief is relational in its nature.

---

4. Kärkkäinen, *Christ and Reconciliation*, 1, 31-32. To Letty M. Russell, hospitality does not impose the life style of the host, but creates a safe and welcoming space for persons to find their own sense of humanity and worth. Russell, *Church in the Round*, 173.

5. Henriksen, *Desire, Gift, and Recognition*, 44-45.

An essential observation is that knowledge, in this context, is relationally oriented (1 Cor 1:9).

Theology, too, is more than an exchange of theory-shaped information. The whole redemptive story, from Genesis onward, is a story of the restoration of a broken relationship. Thus, it is crucial for the well-being of the church that she find her identity as a fellowship of reconciled community life, with her members acting as agents of genuine healing for a broken yet still God-designed creation.[6] In this perspective, hospitality can be regarded as a dramatic enactment of the experience of reconciliation.

A Cross-marked Power

At the heart of the symbolic world of Christianity, there is a cross (1 Cor 1:23–24). Our understanding of the means by which the Spirit works must be distinguished from the source and effect of other kinds of power, which leads us to a paradoxical relationship between power, weakness and vulnerability (1 Cor 2:2–5). The Anglican Communion holds that Christ's raising from the dead is of the same order as the transformation of the disciples, through the Spirit, from a defeated rabble into a dynamic and centrally bounded group of witnesses speaking with authority.[7] It may sound strange, but surrender to the reality of human weakness is the only condition for receiving the Spirit.[8]

Within the writings of Paul, we find his standard for the corporate life of the local congregation and a re-evaluation of the prevailing concept of power (1 Cor 12–14). The ideal and genuine mark of a mature Spirit-oriented church is not self-aggrandizement at the expense of others, but surrender to God through an attitude of gentle and devoted love, reflecting God's creative generosity (Gal 5:22–23). Where else in the world is weakness recognized as being a unique expression of empowerment?

In the kingdom of God it has to be so, because the power of the Spirit is consistently associated with forgiveness, redemption and restoration (Acts 2:38–39, cf. Rom 4:7; Col 1:4). Repentance and baptism are referred to as the primary means by which forgiveness of sins and incorporation into the community of God are promised through the Spirit. The message of God's love for lost human subjects, which defines every being as infinitely precious because of eternal love, was unheard of in pre-Christian antiquity.

---

6. Shaw, "A Welcome Guest," 17.

7. Doctrine Commission of Church of England, *We Believe in the Holy Spirit*, 97.

8. Henri J. M. Nouwen writes that a Christian community is a healing community, not because wounds are cured and pains are alleviated, but because they may be transformed from expression of despair to signs of hope. Nouwen, *Wounded healers*, 93–94.

But it became the Christian root of modern human rights.[9] However, the love of God clearly transcends the level of the individual and seeks to unite others with the new fellowship of God's coming kingdom. Individual self-seeking stands against what might be an achievable metric for measuring the advancement of common good. According to Paul, the only thing that counts is faith; expressed as love (Gal 5:6). The church with a humble and vulnerable identity is reflected in a prayer of Søren Kierkegaard:

> *It is in a fragile vase of clay that we men carry the holy one,*
> *but you, O Holy Spirit, when you dwell in a man,*
> *you dwell in what is infinitely inferior—*
> *you, Spirit of holiness, dwell in impurity and dirt,*
> *you, Spirit of wisdom, dwell in foolishness,*
> *you, Spirit of truth, dwell in deceit!*
> *Oh, dwell in me forever!*
> *O you, who do not look for the comfort of a desirable residence,*
> *something that you would certainly look for in vain,*
> *you, who create and regenerate*
> *and make your dwelling place for yourself*
> *dwell in me forever!*
> *Dwell in me forever, so that you will,*
> *one day, end by being pleased with that dwelling place*
> *that you have prepared for yourself in the impurity,*
> *wickedness and deceitfulness of my heart!*[10]

The far-reaching consensus of seeing the life of the church as a reflection of the love of the Triune God (1 John 4:8)[11] is that the mission of the church is to be a constructive response to God's urging love, shown in creation and redemption and communicated within an atmosphere of love and humility. Doing church is synonymous with sharing the love of God through a compelling ministry of reconciliation. Committed of the message of reconciliation, we become Christ's ambassadors to share this massage on behalf of the LORD of the church (2 Cor 5:14; 18–21).[12]

9. Pannenberg, *Systematic Theology*, vol 3, 180.

10. Based on a French translation of Kierkegaard in Sr. Geneviève, *Le trésor de la prière à travers le tempts*, 119, as cited in Congar, *I Believe in the Holy Spirit*, 150.

11. World Council of Churches, "Together Towards Life," §55.

12. See Jeanrond, *Theology of Love*. In a section of his book, called The Church as Institution of Love, Jeanrond states that the church is characterized primarily by its response to God's gift of love in creation, in Jesus Christ and in the Holy Spirit. In the situation of broken relationships the community of Christians is called to establish

This love of God, manifested by the fruit of the Spirit, is an inspirational gift to all humanity. The commandments to love God and neighbor (Matt 22:37–39) in an attitude of kindness, receptiveness, and generosity are the protective *telos* of life, an invitation to pursue human good.[13] The WCC document, "Together Towards Life" declares that the church, by the Spirit, participates in the mission of love that is at the heart of the life of the Trinity:

> This result is a Christian witness which unceasingly proclaims the salvific power of God through Jesus Christ and constantly affirms God's dynamic involvement through the Holy Spirit, in the whole created world. All who respond to the outpouring of the love of God are invited to join in with the Spirit in the mission of God.[14]

In this sense, the distinctiveness of the Spirit lies precisely in his apparent lack of distinctive substantiality. According to Anselm K. Min, the Spirit is wholly relational and is the divine source of all relations, communions, and solidarities. A world marked by divisions and hostilities is in special need of the Holy Spirit as the spirit of fellowship and solidarity. Min seems to sense a strong yearning for the return of the Spirit of fellowship to turn the individual's helplessness and loneliness into love to the stranger, and suspicion into solidarity and trust. To empower human beings to live with dignity and care shapes a theological understanding of the role of the Spirit, who never calls attention to himself but brings together diverse parties into communion and fellowship (John 15:26; 16: 13–14).[15] As the Spirit proceeds from the Father and the Son as mutual love, the function of the Spirit is to create, inspire and liberate finite beings for solidarity and communion with God and with one another. The personhood of the Spirit lies in the activity of relating, comforting and reconciling (2 Cor 1:3–7).[16]

Thus, the Spirit of God encompasses the members of the church in an act of ever-giving grace, particularly to those who are wounded by injustice and poverty, as an expression of our reconciled relationship with all created life.[17] Acts of reconciliation are the fruit of charismatic gifts, especially the gift of discerning spirits (1 Cor 12:10). The church discerns the Spirit of God "wherever life in its fullness is affirmed in its various dimen-

---

God's kingdom through the pluriform praxis of love. Thus, Christian faith is engaged with God's creative and reconciling love project of universal transformation, 215–16.

13. Smith, *Desiring the Kingdom*, 174–75.
14. World Council of Churches, "Together Towards Life," §18.
15. Min, "Solidarity of Others," 417.
16. Ibid., 418.
17. World Council of Churches, "Together Towards Life," §24–25.

sions, including liberation of the oppressed, healing and reconciliation of broken communities" and the restoration of creation through eco-justice. WCC holds that the church even needs to discern evil spirits wherever forces of death and destruction of life prevail in order to bring about God's reign of justice (Acts 1:5-8).

The church's being-in-world-of-creation and participation in mission need to be woven together as an expression of the transformative life of the Spirit.[18] The apostle Paul expresses this by encouraging the church to bear the fruit of the Spirit, which entail love, joy, peace, patience, kindness, generosity, faithfulness and self-control (Gal. 5:22-23). While bearing these fruits, others may discern the love and power of the Spirit at work both inside and outside the boundaries of the church.[19]

Both Judaism and Christianity have the double commandment of love at the burning heart of their life and faith because of their understanding that love is the most substantial aspect of the nature of God (1 John 4:16). Likewise, God's desire for steadfast love rather than for ceremonial sacrifice (Hos 6:6) is a result of God's very nature, pointing back to the love of God for the world (John 3:16; cf. Col 1:13), a love so grand that it surpasses rational insight (Eph 3:19). The very substance of the Spirit's life has love as its most outstanding fruit (Gal 5:23-24), against which there is no law. From an eschatological perspective the victory of divine love will be all-encompassing (Rom 8:38-39). Because the Spirit is the Spirit of love, we stand face to face with the realities of God (1 Cor 13:12). However, this sanctifying love subdues the temptation to see the Spirit as a means to internally focus religious ecstasy. A love-shaped spirituality looks in the direction of the Other. As such, love as an outpouring of divine compassion seems to be the essence of Spirit baptism (Eph 4:2-4).[20]

According to Macchia, where love is lacking, theological constructions become fragmented abstractions and Christianity may end up as a system in which religious rites becomes goals for their own sake. We could not be certain whether the kingdom of God was a liberating or dominating reign.[21] By aligning ourselves with the Scripture's account, we may ascertain that love is an event, rather than a theoretical description, of God. All that is given through the salvation story is present in God's love and is received as a gift of the Spirit. Michael Welker holds that the presence of the Holy Spirit becomes recognizable from the perspective of Christ's selflessness

---

18. Ibid., §21.
19. Ibid., §28.
20. Macchia, *Baptized in the Spirit*, 258.
21. Ibid., 260.

and suffering. In contrast to an abstract-theistic and metaphysical approach, presenting the Spirit as the Spirit of Christ is both a capacity and a power that persistently works to the universal establishing of justice, mercy and knowledge of God. These take the shape of reciprocal interconnections that grant authority to persons who are publicly powerless and despised. At the same time, this presentation extends beyond imperialistic monocultures and makes possible a prophetic community of the testimony of women and men, old and young, powerful and oppressed.[22] Thus, there is a sense of the multipresence of the Spirit, in which the faith community is assumed to be the physical-finite and fleshly-earthly place of the presence of Christ in the midst of the world's cultural settings. This points to the notion of the Spirit as comfort itself, which in turn points to the common sharing of the Spirit and to the gifts of tenderness and compassion, which all of people united with Christ experience (Phlm 2:1–3; cf. Mark 13:11).

But for Welker, love is the most complete form of expression and communication in accordance with the Spirit. As a fruit of the Spirit, love tolerates no division into hostile camps and vilification of the other along racist, sexist, and other lines.[23] At the same time, love appears to be something that is continually endangered and vulnerable. Nevertheless, as a result of the Spirit's graceful operating, love works toward a more comprehensive righteousness, a more sensitive justice and a more effective practice of mercy (Rom 13:10).

Pentecost, the Welcoming of All

Is it possible to integrate a hospitable embrace of others into the Pentecost narrative? Does a charismatic profile stand in the way of the more inclusive virtues? Daniela C. Augustine holds that the event of Pentecost serves as contextual origin, dialogical anchor, and continual source of inspiration and challenge within Pentecostal theological reflection.[24] The event on the Day of Pentecost established and identified the church's demarcations as a charismatic *koinonia*. We talk of no less than the body of Christ, transformed by the Word and empowered by the Spirit as the teleological creation of

22. Welker, *God the Spirit*, 220.
23. Ibid., 250.
24. Rooted in Eastern European Pentecostalism, Daniela C. Augustine focuses on the work of the Trinity in her balanced presentation of a Pentecostal ecclesiology. She contends that the confession of Christ as Spirit-Baptizer and the corresponding pneumatic-sacramental practices following the encounter of the Spirit, are among the focal points of Pentecostal theology and spirituality. Augustine, "The Empowered Church," 156–80.

the Triune God. The chief mark of the church, outlined in the Pentecost narrative as the unity of the newborn fellowship, is to embrace the other in their ethnic, socio-economic and gender diversity (Acts 2:17–18). A flame from God was distributed upon each of them and became a visible sign of the Spirit's divine presence and a faith community was constituted. The catholicity of Pentecost revealed a radical hospitality, expressed in loving and welcoming all nations into the life of the Trinity.[25]

In the church, the embodiment of the coming age, human history meets an eschatological unfolding. By the transfiguration of the Spirit, the church becomes a sacred but open place, where history is faced with its own future in a proleptic sense. Humanity is invited by the Trinity to partake in the divine communal life and to be transfigured into their likeness (cf. 2 Pet 1:4). According to Augustine, by being a living extension and continuation of the risen LORD in this world, the church has an extroverted orientation in line with the mission of Christ, which is directed outward from the self to the other.

The Pentecost event urges the church to cross the bridge from the private to the public and become a distinct factor of social change (Acts 2:44–47; 4:32–35). In this way the church becomes incarnational, not just a mediator of Christ but an incarnation of his presence and power. The church transitions from reflection and prayer to interaction and transformation, with the Spirit as agent, engine and navigator.[26] In the Pentecost narrative, the voice of the community gave a call to moral responsibility and discernment. Illuminated by the Spirit, they came to know the other in such a way that human dignity and wholeness were restored (Acts 2:42–47; 5:12–16). Augustine writes:

> The descending of the Holy Spirit upon the hundred-and-twenty on the Day of Pentecost is a public statement from the Father to His children of love and affirmation. They are indeed the sons and daughters of God and are, therefore, the recipients of the promise of the Father (Acts 2:39). This is the long anticipated eschatological unveiling of the identity of those who in their corporate existence as the Body of Christ on earth become the instruments of God's justice, healing, and restoration not only to human society but also to all the rest of creation. Through them the consequences of the life of God, in-fleshed in the community of faith, are translated to the rest of the created cosmos.[27]

The redemptive eschatological union with God is experienced in the community of faith through its worship, liturgical practices and anticipation of

---

25. Ibid., 159.
26. Ibid., 163.
27. Ibid., 165.

the concrete and transformative presence of the Spirit. Through the body of Christ heaven descends on earth, and the liturgical celebration gives a foretaste of life in the coming age. From Augustine's point of view, the event of Pentecost presents a vision of the radical, self-giving hospitality present in the community of believers.[28] God welcomes all nations to the Godhead's banquet, and the invitation of God's Word resounds in every ethnic tongue (Acts 2:5–6).

Rightly understood, glossolalia on the Day of Pentecost was an embracing of the language of the Other. As a gift of hospitality, Pentecost is a reminder to include and embrace the language and speech-acts of the other. The fact that God's Word filled the word of the nations with the story of the LORD expresses the church's great missional focus (v. 11). By establishing these conditions for inclusive conversation, the Spirit of Christ welcomes all foreigners on their own terms.[29] Pentecost offers a paradigmatic vision of both the incarnation of God's self-giving hospitality in the community of believers and the outpouring of the Spirit manifested in God's self-sharing with every nation under heaven (Acts 2: 1–6).[30]

The Spirit-saturated church is the embodied experience of the mutual indwelling of heaven and earth. It offers foretaste of the ultimate destiny, when God may be all in all and no barrier of language will separate us (1 Cor 15:28). In the meantime, glossolalia has a sacramental function in the life of that church as a prophetic narrative sign and an eschatological symbol, by which the community may experience the living presence of God in ways that transcend human logic and rationality. It articulates the mystery of the union with Christ and celebrates the experience of God's in-breaking presence. As part of sacramental practice, glossolalia mediates to us the power of the invisible grace that transforms us into a visible extension of Christ on earth.[31]

As such, speaking in tongues can be interpreted as an expression of an eschatological language, signifying the expansive reality of the church under the reign of the coming kingdom of God. The empowered church and prophesying community of faith are embodiments of the future of the world. The church enters the present from the future such that the future

---

28. Ibid., 172.

29. Augustine understands the speech miracle on the Day of Pentecost in two ways: first, as the expression of the differentiation of the ethnic groups which pays attention to their own singularities and diversity. And second, as an affirmation of each separate ethnic identity present in the multiplicity of languages expressed. Ibid.

30. Augustine, *Pentecost, Hospitality, and Transfiguration*, 65.

31. Augustine, "The Empowered Church," 178.

permeates the present as a proleptic vision of the coming of the Kingdom. Or, as Augustine says, the church becomes a living gospel for a needy world.[32]

Mirroring a Hospitable God

Through the coming of the Spirit on the Day of Pentecost, a new kind of community empowerment was made possible. The changed social structure of the church had its own theological justification: the Spirit came upon the entire people. The Spirit no longer privileged a select group of individual prophets (Joel 2:28-29). Rather, the Spirit eliminated social differences and barriers (Acts 2:17-18). This action mirrored the ideals of Jesus. He established and reconciled relations, especially among those who were denied community. He refused to take part in religious-social exclusion, classism and discrimination. According to the New Testament, Jesus associated with rich and poor (Luke 19:1-10; 6:20), educated and uneducated (Luke 14:1-6; Matt 11:25-26), rural and urban (Mark 1:14; Matt 23:37), healthy and sick (Matt 4:23), and righteous and sinful (Luke 16:15; 19:10). He took the side of the poor (Luke 7:22), the hungry, the thirsty, the stranger, the needy, the imprisoned (Matt 25: 31-46), the marginalized, tax collectors (Matt 11:19), prostitutes (Matt 21:31-32), and women and children (Luke 10:25-37; Matt 5:31-32; Mark 10:13-16). In God's kingdom, no one is disqualified; all are recipients, standing on their own feet.

The disciples pursued his ethical and social ideals after Easter, manifesting the togetherness of Jew and Gentile, slave and free, man and woman (Gal 3:28). The reciprocal pronoun "one another/each other" appears as an important part of early Christian vocabulary, especially in the authentic letters of Paul and those letters standing in the Pauline tradition.[33]

Another aspect became evident: the building up of the church happens in conjunction with the responsibility every person in the community has for one another (cf. 1 Cor 14:26). [34] Paul insisted on a liturgical strategy structured in such a way that it edified the whole community. The utterance of charismatic gifts was met by an obvious requirement: an intelligible translation out of consideration for those outside the believing community (1 Cor 14:13-25).

---

32. Ibid., 180.

33. Examples of such passages is Rom 12:10, 16; 15:7; 16:16; 1 Cor 11:33; 12:25; Gal 5:13; 6:2; 1 Thess 5:11, 13, 15; Eph 4:2, 32; 5:21; Col 3:13; James 5:16; 1 Pet 1:22; 4:9; 5:5; 1 John 1:7.

34. That seems to be the main reason why prophetic speech was preferred to speaking in tongues. The first builds up the church while the latter only builds up the individual (1 Cor 14:2-4). Lohfink, *Jesus and Community*, 103.

The eschatological outpouring of the Spirit gave them a distinct feeling of being children of God (Rom 8:14–16; Gal 4:5–7). As God's beloved sons and daughters, they became brothers and sister to one another. Brotherly love was thus a distinctive feature of the new fellowship after Pentecost, realized in the frame of the early Christian house churches (Acts 12:12; 1 Cor 16:15; Col 4:15; Phlm 1:2; cf. Matt 23:8). The self-sacrificing hospitality of the hosts made these open homes into centers of community life, even as they supported those who were travelling with the gospel (2 Cor 8:23–24).[35]

Other biblical sources (like Philemon) make clear the freshness, sincerity, and goodness which flourished wherever people experienced the new reality of sisterly and brotherly community. The new reality of the early church was marked by fraternal, mutual friendship and love (Gal 5:14, Rom 13:8–10). Drawing upon these insights, Lohfink contends that the early church became a divine contrast-society, not because of any self-acquired holiness, cramped efforts or moral achievements, but because of the saving deed of God, who justifies the godless, accepts failures and reconciles himself with the guilty. Only in this gift of reconciliation, in the miracle of the life newly won against all expectation, can the church justify being called an alternative community, open for everyone.[36] Being aliens in the world (1 Pet 2:11), Christians are perpetually guests and thus need to receive hospitality, even when playing the host. A Christian is a servant of all (Matt 23:11), combining the countercultural oppositions inherent in the gospel with hospitable openness (cf. Jer 29:7).

Some basic features of a pneumatological theology of being guest and host are given by Amos Yong. First, for Christians, Christ operates as the exemplary guest who went into the far country and became the model for a church, which is both *ecclesia* (called out from the world) and *koinonia* (inclusive while at work in a strange land). Second, the outpouring of the Spirit signifies and enables the continued reenactment of the meal-fellowship of Jesus through the church (2 Cor 9:6–11). Third, the practice of hospitality embodies the trinitarian character of God: "What is being given and what is being received is not any "thing" but the Triune God, manifested in the body of Christ and animated by the power of the Spirit."[37] Fourth, through this power we are obligated to discern the Spirit's presence and activity when evaluating which practices are most appropriate to represent the hospitable God. Which tongues we speak and what practices

---

35. *Didache* (11.8) remarks that not everyone who speaks in a spirit is a prophet, but only those with the behavior of the Lord or the Lord's manner of life. Niederwimmer and Attridge, *The Didache*.

36. Lohfink, *Jesus and Community*, 147.

37. Yong, *Hospitality*, 124–27.

we engage in depend on where we are, with whom we interact and in which context we find ourselves. The church is to participate in the redemptive hospitality of God.

Concurring with Daniela C. Augustine, I contend that the catholicity of Pentecost reveals the radical hospitality of God to welcome all nations under heaven into the life of the Trinity through the Spirit (Acts 2).[38] The empowered and hospitable church is the extension of the resurrected LORD. Through the agency of the Holy Spirit, the sacraments unite her with Christ so that she may be a living sacrament in the world. With the realization that we all share a global household and a responsibility for the world's health and functionality, there is "an escalating sense of urgency that our survival as a human race depends on our ability to transform the multicultural polyphony of the globe into a purposeful dialogue motivated by a cosmopolitan vision of a just future." [39]

Letty M. Russell says that hospitality is an unconditional "solidarity with strangers." She describes hospitality, which corresponds with the fruit of the Spirit like kindness and generosity (Gal 5:22), as the practice of God's welcome by reaching across differences to participate in God's actions bringing justice and healing to our world in crisis.[40] This hospitality is an expression of unity without uniformity. Through it, communities are built up out of difference and not sameness, sharing a divine communal life with the rest of the world without anticipating any transformation of the other into our likeness.[41] If hospitality can be described as a gift of the Spirit and as a kind of charismatic presence of God on earth, incarnated in the community of faith, then it must be a distinctive feature of the church's basic, open identity.

We may compare this to the obligation of the Jewish people in the Law: "You are to love those who are foreigners, for you yourselves were foreigners in Egypt" (Deut 10:19). Abraham's dependence on the hospitality of others prior to the Canaan settlement gives perspective to the many laws given to remind Israel of her responsibility to the aliens and strangers in her midst. Israel is no longer a guest but a host (Ex 22:21; Lev 19:33–34; Deut 15:15). These ideals may also advocate an interreligious dialogue of hospitality. By referring to biblical wisdom material, there seems to be meaningful points of contact between Christians and representatives of other world religions. Common wisdom literature provides a common platform for discussion, interaction, and perhaps evangelism.[42]

---

38. Augustine, *Pentecost, Hospitality, and Transfiguration*, 18.
39. Ibid., 43.
40. Russell, *Just Hospitality*, 19–20.
41. Ibid., 65.
42. Yong, *Hospitality*, 110–13.

According to the Ten Commandments (Ex 20:12–17), God places the other at the centre of both personal and corporate social redemption.[43] Out of love for God and neighbor emerges a vision for covenantal, global community, marked by a spirituality which is incarnated into the fellowship of faith and expressed through a social reality which reflects God's cheerful grace and self-giving sacrifice in Christ (Matt 27:37–40). Augustine claims that "the fruit of the Holy Spirit is revealed within the human *socium* precisely through the prioritization of the other as a beneficiary of the social capital produced in the believer's life by the Spirit's Christo-forming presence."[44] Thus both the work of the Holy Spirit and the effects of the church can be identified as unconditional hospitality.

The church is where God has the position of being the immediate dwelling place of the other as the very environment in which they live and move and have their being (Acts 17:28).[45] This is evident both in the act of creation by the building of a home for the created human (Gen 2:8), in the seventh day of rest (v. 1), and in the incarnation of Christ where matter meets the redemptive embrace of divine hospitality.[46] Luke understood the graceful life and ministry of Jesus, the authorized representative of God's salvific hospitality, as inspired by the Spirit and thus pneumatologically constituted (Luke 4: 18–19, Acts 10:38). Salvation came to those who welcomed Christ: Pharisees, publicans, prostitutes, the poor and oppressed, women, children, and the sick. They could enjoy his hospitality in terms of healing, forgiveness, acceptance, and inclusion (Luke 1:76–79; 19:1–10; John 3, 4, 8 and 9).

Amos Yong points out three aspects of the hospitality of Christ. Firstly, throughout his life, he was a guest of others. As the "journeying prophet," he changed the role of being guest to that of being host, using situations to talk about the eschatological banquet of God (Luke 24:13–35). Secondly, in the various meal scenes, we observe that the recipients of his divine hospitality were not the religious leaders but the poor and oppressed. He even rebuked religious leaders in order to display his inclusiveness (Luke 7:44–47; cf. 14:21). Thirdly, in the parable of the Good Samaritan (Luke 10) Jesus shows that a representative of another religion and another people can embody divine hospitality as well.[47] Both giving and receiving hospitality became manifested in the New Testament churches. The homes became a new sort

---

43. Augustine, *Pentecost, Hospitality, and Transfiguration*, 46.
44. Ibid., 47.
45. Ibid., 54.
46. Ibid., 57.
47. Yong, *Hospitality*, 101–3.

of sacred space, where the reign of God produced the community of grace and the house of God—*Beth-El*.

This was a place for God's dwelling and a sign of the reconciliation of highly different people, men and women, slave and free (Gal 3:26–29).[48] In a quite extraordinary way, the attitude of hospitality was displayed in the life of the Jerusalem church. They had everything in common (Acts 2:44), they were each other's host and guests (v. 46), and they distributed foods to those in need (6:1). The result was astounding. They enjoyed the favor of all people and experienced a tremendous growth (v. 47).

In light of the household relationships and table fellowship displayed by the New Testament churches, and because of their emphasis on justice and divine grace, the church today is called to develop the same inviting attitude of hospitality with unconditional acceptance and divine support. The church is a sanctuary for the other in the world, a body and a home for the alien. When practicing hospitality not out of the position of ownership and privileged status but out of a position of humble stewardship, hospitality emerges as a gift from God. The differences are leveled; host and guest become equal recipients.[49] Paul asks, "For who sees anything different in you? What do you have that you did not receive?" (1 Cor 4:7). With this insight, the church becomes transformed from being a place where anxious social imaginations rule to a welcoming fellowship of confidence and public respect. By the agency of benevolent hospitality, the church grows in maturity, a graceful sign of the Spirit's dignifying power (Gal 5:16–25). It ought to be so, because the church herself is a community of pilgrims.

Unconditional hospitality may be understood in terms of the fruit of the Spirit, described by Paul in his conversation to the churches in Galatia (Gal 5:22–23). These fruits are characterized by their inter-sociality for the well-being of the other. Either they are turned towards society as an overflow of life (love, joy, kindness, goodness and gentleness), or they represent self-giving inward attitudes and Christ-like behaviors which in turn make the world beautiful (forbearance, faithfulness and self-control). The hospitality of faith, hope, and love contain, Augustine asserts, a vision of making the cosmos a household of all, a home where all have a place in the unconditionally loving embrace of the Trinity.[50]

Pointing to the sanctifying work of the Spirit, the church states that the Spirit involves the totality of the human existence with all of its social and material expressions in actions, relationships, and desires.[51] This points to

---

48. Ibid., 105.
49. Pohl, *Making Room*, 106–107.
50. Augustine, *Pentecost, Hospitality, and Transfiguration*, 97.
51. Ibid., 98.

the ever-shifting sets of human interrelations each member of the body of Christ is called to capture as an extension of God's open arms. By the sensitivity and discernment of the Spirit, the church is encouraged to facilitate new arenas for hospitable practices in order to serve as channels for the mercy of God.

Hospitable Virtues

Is it possible to talk about concrete ecclesial practices of a stranger-centered theology of hospitality? First and foremost, this is a question of humble and sensitive attitudes, displayed as congregational and liturgical practices. According to one of my interlocutors, Amos Yong, congregational hospitality involves a welcoming public "face," a dialogical posture and a commitment to public servanthood (i.e., sharing neighborhood meals as an act of friendship and trust). The liturgy too may emphasize God as the host and the church as the minister of public worship, toning down hard lines between insiders and outsiders since all are in need of God's grace.[52] This call includes an open communion table-attitude, which facilitates the invitation of all people to enjoy the hospitality of God in accordance with the Matthean version of the Great Banquet, in which both good and bad are invited (Matt 22:10; cf. Luke 14:21). This evangelistically-shaped hospitality is something the church does in and through worship, liturgy and sacramental practices.[53] An important insight is that truth in which the Christians are guided by the Spirit is not only propositionally or dogmatically formulated but intersubjectively encountered, interpersonally inhabited, and intercommunally adjusted.[54]

Hauerwas and Wells help us to focus on the inspiring reflection that God wants his people to worship him, to be his friends, and to eat with him. The main eschatological image of the gospel is the *banquet*. The picture of the feast declares that God is longing for his people to worship him in a friendship embodied in the sharing of a meal. The Eucharist offers a model of companionship and friendship. Stanley Hauerwas and Samuel Wells emphasize that disciples gather and greet; are reconciled with God and one another; hear and share their common story; offer their needs and resources; remember Jesus and invoke his Spirit; and then share communion, before being sent out.[55] Through worship, performance and repetition, the people

52. Yong, *Hospitality*, 134–35. See also Keifert, *Welcoming the Stranger*.
53. Yong, *Hospitality*, 137.
54. Ibid., 158.
55. Hauerwas and Wells, "Gifs of Church," 13.

of God are given resources to live in his presence. The church offers these actions—these verbs—through which its members can become distinctive nouns: people, disciples and witnesses.

Ethics begins and ends with a firm belief, not in human scarcity, but in divine abundance, expressed by the gifts of salvation which are given to the church through the means of grace. Christian ethics can be regarded as the study of how God, through the church, meets the needs of those who are seeking what may be seen as the purpose of a devoted life, to fulfill all righteousness (Matt 3:13–17). These theologians understand God's gracious action as particularly crystallized in baptism and in the Eucharist. Here the goal of God's creation and redemption comes to fruition, since the goals of Christian ethics are none other than these very same longings and realizations.[56] The kingdom Jesus pointed to and defined expresses the hope for the church. The harmonious relationship and joyful communion seen in the story of Jesus creates the same longing within the hearts of church members.

Research looking at case studies of life strategies in some growing late modern churches in West Europe corroborates these thoughts. The analyzes of Karl Inge Tangen show that close relationships with significant others were important for the six people studied in identifying with their church. Motives of friendship and other relational qualities played a crucial role in the commitment stories of the respondents as well. The fact that the church was a family-like community, with elements of pleasure, mutual enjoyment, practical support and common beliefs, indicated that they were part of a larger mega-story which included God and others. Relational qualities of love, such as hospitality and service, were verified as well. Among the seven descriptions of why individuals identify with certain organizational foci, Tangen holds that the most important aspect was precisely the churches' abilities to offer a sense of community and friendship with family qualities.[57]

So, if Scripture is about heritage, then kingdom is about destiny. The one crowned on the cross is the one enthroned in eternity. Nobody is outside; the downtrodden and abused may look forward to vindication in times to come. The Spirit brings the remembered word of Scripture to life and transforms the anticipated hope of the kingdom into action.[58] Through the life of the Spirit in the community, the gift of Jesus is made present and ever new. Because of the Spirit, words, stories, and ideas become habits, practices and patterns of action. The Spirit shapes the ways in which the

---

56. Ibid., 16.
57. Tangen, *Ecclesial Identification*, 193–95, 312.
58. Hauerwas and Wells, "Gifs of Church," 17.

church reflects the character of God and expresses itself in the surrounding culture and in the church's wider context. That makes the church something more than an assembly that Jesus happens to visit. She is herself an aspect of God's gift in Christ; a gift delivered and shaped by the incarnate, crucified, and risen LORD. She brings people into the company of the faithful because of the liberating force of the gospel story and accompanying transformative practices.

The church's emphasis on baptism contains a message of freedom instead of slavery, light instead of darkness, and life instead of death. For Hauerwas and Wells, baptism leads in the direction of the regular life of the church, the practices of praise and a response to God's love, all of which in turn cultivate listening ears, singing hearts, and serving attitudes. Worship stretches words to their limits and leads the assembly to express gratitude for God's mercy, which has been extended to the most unworthy and unexpected people. Within the intimacy of God's presence and within the regular rhythm of the celebration of the eucharistic meal, a person is formed to witness; restored to relationship, friendship and hospitality; and equipped to love, serve and share. Each celebration looks back to the last and forward to the next; the regularity secures the church's need for time and space to reflect upon her identity.

Following these thinkers, the church is what she does when she does what she is called to be: the community which responds to God's love by accepting the Godhead's invitation to worship, to be his friend and to eat with him.[59] She inherits the promise to Abraham to bless the whole world (Gen 12:3). She is a gift to the world and she does not exist for her own sake.[60]

When going to the New Testament material and the patristic sources, the references to hospitality and friendship relate to a generalized ethical pattern, which is expected to apply universally. However, Christian hospitality in the early church was not limited to functions related to relieving the poor, the widowed, and the persecuted. It operated also in the transmission of the gospel tradition. In the beginning of the church era, people—not documents—spread the good news of Christ. The migration and travelling of Christian families was frequent, according to different passages of the *Didache* and *Hermas*. Travelling messengers would be welcomed when it was attested that they travelled because of the Name (3 John 1:7).[61]

---

59. Riddle, "Early Christian Hospitality," 143. Ibid., 154.

60. In this regard, the church has a role like the disciples during the feeding of the five thousand men (Matt 14:21): to beg people to bring their resources to Christ, to wonder upon his work and to distribute his blessed gifts. Hauerwas and Wells, "Gifs of Church," 21.

61. Riddle, "Early Christian Hospitality," 143.

The house-church profile in the NT churches is an aspect of both early Christian hospitality and of the effectiveness in the landing of the gospel within the whole household. The first sending out of the apostles and others included instruction to take no money and baggage with them (Mark 6:7–11), because those to whom the message was proclaimed were expected to provide functional hospitality. To a certain degree, one may say that hospitality played a role in the making of the canon. The written documents came after the voiced messages, which in turn affected the social processes in the expansion of Christianity.[62]

The question about the place of the church has only one answer. It is where people are gathered in the name of Jesus (Matt 18:20), where he is with his presence and where his gifts are given through the means of grace. All this is the work of the Holy Spirit. The church should be where Christ would likely have been, according to the story of his earthly life (cf. Matt 25: 31–46).

Here the relationship between worship and ethics comes to fore within an ecclesial context. Formation, participation and rhythm are incorporated in worship, which is key for discipleship on earth and for learning Christian ethics.[63] Humans involved in worship become trained to take the right things for granted, included those issues they regard as a crisis or a dilemma. When I confess my sins, I recall the passion of God and realize that every saint has a past and every sinner has a future.[64] In our common sharing of the bread, we rediscover our common story: that we are beloved and protected because of his glorious work on Calvary. Worship is God's time for training his people to imitate him in habit, instinct, and reflex (Phlm 2:1–11). The people who hear the narrative of the homeless young mother who became a refugee learn to welcome such people whom they meet in their own lives.

Through worship and through the content of the good news for all humankind, we may see how God opens heaven in response to the cry of the oppressed. The church in the Spirit exists to practice the life made possible by Christ and to give that life to the world in witness and deeds. The worldwide church takes part in corporate prayer, honed by traditions and insights through the centuries. A closer look at the church reveals a people in prayer for God's righteousness to be fulfilled.

---

62. Ibid., 154.
63. Ibid., 25.
64. Ibid.

A Church of Compassion

Rooted in the biblical witness, we may ask whether it is possible to state that the Holy Spirit is characterized by solidarity with others.[65] In the Hebrew bible the divine Spirit is pictured as creating, sustaining and renewing the life of all creation (Ps 33:6; 104:29–30); empowering leaders for political leadership; inspiring the prophets to proclaim justice and peace to oppressive kings by pointing to a new covenant (Ezek 11:19–20; Is 59:21); and inaugurating the eschatological age of social justice, reconciliation and harmony with nature (Isa 11:1–9; 32:1–8; 42:1–16; 61:1–11). This particular eschatological presence is manifested by the gift of the prophecy which is equally given to men and women, young and old, masters and servants (Joel 2:28–29; Acts 2:17–18). Anselm K. Min writes:

> The Holy Spirit is a self-effacing, selfless God whose selfhood or personhood seems to lie precisely in transcending herself to empower others likewise to transcend themselves in communion with others, and to liberate humanity and creation from their self-isolation and empower them to transcend themselves toward one another and towards God in union and solidarity.[66]

The Holy Spirit remains the transcendental horizon of our knowledge of God. The purpose for the outpouring of the Spirit is not to call attention to the Spirit himself through wonders and signs, as much as it is to establish prophetic equality between women and men, young and old, servants and masters, in line with the proclamation of Peter on the Day of Pentecost (Acts 2:17–18). The work of the Spirit that very day was centered on the proclamation of the mighty deeds of God through different comprehensible languages (v. 11), a sign of the elimination of the linguistic barriers among different ethnic groups. Thereafter the people of the Spirit were encouraged to communicate the good news of Jesus as the risen LORD (Acts 2:21, 36, 38; 4:2, 12, 18; 5:40, 42; 8:4) in order to bring people closer to God and to one another through repentance, forgiveness, and hope. As servants of one another (Gal 5:13) we carry each other's burdens in the new life of the Spirit (Gal 6:2) by mutual forgiveness (Eph 4:32) and by the fruit of the Spirit, which are indicative of an environment of relational co-existence (Gal 5:22–23). Because of the Spirit's reconciling character, he appears as a threat against every condition of alienation caused by sin and oppressive differences.

---

65. Min, "Solidarity of Others," 423.
66. Ibid., 426.

Saying this raises the questions of where to draw the line between the world and the church and how we perceive the openness of the church. While a radical openness could degenerate into indifference, it is possible to combine openness with clarity. It is part of the church's deepest essence to provide room for the excluded, inspired by the radical sayings and actions of Christ. His bad company signals that the kingdom belongs to the marginalized (Luke 7:34). The periphery becomes the center and the center the periphery. The kernel is the fringe. Only by the church's willingness to take the very nature of a servant (Phlm 2:7) can the church really be the church.

According to Norwegian theologian Sturla Stålsett and his folk church ideal, the church should recognize the places where church happens, often in places and among people we may not expect. Basically, the good news creates church, not the reverse. The question about the line between the world and the church is thus impossible to decide once and for all. In any case, the unity of the church cannot be founded upon a strategy of excluding but only upon a strategy of frankness.[67]

In the story of the way the Gentiles became members of the young faith community, hospitality played a crucial role. Their salvation was evidenced by the actions of Peter as a representative Jewish believer (Acts 10:33) and by his mutual acceptance of Gentile hospitality (Acts 11:3). Because of this reciprocal hospitality, the gate was opened for the presence of the Spirit when it was experienced in quite a similar way to the way it was experienced on the Day of Pentecost (Acts 11:17). As underlined by Gaillardetz, the Johannine literature is known for its love mysticism. The believing community should be distinguished by their life of love (John 13:34–35). In the First Letter of John, love defines the spiritual bonds of the church and the mystical unity between God and humans (1 John 1:3; 4:16b; 20–21).[68] The openness to foreigners was a prominent characteristic of the early Christians.[69]

Christ is the archetype of how the church may reflect upon being the people of the Spirit. In preaching, healing, and table fellowship Jesus identified himself with the outcast others of society, the marginalized "nobodies," excluded from the dominant social system of identity.[70] In that way the new

---

67. Stålsett, "Den krevende evangeliske åpenheten," 21. These reflections may also be grasped through a cheerful concept of hospitality.

68. Gaillardetz, *Global Church*, 28.

69. The document on mission and evangelism from WCC states that the Holy Spirit is present with us as companion, which is not domesticated or "tame." Among the surprises of the Spirit are the ways in which God works from locations which appear to be on the margins and through people who appear to be excluded. World Council of Churches, "Together Towards Life," §35.

70. Min, "Solidarity of Others," 428.

people of God were shaped into the *koinonia* of his Son (1 Cor 1:9), God's chosen people of peace (Eph 2:14–20), holy and dearly loved, is clothed with compassion, kindness, humility, gentleness and patience (Col 3:12). In Christ, all barriers are removed and the stranger becomes a friend (Col 1:21). As Min points out, it is precisely in this work, the filiation of humanity and the reconciliation of all things, that the Spirit reveals the Godhead's most appropriate identity and empowers the church to transcend oppressive distinctions (1 Cor 12:13).

In Luke, there are several passages narrating table fellowships and parties to which Jesus was invited. According to this gospel, it seems that Jesus was often either on his way to a banquet, in the banquet or on his way from a banquet (Luke 5:29; 11:37; 14:1). Heavenly existence is in essence synonymous with partaking in the feast in the Kingdom of God (Luke 13:29–30).

Despite appearances to the contrary, today there are countless ministers in the Holy Spirit, actively engaged in the praxis of uniting and reconciling people through love all over the world. These people are self-sacrificing parents, dedicated teachers, health care workers, family counselors, and relief workers, all of whom are signs of the movement of the Spirit to bring about the solidarity of others. [71] The experiences of the Spirit need to be acknowledged not only in the extraordinary and exciting but also in the ordinary and quotidian, where normal people live normal lives. The Spirit is where self-transcendence and liberating action become concrete expressions on behalf of those who are in need of transformed social relations.

Marginality seems to be an appropriate description of the church's changed position in relation to (post)modern culture. But what does it imply that she has lost her former roles, status and social location at the center of the culture? According to Alan J. Roxburgh, the motion of the church from the mainstream to the margins of culture holds the seed of a renewed witness to the presence of God's kingdom in the world.[72] While secular society may broadly describe the Western church as marginalized, each local church must be conscious of another aspect of marginalization: the fact that many socially, culturally and economically marginalized people are living within the local church's surroundings. The church needs to be constantly reawakened by those groups because they are a gift to the church. One could say that in the midst of the church's own marginalization, the church is only church insofar as she has the margins in her midst.

By doing so, the church facilitates a social sensibility in motion, which may be the result of the relational church in practice. The faith community is

---

71. Ibid., 436.
72. Roxburgh, *Missionary Congregation*, 2–3.

challenged by a concrete commandment, given by Christ, regarding the attitude of hospitality: "When you give a banquet, invite the poor, the crippled, the lame, the blind. And you will be blessed, because they cannot repay you, for you will be repaid at the resurrection of the righteous" (Luke 14:13–14). Because missionary activity encounters secular culture in a decentered context of competing voices and liminal existences, hospitality seems to be the most crucial dimension in designing an embodied pattern of what it means to be stimulated by Jesus in words and deeds.

To avoid a sectarianism characterized by an identity removed from culture and society, Roxburgh suggests the image of a town built on a hill (Matt 5:14). That picture offers a visible society with an alternative form of life, in line with how Christianity in the early church gradually influenced the pluralized culture by practicing a different reality. The church in modernity recovers her communal sense of being God's people, led by the Spirit and by an identity which is not so much institutional as it is relational. Instead of the former churches' focus on status, privileges and law, postmodern churches offer an intersubjectivity of persons formed by a new center, Christ; a new empowering, the Spirit; and a new focus, the long church tradition which stands against being absorbed by the current culture.

Here the role of the pastor/vicar comes to fore. A pastor needs to be a poet more than the mere image of a caregiver. A poet hears voices at a deeper level: the loneliness of our individualism and the fragmentation of the secularization. He or she gives voice to the desire for transformation and renewal.[73] However, without the prophetic dimension, poetic leadership is not much more than adaption and consolation. A Word-anchored fellowship is, by the gift of the Spirit of prophecy, given new visions and fresh definitions of what it means to be God's people in a secular age. The church is a people called out on a missionary journey that is a calling far beyond herself, inspired by the gospel that transcends every context, social order and ideology.[74] The pastorate has also an apostolic role: "The gown of the scholar has to be replaced by the shoes of the apostle," Roxburgh writes, calling for a paradigm shift from theoretical reflections about the well-being of church members toward a contextual engagement with culture.[75] The pastorate functions as a symbol of the ecclesiocentric essence of the church.

---

73. Ibid., 58–59.
74. Ibid., 61.
75. Ibid., 62.

A Feminist Perspective

Because theology is a response to God's presence in the world, the church is called to become the community that uncovers and challenges the forces that hold both women and men captive. Concurring with Dame Mary E. Tanner, I hold that exposing violence, standing for peace with justice and caring for the harmony of creation are indispensable parts of being church.[76] A feminist interpretation of the church has inspired Letty M. Russell to talk about a hot-house ecclesiology: a place for safety, comfort and care and a sanctuary for all who enter, especially for those who are the most marginalized, weak or despised of any community.[77] Her dream is that the church would heal the broken and to live out God's justice by welcoming those of all races, ages, nationalities, and genders rather than to promote the privilege of the few.

This is the theme of another book of Letty Russell, *Church in the Round*. In this book she uses the metaphor of the church as a round table to which the marginalized people of the world are gathered in response to an open and inclusive hospitality, viewing the church through the lens of communities of faith and struggle. She emphasizes relationality as a new style in ministry and as a "spirituality of connection and open hospitality," especially to people on the margins. Our understanding of the church as a community of word and sacrament is transformed when we look at it from the perspectives of those who are suffering from injustice and oppression. As I read her, she transforms the axiom "no salvation outside the church" to "no salvation outside the poor."

Feminist ecclesiology looks at the contradictions between the way biblical and church traditions speak about the church and the way this is actually experienced by women in church. By describing the church as a welcome table, Russell refers to the OT jubilee year and to the Pentecostal gifts of understanding and inclusion (Luke 14:12–14; Acts 2:2–21).[78] God's grace is empowering the church not only to renew hierarchical structures but, even more importantly, to understand the gifts of Christ to the church in ways that make the church a welcoming place for all.

Within an Asian context, Yong Ting Jin writes about the role of the women in church: "We envision a community of women, men and children who are valued and value each other as equally created in the image of

---

76. Tanner, "On Being Church," 70.

77. Russell, "Hot-House Ecclesiology," 48. This church model can be represented by words such as energy, balance, refreshment, and relaxing.

78. Russell, "Hot-House Ecclesiology," 51.

God. (. . .) This new humanity is liberating, inclusive and celebrating."[79] Inspired by the powerful story of Mary Magdalene and Jesus in the garden, the empty tomb tradition is a women-oriented tradition dedicated to the overcoming of death and of socio-cultural structural bondage and violence against women. The practical outcome of this view is given by a South African Pentecostal womanist-activist perspective, Sarojini Nadar, who has studied the problem of inequality among women belonging to the Full Gospel Churches in Southern Africa. At the time of the research project, women were not allowed to participate fully in the church, even to be ordained. To Nadar, the most limiting notion of spirituality is grounded in an understanding of the indisputable, infallible word of God.[80] A one-sided interpretation of the Bible contributes to discrimination against women. They are prevented from enjoying a fullness of humanity equal to that of men, though they are deeply involved and indispensable in the church's spiritual, devotional and diaconal life.

For Nadar, a one-dimensional understanding of the Spirit in the process of interpreting the role of women according to some selected texts restricts the church from engaging with pressing social concerns like the emancipation of women.

Nadar's own contribution towards gender transformation within a Pentecostal context is to promote a more holistic understanding of the Spirit's work in the church, one which takes into consideration the full humanity of all people. Further, the spiritual realm must be seen as being in a complementary and enriching relationship with the physical realm. The Spirit forces the church to have a biblical interpretation which is empowering, not oppressive.[81] Moreover, within the realm of the church, the Spirit produces life, freedom, speech, community and action.[82]

These are all important foundations for discernment. As criteria, they can be used to face questions about the restriction of the ordination of women. According to Michel Paget-Wilkes, life which is divided into matter and Spirit, body and soul may risk for a dualism which leads to an inadequate interpretation of the gospel: "As long as faith can be divorced from reality the demand for the church to face the facts of human existence is unheard."[83] The result of inner and outer realms may be a spiritualization of reality in which the inner church environment provides a form of

---

79. Jin, "On Being Church," 111.
80. Nadar, "Being the Pentecostal Church," 359.
81. Ibid., 361.
82. Comblin, *Spirit and Liberation*, 61.
83. Paget-Wilkes, *Poverty, Revolution*, 44–45.

escape from the reality of oppression and only a temporary relief for the suffering woman.

The consequence is that while the vertical relationship to God may seem correct, the material, social and political aspects of life are moved out of the orbit of God's influence such that poverty and unjust structures continue without serious church resistance.[84] Healing society can be kept separate from what seems to be the more primary mission: soul saving.[85] We should appeal to a re-integration of what has been dichotomized and a liberation of what has been enslaved.

A Public Call for Reconciliation

In theology, as in life, we have nothing that we have not received and continue to receive (1 Cor 4:7). Theology originates in the church and is accountable to the church in the sense that it arises from and points back to liturgical practices and the ongoing life of the church. In a deeper sense, there is no doctrine or theology (*lex credendi*) without a worshipping community (*lex orandi*).[86] The right practice of sustainable spirituality in the church is the practice of the *vita passiva* (the receptive life of faith). Today the word "passive" can be misunderstood to mean inertness. However, in the Lutheran version it means that God is the active subject while humanity is the object of God's action. The Christian life therefore is passive in the sense that it undergoes God's work, meaning it passively receives it.[87]

With the presupposition that the church as the body of Christ represents the presence of Christ in the world (1 Cor 12:27), we are invited to reflect on the nature of that presence. The mediation of this identification and reconstitution may be found through the church's sharing in Christ's anointing by the Spirit. Following Hans Boersma, through faith the church shares the Spirit in which Christ became prophet, priest, and king (*Christus Victor*). By emphasizing the work of the Spirit, we may regard the inner life of the church, with its structure, ministries and charisms, not as something irrelevant but as the God-given means to continue his work of reconciliation in the world.[88] The church is raised up with Christ. She is in Christ (Gal 3:16) and there is a Spirit-given identity between Christ and the church.

---

84. Nadar, "Being the Pentecostal Church," 362.
85. Walker, *Challenging Evangelicalism*, 182.
86. Boersma, *Violence, Hospitality, and the Cross*, 205.
87. Bayer, *Theology the Lutheran*, 22.
88. Boersma, *Violence, Hospitality, and the Cross*, 207.

In that regard, Boersma asks whether the church, as a result of that presence, really is the primary place where reconciliation takes shape. The atonement functions as *telos,* acted out with unprecedented and celebrated hospitality. He proposes various practices of hospitality: *evangelical hospitality* (the proclaiming of the gospel), *baptismal hospitality* (the receiving of forgiveness and renewal, received by faith through the means of grace), *Eucharistic hospitality* (an open table fellowship), *penitential hospitality* (the confession of the sins before God and one another), and what can be termed as *cruciform hospitality* (the sharing of suffering in Christ). By these practices the church constitutes a public call for reconciliation, even if the Spirit-mediated presence of Christ is found outside the boundaries of the ecclesial community.[89] Thus the resurrection life (Rom 1:4; 6:4–5; 1 Pet 1:3; Rev 20:6) is evident in the life, liturgies and ministries of the church.

However, it is through the vertical relationship between Christ and the church that forgiveness and reconciliation make sense, not through a self-absorbed and therapeutic culture preoccupied with the emotional effects of an ideology of intimacy achieved by personal effort and will.[90] However, hospitality that is truly evangelical does not have the personal feelings of individual members as its foremost concern. Rather, the open and public aspect of true hospitality given through the gospel reaches out to the other, since it is an antithesis to the self-enclosed economy of exchange which in its most outstanding version may transform forgiveness into narcissism. The hospitality of the good news is only possible against the backdrop of boundaries that identify the church as a community that is shaped by the gospel.[91]

Hütter explains that the church is the public of the Holy Spirit, constituted through her christological centre and core practices, expressed authoritatively in the proclaimed doctrines and communicated by the universal *koinonia* of locally bound, concrete faith communities.[92] When the hospitality of the gospel loses its centrality, the church loses its public space and its distinctive character. Becoming a hospitable community of other-focused reconciliation represents a continuous call to be on the move and to resist the temptation of self-sufficiency.

---

89. Ibid., 208.

90. Ibid., 209. Boersma warns against a privatized ideology of intimacy in Christian worship, which fails to recognize the need to retain permeable boundaries that enable others to join the community in worship. Jones, *Embodying Forgiveness*, 50–52. See also Keifert, *Welcoming the Stranger*, 24.

91. Boersma, *Violence, Hospitality, and the Cross*, 211.

92. Hütter, *Suffering Divine Things*, 165.

Baptismal Inclusivism

Hospitality also refers to the ecclesiological reflection of the relationship between the local and universal church. Incorporation into Christ and the church through faith, of which water baptism is a visible expression, implies that one becomes a part of his universal body despite every denominational border and distinction. Baptismal hospitality and inclusivism is by definition corporate in character[93] and signifies the attitude of inclusiveness and acceptance necessary to recognize the validity of a baptism performed in another church. This kind of hospitality calls into question the denominational walls and exclusivity that have been erected by churches throughout history.

With Boersma, our mutual recognition of one another's baptismal practices counters our divisions and implies unity of the baptizand with the universal church.[94] The unrepeatable nature of baptism is closely and clearly connected to the unrepeatability of Christ's death and resurrection, claimed by Paul as an ethical demand in Rom 6:8–14 (cf. Heb 7:27; 9:12; 10:10), by which practices of rebaptism become a legitimate and serious issue within ecumenical conversations. The new life given by the Spirit and made visible through the church is based upon the fact that everything has become new and that the old has passed away (2 Cor 5:17). This is clearly demonstrated in baptism. The *one* baptism refers to the *one* faith and the *one* body of Christ (Eph 4:4). There must be no inequality on the basis of race, nationality, social position or gender among the baptized (Gal 3:28; Col 3:11).

This sense of inclusion lays the foundation for regarding baptism as a sacrament of initiation, mission (Matt 28:19) and gracing relationship across denominational lines. In light of the letter to the Ephesians, the age of the baptizand and the order of factors in the initiation process may not be so important, so long as the elements of faith, baptism and discipleship are taken seriously in the different church traditions.[95] In his doctoral dissertation on Pentecostalism from 1956, Nils Bloch-Hoell comments with wonder why baptism became so important when it was not given any sacramental meaning. He presumed that its significance was connected to its ability to act as a confessional demarcation line, indicating a break with the old churches.[96] In light of this, would it be possible to create a theological *modus vivendi*, a new way of living together as churches? How can the

---

93. Boersma, *Violence, Hospitality, and the Cross*, 213.
94. Ibid., 215.
95. Hegertun, "Bridge over Troubled Water," 240.
96. Bloch-Hoell, *Pentecostal Movement*, 164–67.

content of baptismal fullness become theological secured at the same time as new, bridge-building practices are established? Ecumenists, theologians and pastors may provide constructive assistance to one another.

In light of these reflections, it is legitimate to ask whether Christian baptism is satisfactorily realized through more than just one baptismal form. If the two different baptismal acts in use in the global church today apparently do the same work, if they foster a common understanding of the relation between faith and baptism, and if the baptized becomes a disciple of Jesus and a citizen of the kingdom of God, whether faith is fostered before or after the actual time of the baptismal act, what does this mean for the question of rebaptism? Given a common understanding of the theological content of baptism developed through ecumenical dialogues, could in fact these two forms be mutually appreciated as both being valid forms of Christian baptism? Can form really invalidate content? [97] Regarding the question of rebaptism, the following reflection for a wider ecumenical dialogue may be the object of further considerations:[98]

1) *Intentions:* instead of talking about each other's doctrine of baptism as wrong or right, it is more constructive to argue that there are both weak and strong aspects of the various views of baptism, both with regards to content and practice.

2) *Vitalization:* the theological sober-mindedness and attitude of hospitality related to what baptism really is and the theological closeness of faith, baptism and the Spirit represent the most important prerequisites for developing a new practical-theological trail in dialogue with believers of another, sacramental tradition. Without such doctrinal depth, the baptismal consciousness will be further weakened, to no one's benefit.

3) *Invalid baptism:* since a greater understanding of the theological content of baptism is emerging among churches, it is difficult to imagine baptism being used as a proselyte act of separation. Baptism is by its nature a baptism of repentance into the kingdom of God. It belongs to the very beginning of the Christian faith. Baptism is not suitable as a way of becoming a member of another church.[99]

4) *Freedom of conscience:* there are people who, as a matter of conscience, look down on their first (infant) baptism because it does not seem to appropriately link repentance, personal faith and baptism together and therefore ask to be baptized as adult. The same principle applies to churches

---

97. Hegertun, "Bridge over Troubled Water," 243.

98. The following is built upon ibid., 250–52.

99. See a corresponding reflection in Robeck and Sandidge, "The Ecclesiology of *Koinonia* and Baptism."

which perform these baptisms on the basis of the new faith and confession of the baptizands, considering their new baptism to be analogous to the missional character of the New Testament. Thus it is necessary to discuss the problem of rebaptism in light of the freedom of conscience for churches as well as for individuals. Here, pragmatic ideals confront theological normativity. A consistent practice dictates that such a principle would also have to be applied to those who do not want to be baptized again, since they already are living within the sphere of the theological content of baptism, even if they have been baptized in another church and in accordance with a different tradition.[100]

5) *A potential model:* in order to strengthen the theological consciousness related to baptism, church affiliation practices which privatize the doctrine of baptism must be prevented. Baptism will always be an important church affair. Transmitted membership may therefore win distinction as a possible model. That model emphasizes that the church is a congregation of baptized, personal believers. It recognizes that the road to faith and service is a result of the contribution of other baptizing churches. These involved churches have not only brought these persons into baptism but into living faith and discipleship. For me, that seems to be more than enough. For those who previously have been baptized, confirmed and want to be received as members in a another church without being rebaptized because their theological understanding of baptism largely is in agreement with the church they want to attend, there is a need to have a liturgy which emphasizes a commitment to Christ as LORD and the intention to live in loyalty to the new community. A church cannot enforce the use of two different practices.

To express a common understanding and to admit a mutual recognition and responsible commitment are not the same as having a unanimous comprehension in all details. The latter is hardly possible. However, it *is* really possible to approve of an inner factual coherence of what baptism is about in the global church in an attitude of inclusive hospitality. By expanding the theological language and by becoming familiar with the theological grammar already established by churches in the ecumenical dialogues of the last decades, we already have in our possession the most basic insights for succeeding in the baptismal conversation.

Pentecostal scholars Robeck and Sandidge hold that from a Pentecostal point of view, believers' baptism will continue to be affirmed in Pentecostal theology and practices at the same time as infant baptism performed in another Christian confessional family might be viewed as an acceptable

---

100. In accordance with the writing of Roy Kevin in: Kevin, *Baptism, Reconciliation and Unity.*

and equivalent alternative, based upon historical and theological considerations. If a person joining a Pentecostal church were baptized as an infant and if that baptism has been made alive and meaningful through a subsequent spiritual encounter with Christ, then Pentecostals need not insist on water baptism as an adult.[101]

In light of the possibility of recognizing one another as churches on the basis of the degree of unity implied in the performance of the baptismal rites, the following questions are asked in "One Baptism," on behalf of the ecumenical world: how does the liturgical practice of your church reflect its theological understanding of baptism, Christian initiation, and the process of continuing growth into Christ? How far do similar patterns in the life of other churches enable your church to discern common theological understandings which would lead to a mutual recognition of baptism? How does the celebration of baptism in your church make clear that baptism is into the whole body of Christ and not simply into a local congregation and particular denomination? How does your church's understanding of membership reflect an understanding of baptism as entry into the one body of Christ and not as a mode of changing churches? In some places, churches already express their mutual recognition of baptism by issuing Common Baptismal Certificates. World Council of Churches, "One baptism," § 84–85.[102]

Eucharistic Hospitality

Gracious relationship has different dimensions: One of them is the notion of eucharistic hospitality. This perspective regards the discipline of spiritual discernment as an essential category. Wolfgang Vondey talks about eucharistic discernment as a way to recognize in the meal the continuing presence of Christ and thereby the presence of Christ in all churches confessing Christ as LORD, thus making them part of the same body.[103] Both unity and discernment are achieved by the act of self-examination (1 Cor 11:28) and by the act of coming together to participate in table fellowship, despite every social and cultural difference. This exercise is a fundamental ecumenical endeavor and a theological statement expressing emotional, ethical and social responsibility.[104]

The breaking of bread is not an isolated act. We celebrate our common faith and companionship with one another. This celebration of divine

---

101. Robeck and Sandidge, "The Ecclesiology of *Koinonia* and Baptism," 531.
102. World Council of Churches, "One baptism," §84–85.
103. Vondey, "Eucharistic Hospitality," 42.
104. Ibid., 49.

hospitality reaches out as a calling which unites us with others to recognize the continuing presence of Christ's work in death and resurrection.[105] The invocation of the Spirit at the breaking of the bread indicates that the unity of the church is a work of the Spirit and of the sanctified community.

Yves Congar quotes Augustine, saying that we are the body of the church, firstly if we have the spirit of communion and unity, and then, if we eat the sacrament of the body, if we go beyond the visible sign of bread to reach the Reality to which it points.[106] The institutional word of Christ (1 Cor 11:24) does not only refer to that action of eating bread and drinking wine, but to the notion of Christ's being broken and poured out for the sake of the world. Myra Blyth writes that the "liturgy after the liturgy" or "living the liturgy" means to translate the eucharistic actions of receiving, thanking, breaking, and sharing into a deliberate and intentional life-style.[107] The table-fellowship of Jesus became ritualized in the sacrament of the Eucharist. But the significance is lived in highly diverse contexts and gatherings, whereby a stranger is transfigured into a friend. Vondey promotes an ecumenical approach to the question of whether the LORD's Table should be closed or open:

> The visible unity of the churches emerges from the life and homes of the faithful, where any artificial distinction between private and public life, clergy and laity, or sacred and profane is erased at the table of bread and wine. As long as the hospitality of the eucharistic meal is restricted to the ritual celebration of the institutional church, a realization of visible unity remains confined to questions of doctrine, ecclesial office, and liturgical praxis. The heart of the ecumenical movement is the celebration of a companionship of life that invites the challenges and risks of friendship with strangers, a reconciliation of memories, a common experience of faith, a shared responsibility for the church's mission, and a proclamation of the gospel of Jesus Christ.[108]

In this respect, the gathering around the LORD's Table and the breaking of the bread of life are signs of the unreserved sharing of the gospel in a fragmented

---

105. However, the position of the Roman Catholic Church is different. By referring to John 6:53–58, this church highlights the Holy Communion as an intimate encounter with Christ. Because of the believe that the meal is a sign of the oneness of faith, members of those churches with whom the Catholics are not yet fully united, are ordinarily not admitted to Communion. According to Rome, to attend would be to proclaim a unity to that does not exist.

106. Congar, *I Believe in the Holy Spirit*, 259.

107. Blyth, "Liturgy after the Liturgy," 74.

108. Vondey, "Eucharistic Hospitality," 52.

world. It is a sign by which the fellowship of love, equality, freedom, and hope challenges the notions of alienation and loneliness and provides an occasion of renewal, confession and forgiveness. Like the eucharistic meal, church is liberation of the whole of life that cannot stop at the boundaries of faith and praxis created by today's churches and denominations.[109]

By rooting the Christian community more firmly in the notions of hospitality and companionship, the image of the church may exceed her traditional confines and develop an ecclesial vision that begins in the meeting together of strangers, the lost, the dispersed and the separated in any place and at any time. Of course, this is an ecumenical call for an opening of the closed Table, a deeply regrettable situation for many devoted Christians and a gaping wound in the body of Christ. The fact that there are church traditions who do not allow participating in the Eucharist offered at a church different from one's own causes pain in the body of global Christianity.

Communicating the Disclosed Mystery

One the one hand, some churches responsible for this suffering justify their refusal of other believers at the LORD's Table by referring to the alleged mysterious relationship which exists between the church catholic as *communio* and the Eucharist fellowship. On the other hand, Christians of Protestant churches state that churches cannot act as rulers of the means of grace, instituted by Christ as a gracious gift of remembrance and presence. By referring to passages in the New Testament which talk about the mystery of Christ (Rom 16:25f; Eph 3: 4-6; 9-11; Col 1:26-27), Catholic scholar Walter Kasper exerts this mystery as an argument for an exclusive understanding of the Eucharist.[110] However, these NT passages are more relevant when used in quite the opposite way: the mystery is something the church is called to disclose, not to hide. The mystery has nothing to do with celebrating the Eucharist, but is plainly the revelation of the gospel, given to both Jews and Gentiles through the prophetic writings (Rom 16:26), which proclaim salvation in Christ and the notion of eucharistic hospitality. A sacramental understanding of the nature of the church is thus no legitimate argument for maintaining the prevailing position of a closed table.

---

109. Ibid., 53.

110. Kasper, "Ecumenical Implications," 538. While Kasper expresses his hope for a pneumatological delineation of the sacraments and for the breaking down of institutional rigidities between churches, my hope is that the Catholic Church has the courage and the ecumenical sensitivity to tackle the root problems in order to break down the barriers in the way of opening the closed table of the LORD.

Pannenberg points to the Protestant objection regarding the understanding of the term *mysterion* or *sacramentum,* stating that the passages in Col 2:2 and Eph 3:4f do not refer to the church or to the exclusionary use of this term as understood by the oldest churches. The terms refer to Christ as the revelation of the divine plan in history. The mysteries are now open to believers (2 Cor 4:3–6; Matt 13:11), manifested in Christ and brought to the fore by the encompassing of Gentiles in the promise of salvation (Rom 16:25–26; Eph 3:6). Accordingly, it is reasonable to consider that Jesus himself, and not the church as such, is the sacrament of unity.[111] By placing the mystery of salvation within the frame of salvation history (Col:20), the Eucharist comes into a renewed understanding. It is the message of salvation *per se* which is the very foundation of the life of the church. Christ and church belong together inasmuch as Christ is present in the church.

In that way, the church has a place in the mystery of salvation, but not as an independent jurisdiction with the alleged strength to close the access to the Lord's Table. I make the words of the departed prominent Swedish Catholic, Gunnel Vallquist, my own: "No scandal is greater, no sorrow deeper than the ongoing division that still prevents Christians from meeting at the same Table of the Lord."[112] Only God has ownership of the Lord's Table. The churches' right of disposal is given by commission of a merciful God. The participants ought to be met with corresponding behavior.

Drawing upon the thoughts of Stanley Hauerwas, the church is a sanctified people of peace who live the life of the forgiven. She is charged to be faithful to the calling of God as a foretaste of the kingdom. In this sense sanctification is a life of service that the world cannot account for on its own grounds.[113] Claims for the distinctiveness of the church and her ethics are not equivalent to any assumptions of superiority. She is church just because she is populated by followers of Christ, by which the church is transformed to be God's peaceable people. Stating that stories are lived before they are told, Hauerwas claims that everyone is embedded in the story of those communities from which they derive their identity. Christian ethics entails a claim of being part of the shared history that God intends for his creation.

Thus, morals and convictions are anchored within the narrative of God's relationship to his creation. The church is a distinctive people formed by the narrative of God. Furthermore, by denoting the church as the social reality of being disciples of Christ, Christian ethics will always be a social ethic and the responding church is the place for ethical

---

111. Pannenberg, *Systematic Theology*, vol 3, 40.
112. Cited by Peter Halldorf in *Dagen*, Stockholm, January 12., 2016.
113. Hauerwas, *Peaceable Kingdom*, 60.

reflection. Our identity as social and relational beings forms our personal individuality. The Christian life is about sharing a life together. Among the distinctive features for a community of ethical virtues is to be at peace with themselves, with one another, with the stranger, and with God in a humble attitude of hospitality.

Constructive Reflections

Informed by this notion of God as the giver and sustainer of life, the Spirit-driven church has an orientation of hospitality, of friendship, and of giving and receiving gifts in an environment of kindness and generosity. Gracing relationship and cheerful inclusiveness have the theology of love as their grounding. In its concrete manifestation, love is the ultimate expression of Pentecost and of a cross-marked power. A shared table fellowship is an expression of a gracing relationship and friendship towards the marginalized, assuming that it is initiated without any expectation of returned favor.

The Hebrew ideal from the OT is clear: "The alien who resides with you shall be to you as the citizen among you; you shall love the alien as yourself . . . " (Lev 19:34). Lavish hospitality may in turn yield a divine visitation, as was the case with Abraham (Gen 18:1–15), because the risen LORD himself is embodied in the stranger. The arrangement of an open Eucharist meal opened the closed eyes of the disciples to this kind of hospitality (Luke 24:28–35). This Christian hospitality is based on the idea that each person bears the image of Christ and should be received accordingly (Rom 15:7).[114] In light of one of the most expressive stories of Jesus, the parable of the Good Samaritan (Luke 10:25–37), it appears that the person we imitate in showing mercy is a stranger and alien himself.

The ecclesial dimension of the fostering of gracing relationship is connected to symbolic actions within liturgy, diaconal practices and involvement in society in general. However, according to Scripture, some early Christian groups were criticized for their eucharistic insensitivity (1 Cor 11:21), despite their otherwise charismatic church profile. The conflict between what is learned and what is practiced became an issue in need of adjustment, which later happened through the writings of Paul. The genuine mark of a mature Spirit-oriented believer is not self-aggrandizement at the expense of other, but submission to God and the fellowship through an attitude of devoted love, joy, peace, patience, and kindness. These are all described as fruits given by the Spirit for friendly relationships and for reflecting God's creative generosity (Gal 5:22–23). That demands a humble

---

114. Kessler, "Hospitality and Christian Unity," 378.

recognition: the claim that "the Spirit is with us" is not for the church to make, but for others to recognize."

The multipresence of the Spirit is made visible in the diverse acts of making Christ present through the Johannine understanding of the Spirit as the Paraclete, an understanding which assumes the faith community to be the physically-finite and fleshly-earthly place that Christ inhabits in the midst of culture and society. Far from any stance of triumphalism, the Spirit is the power of comfort, a fact which points to the common sharing of the Spirit and to the gifts of tenderness and compassion, all of which all are experienced by those united with Christ.

Is it possible to integrate a hospitable embracing of others with the Pentecost narrative? In this narrative, the voice of the community was a call to moral responsibility and discernment. Illuminated by the Spirit, they came to know the other in a relationship in which human dignity and wholeness were restored. The event of Pentecost offered a paradigmatic vision of self-giving hospitality in the community of believers. God welcomes all nations to the Godhead's banquet by submitting God's Word to the sound of their specific ethnic tongues. The celebration of divine hospitality reaches out as a calling to unite with others in recognizing the continuing presence of Christ's work in death and resurrection within churches other than our own.

Among the different aspects of gracing relationship, the dimensions of eucharistic hospitality and baptismal inclusivism are crucial. Eucharist and baptism are not isolated acts. We celebrate our common faith and therefore our companionship with one another and with God. The Eucharist belongs to God and cannot be captured by any church. Having a sacramental understanding of the nature of the church is thus no legitimate argument for maintaining the position of a closed table. A closed table appears as a sign of disunity, not as the church's given unity in the Spirit.

The main eschatological image of the gospel is the banquet in which the enemy is a friend waiting to be made. The picture of the feast declares that God is longing for his people to worship him through friendships embodied in the mutual sharing of the meal. If Scripture is about heritage, then kingdom is about destiny. The one crowned on the cross is the one enthroned in eternity. Nobody is outside; those trodden down and abused may look forward to the vindication in times to come. This is the work of the Spirit. He brings the remembered word of Scripture to life and transforms the anticipated hope of the kingdom into action. So, this is our hope, that "the sun of righteousness shall rise, with healing in its wings" (Mal 4:2).

Nouwen has right when pointing to the fact that hospitality is the virtue that allows us to break through the narrowness of our fear and to open our rooms to the stranger.[115] Anxious friends of Christ become powerful witnesses. Suspicious owners become generous givers, and closed-minded sectarians become interested recipients of new ideas and insights.

The last chapter focuses on unity and mission as essential elements of a Spirit shaped church. Both mission and ecumenism are matters of love, not of mutual convergence, since the Spirit is the comprehensible principle of Christian unity across all denominational lines. Unity is a received gift of the Spirit, while mission is a gracious gift to the world.

---

115. Nouwen, *Wounded Healers*, 89.

10

Unified and Missional

> We are being pointed to the work of the Holy Spirit, who as the gift of the last days, shows up our world in its finitude, creates fellowship between the abidingly different, and precisely thus enables us to experience new life, life in its fullness.[1]

Introduction

THE CHURCH IS BOTH a missional community and a lived reality of unity in reconciled diversity. Its unified essence is the result of a shared faith in Christ, a confession of the gospel and a fruit of the Spirit. Unity is an accomplished theological fact in the spiritual realm rather than a goal to reach in the physical (Eph 4:4–6). Strangely enough, the precondition of spiritual unity in Christ seems tantamount to recognizing diversity, plurality and difference.[2] Unity is part of God's redemptive plan and is characteristic of the distinctive mission of the Spirit. Because unity is an intrinsic component of a Spirit-driven church, it has to be seen as a lived reality in the church's visible expressions and celebrations. And though Calvin may have said that the church consists of a manifold unity similar to a harmony of different music sounds, the witness of the church's unity is broken in the world. Yet, the church is "catholic" in terms of being universally spread out in space, across cultures and throughout time. To be aware of her diversity, the question of unity must be seen through those lenses.[3]

---

1. Raiser, *Ecumenism in Transition*, 78.
2. Abdul-Moan, "Christian Unity," 9.
3. Vanhoozer, *Drama of Doctrine*, 27.

As shown in the previous chapter, the gospel and sacraments are not equally shared treasures because some traditions restrict access to the Lord's Table. However, there seems to be no future for any denominational identity which dismisses ecumenical accountability and global responsibility. An invariable ecumenical precondition is to let as many people as possible be involved in building the church and in seeking the truth, so that the world may believe (John 17:21), because the ecumenical life of churches is rooted in relationships. Intentional acts and public kindness provide a fertile seedbed for growing reconciliation and further cooperation.

Or as Diane C. Kessler writes, a social system is based on the concept of reciprocal hospitality and reciprocal need.[4] By being part of the same human family and by experiencing the sign of compassion and fairness in the eyes of the Other, we can get a glimpse of the encounter of the Holy.[5] Therefore, ecumenical hospitality must be a foundational quality of church leaders. For our purposes, this aspect of gracing relationship can be defined as the longing for Christian unity that is combined with the mandate to be loving hosts and guests in the midst of reconciliation and bridge-building.

This chapter is preoccupied with ecumenical issues and with understanding how the church has been given to the world as a fruit of the Spirit's presence. How is the New Testament description of the unity of the Spirit to be perceived in light of the missional nature of the church? And what should be the ecumenical ideals for the twenty-first century?

Unity as Mutual Responsibility

The mission of the church is to visibly demonstrate God's healing and restoring work in this world. In this mission, Paul boldly states a demand for love in perfect unity (Col 3:14). Rooted in the gospel, these virtues are compassion, kindness, humility, gentleness, patience, and forgiveness (vv. 12–13). To put it in line with the work of Matthias Wenk, unity is not achieved through doctrinal agreement, but rather by Christians accepting each other as Christ has accepted them (Rom 14:1–3).[6] Unity is a matter of love, not of mutual convergence, first and foremost linked to the church's ethics and then to dogmatics.[7] Love is lived solidarity, mutual responsibil-

---

4. Kessler, "Hospitality and Christian Unity," 376.
5. Carmichael, *Friendship*, 201.
6. Wenk, "Reconciliation and Renunciation," 44.
7. In Israel, an ethics of solidarity was developed contrary to the Greek sense of ethics as self-control. The Hebrew virtues were concerned with caring for one's neighbor and expressing love in action rather than in self-discipline. Ibid.

ity, shared accountability and renunciation of status. Since the church wants to give some glimpses of God's presence in the world, the mission of the church is closely linked to the issue of unity. According to John, Christ died for the scattered children of God, to bring them together and make them one (John 11:52; cf. Acts 4:32). In other words, this unity is influenced by the Christ narrative and his radical promotion of a renewed and reconciled community characterized by inclusiveness.[8]

D. L. Dabney talks about a condition of not being conformed to the age but instead acting in a manner appropriate and authentic to the time and place in which global Christianity now finds itself. It is a theology of transformation, such as is attested to in the third article of the creedal tradition: that of the church, of communion and of forgiveness as signs of the resurrection of the new creation. This is a theology of relationality and continuity, and it tends to have an ecumenical approach. In line with these positions, I express that the time for polemics and party-spirit in Christian theology is over.[9] If the challenges posed by ecumenical divisions do not seem capable of being resolved through structural-institutional organization or through doctrinal-theological agreement, perhaps the many tongues of Pentecost is paradigmatic and suggestive of a new model for ecumenical relationships featuring functional unity through diversity.[10]

The great theologians and reformers from the past all sought to employ the tools available in their own time and context to impart the reconciling grace of Christ. We have to do now what they did then: act within the context of our own age and participate in God's mission of reconciliation in humble cooperation with the worldwide church.

Normally, when talking about ecumenical visions, we refer to Jesus' priestly prayer in John 17:21. With the ecclesial ideals of John as a backdrop, the ideals of Paul in his letter to the Ephesians are more relevant for reflecting upon the interrelatedness of the church's unity and mission. The position of Paul functions as a crucial antireductionist qualifier, prohibiting any single church tradition from understanding its conception of the gospel and of the church as paramount. According to Paul, every Christian has a call to be humble and gentle and patient, bearing with one another in love (Eph 4:2–16). He urges the congregation to keep the unity of the Spirit through the bond of peace (v. 3). The reason is unchallengeable: there is only one body and one Spirit, one LORD, one faith, and one baptism (v. 5). There exists only one God and Father of all, who is over all and through all and in all

---

8. Burridge, *Imitating Jesus*, 73.
9. Dabney, "Priority of Pneumatology," 257.
10. Yong, "Poured Out on All Flesh," 22.

(v. 6). The goal is quite clear: through the highly different ministries given to the church, the body of Christ is to be built up and to reach unity in the faith and in the knowledge of the Son of God (v. 13). The church becomes mature in the fullness of Christ. The result is impressive. By speaking the truth in love, the church will be healed by the interdependent strength of every supporting ligament, and she grows and builds herself up in love (vv. 15–16).

According to Stig Hanson, these verses have to be understood against the background of the Old Testament, in which the universe was the creation of God, the One by whom the universe would be restored in harmony. As such, the new community within the new covenant is characterized by reconciliation, unity, and peace (Eph 4:1–6; see also Eph 2:11–18).[11] The unity corpus of Paul in Eph 4:1–6 presents the mission of the church primarily as a visible demonstration of God's reconciling power in Christ, a gift of the Spirit. If so, then it should be expected that the same reconciling power be utilized as an ecumenical resource and as a pathway into serious conversation between churches. Do churches ask themselves what it means to keep the unity in the Spirit through the bond of peace (Eph 4:3)? How can we understand the two existing baptismal forms as being substantially *one* baptism? In what ways could we be more visibly unified in faith and in the fullness of Christ?

The apostolic guidelines in Acts 15, by which unity was attained, have a pneumatological origin (Act 15:28). It may correlate with the Pauline phrase, "the unity in the Spirit" (Eph 4:3), and with a more pluralistic approach for engage with each other on different questions. An important observation is that unity in the Spirit must be in accordance with unity in Christ (John 15:1–8; 17:21). This unity is not result of an idea, but is a pure gift manifested in love for each other (1 John 2:10) and shaped by care and reciprocal responsibility. In all likelihood, we will not achieve one uniform church that holds all the same beliefs. But to an increasing extent, churches have achieved that kind of deep unity which consists of living a responsible life of mutual and supportive respect. They have learned to activate many constructive and interpersonal scriptural virtues and sensitive attitudes.

These churches exist in accordance to ethical standards and in line with the graceful nature of the gospel. The mutual acceptance of each other's differences is just an expression of unity in diversity and a release from the pressures of uniformity.[12] Diversity is not a problem for churches aware

11. Hanson, *The Unity of Church*, 56.

12. The ecumenical ideals of the Global Christian Forum (GCF) articulate what may be referred to as a new ecumenism, encouraging different expression of faith coming to the table with mutual respect and good will for the Other. For an introduction of this particular dialogue-sensitive platform, see Sarah Rowland Jones in: Jones, "Global Christian Forum," 140–81.

of their purpose. Unity allows diversity by opposing monolithic conformity and by promoting the interplay of interpretations and creativity, which come to the fore within the worldwide church at a scale never seen before.

According to James J. Buckley, there is no ecumenical movement prior to the Holy Spirit who moves it. Our participation in this movement depends crucially on how we respond to and identify with this Spirit. With this in mind, the ecumenical movement may be defined as the narratives and practices and teachings necessary and sufficient for visible unity, or reconciled diversity.[13] This movement depends on God's movement toward us and on our continual conversion to the Triune God. In a similar way, Frank D. Macchia holds that the relational quality of Spirit baptism is to be found in the concept of *koinonia* and not just in the event of Pentecost. This understanding of the relational aspects of that concept implies that a distinctive characteristic of any Spirit-driven community is interactions and relationships among the thrilling diversity of the people of God.[14]

In line with Arthur M. Ramsey, there is a kind of real unity between Christians. Thus, questions about the church must involve questions of the inner unity of the church. Local communities are not allowed to forget the existence of the others in their midst and their close relationships in life, work, worship, wealth and poverty (2 Cor 1:7; 1 Thess 2:14).[15] To put it differently, we are not talking about a unity in similarity and convenience, but about the unity of the church as one organism of joy and sorrow (2 Cor 4:12). Christian love and sacrificial giving proclaim the gospel of Christ. Love is among the most distinguishing marks of the church in the eyes of the world.[16]

These reflections on the nature and function of the church are necessary, not only for an adequate understanding of the church, but also for a further development towards Christian unity. As part of the church's core identity, a proper balance between pneumatology and Christology is required. Referencing Congar, Douglas M. Koskela asserts that if the Spirit who is the principle of unity in the church is moving in new and surprising ways, constantly developing and shaping the very being of the community in faith, then fresh hope emerges for overcoming deep and long disunity between Christian communities.[17]

---

13. Buckley, "Wounded Body," 224–25.
14. Macchia, *Baptized in the Spirit*, 165.
15. Ramsey, *Gospel and Catholic Church*, 45.
16. Lord, "Gospel Shaped Church," 16.
17. Koskela, *Ecclesiality and Ecumenism*, 150.

Clearly, there is a link between the work of the Spirit and the unity of the church. The work of Christ in history cannot be reduced to what has been instituted during the constitutive history of biblical revelation. The move of the Spirit shapes new realities, new reforms, new relations and networks, new approaches and attitudes, revitalizations and renewals. Together, these pave the way for more mature reflections on the condition of the developing, visible ecclesiological unity, based upon an ecclesiality which is grounded in the living and active presence of the Triune God.

When Catholicos of Cilicia, Aram I, talks about the need for an ecumenism that transforms the life of the people and brings churches out of self-centeredness, he calls for a kind of unity which resists what he refers to as ecumenical dogmatism.[18] He looks for something that emerges as a pro-active and prophetic ecumenism and as the next step to maximizing the fruitfulness of ecumenical encounters in the full ecumenical potential of the Spirit-driven church. According to him, ecumenism is a challenge in the power of the Holy Spirit for common witness in faithful obedience to the gospel. He writes:

> The churches can no longer afford to take refuge in their own confessions and to live in self-isolation. They must coexist; otherwise they cannot meaningfully exist. They must interact; otherwise they cannot properly act. They must share their experiences and resources; otherwise they cannot grow towards visible unity. (. . .) Growing together is, indeed, a costly process. It calls for a conversation, renewal and transformation. Ecumenism is no more a dimension, a function of the church. It is essentially a mark of what it means to be church because it affirms and serves the oneness of the church. Ecumenism is no longer a question of choice, but the way we respond to the call of God. Being church means being ecumenical, i.e., being embarked on a common journey.[19]

On that background, Aram I pictures ecumenism as an opening to the Other. It is a dialogue which is existential, a learning process, a mutual call and a pilgrimage towards visible unity. An existential part of the missional nature of the church is thus to fulfill her mission in unity (Eph 1:10). Inspired by God's reconciling power in the midst of church life, unity is both a divine gift and an imperative for the church to accomplish. According to Aram I, the future of the ecumenical movement lies in the hands of committed and visionary young people, not in the changing of church structures and programs.

18. Aram I, *Ecumenical Vision*, coverpage.
19. Ibid.

Ecumenical Contributions

The worldwide ecumenical movement has made substantial contributions to a renewed understanding of the church. Different ecumenical bodies have shed light on the doctrine of the church by stressing the aspect of the *koinonia* relationship with the Trinity, displayed in the committed fellowship of the believers. The church's existence is enabled by God's grace, made visible in worship and through the operation of liturgical elements. This perspective marks a paradigm shift from organizational unity to a more realistic but still substantial position of seeking a pneumatologically distinguished unity.[20]

Karl Rahner gave a substantial contribution to a more dynamic Catholic ecclesiology by insisting on seeing the church as more than a hierarchical structured institution. The church is also a symbol. The salvific work of Christ is given to all by the Holy Spirit. We are related to the Spirit at our deepest level and we are all given a genuine unity, fully realized only in the church. The inclusive ecclesiology of Rahner opens up a mixed perspective: membership in the church is necessary for salvation, yet salvation is available to all, because all people of good will are related to Christ and also to the church, though they are not conscious of their belonging. According to Rahner, questions about faith are both a factual issue and a dawning phenomenon of growing consciousness and conviction. That is why the church has to be as close to human beings in their cultural and sociological contexts as possible.

During the last twenty years or so, the ecumenical fellowship within the framework of the World Council of Churches (WCC) has produced significant convergence texts and documents concerning the purpose and nature of the church.[21] Parts of these documents have clear pneumatological connotations, influenced by the dynamic of the present church. "The Church: Towards a Common Vision" anchors its biblical vision of Christian unity in the Pauline teaching on the one church, baptized in one Spirit in order to be one body where all drink of one Spirit (1 Cor 12:12–13). Expressed by worship, common life in Christ, and her witness to the world, the search for unity in one eucharistic fellowship entails a mutual recognition of other churches as true expressions of the one holy, catholic and apostolic church.

---

20. Rahner, *Church and Sacraments*, 23, 34. See also Healy, "Church in Modern Theology," 119.

21. Three of the most important documents from WCC, produced during the last years, are "The Church: Towards a Common Vision," "One Baptism: Towards Mutual Recognition," and "Together Towards Life: Mission and Evangelism in Changing Landscapes".

The document points to scriptural witnesses and holds that although the New Testament provides no systematic ecclesiology, it does offer accounts of the faith of the early communities, of their worship, of their practice of discipleship, of various roles of service and leadership, and of the images and metaphors they used to express the identity of the church.[22]

"The living tradition" is a phrase denoting how the same Holy Spirit who guided the earliest communities in producing the inspired biblical text, continues to do so by supporting new generations in their efforts to be faithful to the gospel. The Spirit indeed forms relevant Christian communities which live alongside prevailing cultures and current contexts. However, legitimate pluriformity is not accidental in the life of the church. Rather, it is an aspect of her catholicity and of her incarnated identity to be present wherever the kingdom of God is rooted. The Faith and Order Commission states that the ongoing work on ecclesiological issues takes place under the guidance of the Holy Spirit. Furthermore, the church is shaped in the design of God:

> The Church, as the body of Christ, acts by the power of the Holy Spirit to continue his life-giving mission in prophetic and compassionate ministry and so participates in God's work of healing a broken world. Communion, whose source is the very life of the Holy Trinity, is both the gift by which the Church lives and, at the same time, the gift that God calls the Church to offer to a wounded and divided humanity in hope of reconciliation and healing.[23]

In other words, the church takes it mandate from the promise of Christ, who empowered men and women by the Spirit (John 20:19-20; Acts 1:8) in order to realize the missionary mandate (Matt 28:18-20). The church was formed as a community of witness and worship, initiating new members by baptizing them in the name of the Holy Trinity.

When it comes to the question of the role of the Spirit after the Day of Pentecost, the WCC document states that the Holy Spirit came upon the disciples for the purpose of equipping them to begin the mission entrusted to them. The Spirit not only bestows faith and other charisms upon individual believers, but also equips the church with its essential gifts, qualities and

---

22. World Council of Churches, "The Church," §11. Remark the words of Nouwen, that "the paradox of Christian leadership is that the way out is the way in, that only by entering into communion with human suffering can relief be found." Nouwen, *Wounded Healers*, 77.

23. Ibid., §1.

order.²⁴ The Holy Spirit nourishes and enlivens the body of Christ through the living voice of the preached gospel, through sacramental communion in the Eucharist, and through ministries of service and leadership.

Accordingly, there is an indissoluble link between the work of God in Christ through the Holy Spirit and the church as a reality. One of the images used in the broader conversation of worldwide ecumenists is that the church is a temple of the Holy Spirit, who brings forth inner unity and renews hearts, equipping and calling believers to good works and serving the LORD for the growth of God's kingdom in the world. By the power of the Holy Spirit, believers grow into a holy temple in the LORD (Eph. 2:21-22) and into a spiritual house (1 Pet 2:5). Filled with the Spirit, they are called to lead a life worthy of their calling in worship, witness and service, eager to maintain the unity of the Spirit in the bond of peace (Eph 4:1-3). The Holy Spirit thus enlivens and equips the church to play its role in proclaiming and bringing about that general transformation for which all creation groans (cf. Rom 8:22-23).²⁵

And illustrative comparison may be made to the Pentecost narrative, in which a unified testimony about the mighty deed of God was given through the cacophony of many tongues and languages. According to Michael Welker, by starting with the Spirit, God affects a world-encompassing, multilingual, polyindividual testimony to Godself.²⁶ A pneumatologically oriented ecclesiology is capable of speaking into the postmodern sense of awareness of reality marked by its dynamic, processive, relational and pluralistic character.²⁷

In this way, an ecumenical theology may be able to celebrate the diversity of various churches as it tries to overcome the divisions between those churches. Yong proposes the following hypothesis: Insofar as Christian conversion is a complex and multifaceted process and Christian salvation is a holistic and multidimensional work of the Holy Spirit, Christian praxis to a postmodern world needs to take many forms.²⁸ This multiplicity of forms

---

24. Ibid., §3. See also Stronstad, *Charismatic Theology of Luke*, 75-83. and Menzies, *Empowered for Witness*, 201-25.

25. World Council of Churches, "The Church," §21. The Holy Spirit is considered the principal agent in establishing the kingdom and in guiding the Church to be a servant of God's work in this process: "Only as we view the present in the light of the activity of the Holy Spirit, guiding the whole process of salvation history to its final recapitulation in Christ to the glory of the Father, do we begin to grasp something of the mystery of the Church." Ibid., §33.

26. Welker, *God the Spirit*, 235.

27. Dabney, "Starting with the Spirit," 26-27.

28. Yong, *Hospitality*, 64.

is manifested in the pluriformity of tongues and gifts of the Spirit, including many languages and discourses through which the salvation of the world is effected. The many tongues of Pentecost make possible highly different Christian practices in a pluralistic world.

Ecumenical re-imagining among Pentecostals

Taking seriously the freedom and movement of the Spirit is one of the constitutive elements in the ongoing ecumenical conversations in which Pentecostals are involved. The pioneers in the pre-constitutional phase of the Pentecostal movement in Europe were not concerned with the establishment of a new church but precisely the contrary. They considered it intuitively to be a tool for spiritual renewals which encompassed the already-existing churches. It was pneumatology—not ecclesiology—that was the primary focus of that young movement. Thus, from its very beginning, the movement possessed a specific ecumenical potential which now seems to be acknowledged and rediscovered worldwide.[29]

The Pentecostal movement obviously benefits from being engaged in the brotherly ecclesiological conversations because those conversations strengthen its understanding of the church as church. Chris E. Green, for instance, refers to the weak ecclesiology within Pentecostalism. Pentecostal spirituality seems to have been divorced from an adequate theology of the church, which has led some to consider the church as a service provider catering to the need of individual Christians.[30] In a conversation with Robert Jensen, Green refers to different, re-imagined perspectives received as a result of the ecumenical and theological dialogue across denominational lines.

For a re-visioning of ecclesiology, the Pentecostals need to place their own historical narrative in the one history of the one people of God. They must come to terms with the role of post-apostolic positioning and their suspicious relation to the existence of creeds and dogmas. Thus, the understanding of the christological dogma in the mainline denominations may obviously be regarded as the work of the Spirit. If not, how are we to trust them now?[31] Can the dogmatic decisions which have been embraced as common ecumenical insights say something to Pentecostals about the role of the Spirit in church history?

---

29. Hegertun, "Thomas Ball Barratt," 37.
30. Green, "Re-Visioning Pentecostal Ecclesiology," 16.
31. Ibid., 17.

Another challenge coming from the ecumenical circles towards Pentecostal ecclesiology relates to the more general view of the church and to her bearing of the truth of Christ. Green states that Pentecostals tends to trust the principle of *sola Scriptura* in a way that fragments soteriology and ecclesiology by giving the individual's devotion to Christ a status which precedes and supersedes commitment to life in churchly community. However, from my position, this seems to be an overstatement from Green. The understanding of the church as determined and formed by the Spirit leads, to be sure, to an understanding of the need for personal experiences, but at the same time the church fellowship is understood as a communal participation in the Spirit by which a strong and voluntary commitment to the local community is fostered. When Steven Land states that the church is more a movement of the Spirit than a structure wedded to the present age, he consciously warns against institutionalism of the dynamic body of Christ and against any adaptation to secular surroundings.[32]

However, both Christ and Spirit must be known in their ecclesially founding roles. As I see it, the church is a pneumatic reality that has her (different) established structures and institutions for rational and practical reasons, rooted in historical continuity and traditions. While the essence of the church is of christological and pneumatological character with a diversity of gifts and ministries, her outward structures of form and stability are adjusted differently from time to time and from place to place.

The church is both movement and structure. Both are creations of the Spirit insofar they serve the nature and mission of the church and foster sustainable, renewable dimensions. The Pentecostal protest against an apparent formalization and objectification of the Spirit's work in liturgical life has been challenged by a more sensitive approach, which may be seen as a fruit of the ecumenical exchange of experiences and a constructive outcome of visiting each other's rooms. The influence of Orthodox spirituality mirrors the reflection that, in the liturgy, people are transformed into church. However, the Pentecostal contribution is that worship always becomes more than what it is restricted to in formal liturgical observance.[33]

The question about whether communion with God is mediated or unmediated is also an issue raised within the ecumenical common room of reflection and mutual sharing. Pentecostals have a sense of unmediated intimacy with Christ through the Spirit,[34] and Harvey Cox holds that the core of all Pentecostal conviction is that there is no need for a mediator in

---

32. Land, *Pentecostal Spirituality*, 178.
33. Castelo, "Ecclesial Holiness," 89.
34. Jacobsen, *Thinking in Spirit*, 287.

order to experience the Spirit in an immediate way.[35] My proposal, in line with Green, is to consider a double aspect. Firstly, we might understand the receiving of the sacraments as a way into Christ's immediate presence, given by the Spirit in the midst of the faith community. And secondly, there may be room within the liturgy for some charismatic elements which serve and enrich the service.[36] Pentecostals do not need to adapt the metaphysics presupposed in traditional sacramentalism.

At any rate, it is possible to reflect upon the theological status of the *communio sanctorum* (the communion of the saints) while gathered around the LORD's Table and upon what it really means to be the living body of Christ in general. The whole ecumenical family seems to state that the presence of the risen Christ is caused by the energies of the Spirit, revealed as the heartbeat of the gathered assembly and made visible through manifold expressions, liturgies and manifestations.

An Ecumenically-minded Ecclesiology

In all its diversity, we may at least indicate some perspectives which are characteristic of an ecumenically-minded church that lives by and through the gracious gift of the Spirit from on high. My proposals are, of course, not all-encompassing but give some clues for at least a direction to go. Firstly, a church open to the variety of branches and traditions has an understanding of the trinitarian shaping of the church. Her potential for a missional ecclesiology is based on this tripartite understanding of her characteristics: the church as *kerygma* (the giving of the good news), *koinonia* (the involvement in fellowship), and *diakonia* (the sharing in service). Together these perspectives are expressions of an holistic approach to reality shaped by the love of the Triune God. As such, mission is the proleptic articulation of the Kingdom and the foretaste, sign and witness inaugurated in the resurrection of the crucified Christ and in the coming reign of the LORD. Peter Althouse writes:

> The *kerygma, koinonia* and *diakonia* ministries of the Church reflect the Trinitarian being and mission of God: the proclamation of the Word made flesh in Christ Jesus, who ultimately gives himself to the world for the world; the fellowship we have inside and outside the Church for the other, founded in the

35. Cox, *Fire From Heaven*, 87.

36. Green, "Re-Visioning Pentecostal Ecclesiology," 24. See also Green's extensive introduction of a classical Pentecostal position of the Eucharist in Green, *Pentecostal Theology of the Lord's Supper*.

perichoretic fellowship of God; and the service we give to others reflected in the kenotic self-giving of God in Christ Jesus by the Spirit, so that the world and the entire universe might be brought into communion with God.[37]

The church is thus constituted by the Triune God, who establishes the framework for communal relationships in the body of Christ.[38] The church has unity in the same way that God has unity within the Trinity, in which the divine persons exist in relation to one another. Unity resides in the relation of persons to one another as a pathically constructed reception of identity through the other.[39] The outpouring of the Spirit on the Day of Pentecost represents the Spirit's continuous presence in the ongoing, everyday life of the church. It is both a pledge and a dawning of the kingdom in the world, which groans for its coming redemption (Rom 8). I affirm Althouse's position that the world—not the church—is the main focus for God's redemptive activity.[40] That is why the church always needs to be missional, open, encompassing and hospitable.

A complacent church has lost her credibility. The church is a sent and sending fellowship. The missional life of the church is her honor and crown. It is the activity of the Triune God, the *missio Dei*.[41] God is not so much the agent as the locus of the mission. God calls and sends, guides and gathers. Using the church as one of his instruments, the Son is sent into the world. In light of this, the Spirit is bound to his role as pointer to Christ for his glorification (John 16:14). Any charismatic aspect of the church will never be more than *signs* which serve to stimulate the church's inner life and dynamic. These gifts cannot play the lead, but have supportive and edifying functions for an intention which is always greater than the gifts themselves. The face of the church is turned beyond her own limited agenda of activities. The nature of the church as missional is more than a question of extension and growth, inspired from time to time by self-aggrandizing endeavors.

Being part of the kenotic mission of God means being a part of the broken and missionary activity *in* God and *with* the suffering of the world. The church bears a divine witness of hope and compassion. She shares the weakness of Christ. She is sensitive to the need for social action and justice.[42]

---

37. Althouse, "Pentecostal Ecclesiology," 245.

38. For some reflection about ecumenical aspect in the building of a Pentecostal ecclesiology, see ibid.

39. Hütter, *Suffering Divine Things*, 117.

40. Althouse, "Pentecostal Ecclesiology," 231.

41. Bosch, *Transforming Mission*, 389–93.

42. Newbigin, *Pluralist Society*, 121.

Newbigin emphasizes an important aspect in balancing the church's self-understanding by saying that it is impossible to stress too strongly that the beginning of mission is not an action of ours, but the presence of a new reality, the presence of the Spirit of God in power.[43] He states that mission is the action of the Holy Spirit to bring the universal work of Christ for the salvation of the world nearer to its completion.[44] The inbreaking of the kingdom and mission of Christ operates with values reverse of the prevailing circumstances. God gives priority to the poor and to the downtrodden, and calls for participation in self-giving service (1 Cor 1: 18–29).[45]

Secondly, an earth-grounded, mature spirituality informed by ecumenical conversations over decades is needed to anchor the tangible mercy of God in the message of grace, through which the sacraments are visible signs. Kenneth J. Archer asserts that it is through sacramental ordinances that we are supplied by the Spirit with the kinds of insights that help the community on the right path, the way of salvation (cf. Wesley's *via salutis*). While refusing both the magical and the merely symbolic, Archer refers to the sacraments as effective means of grace when inspired by the Holy Spirit and received by genuine human response in faith.[46] They are prophetic, narrative signs involving words and deeds. As metaphorical-narrative signs that re-enact the redemptive story of Christ, time and space are fused and transcended in the Spirit through proleptic and playful foretastes of the coming future. The sacraments, when received by faith, provide nourishment for the pilgrimage. They reshape the church identity as an eschatological community, bearing the kind of reconciling power that fosters freedom, peace, mercy and justice.[47]

Thirdly, a biblical theology of Christian unity begins with the unity presented by the New Testament writings, which recognize that we are all one in Christ through the Spirit. This unity is tantamount to the unity of the very life of God, of the mind of God and of the works of God. In line with this, Rowan Williams talks about the unity of the work, prayer and mind of Christ, which is itself delivered to the church as a gift through the Spirit. This unity should then be a unity with one another in the body of Christ as a dimension in which we recognize the mutuality of the gifts of the Spirit. In receiving communion, we see that the fullness of life in the body of Christ comes from the love of the community and entails the freedom both to give

---

43. Ibid., 119
44. Newbigin, cited in: Althouse, "Pentecostal Ecclesiology," 234.
45. Ibid.
46. Archer, *Gospel Revisited*, 68.
47. Wenk, "Reconciliation and Renunciation," 44–58.

and to receive what we already have been given through Christ and through the outpouring of the Holy Spirit. Finally, with Williams, we may talk about a unity with the apostolic witness, the proclamation of a resurrected Christ, in whom the history of the world is transformed.[48]

Fourthly, regarding the question of ecumenical methodology, it is possible to define this engagement as a conversation between mutual travellers. Ecumenical theology is the fruit of the common understanding that results from being on the road together, because the church is a pilgrim church.[49] On this road, believers find each other's heart across denominational lines by listening to each other with humble respect. The outcome is a language that is not necessarily shaped by consensus agreement or by academic formulations. A profound feeling of interdependence and friendship seems to be a precondition for seeking the unity that has yet to be fully grasped. The performative effect of this ecumenical solidarity is stated by The World Conference of Faith and Order of 1993 in Santiago de Compostela:

> As we strip ourselves of false securities, finding in God our true and only identity, daring to be open and vulnerable to each other, we will begin to live as pilgrims on a journey, discovering the God of surprises who leads us into roads which we have not travelled, and we will find in each other true companions on the way.[50]

Different church traditions continuously borrow theological insights from one other. Through these unfamiliar experiences with one another, the ecumenical language and theological reflections are provided with new linguistic resources for interpretation. An ecumenism which does not lead in the direction of worship appears to be a remote exercise with limited interest. However, when I observe the richness of the faith of the other, I am stimulated to pursue a relational identity of networks and alliances which is dynamic, flexible and dialogical. Catholic Walter Kasper says that it is a pleasure to recognize that which was forgotten in our own tradition still preserved in another.[51] This is a form of acknowledging the other which is based on love and consideration, and thus is responsive and relational in its character. We are also responsible for healing the wounds we caused. By a common feeling of pain, the sore of the church can began to heal. One church might have the medicine to the other church's weakness and disease.

---

48. Presented in Williams, "Archbishop's address," line 25–92.

49. "Porvoo Statement," §20.

50. A similar statement was given at General Assembly of the World Council of Churches in Porto Alegre in 2006.

51. For a broader presentation, see Kasper, *Spiritual Ecumenism*.

Fifthly, in the Pentecost narrative of Acts, integration and uniqueness are drawn together, diversity is affirmed, and a community of harmony is shaped. The terms "each" and "all" are placed in a creative tension, as Christopher Duraisingh points out. Different cultures and languages are affirmed, thus Pentecost both destigmatizes and relativizes cultures, forming a communion of diversity. The Spirit brings about not a homogenized, safe and secure uniformity but a differentiated and costly unity of all people; Jews, Arabs and people from many nations. The gospel is heard in the interwoveness of the plurality of peoples, in cultures in collision.[52] This is the multicolored wisdom of God (Eph 3:10), a Pentecost paradigm and a pathway for ecumenical progress. According to Duraisingh, Pentecost points to a de-centering of centers and identities that exclude a courageous crossing of borders, instead promoting a multi-voiced, polyphonic community.

When the Spirit came on the Day of Pentecost, the disciples' question about the restoration of the kingdom of Israel was answered by their own dispersal to the ends of the earth. A centripetal longing is met with the promise of centrifugal dispersal. There is no central place, no single language, and no single authoritative seat of power, not even in Jerusalem. The young church found her new common identity in the baptismal act, in a burial and in a resurrection. According to Duraisingh,

> our many voices of heteroglossia offer us a richness of thinking, knowing and experiencing ourselves and all that is around us. It is through the multivoicedness we are made as social selves. The absence of multivoicedness leads a community to dominant modes of discourse; its definitions of truth will remain static and exclusive.[53]

Ecumenism begins with friendship. It offers a call to cross boundaries of culture and tradition that divide us, in the pattern and power of the One who crossed every human boundary and broke every dividing wall. He did so in order that the one new humanity, in which there is no longer Jew or Greek, slave or free, male or female, may be brought about. That kind of border-crossing displayed in the Pentecost narrative cannot be imagined apart from the power of the Spirit, given to humanity by the risen Christ.

So, as asked by Wesley Granberg-Michaelson, who is sitting around the ecumenical table?[54] In the coming years, the expansion of fruitful

---

52. Duraisingh, "Mission in a Pluralistic World," line 170–300. Se also a broader presentation of his missional oriented ecclesiology in Duraisingh, *Mission-Shaped Church*.

53. Ibid., line 318–23.

54. See the analysis in Granberg-Michaelson, *From Times Square to Timbuktu*, 137–52.

relations presupposes a change in the traditional way of working and a critical consideration of ecumenical style, culture and practical priorities. What we could call the "new" ecumenism must be deeply rooted and incorporated in the breadth of the global church in her great diversity, adjusted in accordance to how the worldwide church is really compounded.

This is to say that the two church bodies which are standing outside the formal fellowship of the World Council of Churches, the Roman Catholic Church and the Pentecostal movement, must be included. These church bodies are invited, but, with the exception of some national Pentecostal denominations, Catholics and Pentecostals have refused to be part of that worldwide ecumenical body. However, the matter of representation becomes a pressing issue when churches who evidently will have a central role to play in world Christianity in the years to come are missing.

An ecumenism designed for the future wants to commit itself in line with what is already recognized as important in the global church: practical cooperation on the local level, a common witness of the good news, a voice of hope in a risky world, a demonstration of visible unity and a supportive engagement in questions that affect the church's well-being in general.[55] In the days ahead, there are questions and challenges which need to be addressed by a clear voice from the worldwide church. From a broader perspective, her desire to unite and cooperate must be in accordance with the challenges that need to be solved. Her prophetic voice has to be heard since she is an agent responsible for stewarding the created world, defending the integrity and dignity of human beings—regardless of status, gender, race and functional ability—projecting the voice of the voiceless and persecuted, and acting boldly for the freedom of belief.

Unity seems to be a matter of love linked to the church's ethical consciousness. And since the Spirit blows wherever it chooses (John 3:8), the decisive question is to what extent the churches are able to move together towards Christ for the sake of the world. We do not know what may be the result but, as a religious impulse, unity is something given and received, and thus it is something shared.

The Church's Missional Disposition

Nothing is really ours before it is shared with someone. The mission of the church is to be a visible demonstration of God's healing and restorative

---

55. According to the Indian Bishop D. K. Sahu, ecumenism is nothing less that everything that relates to the whole task of the whole church to bring the gospel to the whole world. Sahu, "Gathered Community," 132.

work in the world. Today, mission is considered to be the inherent nature of the church. God's missionary character is expressed in the work of creation and in the work of redemption. The Spirit leads and teaches the church to live as a distinct people of God. Mission is not a function of the church. It is part of the church's very nature and essence. Considering the church as missional in her nature rather than in her actions represents a more holistic view for the church as the Spirit-created community, living as the very body of Christ in the world. Her existence declares that the effects of God's redemptive work by the Spirit are already felt in the world prior to the launch of any missional program.

Thus, the community of the Spirit may have the confidence that it possesses all of the power of God's presence for concrete ministry. Mission and church address the same reality. The church *is* mission. These are not two distinct entities but are merged as a common concept. Thus, ecclesiology and missiology are interrelated and complementary, as a distinct theology of missiological ecclesiology.[56] In one sense, all theology is inherently missional theology, because the missionary nature of the church is linked to the mission of the Triune God, proposed under the title *missio Dei* by missiologists from the 1960s onwards.[57] The redemption of creation is carried out through the church in the power of the Spirit, a position that today represents a broad convergence within the church worldwide. Craig Van Gelder writes:

> The church is. The church does what it is. The church organizes what it does. The nature of the church is based on God's presence through the Spirit. The ministry of the church flows out of the church's nature. The organization of the church is designed to support the ministry of the church. Keeping these three aspects in the right sequence is important when considering the development of a missiological ecclesiology.[58]

So, what the church believes and confesses forms her identity and gives direction to her life and ministry. In theological terms, the church confesses the LORD Jesus Christ as God and Savior, in accordance with Scripture. She seeks to fulfill a common call to glorify the one God, Father, Son, and Holy Spirit.[59]

---

56. Van Gelder, *Essence of the Church*, 31. For an extensive reflection of the missional church, see Regnum Edinburg Centenary Series: Mission in the Twenty-First Century.

57. Bosch, *Transforming Mission*, 389–93.

58. Van Gelder, *Essence of the Church*, 37.

59. This basis definition of what it means to be a church, together with other

The church exists in history as an actual and visible reality in all her multiple forms and structures, in all her different contexts, and by virtue of quite different cultural expressions. Though she is universal, the contextual character of the church must continually be addressed. New historical, social, and cultural contexts require new expressions for understanding the church as missional and communicating her compassionate message for the sake of the world. The work of the Holy Spirit is the key resource for the ongoing development of the church. As a changing and maturing living organism, the church is led, taught, and nurtured by the Spirit of God. The fact that the church is made by the Spirit implies a readiness to find new ways to organize the church's life and to respond creatively to altering contextual realities.

In the Apostolic Creed the church is identified as a spiritual community; the community of saints. This refers to an ecclesiological identity in which the church is a social fellowship of Spirit-filled persons, a *koinonia*, spread around the world in countless variations. In fact, it was self-evident to the early leaders that the church was catholic as well, a universal and apostolic church authoritatively representing God in the world. Though the encounter with the Triune God is inward, personal, and communal, it is directed outwards in the missionary endeavour. However, the traditional symbols and titles of the Spirit (such as fire, light, dew, fountain, anointing, healing, melting, warming, solace, comfort, strength, rest, washing and shining) connect with the life of the believer and with all the aspects of relationship, life, and creation with which mission is concerned. The church is led by the Spirit into various situations and moments, into meeting points with others, into spaces of encounter and into critical locations of human struggle.[60]

The church exists by mission, just as fire exists by burning: If it does not engage in mission, it ceases to be church.[61] Thus, it is not the church that has mission, but the mission that has church. The church is the coming together in joy and the going forth in peace. According to the Christian tradition, though the Holy Spirit chooses to work in partnership with people's preaching and demonstration of the good news (Rom 10:14–15; 2 Cor 4:2–6), it is only God's Spirit who creates new life and brings about rebirth (John 3:5–8;

---

churches, have also been used by the World Council of Churches as their confessional formulation. https://www.oikoumene.org/en/about-us.

60. Accordingly, the Spirit inspires human cultures and creativity, so it is part of the mission to acknowledge, respect, and cooperate with the life-giving wisdoms in every culture and context. See World Council of Churches, "Together Towards Life," §26–27.

61. Ibid., §57.

1 Thess 1:4–6). God deserves all the glory for every victory achieved in the name of the Triune God.

> God's hospitality calls us to move beyond binary notions of culturally dominant groups as hosts and migrant and minority peoples as guests. Instead, in God's hospitality, God is host and we are all invited by the Spirit to participate with humility and mutuality in God's mission.[62]

Based on these distinctive marks of the church, it is legitimate to ask, where does the Spirit lead the church? If we speak of the *Missio Dei* (God's mission), we also have to speak about the *Missio Spiritu* (The Spirit's mission). Within trinitarian theology, the Spirit is an actor in his own right. A second question is, how can the church follow the leading of the Spirit in order to follow the mission of the Spirit (Rom 8:14; Gal 5:18)?[63] According to Matthias Wenk, this shift in the question of the relation between pneumatology and ecclesiology brings to light some presuppositions. The term "Spirit" appears in the biblical texts as something tangible and specific (Gen 1.1; Ezek 36–39). The Holy Spirit is the Spirit of communion (1 Cor 12:13; 2 Cor 13:13) and of manifested fruits (Gal 5:22–26). He is materialized through distinctiveness, otherness and particularity, which is a prerequisite for talking about individuality and self-identity. However, at the same time as the Spirit leads to affirmation of the particular, he is also the Spirit of the reconciled community.

An ecclesiological self-identity based on what happened at the Day of Pentecost sees the narrative of speaking in many tongues (Acts 2:1–4) as a fundamental characteristic of the people of God (2 Cor 6:16; 1 Pet 2:9–10). Because the church is the people of God, she is a trinitarian communion of the Holy Spirit.[64] Within a new ecumenical horizon, we are able to observe an ecumenical, worldwide church speaking in different tongues by virtue of their different traditions while still making a common declaration of the wonders of God (Acts 2:11). This was an encounter with the divine, which signaled the transcendence of any ecclesial particularity.[65] Thus, a common language is not necessarily the primary marker of self-identity for a new ecumenical consciousness. The presence of the Spirit and the many tongues has replaced that role. After Pentecost, the church has been able to

---

62. Ibid., §71.
63. Wenk, "Mission Spiritu," 2.
64. Alvarado, "Worship in the Spirit," 138.
65. Wenk, "Mission Spiritu," 5.

speak the language of the others (v. 8) and affirm them into a local-ecclesial particularity:

> Today no church denomination needs to lose its own identity and distinctiveness in order to participate in the higher and transcending 'ecumenical identity' of all Christian churches. A pneumatological-based ecumenical process will be able to foster an ecclesial self-identity that is both characterized by in-group love and out-group love.[66]

According to Wenk, the Spirit has a tendency to work towards the kind of reification and materialization which is evident in the writings of both Luke (Acts 2:41-47) and Paul (Rom 8:18-30). Characteristic of the *Missio Spiritu* is an active solidarity, stirring up hope and interceding on behalf of those groaning in pain. Here we find pneumatological grounds to ascribe to the Spirit the motive of God's solidarity with all of creation. In particular, the Pentecostal tradition is challenged to reconsider its perception of the Spirit as mainly a means of empowerment and to redefine its perception of the Spirit as an agent in solidarity with a groaning creation until its final redemption.[67] It is not appropriate to associate the Spirit only with different kinds of power. Any pneumatologically based ecclesiology must practice solidarity of one concrete, particular ecclesial body with another in *their* particularity. The focus moves from discussing dogmatic differences and attempts to agree on common declarations towards finding ways to express unity in the Spirit with one another and with those in need. It can be done, for instance, by placing one's resources at the disposal of other church bodies, providing training programs and being involved in specific ecumenical projects and social collaborations rather than only engaging in formal, theological discussions. In this way, one church allows herself to be enriched by other traditions and to be challenged by other forms of spirituality.

The Role of the Spirit in Ecumenical Ecclesiology

Presupposing that the disunity among Christians is a scandal which handicaps the witness of the church to the gospel of Christ and distorts her pneumatic vitality, what kind of pneumatological elements seem to

---

66. Ibid., 6. Wenk draws from the theory of social identity formation presented by Kuecker in his use of terms like categorization, identification and comparison. See Kuecker, *The Spirit and the Other*, 24-32.

67. Wenk, "Mission Spiritu," 6.

be particularly decisive for furthering ecumenical progress in uniting the church? How does pneumatology contribute to some form of ecclesial unity?

The Catholic scholar Ralph del Colle was, during his relatively short lifetime, engaged in these kind of questions. As a basic thesis of some foundational ecclesiological issues of the church's existence, he stated that the church exists only as a result of the outpouring of the Holy Spirit.[68] With the help of his pneumatologically-oriented Christology, he regarded the church as being a direct consequence of the joint mission of the Son and the Holy Spirit. Liturgy takes its lead from the Lukan narrative by structuring the Easter season around the resurrection of Christ and the coming of the Spirit: Pentecost is not some additional feast on the Church's calendar after Easter but is integral to fulfilment of the Easter mystery.[69] Thus, pneumatology and Christology inform each other reciprocally.

That fact that the outpouring of the Spirit was a presupposition for the formation of the church (Luke 24:49), raises the question of which came first. Since the Spirit's outpouring occurred first as a matter of priority, the church exists in a larger context of eschatological promise and fulfilment (2 Pet 3:13; 2 Cor 1:22).[70] This pneumatological focus reminds us that the Spirit is the agent of the ecclesial witness to Christ through the church's missional calling until that mission is fulfilled (Matt 28:18–20).[71] The internal and external dimensions of ecclesial life—the inner life and the outward structures—are simultaneously attributed to Christ and to the Spirit. By the impartation of the Spirit, the disciples became church because they were missioned by Christ (John 20:21). Therefore, the historical genesis of the church requires continuous, pneumatic actualization. It is through the church that the reality of Christ is both heard and seen, and it is through the Spirit and the radiation of the divine image of Christ, that this reality is experienced in the community. As the gift given to all (Joel 2:28), the Spirit glorifies Christ (John 16:14) and distributes his grace, gifts, and charisms (1 Cor 12:11).

---

68. Del Colle, "The Outpouring of Spirit," 247.

69. Ibid., 249.

70. Ibid., 250.

71. Ralph del Colle refers to Schleiermacher when he assigns a person-forming potency to the God-consciousness in Jesus and the fellowship-forming potency to the Holy Spirit. The distinctiveness of the Son appears as the created reality of Jesus' human nature, while the created reality that manifests the person of the Spirit is gathered in community. The world-forming missional activity of the Spirit is sustained by the communion of the same Spirit within the corporate life of the community. See Schleiermacher, *Christian Faith*, 573. Del Colle, "The Outpouring of Spirit," 253–54.

As said above, it is not because of Christ that we can talk about the presence of the Spirit; it is because of the Spirit that we can talk about the presence of Christ (Matt 18:20). The Spirit is without face, while Christ is not (cf. Num 6:26). The responsibility of the Spirit is to make Christ visible through the life and deeds of the church. According to del Colle, the effusion of divine love can be characterized as the internal mission of the Spirit to shape the church's communal life and to foster a diversity of gifts, offices, charisms and prophetic initiative for her upbuilding and well-being. Signs, in the modality of charisms and gifts, give evidence that the power of God is at work and that the face of Christ is revealed.[72] But if signs demonstrate the presence in terms of power, it is the caritative dimension which bespeaks the Spirit's relationality in love of one to the other, realized in deeds (1 John 3:18).

Apostolic life and caritative praxis communicate the gospel as a living reality (Col 16). A fitting description is therefore that the church always is obligated to pray for a new outpouring of the Spirit. She is dependent upon fresh inspiration to impel the work ahead and to foster a dependent relationship on the gifts and fruits of the Spirit, so that she may grow into maturity of love and truth (Eph 4:13–16). Despite any church division, a glimpse of unity is visibly expressed every time a clear confession of Christ comes out of the lips of believers. For no one can say, "Jesus is LORD," except by the Holy Spirit (1 Cor 12:3).

The ecumenical task is a matter of divine intent and holy desire,[73] in concert with a hope for some surprises. This commitment to unity in the Spirit is based on the theological reality that there is only one body and one Spirit (Eph 4:3–4). Our time is ecumenically loaded.[74] The unity we have been given grows when the reciprocal and mutual recognition of our common gifts and callings becomes a part of our shared language.

Constructive Reflections

Christianity is not a system of beliefs but a way of life.[75] The time of harsh confessionalism, claims of likeness and vague pluralism is over. Instead, we must gather the courage to transgress human borders and historical divisions. The unity of the Spirit is already a theological and spiritual reality. Unity is a substantial and distinctive mark of the church's identity. Within

---

72. Ibid., 261.
73. Ibid., 263.
74. Tjørhom, *Kirkens enhet*, 11.
75. Smith, *Desiring the Kingdom*, 134.

ecumenical circles, there is a loving knowledge which appears as a desire for solidarity, union, relation and fellowship. This seems to be the main factor for the coming ecumenical dialogue. Thus, only those who recognize the basic characteristic of our common Christian belief will appear as interesting ecumenical dialogue partners. Ecumenical hospitality is expected to be an advisable quality among the Christian church leaders of today. Carl E. Braaten and Robert W. Jenson state:

> Visible Christian unity is not a modern dream, but a permanent and central aspect of Christian life. It exists already, in virtue of our common faith which unites us in a single Savior; and it continues to call us beyond our differences of theology and worship, to a deeper unity of common prayer, common witness, shared conviction, and mutual acceptance.[76]

The Holy Spirit is the comprehensible principle of Christian unity across denominational lines. As given by God through the Holy Spirit, ecumenism can be perceived as a received unity in the Spirit. By affirming both unity-in-diversity and diversity-as-unity, a differentiated consensus may be achieved. From a broader perspective, the church's desire to unite and cooperate must be in accordance with the huge challenges that need to be solved in society and the public arena.

Because of the ecclesial character of salvation and the communion-shaped distinctive of the Spirit, an inevitable ecumenical precondition is to let as many people as possible be involved in making the church visible as a reconciled fellowship. The new ecumenism is a matter of love, not of mutual convergence, linked first and foremost to the church's ethics and then to her dogmatics. It is influenced by the Christ narrative and his promotion of a renewed and reconciled community characterized by radical inclusiveness. That mutual acceptance of each other's differences is a release from the pressure of uniformity. This kind of unity is like a journey guided by the Spirit. Though we do not know exactly what the result will be, unity is a religious impulse that has been given to us. That unity will be revealed when the fellowship of faith searches for God through divine reflection and mature considerations.

Mission and church address the same reality of unity in reconciled diversity. A self-complacent church will lose her credibility. The church is a sent and sending fellowship. As a reflection of the activity of the Triune God, the missional life of the church is her honor and crown. God is not so much the agent as the locus of the mission. God calls and sends, guides and gathers. By the church as one of his instruments, the Son is sent into the

---

76. Braaten and Jenson, *In One Body*, 12–13.

world. In light of this, the Spirit is bound to his role as pointer to the glory and glorification of Christ. There seems to be no future for a denominational identity which dismisses the need to develop a solid sense of ecumenical accountability and global responsibility.

The secular age is an age of possibilities. When the church no longer serves society from her position of power and juridical privileges, she operates as a friendly guest. The minority position ought to be the preferred point of entrance, because only the Spirit of God will be able to convince the world (John 16:7–11). By abstaining from forcible means, there is but one possibility left: trusting God's power to lead, to convince, and to affirm the calling from God. Thus, the church's gift is to bless the world with the good news of salvation and liberation.

A graceful greeting has followed the worldwide church, transmitted from generation to generation over a period of 2000 years: "The grace of the LORD Jesus Christ, the love of God, and the communion of the Holy Spirit be with all you" (2 Cor 13:13). Building the church is a never-ending process. In fact, the existence of the church is never more than one generation away from falling through. That is why good church leadership needs to have the next generation in mind. We have already been given the tools for the continuous receiving and sharing of God's graceful gifts.

An over-specialization of service runs the risk of pacifying the church's life, shaping an audience instead of fostering participants. We must remember that a church service is a mutual work, something we do together.[77] The Free Church tradition needs to feel safe in the fact that fixed elements in the service do not threaten the inner structure of worship, but rather stabilize it. It is highly possible to develop forms and elements without letting go of one's identity. Even though various churches have their own ways of worshipping, they can agree that the church service exists in some basic elements: in the gathering, in the Word and prayer, in response, and in the sending out.

Based on these elements, churches are searching for a liturgical grammar by which the language of worship can come to the fore in an understandable and dynamic way. A church service is—and will always be—an encounter between heaven and earth. The King invites his people to enjoy God's presence, to listen to the Godhead's word and to share a common meal. These encounters are shaped in highly different ways in various church traditions. Thanks to the expansion of ecumenical relations, church leaders have been stimulated by each other's stories, practices and testimonies.

---

77. In line with the Greek *leitourgia*, denoting service, ministry, liturgy, charitable gift, ritual performed together, or something done on behalf of someone.

In this work I have analyzed the church as a graceful fellowship, identified and qualified as a lived reality with recognizable fruits. By going behind the different external and structural frameworks that normally define various church traditions, I have portrayed the church as Spirit-driven. She has an identity which is both charismatic and sacramental. As a dwelling place for God's Spirit, she reflects this double identity. The essence of the church is marked by her consciousness of being sustained by graceful gifts and recognized by gracious relations.

The church lives thanks to these dynamic and objective dimensions of being. Her charismatic-sacramental identity is necessary in order to face an inner secularization and an attitude of consumerism, both of which may be greater challenges for the development of the inward qualities of the faith community than declining support.

Epilogue

Amor ipse notitia est (love is itself a form of knowledge).[1]

FROM THE LIPS OF the faith community, you may hear a broken hallelujah. For me, this is a divine atmosphere of faith, a pulse of grace functioning as the rhythm of my life. My hope is that you have heard these tones while reading this book. I have been preoccupied with addressing the deep relationship that exists between the Spirit and the church. Despite her brokenness and failure, the worldwide community of faith is a composition of the Spirit. Indeed, she is a place where God's graceful presence is tangible in worship and in the hospitable deeds of those who love and serve Christ in humility, honesty and frankness.

Through the interaction with Scripture and by attending to insights and reflections of theologians from different church traditions, the role of the Spirit in the ongoing life of the church has been manifested. When placed together within a framework like this, you may be surprised at the extent to which these positions enrich and complement each other. To a considerable degree, these different perspectives have broadened my perceptions and deepened my persuasions. If for a moment we could ignore church divisions, we could imagine that there is a unity capable of incorporating a range of differences after all. That surprising fact is based upon the recognition that every ecclesial doctrine must be considered in light of what it is that constitutes the church. All Christians have a distinct sensation of a common ground by which the church exists: the work of Christ in death and resurrection, and the powerful presence of the Spirit.

In truth, the church has never left the Upper Room at the Day of Pentecost.[2] That event formed her identity and shaped her conviction of being

---

1. Homily 27 on John 15:12–16. Gregory the Great, *Gospel Homilies*, 115.
2. Murray, "Dominum et vivificantem," 147.

lifted on the arms of grace and pushed forward by the power from on high. Although she is a composition of the Spirit, she is a vulnerable fellowship in which the human resources are confined and her failures are acknowledged. Is that a problem? Not at all! One of the greatest gifts the church may offer the world is simply to be church: a charismatic, sacramental fellowship and a room of God's Spirit. This way she may be recognized and qualified as a Word-anchored, concrete, local, visible and compassionate reality. Surely, the church is a composition of the Triune God. In a deep sense, she is out of human control. The best is always yet to come.

The banner hanging over the church is formulated by the prophet Micah, who said, *He has told you, O mortal, what is good; and what does the Lord require of you but to do justice, and to love kindness, and to walk humbly with your God?* (Mic 6:8). In line with an African proverb, which says, "we participate, therefore I am," the church arises where she is practiced. She connects ordinary people living their ordinary lives. She is not an institution of human preservation but of the reality of God's presence, experienced by the mystery of God's grace. Indeed, the local church is the hope for the world.

So it will be, today and forever.

Bibliography

Abdul-Moan, Joy Evelyn. "Christian Unity—a Lived Reality: A Reformed/Protestant Perspective." In *Transformation: An International Journal of Holistic Mission Studies* 27 1 (2010) 8–13.
Albrecht, Daniel E. "Pentecostal Spirituality: Ecumenical Potential and Challenge." In *Cyberjournal for Pentecostal-Charismatic Research.* http://www.pctii.org/cyberj/cyberj2/albrecht.html.
———. "Pentecostal Spirituality: Looking through the Lens of Ritual." In *PNEUMA: The Journal of the Society for Pentecostal Studies* 14 2 (1992) 107–25.
Alexander, Kimberly Ervin. *Pentecostal Healing: Models in Theology and Practice.* Dorset: Deo, 2006.
Althouse, Peter. "Towards a Pentecostal Ecclesiology: Participation in the Missional Life of the Triune God." In *Journal of Pentecostal Theology* 18 (2009) 230–45.
Alvarado, Johnathan E. "Worship in the Spirit: Pentecostal Perspectives on Liturgical Theology and Praxis." In *PNEUMA: The Journal of the Society for Pentecostal Studies* 21 (2012) 135–51.
Aram I, Catholicos. *In Search of Ecumenical Vision.* Antelias: Armenian Catholicosate of Cilicia, 2000.
Archer, Kenneth J. *The Gospel Revisited: Towards a Pentecostal Theology of Worship and Witness.* Eugene, OR: Pickwick, 2011.
Arjona, Ruben. "A Time to Sing and a Time to Dance: Activating Hope and Wisdom." In *Pastoral Psychol* 62 (2013) 781–90.
Aronson, Torbjörn. "Spirit and Church in the Ecclesiology of Lewi Pethrus." In *PentecoStudies* 11 2 (2012) 192–211.
Atkinson, William. *Baptism in the Spirit: Luke-Acts and the Dunn Debate.* Cambridge: Lutterworth, 2012.
———. "Pentecostal Responses to Dunn's *Baptism in The Holy Spirit*: Luke-Acts." In *Journal of Pentecostal Theology* 6 (1995) 87–131.
Augustine, Daniela C. "The Empowered Church: Ecclesiological Dimensions of the Events of Pentecost." In *Toward a Pentecostal Ecclesiology: The Church and the Fivefold Gospel,* edited by John Christopher Thomas, 157–80. Cleveland: CPT, 2010.
———. *Pentecost, Hospitality, and Transfiguration: Toward a Spirit-inspired Vision of Social Transformation.* Cleveland: CPT, 2012.

Baer Jr., Richard A. "The Dictionary and Modes of Worship." In *Theology Today* 31:3 (1974) 220–27.
Balthasar, Hans Urs von. "The Spirit of Truth." In *Theo-Logic: Theological Logical Theory*. Vol. 3. San Francisco: Ignatius, 2005.
Barr, James. *Holy Scripture: Canon, Authority, Criticism*. Oxford: Clarendon, 1983.
Barrett, C.K. *Church, Ministry and Sacraments in the New Testament*. The Didsbury Lectures. Carlisle: The Paternoster, 1985.
Bartchy, S. Scott. "Divine Power, Community Formation, and Leadership in the Acts of the Apostles." In *Community Formation in the Early Church and in the Church Today*, edited by Richard N. Longenecker, 89–104. Peabody: Hendrickson, 2002.
Baumert, Norbert. "'Charism' and 'Spirit-baptism': Presentation of an Analysis." In *Journal of Pentecostal Theology* 12 2 (2004) 147–79.
Bayer, Oswald. *Autorität und Kritik: Zur Hermeneutik und Wissenschaftstheorie*. Tübingen: J. C.B. Mohr, 1991.
Bayer, Oswald. *Theology the Lutheran Way*. Edited and translated by Mark C. Mattes and Jeffrey G. Silcock. Grand Rapids: Eerdmans, 2007.
Beasley-Murray, G. R. *Baptism in the New Testament*. Grand Rapids: Eerdmans, 1962.
Beek, Huibert van, ed. *Revisioning Christian Unity: The Global Christian Forum*. Studies in Global Christianity. Oxford: Regnum, 2009.
Belcher, Jim. *Deep Church: A Third Way Beyond Emerging and Traditional*. Downers Grove: IVP, 2009.
Biddy, Wesley Scott. "Re-envisioning the Pentecostal Understanding of the Eucharist: An Ecumenical Proposal." In *PNEUMA: The Journal of the Society for Pentecostal Studies* 28 2 (2006) 228–52.
Birkedal, Erling, et al. *Menighetsutvikling i folkekirken: erfaringer og muligheter (Church Development in the Folk Church: Experiences and Possibilites)*. Oslo: IKO, 2012.
Bittlinger, Arnold. *The Church is Charismatic*. Geneva: WCC, 1981.
Bloch-Hoell, Nils. *The Pentecostal Movement: Its Origin, Development and Distinctive Character*. Oslo: Universitetsforlaget, 1964.
Bloesch, Donald G. *The Holy Spirit: Works & Gifts*. Downers Grove: IVP, 2000.
Blyth, Myra. "Liturgy after the Liturgy: An Ecumenical Perspective." In *The Ecumenical Review* 44 1 (1992) 73–79.
Bobrinskoy, Boris. "Holy Spirit." In *Dictionary of the Ecumenical Movement*, edited by Nicholas Lossky et al. Grand Rapids: Eerdmans, 1991.
Boersma, Hans. *Violence, Hospitality, and the Cross: Reappropriating the Atonement Tradition*. Grand Rapids: Baker, 2004.
Boff, Leonardo. *Ecclesiogenesis: The Base Community Reinvent the Church*. New York: Orbis, 1986.
Bolli, Heinz, ed. *Schleiermacher-Auswahl mit einem Nachworth von Karl Barth*. Munich: Siebenstern-Taschenbuch, 1968.
Boone, R. Jerome. "Community and Worship: The Key Components of Pentecostal Christian Worship." In *Journal of Pentecostal Theology* 8 (1996) 129–43.
Bosch, David J. *Transforming Mission: Paradigm Shifts in Theology of Mission*. New York: Orbis, 1991.
Braaten, Carl E., and Robert W. Jenson, eds. *In One Body Through the Cross: The Princeton Propsal for Christian Unity*. Grand Rapids: Eerdmans, 2003.
Bradshaw, Paul F. et al. *The Apostolic Tradition: A Commentary*. Minneapolis: Fortress, 2002.

Breck, John. "'The Two Hands of God': Christ and the Spirit in Orthodox Theology." In *St Vladimir's Theological Quarterly* 40 4 (1996) 231–46.
Brown, Raymond E. *The Churches the Apostles Left Behind*. New York: Paulist, 1984.
Bruner, Frederick Dale. *A Theology of the Holy Spirit: The Pentecostal Experience and the New Testament Witness*. London: Hodder and Stoughton, 1971.
Brunner, Emil. *The Misunderstanding of the Church*. London: Lutterworth, 1952.
Brunner, Peter. *Worship in the Name of Jesus*. St. Louis: Concordia, 1968/2003.
Buckley, James J. "The Wounded Body: The Spirit's Ecumenical Work on Divisions among Christians." In *Knowing the Trinune God: The Work of the Spirit in the Practices of the Church*, edited by James J. Buckley and David S. Yeago, 205–30. Grand Rapids: Eerdmans, 2001.
Burgess, Stanley M., and Eduard M. van der Maas, eds. *The New International Dictionary of Pentecostal and Charismatic Movements*. Grand Rapids: Zondervan, 2002.
Burridge, R. A. *Imitating Jesus. An Inclusive Approach to New Testament Ethics*. Grand Rapids: Eerdmans, 2007.
Burtchaell, James T. *From Synagogue to Church: Public Services and Offices in the Earliest Christian Communities*. Cambridge: Cambridge University Press, 1992.
Calvin, John. *Institutes of the Christian Religion, IV, 14, 1–26*, edited by John Baillie, et al. Vol. 26, The Library of Christian Classics. London: SCM, 1953/1966.
Carmichael, Liz. *Friendship: Interpreting Christian Love*. London: T & T Clark, 2004.
Castelo, Daniel. "The Improvisational Quality of Ecclesial Holiness." In *Toward a Pentecostal Ecclesiology: The Church and the Fivefold Gospel*, edited by John Christopher Thomas, 87–103. Cleveland: CPT, 2010.
Chan, Simon. "The Church and the Development of Doctrine."In *Journal of Pentecostal Theology* 13 1 (2004) 57–77.
———. "Jesus as Spirit Baptizer: Its Significance for Pentecostal Ecclesiology." In *Toward a Pentecostal Ecclesiology: The Church and the Fivefold Gospel*, edited by John Christopher Thomas, 139–56. Cleveland: CPT, 2010.
———. "Mother Church: Toward a Pentecostal Ecclesiology." In *PNEUMA: The Journal of the Society for Pentecostal Studies* 22 2 (2000) 177–208.
Chauvet, Luis-Marie. *The Sacraments: The Word of God at the Mercy of the Body*. Collegeville: Liturgical, 2001.
Cheung, Tak-Ming. "Understandings of Spirit-Baptism." In *Journal of Pentecostal Theology* 8 (1996) 115–28.
Clifton, Shane. "Pentecostal Ecclesiology: A Methodological Proposal for a Diverse Movement." In *Journal of Pentecostal Theology* 15 2 (2007) 214–32.
Comblin, José. *The Holy Spirit and Liberation*. New York: Orbis, 1989.
Congar, Yves. "The Council as an Assembly and the Church as Essentially Conciliar." In *One, Holy, Catholic and Apostolic: Studies on the Nature and Role of the Church in the Modern World*, edited by Herbert Vorgrimler, 44–88. London: Sheed and Ward, 1968.
———. *I Believe in the Holy Spirit*. New York: Crossroad, 1997.
———. *The Mystery of the Temple*. Translated by Reginal Trevett. London: Burns and Oates, 1962.
———. *The Word and the Spirit*. Translated by David Smith. London: Geoffrey Chapman, 1986.
Conniry, Charles J. "Identifying Apostolic Christianity: A Synthesis of Viewpoints." In *Journal of the Evangelical Society* 37 (1994) 247–61.

Cox, Harvey. *Fire From Heaven: The Rise of Pentecostal Spirituality and the Reshaping of Religion in the Twenty-First Century.* Cambridge: Da Capo, 2001.
Crawford, Janet. "Women and Ecclesiology: Two Ecumenical Streams?" In *One in Christ* 35 (1999) 101–8.
Creech, Joe. "Visions of Glory: The Place of the Azusa Street Revival in Pentecostal History." In *Church History* 65 3 (1996) 405–24.
Dabney, D. Lyle. "Starting with the Spirit: Why the Last Should Now Be First." In *Starting with the Spirit*, edited by Gordon R. Preece and Stephen K. Pickard. Adelaide: Openbook, 2001.
———. "Why Should the Last Be First? The Priority of Pneumatology in Recent Theological Dicussion." In *Advents of the Spirit: An Introduction to the Current Study of Pneumatology*, edited by D. Lyle Dabney and Bradford E. Hinze, 240–61. Milwaukee: Marquette University Press, 2001.
Dawn, Marva J. *Reaching Out without Dumbing Down: A Theology of Worship for the Turn-of-the-Century Culture.* Grand Rapids: Eerdmans, 1995.
Del Colle, Ralph. *Christ and the Spirit: Spirit-Christology in Trinitarian Perspective.* Oxford: Oxford University Press, 1994.
———. "The Outpouring of the Holy Spirit: Implications for the Church and Ecumenism." In *The Holy Spirit, the Church, and Christian Unity: Proceedings of the Consultation Held at the Monastery of Bose, Italy, 14–20. October 2002*, edited by Doris Donnelly, et al. 247–65. Leuven: Leuven University Press, 2002.
Dempster, Murray W. "The Church's Moral Witness: A Study of Glossolalia in Luke's Theology of Acts." *Paraclete* 23 (1989) 1–7.
Dempster, Murray W. et al. *Called and Empowered: Global Mission in Pentecostal Perspective.* Peabody: Hendrickson, 1991.
Dockery, David S. "The Thology of Acts." In *Criswell Theological Review* 5 1 (1990) 43–55.
Doctrine Commission of the General Synod of the Church of England. *We Believe in the Holy Spirit: A Report.* London: Church House, 1991.
Dokka, Trond Skard, et al. *Kirke nå: Den norske kirke som evangelisk-luthersk kirke (Church Now: The Church of Norway as Evangelical-Lutheran Church).* Trondheim: Tapir, 2011.
Doran, Robert M. *Theology and the Dialectics of History.* Toronto: University of Toronto Press, 1990.
Dulles, Avery. "The Church is 'One, Holy, Catholic, and Apostolic.'" In *Evangelical Review of Theology* 23 1 (1999) 14–27.
Dunn, James D. G. *Baptism in the Holy Spirit: A Re-Examination of the New Testament Teaching on the Gift of the Spirit in Relation to Pentecostalism Today.* Philadelphia: Westminster, 1970.
———. "Baptism in the Holy Spirit: Yet Once More-Again." In *Journal of Pastoral Theology* 19 (2010) 32–43.
———. "Baptism in the Spirit: A Reponse to Pentecostal Scholarship on Luke-Acts." In *Journal of Pastoral Theology* 3 (1993) 3–27.
———. *Jesus and the Spirit: A Study of the Religious and Charismatic Experience of Jesus and the First Christians as Reflected in the New Testament.* Grand Rapids: Eerdmans, 1997.
———. *Pneumatology: The Christ and the Spirit: Collected Essays of James D. G. Dunn.* Vol. 2. Grand Rapids: Eerdmans, 1998.

———. *Unity and Diversity in the New Testament: An Inquiry into the Character of Earliest Christianity*. London: SCM, 2006.

Duraisingh, Christopher. "Christian Mission in a Pluralistic World." In *Holy Cross Greek Orthodox School of Theology* (2002). http://www.goarch.org/special/pluralistic2002/presentations/duraisingh.

———. "From Chrch-Chaped Mission to Mission-Shaped Church." In *Anglican Theological Review* 92 1 (2010) 7–27.

Elowsky, Joel C. *We Believe in the Holy Spirit*, edited by Thomas C. Oden. Vol. 4 of Ancient Christian Doctrine. Downers Grove: IVP, 2009.

Engelsviken, Tormod. "The Gift of the Spirit: An Analysis and Evaluation of the Charismatic Movement from a Lutheran Theological Perspective." PhD diss., Aquinas Institute of Theology, 1981.

Evans, G. R. "The Church in the Early Christian Centuries." In *The Routledge Companion of the Christian Church*, edited by Gerard Mannion and Lewis S. Mudge, 28–47. New York: Routledge, 2008.

Farrow, Douglas. *Ascension and Ecclesia: On the Significance of the Doctrine of the Ascension for Ecclesiology and Christian Cosmology*. Edinburgh: T & T Clark, 1999.

Fee, Gordon D. *God's Empowering Presence: The Holy Spirit in the Letters of Paul*. Peabody: Hendrickson, 1994.

———. *Gospel and Spirit: Issues in New Testament Hermeneutics*. Peabody: Hendrickson, 1991.

———. "The Spirit as the Renewed Presence of God." In *CRUX* 44 2 (2008) 2–7.

Fung, Ronald Y. K. *The Epostle to the Galatians*. New International Commentary on the New Testament. Grand Rapids: Eerdmans, 1988.

Gaillardetz, Richard R. *Ecclesiology for a Global Church: A People Called and Sent*. Maryknoll: Orbis, 2008.

Gelpi, Donald. *The Turn to Experience in Contemporary Theology*. New York: Paulist, 2000.

Gibbs, Eddie. *Church Next. Quantum Changes in How We Do Ministry*. Downers Grove: InterVarsity, 2000.

Granberg-Michaelson, Wesley. *From Times Square to Timbuktu: The Post-Christian West Meets the Non-Western Church*. Grand Rapids: Eerdmans, 2013.

Gregory, the Great. *Forty Gospel Homilies*. Translated by David Hurst. Kalamazoo: Cistercian, 1990.

Green, Chris E. W. "'The Body of Christ, the Spirit of Communion': Re-Visioning Pentecostal Ecclesiology in Conversation with Robert Jensen." In *Journal of Pentecostal Theology* 20 (2011) 15–26.

———. *Toward a Pentecostal Theology of the Lord's Supper*. Cleveland: CPT, 2012.

Green, Joel, and Max Turner, eds. *Between Two Horizons: Spanning New Testament Studies and Systematic Theology*. Grand Rapids: Eerdmans, 2000.

Green, Stefan. "Församling och medlemskap ur ett bibelteologisk perspektiv (Congregation and Membership from the Perspective of Biblical Theology)." In *Medlemskap. En tvärvetenskaplig studie av medlemskap i Pingströrelsen (Membership: A Cross-Scientific Study of Membership in the Pentecostal Movement of Sweden)*, edited by Jan-Åke Alvarsson, 17–37. Uppsala: Institutet för Pentekostala Studier, 2011.

Groppe, Elisabeth. "The Contribution of Yves Congar's Theology of the Holy Spirit." In *Theological Studies* 62 3 (2001) 451–78.

Gudstjeneste for Den norske kirke (Handbook for the Service in Church of Norway). Stavanger: Eide, 2011.

Gudstjenestebok for Den norske kirke – del 2 – Kirkelige handlinger. Oslo: Verbum, 1992.

Gunkel, Hermann. *The Influence of the Holy Spirit: The Popular View of the Apostolic Age and the Teaching of the Apostle Paul.* Philadelphia: Fortress, 1888/1979.

Hagman, Patrik. *Efter folkkyrkan: en teologi om kyrkan i det efterkristna samhället (After the Folk Church: A Theology of the Church in the Post-Christian Society).* Skellefteå: Artos, 2013.

Halldorf, Joel. "Lewi Pethrus and the Creation of a Christian Counterculture." In *PNEUMA: The Journal of the Society of Pentecostal Studies* 32 3 (2010) 354–68.

Hanson, Stig. *The Unity of the Church in the New Testament: Colossians and Ephesians.* Uppsala: Alqvist, 1946.

Hardy, Daniel W. *God's Way with the World: Thinking and Practising Christian Faith.* Edinburgh: T & T Clark, 1996.

Hauerwas, Stanley. *Character and the Christian Life: A Study in Theological Ethics.* San Antonio: Trinity University Press, 1975.

———. *A Community of Character: Toward a Constructive Christian Social Ethics.* Notre Dame: University of Notre Dame Press, 1981.

———. *The Peaceable Kingdom. A Primer in Christian Etics.* Notre Dame: University of Notre Dame, 1983.

Hauerwas, Stanley, and Samuel Wells. "Christian Ethics as Informed Prayer." In *The Blackwell Companion to Christian Ethics. Blackwell Companions to Religion.* 2nd ed. Edited by Samuel Wells and Stanley Hauerwas, 3–12. Malden: Wiley-Blackwell, 2011.

———. "The Gifs of the Church and the Gifts God Gives It." In *The Blackwell Companion to Christian Ethics. Blackwell Companions to Religion.* 2nd ed. Edited by Samuel Wells and Stanley Hauerwas, 13–27. Malden: Wiley-Blackwell, 2011.

Healy, Nicholas M. *Church, World and the Christian Life: Practical-Prophetic Ecclesiology.* Cambridge: Cambridge University Press, 2000.

Healy, Nicholas M. "The Church in Modern Theology." In *The Routledge Companion of the Christian Church,* edited by Gerhard Mannion and Lewis S. Mudge, 106–26. New York: Routledge, 2008.

Hegertun, Terje. "Bridge over Troubled Water? Rebaptism in a Nordic Context—Reflections and Proposals." In *PNEUMA: The Journal of the Society for Pentecostal Studies* 35 2 (2013) 235–52.

———. "Menigheten i lys av den tredje trosartikkel. Elementer i en pentekostal ekklesiologi (The Church in Light of article 3 of the Creed. Elements of a Pentecostal Ecclesiology)." In *Pentekostale perspektiver (Pentecostal Perspectives),* edited by Knut-Willy Sæther, and Karl-Inge Tangen, 165–86. Bergen: Fagbokforlaget, 2015.

———. "Thomas Ball Barratt and 'the Spirit of Unity.'" In *Journal of the European Pentecostal Theological Association* 35 1 (2015) 34–47.

———. "When a Theological Institution becomes Ecumenical: A Focus on the Process and Experience." In *Dialog: A Journal of Theology* 55 4 (2016) 364–71.

Hegstad, Harald. *The Real Church: An Ecclesiology of the Visible.* Eugene, OR: Pickwick, 2013.

Heidegger, Martin. *Being and Time.* Translated by Joan Stambaugh. New York: State University of New York, 1996.

Heim, David. "Sophia's Choice." In *The Christian Century* 111 11 (1994) 339–40.

Hendry, George S. *The Holy Spirit in Christian Theology.* Philadelphia: Westminster, 1956.
Henriksen, Jan-Olav. *Desire, Gift, and Recognition: Christology and Postmodern Philosophy.* Grand Rapids: Eerdmans, 2009.
———. *Live, Love & Hope: God and Human Experience.* Grand Rapids: Eerdmans, 2014.
Hollenweger, Walter J. "After Twenty Years of Research on Pentecostalism." In *International Review of Mission* 75 297 (1986) 3–12.
———. *Pentecostalism: Origins and Developments Worldwide.* Peabody: Hendrickson, 1997.
———. *The Pentecostals.* London: SCM, 1972.
Huyssteen, J. Wentzel van. *Essays in Postfoundationalist Theology.* Grand Rapids: Eerdmans, 1997.
Hütter, Reinhard. "The Church. The Knowledge of the Triune God: Practices, Doctrine, Theology." In *Knowing the Triune God: The Work of the Spirit in the Practices of the Church*, edited by James J. Buckley and David S. Yeago, 23–47. Grand Rapids: Eerdmans, 2001.
Hütter, Reinhard. *Suffering Divine Things: Theology as Church Practice.* Translated by Doug Stott. Grand Rapids: Eerdmans, 2000.
Innerdal, Gunnar. "Spirit and Truth: A Systematic Reconstruction of Hans Urs von Balthasar's Doctrine of the Spirit of Truth and Its Connections to the Philosphy and Theology of Truth by the Theoretical Framework of Lorenz B. Puntel." PhD diss., MF Norwegian School of Theology, 2014.
Isaacs, Marie E. *The Concept of Spirit: A Study on Pneuma in Hellenistic Judaism and Its Bearing on the New Testament.* London: Heythrop College, 1976.
Jacobsen, Douglas. *Thinking in the Spirit: The Theologies of the Early Pentecostal Movement.* Bloomington: Indiana University, 2003.
Jaichandran, Rebecca, and B. D. Madhav. "Pentecostal Spirituality in a Postmodern World." In *Asian Journal of Pentecostal Studies* 6 1 (2003) 39–61.
Jeanrond, Werner G. *A Theology of Love.* London: T & T Clark, 2010.
Jensen, Richard A. *Touch by the Spirit.* Minneapolis: Augsburg, 1975.
Jin, Yong Ting. "On Being Church: Asian Women's Voices and Visions." In *The Ecumenical Review* 53 1 (2001) 109–13.
Johnson, Luke Timothy. *The Acts of the Apostles.* Collegeville: Liturgical, 1992.
Johnson, Maxwell E., ed. *Sacraments and Worship.* Louisville: WJK, 2012.
Jones, Gregory. *Embodying Forgiveness: A Theological Analysis.* Grand Rapids: Eerdmans, 1995.
Jones, Sarah Rowland. "The Global Christian Forum renewing Our Global Ecumenical Method." In *Global Christian Forum: Transforming Ecumenism*, edited by Richard Howell, 140–81. New Delhi: Evangelical Fellowship of India, 2007.
Josefsson, Ulrik. *Liv och över nog: den tidiga pingströrelsens spiritualitet (Life and Overflow: The Early Spirituality of the Swedish Pentecostal Movement).* Bibliotheca theologiae practicae. Skellefteå: Artos, 2005.
Kasper, Walter. "Ecclesiological and Ecumenical Implications of Baptism." In *Ecumenical Review* 52 (2000) 526–41.
———. *The God of Jesus.* London: SCM, 1984.
———. *A Handbook of Spiritual Ecumenism.* New York: New City, 2007.

Kaufman, John. "Diverging Trajectories or Emerging Mainstream? Unity and Diversity in Second Century Christianity." In *Among Jews, Gentiles and Christians in Antiquity and the Middle Ages: Studies in Honour of Professor Oskar Skarsaune*, edited by Reidar Hvalvik and John Kaufman, 113–28. Trondheim: Tapir, 2011.

Keifert, Patrick R. *Welcoming the Stranger: A Public Theology of Worship and Evangelism.* Minneapolis: Fortress, 1992.

Kelly, Gerard. "Spirit, Church and the Ecumenical Endeavour." In *Starting With the Spirit*, edited by Stephen Pickard and Gordon Preece. Hindmarsh: Australian Theological Forum, 2001.

Kelly, J. N. D. *Early Christian Doctrines.* London: Continuum, 1958/1977.

Kenneson, Philip. "Gathering: Worship, Imagination, and Formation." In *The Blackwell Companion to Christian Ethics*. Blackwell Companions to Religion. 2nd ed. Edited by Samuel Wells and Stanley Hauerwas, 53–67. Malden: Wiley-Blackwell, 2011.

Kessler, Diane C. "'Receive one Another . . .': Honoring the Relationship between Hospitality and Christian Unity." In *Journal of Ecumenical Studies* 47 3 (2013) 376–84.

Kevin, Roy. *Baptism, Reconciliation and Unity.* Carlisle: Paternoster, 1997.

Kolnes, Ralph Ditlef. "Ralphs femte brev til Notto" (Ralph's 5 letter to Notto). In *Vårt Land* 16 (2010) 19.

Komonchak, Joseph A. *Foundations in Ecclesiology.* Boston: Boston College, 1995.

Koskela, Douglas M. *Ecclesiality and Ecumenism: Yves Congar and the Road to Unity.* Milwaukee: Marquette University Press, 2008.

Kraft, Charles H. *Christianity in Culture.* Maryknoll: Orbis, 1979.

Kristiansen, Staale Johannes, and Svein Rise. *Key Theological Thinkers: From Modern to Postmodern.* Farnham: Ashgate, 2013.

Kubac, H. de. *Splendour of the Church.* New York: Sheed & Ward, 1956.

Kuecker, Aaron J. *The Spirit and the "Other": Social Identity, Ethnicity and Intergroup Reconciliation in Luke-Acts.* London: T & T Clark, 2011.

Küng, Hans. *The Church.* London: Search, 1981.

Kärkkäinen, Veli-Matti. *Christ and Reconciliation: A Contructive Christian Theology for the Pluralistic World.* Vol. 1. Grand Rapids: Eerdmans, 2013.

———. "Pentecostal Ecclesiology—Does it Exist?" In *International Journal for the Study of the Christian Church* 11 4 (2011) 248–55.

———. "Pentecostals and the Claim for Apostolicity." In *Pentecostal Issues, Ecclesiology & Ecumenism*, edited by Riku Tuppurainen, 57–76. Sint-Pieters-Leeuw: Continental Theological Seminary, 2011.

———. *Pneumatology: The Holy Spirit in Ecumenical, International, and Contextual Perspective.* Grand Rapids: Baker, 2002.

———, ed. *The Spirit in the World: Emerging Pentecostal Theologies in the Global Contexts.* Grand Rapids: Eerdmans, 2009.

———. "Toward a Pneumatological Theology." In *Pentecostal and Ecumenical Perspectives on Ecclesiology, Soteriology, and Theology of Mission*, edited by Amos Yong. Lanham: University Press of America, 2002.

Käsemann, Ernst. *Commentary on Romans.* Grand Rapids: Eerdmans, 1980.

Ladd, George E. *A Theology of the New Testament.* Grand Rapids: Eerdmans, 1993.

Land, Steven J. "A Passion for the Kingdom: Revisioning Pentecostal Spirituality." In *Journal of Pentecostal Theology* 1 (1992) 19–46.

———. *Pentecostal Spirituality: A Passion for the Kingdom.* Sheffield: Sheffield Academic, 1993.

Lee, Paul D. "Pneumatologcial Ecclesiology in the Roman Catholic-Pentecostal Dialogue." PhD diss., Pontificia Studiorum Universitas/Saint Paul School of Theology, 1994.

Lohfink, Gerhard. *Jesus and Community: The Social Dimension of Christian Faith.* London: SPCK, 1985.

Longenecker, Richard N. *Galatians: Word Biblical Commentary.* Vol. 41, Dallas: Word, 1990.

Lord, Andy. "Gospel Shaped Church: Developing a Trinitarian Pentecostal Ecclesiology." In *Society for Pentecostal Studies, 41st Annual Meeting,* 1–25. Regent University, VA., 2012.

Lossky, Vladimir. *The Mystical Theology of the Eastern Church.* Cambridge: J. Clarke, 1957.

Lubac, Henri de, et al. *Corpus Mysticum: the Eucharist and the Church in the Middle Ages: Historical Survey.* Notre Dame: University of Notre Dame Press, 2007.

Luther, Martin. *Large Catechism.* Philadelphia: Fortress, 1959.

———. *Lectures on Titus, Philemon, and Hebrews.* Luther's Work, edited by Jaroslav Pelikan. Vol. 29. Saint Louis: Concordia, 1968.

Macchia, Frank D. *Baptized in the Spirit: A Global Pentecostal Theology.* Grand Rapids: Zondervan, 2006.

———. "Groans Too Deep for Words: Towards a Theology of Tongues as Initial Evidence." http://www.apts.edu/aeimages/File/AJPS_PDF/98-2-macchia.pdf.

———. "The Kingdom and the Power: Spirit Baptism in Pentecostal and Ecumenical Perspective." In *The Work of the Spirit: Pneumatology and Pentecostalism,* edited by Michael Welker, 109–25. Grand Rapids: Eerdmans, 2006.

———. "The Question of Tongues as Initial Evidence: A Review of Initial Evidence, edited by Gary B. Mcgee." In *Journal of Pentecostal Theology* 2 (1993) 117–27.

———. "Sigh too Deep for Words: Towards a Theology of Glossolalia." In *Journal of Pentecostal Theology* 1 (1992) 47–73.

———. "The Struggle for Global Witness: Shifting Paradigms in Pentecostal Theology." In *The Globalization of Pentecostalism: A Religion Made to Travel,* edited by Byron D. Klaus, et al., 8–29. Oxford: Regnum.

———. "Tongues as a Sign: Towards a Sacramental Understanding of Pentecostal Experience." In *PNEUMA: The Journal of the Society for Pentecostal Studies* 15 1 (1993) 61–76.

Marshall, I. Howard. "Congregation and Ministry in the Pastoral Epistles." In *Community Formation in the Early Church and in the Church Today,* edited by Richard N. Longenecker, 105–26. Peabody: Hendrickson, 2002.

———. *Luke: Historian and Theologian.* Exeter: Pasternoster, 1989.

McCarthy, M. "Spirituality in a Postmodern Era." In *The Blackwell Reader in Pastoral and Practical Theology,* edited by James Woodward and Stephen Pattison, 192–205. Oxford: Blackwell, 2000.

McDonnell, Kilian. *Presence, Power, Praise: Documents on the Charismatic Renewal.* Collegeville: Liturgical, 1980.

———. "A Trinitarian Theology of the Holy Spirit?" In *Theological Studies* 46 (1985) 191–227.

McGee, Gary B. "Early Pentecostal Hermeneutics Tongues as Evidence in the Book of Acts." In *Initial Evidence*, edited by G. M. McGee, 96–118. Peabody: Hendrickson, 1991.

McGrath, Alister E. *The Science of God*. London: T. & T. Clark, 2004.

Menzies, Robert P. *Empowered for Witness: The Spirit in Luke-Acts*. London: T & T Clark, 2004.

Milavec, Aaron. *The Didache: Text, Translation, Analysis, and Commentary*. Collegeville: Liturgical, 2003.

Min, Anselm K. "Solidarity of Others in the Power of the Holy Spirit: Pneumatology in a Divided World." In *Advents of the Spirit: An Introduction to the Current Study of Pneumatology*, edited by D. Lyle Dabney and Bradford E. Hinze, 416–43. Milwaukee: Marquette University Press, 2001.

Moltmann, Jürgen. *The Church in the Power of the Spirit: A Contribution to Messianic Ecclesiology*. London: SCM, 1992.

———. *The Source of Life: The Holy Spirit and the Theology of Life*. London: SCM, 1997.

———. *The Spirit of Life: A Universal Affirmation*. Minneapolis: Fortress, 2001.

Mouw, Richard J., and Mark Noll, eds. *Wonderful Words of Life: Hymns in American Protestant History and Theology*. Gran Rapids: Eerdmans, 2004.

Murray, P. D., ed. *Receptive Ecumenism and the Call to Catholic Learning: Exploring a Way for Contemporary Ecumenism*. Oxford: Oxford University Press, 2008.

Murray, Paul. "Dominum et vivificantem. Read Today." In *Concilium* 4 (2011) 143–47.

Mühlen, Heribert. *Una Mystica Persona: Die Kirche als das Mysterium der heilsgeschichtlichen Identität das heligen Geistes: eine Person in vielen Personen*. Munich: Schöningh, 1968.

Nadar, Sarojini. "On Being the Pentecostal Church. Pentecostal Women's voices and Visions." In *Ecumenical Review* 56 3 (2004) 354–67.

Nelson, Douglas J. "For Such a Time as This: The Story of Bishop William J. Seymour and the Azusa Street Revival." PhD diss., University of Birmingham, 1981.

Newbigin, Lesslie. *The Gospel in a Pluralist Society*. Grand Rapids: Eerdmans, 1989.

———. *The Household of God: Lectures on the Nature of the Church*. London: SCM, 1958/64.

Niederwimmer, Kurt, and Harold W. Attridge. *The Didache: A Commentary*. Minneapolis: Fortress, 1998.

Nikolajsen, Jeppe Bach. *The Distinctive Identity of the Church*. Eugene, OR: Pickwick, 2015.

Nissiotis, Nikos A. *Die Theologie der Ostkirche im ökumenischen Dialog. Kirche und Welt in orthodoxer Sicht*. Stuttgard: Evangelisches Verlagswerk, 1968.

Nouwen, Henri J. M. *The Wounded Healer: Ministry in Contemporary Society*. New York: Image Books Doubleday, 1979.

Nørgaard-Højen, Peder. *Den danske folkekirkes bekendelsesskrifter: Kommentar (The Confessions of the Danish National Church: A Commentary)*. Copenhagen: Anis, 2001.

O'Collins, Gerald, and Daniel Kendall. *The Bible for Theology: Ten Principles for the Theological Use of Scripture*. New York: Paulist, 1997.

Opsahl, Paul D. *The Holy Spirit in the Life of the Church: From Biblical Times to the Present*. Minneapolis: Augsburg, 1978.

Osborne, Grant R. *The Hermeneutical Spiral: A Comprehensive Introduction to Biblical Interpretation*. Downers Grove: InterVarsity, 2006.

Paget-Wilkes, Michael. *Poverty, Revolution and the Church*. Exeter: Paternoster, 1981.
Pannenberg, Wolfhart. *Systematic Theology*. Translated by Geoffrey W. Bromiley, vol. 1. Edinburgh: T & T Clark, 1991.
———. *Systematic Theology*. Translated by Geoffrey W. Bromiley, vol 3. Grand Rapids: Eerdmans, 1991.
Pawson, David. *The Normal Christian Birth*. London: Hodder and Stoughton, 1989.
Peterson, Cheryl M. *Who is the Church? An Ecclesiology for the Twenty-First Century*. Minneapolis: Fortress, 2013.
Pethrus, Lewi. *Brytningstider, Segertider (Times of Changes, Times of Victory)*. Stockholm: Lewi Pethrus, 1969.
Pinnock, Clark H. "Church in the Power of the Holy Spirit: The Promise of Pentecostal Ecclesiology." In *Journal of Pentecostal Theology* 14 2 (2006) 147–65.
———. "The Work of the Holy Spirit in Hermeneutics." In *Journal of Pentecostal Theology* 2 (1993) 3–23.
———. "The Work of the Spirit in the Interpretation of the Holy Scripture from the Perspective of a Charismatic Biblical Tradition." In *Journal of Pentecostal Theology* 18 (2009) 157–71.
Pohl, Christine D. *Making Room: Recovering Hospitality as a Christian Tradition*. Grand Rapids: Eerdmans, 1999.
Porvoo Statement. http://www.porvoocommunion.org/porvoo_communion/statement/the-statement-in-english/.
Preisker, Herbert. "Apollos und die Johannesjünger in Act 18,24–19,6." In *Zeitschrift für die neutestamentliche Wissenschaft* 30 (1931) 301–04.
Rahner, Karl. *The Church and the Sacraments*. Germany: Freiburg Herder, 1963.
———. "What Is a Sacrament?" In *Worship* 47 5 (1973) 274–84.
Raiser, Konrad. *Ecumenism in Transition: A Paradigm Shift in the Ecumenical Movement*. Geneva: WCC, 1991.
Ramsey, Arthur Michael. *Holy Spirit: A Biblical Study*. London: SPCK, 1977.
Ramsey, Michael. *The Gospel and the Catholic Church*. Peabody: Hendrickson, 1935/2009.
Ratzinger, Joseph. *Called to Communion: Understanding the Church Today*. San Francisco: Ignatius, 1996.
———. *Introduction to Christianity*. San Francisco: Ignatius, 2004.
Riddle, Donald W. "Early Christian Hospitality: A Factor in the Gospel Transmission." In *Journal of Biblical Literature* 57 2 (1938) 141–54.
Robeck, Cecil M. "The Nature of Pentecostal Spirituality." In *PNEUMA: The Journal of the Society for Pentecostal Studies* 14 2 (1992) 103–6.
Robeck, Cecil M. Jr., and Jerry L. Sandidge. "The Ecclesiology of *Koinonia* and Baptism: A Pentecostal Perspective." In *Journal of Ecumenical Studies* 27 3 (1990) 504–34.
Robinson, Anthony B., and Robert W. Wall. *Called to be Church: The Book of Acts for a New Day*. Grand Rapids: Eerdmans, 2006.
Roxburgh, Alan J. *The Missionary Congregation, Leadership, & Liminality*. Harrisburg: Trinity, 1997.
Russell, Letty M. *Church in the Round: Feminist Interpretation of the Church*. Louisville: WJK, 1993.
———. "Hot-House Ecclesiology." In *The Ecumenical Review* 53 1 (2001) 48–56.
———. *Just Hospitality: God's Welcome in a World of Difference*. Louisville: WJK, 2009.

Rybarczyk, Edmund J. *The Spirit Unfettered: Protestant Views on the Holy Spirit.* Brewster: Paraclete, 2012.

Sahu, D. K. "A Gathered Community of Witness and Service." In *Global Christian Forum. Transforming Ecumenism*, edited by Richard Howell, 130–39. New Delhi: Evangelical Fellowship of India, 2007.

Saliers, Don. "Singing our Lives." In *Practicing Our Faith: A Way of Life for a Searching People*, edited by Dorothy C. Bass, 179–93. San Francisco: Jossey-Bass, 1997.

Saliers, Don, and Emily Saliers. *A Song to Sing, A Life to Live: Reflections on Music as Spiritual Practice.* San Francisco: Jossey-Bass, 2005.

Samarin, William. *Tongues of Men and Angels.* New York: Macmillian, 1972.

Sandidge, Jerry L. *Roman Catholic/Pentecostal Dialogue (1977–1982): A Study in Developing Ecumenism*, vol. 1. Studien zur interkulturellen Geschichte des Christentums, Band 44. Frankfurt am Main: Peter Lang, 1987.

Schleiermacher, Friedrich. *The Christian Faith.* Edited by H. R. Mackintosh and J. S. Stewart. Edinburgh: T & T Clark, 1928.

Schlink, Edmund. *The Coming Christ and the Coming Church.* Philadelphia: Fortress, 1968.

———. Ökumenische Dogmatik: Grundzüge. Göttingen. Vandenhoeck & Ruprecht, 1983.

Schlink, Edmund. *The Doctrine of Baptism.* Translated by Herbert J. A. Bouman. Saint Louis: Concordia, 1972.

Schmemann, Alexander. *For The Life of the World: Sacraments and Orthodoxy.* New York: St. Vladimirs Seminary, 1973.

Schweizer, Eduard. *Church Order in the New Testament.* Norwich: SCM, 1961.

———. "Pneuma." In *Theological Dictionary of the New Testament (TDNT)* 6 396–455. Grand Rapids: Eerdmans, 1968.

Shaw, Perry W. H. "A Welcome Guest: Ministerial Training as an Act of Hospitality." In *Christian Educational Journal* 8 1 (2011) 8–26.

Sheldrake, Philip, and Megan McKenna. *Spirituality and Theology: Christian Living and the Doctrine of God.* New York: Orbits, 1998.

Smith, James K. A. "Confessions of an Existentialist: Reading Augustine after Heidegger." In *The Influence of Augustine and Heidegger: The Emergence of an Augustinian Phenomenology*, edited by Craig J. N. DePaulo, 221–57. New York: Edwin Mellen, 2006.

———. *Desiring the Kingdom: Worship, Worldview, and Cultural Formation.* Grand Rapids: Baker, 2009.

———. *Thinking in Tongues. Pentecostal Contributions to Christian Philosophy.* Grand Rapids: Eerdmans, 2010.

———. *Who's Afraid of Postmodernism? Taking Derrida, Lyotard, and Foucault to Church.* Grand Rapids: Baker, 2006.

Strawley, James Herbert, ed. *St. Ambrose, On the Mysteries and the Treatise on the Sacraments.* Translated by T. Thompsen. London: SPCK, 1919/1950.

Stronstad, Roger. *The Charismatic Theology of St. Luke.* Peabody: Hendrickson, 1984.

Stålsett, Sturla. "Den krevende evangeliske åpenheten (The Demanding Evangelical Receptiveness)." In *Vårt Land 21*, 2014.

Suurmond, Jean-Jacques. *Word and Spirit at Play: Towards a Charismatic Theology.* Grand Rapids: Eerdmans, 1994.

Svenungsson, Jayne. "Transcending tradition: Towards a critical theology of the Spirit." In *Studia Theologica* 62 (2008) 63–79.
Swete, H. B. *Theodore of Mopsuestia. On the Minor Epistles of St. Paul*, vol 11. Cambridge: Cambridge 1990.
Tan-Chow, MayLing. *Pentecostal Theology for the Twenty-First Century. Engaging With Multi-Faith Singapore*. Aldershot: Ashgate, 2007.
Tangen, Karl Inge. *Ecclesial Identification Beyond Late Modern Individualism? A Case Study of Life Strategies in Growing Late Modern Churches*. Leiden: Brill, 2012.
Tanner, Mary E. "On Being Church: Some Thoughts Inspired by the Ecumenical Community." In *The Ecumenical Review* 53 1 (2001) 48–56.
Tappert, Theodore G., transl. and ed. *The Book of Concord: The Confessions and the Evangelical Lutheran Church*. Minneapolis: Fortress, 1989.
Tarasar, Constance J. "Worship, Spirituality and Biblical Reflection: Their Significance for the Churches' Search for Koinonia." In *The Ecumenical Review* 45 2 218–25.
Tertullian. "On baptism." http://www.newadvent.org/fathers/0321.htm.
Thiselton, Anthony. "Communicative Action and Promise in Interdisciplinary Biblical and Theological Hermeneutics." In *The Promise of Hermeneutics*, edited by Antony Thiselton et al., 133–239. Grand Rapids: Eerdmans, 1999.
Thiselton, Anthony C. *The Holy Spirit: In Biblical Teaching, Through the Centuries, and Today*. London: SPCK, 2013.
———. *New Horizons in Hermeneutics*. Grand Rapids: Zondervan, 1992.
Thurian, Max. *Churches Respond to BEM: Official Responses to the Baptism, Eucharist and Ministry Text*, vol. 1–5. Geneva: WCC, 1986–88.
Tillich, Paul. *The Protestant Era*. Chicago: University of Chicago Press, 1957.
———. *Systematic Theology*, vol. 3. Chicago: University of Chicago Press, 1968.
Tjørhom, Ola. *Kirkens enhet-for at verden skal se og tro: en innføring i økumenisk tenkning (Church Unity—so the World May Observe and Believe: An Introduction to Ecumenical Reflection)*. Oslo: Verbum, 2005.
Turner, Max. "James Dunn's *Baptism in the Holy Spirit*: Appreciation and Response." In *Journal of Pentecostal Theology* 19 (2010) 25–31.
Van Gelder, Craig. *The Essence of the Church: A Community Created by the Spirit*. Grand Rapids: Baker, 2000.
Vanhoozer, Kevin J. *The Drama of Doctrine: A Canonical-Linguistic Approach to Christian Theology*. Louisville: WJK, 2005.
Volf, Miroslav. *After our Likeness: The Church as the Image of the Trinity*. Grand Rapids: Eerdmans, 1998.
———. "Community Formation as an Image of the Triune God: A Congregational Model of Church Order and Life." In *Community Formation in the Early Church and in the Church Today*, edited by Richard N. Longenecker, 213–37. Peabody: Hendrickson, 2002.
———. *Exclusion and Embrace: A Theological Exploration of Identity, Otherness, and Reconsiliation*. Nashville: Abingdon, 1996.
———. *Wir sind die Kirche*. Habilitationsschrift. Tübingen: Tübingen, 1992.
Volf, Miroslav, and Maurice Lee. "The Spirit and the Church." In *Advents of the Spirit: An Introduction to the Current Study of Pneumatology*, edited by D. Lyle Dabney and Bradford E. Hinze, 382-409. Milwaukee: Marquette University Press, 2001.

Vondey, Wolfgang. "Pentecostal Ecclesiology and Eucharistic Hospitality: Toward a Systematic and Ecumenical Account of the Church." In *PNEUMA: The Journal of the Society for Pentecostal Studies* 32 (2010) 41–55.
Wacker, Grant. *Heaven Below: Early Pentecostals and American Culture.* Cambridge: Harvard University Press, 2001.
Wainwright, Geoffrey. "Church." In *Dictionary of the Ecumenical Movement*, edited by Nicholas Lossky et al., 159–67. Geneva: WCC, 1991.
———. *Doxology: The Praise of God in Worship, Doctrine and Life: A Systematic Theology.* London: Epworth, 1980.
Walker, David S. *Challenging Evangelicalism.* Pietermaritzburg: Cluster, 1993.
Wall, Robert W. *Why the Church? Reframing New Testament Theology.* Edited by Joel B. Green. Nashville: Abingdon, 2015.
Ward, Pete. *Selling Worship: How What we Sing has Changed the Church.* Waynesboro: Paternoster, 2005.
Webster, John. "The 'Self-Organizing' Power of the Gospel: Episcopacy and Community Formation." In *Community Formation in the Early Church and in the Church Today*, edited by Richard N. Longenecker, 179–94. Peabody: Hendrickson, 2002.
Welker, Michael. *God the Spirit.* Minneapolis: Fortress, 1994.
———. *The Work of the Spirit: Pneumatology and Pentecostalism.* Grand Rapids: Eerdmans, 2006.
Wenk, Matthias. *Community-Forming Power: The Socio-Ethical Role of the Spirit in Luke–Acts.* Sheffield: Sheffield Academic, 2000.
———. "Mission Spiritu: Why Pentecostals have an Ecumenical Resonsibility." In *Journal of the European Pentecostal Theological Association* 35 1 (2015) 26–33.
———. "Reconciliation and Renunciation of Status as God's Final Aim for Humanity: New Testament Thoughts on the Church's Mission and Unity." In *Journal of Pentecostal Theology* 19 1 (2010) 44–58.
Weston, Paul. *Lesslie Newbigin, Missionary Theologian.* London: SPCK, 2006.
Wilken, Robert Louis. *The Spirit of Early Christian Thought: Seeking the Face of God.* New Haven: Yale University Press, 2003.
Williams, J. Rodman. *The Pentecostal Reality.* Plainfield: Loges International, 1972.
Williams, Rowan. "Archbishop's address at 50th anniversary of PCPCU." (2010). http://rowanwilliams.archbishopofcanterbury.org/.
Williams, Rowan. *On Christian Theology.* Oxford: Blackwell, 2000.
———. *Silence and Honey Cakes: The Wisdom of the Desert.* Oxford: Lion, 2004.
———. *Wound of Knowledge: Christian Spirituality from the New Testament to St John of the Cross.* London: DLT, 1979.
Wolterstorff, Nicholas. *Educating for Shalom: Essays on Christian Higher Education.* Edited by Clarence W. Joldersma and Gloria Goris Stronks. Grand Rapids: Eerdmans, 2004.
World Council of Churches. *Baptism, Eucharist and Ministry (BEM).* Faith and Order Paper No. 111. Geneva: WCC, 1982.
———. "The Church: Towards a Common Vision." http://www.oikoumene.org/en/resources/documents/wcc-commissions/faith-and-order-commission/i-unity-the-church-and-its-mission/the-church-towards-a-common-vision, 2013.
———. "One Baptism: Towards Mutual Recognition." http://www.oikoumene.org/en/resources/documents/wcc-commissions/faith-and-order-commission/ii-worship-and-baptism/one-baptism-towards-mutual-recognition, 2011.

———. "Together Towards Life: Mission and Evangelism in Changing Landscapes." http://www.oikoumene.org/en/resources/documents/wcc-commissions/mission-and-evangelism/together-towards-life-mission-and-evangelism-in-changing-landscapes, 2012.

World Study Report. "Challenges and Opportunities in Theological Education in the 21st Century: Pointers for a New International Debate on Theological Education." Edited by International Study Group on Theological Education, 2010.

Wyckoff, John W. "The Baptism in the Holy Spirit." In *Systematic theology*, edited by Stanley M. Horton, 423–55. Springfield: Logion, 1995.

Yong, Amos. *Hospitality and the Other: Pentecost, Christian Practices, and the Neighbor*. Maryknoll: Orbis, 2008.

———. "Poured Out on All Flesh: The Spirit, World Pentecostalism, and the Renewal of Theology and Praxis in the 21st Century." *PentecoStudies* 6 1 (2007) 16–46.

———. *Renewing Christian Theology: Systematics for a Global Christianity*. Waco: Baylor, 2014.

———. *Spirit-Word-Community: Theological Hermeneutics in Trinitarian Perspective*. Aldershot: Ashgate, 2002.

———. *Spirit of Love: A Trinitarian Theology of Grace*. Waco: Baylor University Press, 2012.

———. *The Spirit Poured Out on All Flesh: Pentecostalism and the Possibility of Global Theology*. Grand Rapids: Baker, 2005.

———. *Theology and Down Syndrome: Reimagining Disability in Late Modernity*. Waco: Baylor University Press, 2007.

Zizioulas, John D. *Being as Communion: Studies in Personhood and the Church*. London: Darton, Longman and Todd, 1985/2004.

Zizioulas, John D. *Eucharist, Bishop, Church: The Unity of the Church in the Divine Eucharist and the Bishop During the First Three Centuries*. Translated by Elisabeth Theokritoff. Brookline: Holy Cross Orthodox Press, 2001.

Zizioulas, John D., and Douglas H. Knight, ed. *Communion & Otherness: Further Studies in Personhood and the Church*. London: T & T Clark, 2006.

———. *Lectures in Christian Dogmatics*. London: T & T Clark, 2008.

Zwingli, Ulrich. *Commentary on the True and False Religion*. Translated by Samuel Macauley Jackson and Clarence Nevin Heller. Durham: Labyrinth, 1981.

Index

Adoration, 21, 34, 104, 144, 148, 167, 169, 175, 187
Albrecht, Daniel E., 144, 147
Alexander, Kimberly E., 169, 186–87, 212
Althouse, Peter, 264–65
Ambrose, 122, 204, 205
Anglican, 26, 209, 218
Anointing, 43, 52, 56, 86–88, 103, 114, 124, 149, 151, 194, 199, 209, 212, 241, 270
Anselm, 220, 234
anthropology, 40, 118–19, 165, 170
apostasy, 64, 82
apostolic, apostolicity, 3, 7, 24, 28–30, 33, 36, 43, 47, 48–53–68, 81–82, 89, 109–110, 135, 149, 151, 157, 173, 194–95, 238, 255, 258, 261, 266, 270, 274
Aquinas, 122
Aram, I, 24, 257
Aristotelian, Aristotle, 176, 210
Aronson, Torbjörn, 156–58
assembly, 62, 65, 74, 76–77, 111, 119, 128, 132, 156, 200, 232, 263, 266
Atkinson, William, 85, 94
atonement, 241
Augsburg Confession, Confessio Augustana 7, 45, 112, 126, 189
Augustine, Daniela, 30, 54, 209, 222–25, 227–28, 230, 246
Augustine, 2, 31, 122, 189, 192–93, 209

authority, 14, 16–17, 26, 30, 49, 57–59, 70, 74, 81, 111, 177, 210, 218, 222
Azusa Street, 96

Baer Jr., Richard A., 152–53
Balthasar, Hans Urs von, 11, 39
baptism, 3, 22, 28–29, 32–35, 37, 43, 48, 50, 55, 57, 60–61, 63, 65, 67, 73, 78–79, 81, 82– 90, 92–106, 114, 116, 123–29, 135, 137–38, 146, 150–51, 155–56, 158, 160, 170, 174–75, 177, 183–84, 188, 189, 190–205, 213–15, 218, 221, 231–32, 242–45, 250, 254–56, 258
Bartchy, S. Scott, 70, 71
Baumert, Norbert, 104, 106
Bayer, Oswald, 169, 170, 240
believe, 3, 6, 26, 48, 65, 72, 99, 102, 103–4, 106, 109–110, 118–19, 124, 125–27, 132, 135, 163, 165, 168–69, 175, 184, 188, 191, 198, 203, 208, 218–19, 246, 253
believer, 4, 7, 13, 19, 45, 55, 66– 77, 93, 97, 100, 103, 105, 109, 112, 115–117, 121, 127, 137–38, 141, 150, 170–71, 175–76, 178–79, 182, 184, 197–98, 200–201, 205, 214, 228, 235, 250, 270
BEM, 23, 28, 50, 130, 197, 198, 203, 204
Bible, iv, xiv, 10, 12–20, 24, 31–32, 34, 44, 169, 192, 234, 239

biblical, 8, 11–12, 14–17, 30–31, 33–34, 41, 44, 49, 52, 56, 59–60, 91, 97, 149, 157, 160, 165, 169, 171, 173–74, 177, 180, 195–96, 210, 226, 228, 234, 238–39, 257, 258, 259, 265, 271
bishop, bishops, 33, 32, 52, 65, 116–17, 208, 268
blessing, blessings, ix, xi, xiv, 29, 72, 87–88, 102–3, 106, 112, 126–27, 133, 151, 178, 182, 185, 200, 202–3, 206, 211, 214
Bloesch, Donald G., 19, 20, 101–3, 145, 191, 196–97
Blueprint ecclesiology, 40, 41, 60
Body of Christ, xiv, 4, 5, 6, 9, 21, 23, 25–30, 32–33, 35, 37, 39, 43, 46, 48, 51, 58, 60, 63, 65, 69, 72, 74, 78–79, 80, 83, 85, 87–89, 97–98, 109, 111–13, 117–18, 123–24, 127–31, 146–47, 157–58, 171, 175, 177, 184–85, 187, 189–90, 197, 202, 204–5, 207–9, 210, 212–14, 223–24, 227, 229–30, 241–42, 245, 247, 254, 258–60, 262–65, 269, 272
Boersma, Hans, 183, 240, 241, 242
Boone, Jerome, 139, 142–45
Bosch, David, 264, 269
Bradshaw, Paul F., 33, 43
Breck, John, 108, 174, 175
Brunner, Emil, 25, 123, 130, 162, 163

calling, 27, 47, 49, 52, 56, 63, 106, 111, 159, 178, 213, 238, 246, 248, 250, 260, 273, 276
Calvin, Calvinist, 196, 205, 211, 252
canon, canonical, 14, 16–17, 59, 117, 171, 233
Catholic, Roman, catholicity, 7–8, 10–11, 24, 32, 48–51, 65–66, 68, 90, 102–3, 108–110, 113, 116–20, 127, 129, 136, 139, 141, 145, 149, 152, 157, 172, 188–89, 191–92, 195, 202–3, 207–8, 223, 227, 246–48, 252, 256, 258–59, 266, 268, 270, 273
celebration, 32–33, 43, 50, 110, 124, 128, 144–45, 151, 165, 174, 185, 189, 194, 204, 208, 210–11, 215, 224, 232, 245–47, 250
Chan, Simon, 25–26, 35–36, 98, 146, 155–56, 185, 188
charism, charisms, charisma, 9, 49–51, 68, 70–72, 77–78, 80, 83, 88, 93, 104–6, 110, 116, 120, 127, 131–33, 136, 138, 153, 170, 173, 241, 259, 273–74
charismatic, charismatics, xiv–xv, 2–9, 13, 19, 25, 34, 40, 43, 47, 49–54, 57–59, 63, 68–69, 71–73, 75–77, 79–83, 86, 90–99, 101–2, 104–6, 109, 113, 116, 118–19, 121, 127, 129, 131–36, 138–39, 141–42, 152–53, 156–60, 173, 183, 188, 210, 214–17, 221–23, 226–27, 250, 260, 263–64, 277, 280
Cheung, Tak-Ming, 85, 103–5, 114
children, 24, 64, 114, 126–27, 156, 168, 172, 191, 194, 204, 223, 225–26, 228, 239, 254
chrismation, 116, 175, 184, 189
christological, Christology, 6, 8, 16, 28, 42, 55, 81, 109–110, 116, 121, 133, 135, 149, 212, 215, 242, 256, 261–62, 273
Colle, Ralph del, 25, 104, 273–74
commitment, 15–16, 19–20, 26, 51, 70, 74, 89, 123, 142, 166, 171, 178, 190, 199, 201, 230–31, 244–45, 262, 274
communion, 3, 6, 23–24, 29, 31–32, 37–38, 45, 50–51, 64, 66, 78, 98–99, 109–111, 116–18, 120, 125, 128, 131, 135, 156, 167, 169, 173, 178, 182, 185, 187–88, 190, 192, 206–210, 218, 220, 230–31, 234, 246, 254, 259–60, 262–65, 267, 271, 273, 276
community, xiii, 2–3, 5, 7–9, 11, 13–14, 17, 19–20, 22–32, 34–35, 37–38, 42–48, 52–53, 56–66, 68–72, 74–76, 78–82, 85, 88, 91–93, 98–99, 103, 106, 110, 113, 115–18, 121–22, 124, 126, 128–29, 131–34, 136, 138–39, 141–46, 148–51, 154, 159–65, 168–69, 171–72, 178, 180–81, 184, 186,

188, 190–92, 194, 203, 207–8, 210, 212–18, 220, 222–29, 231–32, 235, 237–42, 244, 246–47, 249–50, 252, 254–56, 259, 262–63, 265, 267–71, 273, 275, 277, 279
confession, confessional, x–xi, 3, 7–8, 11, 18, 40, 42–43, 52, 55, 62, 65–66, 79, 89, 107, 112, 123, 126–27, 129, 141, 143–44, 183, 185, 188–91, 197, 203–4, 212, 214, 222, 241, 243–45, 247, 252, 270, 274
confirmation, 103, 106, 116, 127, 135, 143
Congar, Yves, 8, 38, 108–110, 118–20, 123–25, 131–32, 134, 136, 192, 219, 246, 256
congregation, xi, 8, 27, 34, 37, 47–48, 51–52, 64–68, 77, 82, 93, 112, 127–28, 132, 140, 143, 158–59, 164, 167, 171, 178–80, 182, 187–88, 192, 212, 218, 237, 244–45, 254
Constantinopolitan, 36, 175
constitution, 6, 54, 109–110
conversion, 55, 58, 61, 64, 78, 87–89, 94–96, 102, 104–5, 123–24, 138, 150, 181, 197–202, 204, 209, 256, 260
covenant, covenantal, 24, 29, 39, 60, 88–89, 125, 201–2, 213, 228, 234, 255
Cox, Harvey, 139, 262–63
creed, creedal, creeds, xiii, 3, 20, 24, 26, 33, 36–37, 43, 49–50, 54, 84, 145, 153, 160, 163, 173–75, 178, 182, 203, 207, 254, 261, 270
cross, xv, 9, 19, 21, 45, 73, 121, 129, 133, 155, 158, 169, 183, 200, 210, 218, 223, 232, 240–42, 249, 251, 267
crucified, 8, 41–42, 73, 122, 129–30, 134, 162, 192, 212, 232, 263
culture, xiii, 9, 13, 18–19, 38, 41, 46, 51, 67, 112, 142, 149, 162, 179, 187, 209, 232, 236–38, 241, 250, 267–68, 270

Cyprian, 195
Cyril, 31

Dabney, D. L., 254, 260
Dawn, Marva J., 12, 163–64, 187
death, 33–35, 62, 73, 89–90, 98, 106, 112, 114, 125, 130, 148, 155, 158, 174, 185, 190, 204, 206, 209–211, 213, 215, 221, 232, 239, 242, 246, 250, 279
deeds, 22, 24, 37, 56, 58, 69, 78, 81, 160, 179, 182, 234–35, 237, 265, 274, 279
Dempster, Murray W., 101, 156
denomination, denominational, denominations, 2, 6, 49, 93, 122, 129, 140, 156–58, 173, 205, 242–43, 245, 247, 251, 253, 261, 266, 268, 272, 275–76
desire, desiring, 35, 70, 74, 80, 109, 121, 148, 152, 156, 162, 164–66, 170–72, 178–79, 181, 186–88, 201–2, 206, 217, 220–21, 237, 268, 274–75
development, 3, 35–36, 38, 111, 156, 196, 256, 269–70, 277
devotion, devotional, 10, 19, 31, 52, 113, 155, 239, 262
diaconal, *diaconia*, 2, 9, 22, 24, 32, 90, 122, 126–27, 131, 134, 160, 210, 217, 239, 250, 263
dialogical, dialogue, 2–3, 5, 7, 19–20, 36, 42, 46, 53–54, 122, 124, 135, 141, 144, 178, 190, 203, 222, 227–28, 230, 243, 255, 257, 261, 266, 275
Didache, 34, 131, 194, 226, 233
dignity, 122, 176, 181, 220, 223, 250, 268
discernment, 2, 11, 44, 46, 52, 57, 74, 77, 92, 132, 165–66, 176, 223, 230, 240, 246, 250
discipleship, 2, 39, 45, 50, 53, 88, 127, 172, 181, 203, 213, 233, 243–44, 259
diversity, x, 2, 10, 20, 24, 32, 35, 37, 46, 54, 62, 110, 113, 117, 135–36, 140, 145, 161, 193, 223–24, 252, 254–56, 260, 262–63, 267–68, 274–75

divisions, 41, 157, 167, 173, 220, 242, 254, 260, 274, 279
doctrine, doctrines, xiii, 1, 4, 7, 14, 20, 26, 30, 32, 35–36, 40, 48, 51, 54–56, 62, 90, 96, 108, 112–13, 120, 127, 136, 148, 158, 160, 162–63, 165, 167, 171, 173, 183–84, 191, 195, 197–99, 202, 208, 213, 217–18, 240, 242–44, 247, 252, 258, 279
dogma, dogmatic, dogmatics, 4, 11, 26, 36, 50, 94–95, 110, 134, 190, 253, 261, 272, 275
doxological, doxology, 21, 109, 119, 163, 166, 209
Dulles, Avery, 50–51, 53
Dunn, James D. G., 57–59, 61, 68, 71–73, 75–80, 84–90, 94–96, 102, 124, 188, 193, 196, 199–202

Eastern Christianity, 4, 6, 31, 65, 116–17, 128, 135, 174–75, 208, 210
ecclesial, ecclesiological, xiv, 1, 8–11, 13, 16, 20, 28, 30, 36–41, 43, 45–46, 48–49, 53–54, 65–66, 81, 83, 90, 97–98, 104, 106, 109, 111, 115–16, 119, 125, 129, 132, 136, 139, 141, 146–48, 154, 156, 160, 169, 173, 183, 185, 188–90, 212, 217, 230, 232–33, 241–42, 247, 250, 254, 257, 259, 261–62, 270–73, 275, 279
ecclesiology, 2–7, 9, 11, 13, 23, 25–27, 30, 36, 38–43, 45–47, 49, 52–55, 61, 65, 80, 90, 99, 104, 108–110, 116, 118, 120–21, 135–38, 140–41, 143, 147, 155–56, 158–61, 164, 173–74, 180, 203, 222, 238–39, 244–45, 258–65, 267, 269, 271–72
ecstatic, 57, 62, 74, 76–77, 115, 130, 150, 184
ecumenical, ecumenism, ix–x, xv, 2–3, 5–6, 24, 29–30, 36, 46, 50–51, 53, 95, 106, 109–110, 118, 125, 135, 139–41, 147, 189–91, 195, 197, 203, 205, 212, 215, 242–43, 245–48, 251–58, 260–68, 271–76
elders, 67–68, 70
Elowsky, Joel C., 163, 184
embodied, embodiment, 7, 9, 19, 24, 26, 46, 51, 63, 101, 110, 134–35, 141–42, 149, 165–67, 170–71, 173, 177, 179, 182, 185, 223–24, 231, 237, 249, 251
emotional, 53, 91, 96, 142, 154, 241, 246
empowering, empowerment, xiii, 26, 49, 63, 79, 86, 90, 95–97, 101–6, 110, 124, 145, 149, 160, 178, 189, 217–18, 225, 234, 237, 239, 272
endowment, 57, 93–95, 103–5, 114
Engelsviken, x, 90–95
enlightenment, 18, 44, 141
enthusiasm, 77, 115, 122
episcopacy, episcopal, 47–48, 50, 141, 152
epistemological, epistemology, 14, 16, 142, 165
equipment, equipped, 15, 61, 68, 70, 94, 115, 199, 201, 232
eschatological, eschatology, 8, 37, 41, 56, 58–59, 63–64, 66, 69–70, 82, 86, 88, 94–96, 99, 106, 114, 120–21, 123, 128–29, 133, 139–40, 142, 159–60, 163, 169, 177, 187, 191, 195, 207, 213–14, 221, 223–26, 229, 231, 234, 251, 265, 273
ethical, ethics, 44, 57–58, 63, 77–78, 81–82, 92–94, 105, 117, 143, 162, 166–67, 175–78, 190, 225, 231, 233, 242, 246, 249, 253, 255, 268, 275
eucharist, eucharistic, 3, 28–29, 32–34, 43, 50, 53, 65, 67, 73, 109, 116, 122, 127–31, 137, 144, 151, 155, 165, 167, 170, 172, 174, 176, 178, 183–84, 188, 192–93, 205–211, 214–15, 231–32, 241, 245–50, 258, 260, 263
evangelical, 51, 101, 139, 145, 186, 191, 241
evidence, 63, 91–92, 95, 100, 103, 149, 151–52, 165, 274

INDEX 301

experience, experiences, x, xiv, 1, 3–5, 7–11, 13–16, 19–21, 26–27, 29–32, 34, 40, 44, 53–54, 57–61, 63–64, 66, 70–73, 78–79, 82, 84–88, 90–95, 97–98, 101, 103–5, 109, 113, 115, 120–21, 123, 128, 130–31, 136, 138–39, 141–43, 146–47, 150–55, 159–60, 164, 170–71, 174, 177, 187, 194, 196–200, 204, 213, 218, 222, 224, 236, 247, 252, 257, 262–63, 266

faith, xiii–xv, 1–3, 5, 7, 11–20, 23–24, 26–31, 35–36, 42, 46, 48–51, 53, 55–58, 65–67, 69, 71–75, 81, 84–88, 94, 96, 102–4, 106, 110, 113, 115, 120–21, 124–27, 134–37, 139, 142–44, 148, 150–51, 156, 159, 161–63, 168, 170–72, 174, 179, 181, 183–85, 187–91, 193–94, 196–207, 211–15, 219–25, 227–28, 230, 235, 237–38, 240–44, 246–47, 250, 252, 254–56, 258–59, 263, 265–66, 273, 275, 277, 279
faithful, faithfulness, 14, 32, 37, 43, 46, 49, 52, 56, 103, 119–20, 164, 175, 179, 192, 198, 221, 230, 232, 246, 248, 257, 259
Fee, Gordon D., 2, 67, 79
feeling, feelings, ix, xv, 2, 11, 34, 74–75, 81, 93, 113, 115, 150, 154, 159, 164–65, 178, 182, 187, 197, 226, 241, 266
fellowship, x–xi, xv, 2, 4–7, 9–11, 21, 25, 27–31, 35, 37, 43, 46–47, 52–53, 59–60, 72, 80, 82, 87, 89–90, 92–93, 97–99, 110–11, 113, 116, 118, 121–24, 126–27, 129–31, 133–34, 137–38, 143, 145–47, 157, 160–61, 163, 173, 180–82, 185, 190, 192, 201–2, 207, 215–20, 223, 226, 228–29, 236–37, 241, 246–47, 249–50, 252, 258, 262–64, 268, 270, 273, 275, 277, 280
feminist, 18, 238

forgiveness, 3, 27, 40, 44, 62–63, 82, 85–86, 94, 110, 124, 145, 149, 165, 188, 198–99, 207, 215, 218, 228, 235, 241, 247, 253–54
formation, x, 15, 21, 27, 39, 47, 62, 64–65, 105, 109, 139, 142–43, 155, 159–60, 162, 164–66, 168, 171–72, 179–81, 233, 272–73
freedom, 49, 59, 100, 113, 118, 122, 127, 131, 133, 142–43, 148–49, 151–52, 154, 157, 170, 175, 193, 197, 232, 240, 244, 247, 261, 265, 268
friendship, 8, 106, 120–22, 129, 216–17, 226, 230–33, 247, 249, 251, 253, 266–67
fruit of the Spirit, 37, 93, 103, 106, 132, 134, 176, 216, 220–22, 227, 229, 235, 252–53

Gaillardetz, Richard R., 43, 45, 235–36
gathering, gatherings, 10, 28, 45, 56, 64, 128, 145, 166–67, 171, 178, 206, 208, 246–47, 276
Gelder, Craig Van, 38, 53, 269
gender, 44, 63, 202, 213, 223, 239, 242, 268
generosity, 37, 78, 103, 216, 218, 220–21, 227, 249–50
gifts, charismatic, xiv, 9, 25, 43, 51–52, 71, 77, 92, 94–95, 119, 131, 134, 142, 152, 221, 226
global, x–xi, 6, 13, 23, 30, 43, 45–46, 91, 98, 119–20, 136, 140, 158, 197, 227–28, 236, 243, 245, 247, 253–55, 268, 276
glossolalia, glossolalic, 73–77, 95, 100, 134, 147–53, 155, 224
gospel, xiv–xv, 6, 8, 18, 20–22, 24, 27, 29, 35–36, 42–51, 53, 58, 63–64, 67–69, 73–74, 85–86, 89, 106, 111–12, 115, 119, 122, 138, 150, 152, 158–60, 174, 178, 181, 183, 185, 188–89, 193, 198, 201, 206, 211–12, 214, 225–26, 231–33, 236, 238–42, 247–48, 251–57, 259–60, 265, 267–68, 272, 274, 279

INDEX

grace, xiv–xv, 2, 8–9, 24, 27, 31–32, 34, 39–42, 45–46, 52–53, 56, 58, 67, 71–73, 78–83, 85, 98, 100–103, 105–6, 109–110, 115, 117, 119–21, 126–27, 129, 131–32, 134, 136, 144–45, 148, 151–52, 154, 160, 163, 172, 176, 178, 181–84, 186–87, 189, 191–93, 195–97, 200–201, 203, 205–7, 209–216, 220, 225, 228–31, 233, 239, 241, 247, 254, 258, 265, 273, 276, 279–80

Green, Joel, x, 11–12

Groppe, Elisabeth, 109, 119

growth, 5, 62, 92–93, 98, 103, 143, 145, 197, 205, 229, 245, 260, 264

guidance, 17, 26, 47, 72, 74, 77–78, 80, 95, 110, 131, 168, 210, 259

Gunkel, Hermann, 76, 150–51

Halldorf, Joel, x, 158, 248

Hauerwas, Stanley, 44, 176–77, 190, 208, 231–33, 248–49

healing, 24, 40, 42–43, 50, 52, 57, 69, 81, 88, 90, 92, 98, 101–2, 139, 142, 152, 154–55, 160, 165, 167, 188, 210, 212, 218, 221, 224, 227–28, 236, 240, 251, 253, 259, 266, 268, 270

Healy, Nicholas M., 4, 27, 38–43, 45, 53, 258

heaven, xv, 18, 122, 139, 142, 152, 224, 227, 234, 263, 276

Hegstad, Harald, x, xiv, 10, 38, 65

Henriksen, Jan-Olav, x, 28, 217

hermeneutic, hermeneutical, hermeneutics, 9–11, 13, 16–17, 44, 55, 58, 64, 82, 95, 100, 149, 169, 187

hierarchical, hierarchy, 72, 80, 108, 111, 117, 131, 143, 157, 205, 217, 239, 258

holiness, 41, 49–50, 113, 219, 226, 262

holistic, 27, 112–13, 142, 166, 171, 182, 239, 260, 263, 269

Hollenweger, Walter J., 76, 139, 141, 154–55, 165

Holy Spirit, 13–14, 17, 19–23, 27–28, 33–46, 48–49, 53, 55, 58, 61, 67, 71–72, 74, 76–80, 83, 89, 94, 98, 100–103, 105, 108–9, 111, 117, 120–22, 124–31, 133–37, 139–42, 144, 146, 148–49, 151–52, 154–55, 157, 161, 163, 166, 171, 174–75, 179, 181, 188–91, 197–98, 200, 205, 207, 209–216, 220–22, 224–27, 230–32, 234–36, 238–39, 243–44, 249–50, 252, 258, 262, 268, 272–76

hope, xv, 5, 26, 28, 31, 39, 44, 48, 60, 62, 64, 71, 83, 101, 106, 109, 113, 120–21, 126–27, 129, 136, 155, 168, 170, 179, 182, 187, 189, 207–8, 212, 214, 216, 218, 230–32, 235, 247–48, 251, 256, 259, 264, 268, 272, 274, 279–80

hospitable, hospitality, xi, 8, 67, 80, 106, 121, 129, 131, 143, 161, 163, 167, 179, 181, 183, 209, 213, 215–18, 222–33, 235, 237–38, 240–43, 245–51, 253, 260, 264, 271, 275, 279

humanity, 15, 37, 99, 113, 123, 169, 187, 201, 208, 217, 220, 223, 234, 236, 239–40, 259, 267

humble, xi, 41, 99, 136, 219, 229–30, 249–50, 254, 266

humility, 21, 74, 99, 122, 134, 163–64, 168, 174, 179, 181–82, 219, 236, 253, 271, 279

hymns, 61, 75, 171–72, 179, 203

Hütter, Reinhard, xiii, 25, 26, 27, 28, 47, 135, 163, 169, 170, 242, 264

identity, 5, 7, 9, 12, 23–25, 27, 30, 38–45, 47–48, 55–56, 58–59, 63, 66, 69, 79, 82, 87, 91, 98, 103, 109–110, 113, 116, 122, 124–25, 127–28, 130–31, 134–35, 137–41, 145–46, 149, 156, 160–61, 165–66, 170–71, 178–80, 183, 185–86, 190, 197, 200–201, 210, 212–14, 218–19, 223–24, 227, 232, 236–37, 241, 249, 253,

256, 259, 264–67, 269–72, 274, 276–77, 279
Ignatius, 64, 111
imagination, imaginative, 15–16, 31, 42–44, 46, 52, 142, 144, 162, 164, 166–68, 170–72, 178–79, 181, 184
incarnation, incarnational, 30, 63, 129, 135, 186–87, 209, 212, 223–24, 228
inclusiveness, 9, 174, 206, 215, 217, 229, 242, 249, 254, 275
individualism, individualistic, 7, 47, 52, 61, 66, 98, 116, 128, 131, 146, 152, 156, 237
individuality, 59, 249, 271
infant baptism, 59, 124–27, 195, 203, 244–45
initiation, 43, 61, 64, 78, 87–89, 94–98, 101, 103, 105, 116, 123–24, 159–60, 184, 189, 197–202, 204–5, 211, 214, 243, 245
inspiration, 17, 34, 54, 68, 74, 79, 94, 114, 199, 209, 222, 274
institutional, 47, 49, 59, 116, 132, 136, 149, 210, 215, 237, 246–48, 254
interpretation, 1, 13, 15, 17, 19, 27, 35, 44, 50, 61, 64, 76–77, 91, 95, 99, 119, 129, 132, 146, 149, 153, 155, 171, 195, 238–40, 266
invocation, 33, 68, 173, 191, 204–5, 210–12, 214, 246

Jewish, 33, 45, 60, 73, 81, 102, 149, 194, 202, 228, 235
Johnson, Luke T., 67, 70
Jones, Gregory, 39–40, 241
joy, 37, 50, 70, 87, 103, 133–34, 153, 179–80, 188, 208–9, 221, 230, 250, 256, 270
judgment, 74, 113, 166, 177, 193
justification, justified, 18, 62–63, 75, 125–26, 136, 188–89, 202, 225

Kärkkäinen, Veli-Matti, x, 6, 49, 50, 53, 54, 112, 140, 141, 147, 159, 217

Kasper, 4, 189–91, 247–48, 266
Keifert, Patrick R., 230, 241
Kelly, J. N. D., 183–84, 194–95
kerygma, kerygmatic, 49, 81, 99, 135, 142, 148, 159, 263
Kessler, Diane C., 249, 253
kingdom of God, 9, 22, 24, 27, 50, 56, 96, 109, 121–24, 133, 140, 143, 150, 185, 195, 199, 206, 209, 212–13, 218, 221, 225, 236, 243–44, 259
koinonia, 28–30, 35, 52, 90, 97, 109, 138, 147, 190, 202–3, 223, 226, 236, 242, 244–45, 256, 258, 263, 270
Koskela, Douglas M., 109–110, 118, 256

Land, Steven, x, 37, 56–57, 138–40, 142–44, 227, 262
leadership, ix, 46, 48, 51, 64, 67–68, 70–71, 114, 157–58, 210, 234, 237, 259–60, 276
liberation, liberation theology, 18, 27, 30, 110, 120, 132, 134, 154, 159, 217, 221, 240, 247, 276
liturgical, liturgy, 5–8, 26, 32–34, 43, 60, 68, 75, 100, 111, 116–18, 120, 122–24, 127–28, 132, 135–38, 141, 143–44, 147–49, 151–56, 161–65, 167–68, 171–72, 174, 177–84, 187, 189, 206–212, 215, 224, 226, 230, 240, 244–47, 250, 258, 262–63, 273, 276
Lohfink, Gerhard, 69–70, 82, 143, 226
Lord, v, x, 23–24, 26, 29, 33, 35, 37, 41, 43, 46, 48, 50–52, 55, 58–59, 64–66, 75, 86, 89, 94, 111, 122, 124–25, 128–31, 148, 150, 156, 159, 163, 167, 175, 177, 180–81, 183, 185, 187, 191, 193, 196–97, 201, 206, 208–212, 215, 220, 223–24, 226–27, 232, 235, 244, 246–49, 253–54, 256, 260, 263, 269, 274, 276, 280
Lossky, Vladimir, 6, 62, 116, 135

love, ix, xiii–xiv, 2, 9, 19, 21, 25, 27–29, 31, 33, 37, 46, 50–51, 63, 72, 74, 77–78, 80–81, 87, 92, 96, 98–99, 103, 106, 109–110, 112–15, 118, 122, 133, 141, 143, 145, 160, 162, 164–66, 169–70, 173, 175–76, 178, 181–82, 202, 207, 210, 214, 216–23, 226, 228, 230–32, 235–36, 247, 249–51, 253–56, 263, 265–66, 268, 272, 274–76, 279–80
Luther, Martin, 20, 102, 189, 193, 197

Macchia, Frank D., x, 51, 55, 74, 76, 95–101, 140, 148–49, 151–54, 158, 160, 221, 256
magical, 130, 182, 186, 197, 203, 205, 215, 265
manifestation, manifestations, 7, 10, 20, 24, 51, 57–58, 62–63, 71–72, 77–83, 92, 96, 99–100, 103, 105, 114–15, 117, 132, 136, 141, 144–45, 149, 155, 176–77, 181, 249, 263
marginalized, margins, 201, 225, 235–38, 249
Marshall, I. Howard, 60, 67–68
McDonnell, Kilian, 55, 81, 90–91
mediation, 62, 66, 100–101, 121, 148, 173, 241
membership, 46, 79, 87, 95, 183, 190, 244–45, 258
Menzies, Robert, 96, 115, 260
mercy, 8, 20, 45, 70, 78, 113, 131, 178, 192, 195, 211, 222, 230, 232, 250, 265
message, 18, 27, 35, 45, 48, 80–81, 103, 110–11, 130, 133, 170, 180–81, 198, 206, 218–19, 232–33, 248, 265, 270
messianic, 88, 111, 121, 124, 126–27, 133, 199
Min, Anselm K., 173, 220, 234, 236
ministry, ix, xiv, 7, 19, 28, 34–35, 38, 47–51, 53, 56–58, 63–64, 67–69, 78, 80–82, 86–89, 91–92, 94–97, 102–6, 115, 117–18, 127, 131, 146, 149, 184, 187, 189, 192, 197, 199, 210, 219, 228, 238, 259, 269, 276
miracle, miraculous, xiv, 31, 69, 72, 89, 155, 224, 226
mission, missional, vii, 9, 21, 24, 27, 30–31, 45, 48–49, 52, 55, 57, 61, 82, 87, 92, 94, 98, 105–6, 110–12, 119, 127, 142, 145, 156, 163, 189, 202, 209, 212, 219–21, 223–24, 236, 240, 243–44, 247, 251–55, 257–59, 261–65, 267–75, 277
Moltmann, Jürgen, 8, 57, 108–9, 111–14, 120–21, 126–27, 129, 133–34, 136, 159, 216
mystery, xv, 21, 29, 63, 108–9, 111, 119, 126, 128, 130, 153, 175, 182, 184, 189–90, 224, 247–48, 260, 273, 280
mystical, 6, 31–32, 43, 76, 110, 116–17, 121, 128, 131, 135, 145, 147, 236

narrative, 8–9, 30, 33, 37, 40, 44, 52, 55, 80, 87–88, 95, 105, 115, 120, 142, 150, 159, 198–200, 213, 222–24, 234, 249–50, 254, 260–61, 265, 267, 271, 273, 275
Newbigin, Lesslie, 24, 28, 37, 52, 84, 147, 264–65
Nicene Creed, 24, 36, 175
Nouwen, Henri J. M., 99, 218, 251, 259

obedience, 50–51, 57, 68, 127, 131, 204, 210, 257
office, 37, 47–49, 51, 53, 66, 68, 71–72, 83, 111, 116, 135, 211, 247
ontological, 17, 26, 109, 118, 125, 187
ordained, ordinancies, ordination, ix, 30, 32–33, 51, 64, 67–68, 70, 82, 127, 136, 184, 210, 213, 239–40, 265
orthodox, ortodoxy, 4–6, 8, 30, 49, 54, 65, 108–9, 116–18, 121, 128, 131, 135, 159, 169, 172, 174–75, 186–87, 189, 208–9, 211, 262

INDEX

Pannenberg, Wolfhart, 8, 106, 108–9, 114–15, 122–23, 125–26, 129–31, 134, 136, 184, 191, 219, 248
Paraclete, 20–21, 250
paradigm, paradigmatic, 61, 64, 71, 167, 224, 238, 250, 254, 258, 267
participation, 25, 28–30, 37, 43, 64, 66–67, 73, 78, 82, 87, 95, 97–98, 104, 109, 114, 123, 131, 141, 162, 184, 198, 210, 212, 215, 221, 233, 256, 262, 265
pastoral, 21, 67–68, 71, 97, 170, 179
Penteost, vii, 8–9, 12, 25–26, 30, 36, 45, 50–56, 58–61, 63–64, 69, 78, 80–83, 86, 88–91, 94, 96, 98, 102–5, 108–113, 115–16, 118–20, 122, 135, 137–39, 141, 143, 145–47, 149–53, 155, 157–59, 161, 173–75, 188, 190, 199, 204–5, 209, 214, 217, 222–28, 230, 234–35, 249–50, 254, 256, 259–61, 264, 267, 271, 273, 279
pentecostal, Pentecostalism, ix–x, 8, 18–19, 30, 37, 40, 56, 58, 63, 66, 76, 83–88, 90–91, 93–97, 101–3, 116–17, 120, 124, 132, 137–61, 165, 172–74, 186, 188, 195, 203–4, 209, 211–12, 222–23, 239–40, 243, 245, 261–65, 268, 272
Peterson, Cheryl M., x, 12, 30, 42
Pethrus, Lewi, 156–58
philosophical, 73, 141, 164
Pinnock, Clark, 17, 27
pluralistic, 56, 255, 260–61, 267
plurality, 42, 67, 82, 110, 252, 267
pneumatological, pneumatology, xiii, 1–9, 13, 20, 23, 25–27, 30, 35–36, 44–45, 49, 51, 54, 56, 62–64, 67, 81, 87, 91, 96–97, 104, 109, 112, 116–21, 123, 130, 133, 135, 140, 142, 145–46, 155, 169, 173–74, 185, 188–90, 205, 208, 210–12, 215, 226, 248, 254–56, 258, 261–62, 271–73
poor, 57, 70, 78, 100, 132, 134, 167, 174, 192, 217, 225, 228–29, 233, 237–38, 265
postfoundationalist, 14–16

postmodern, xi, 19, 38, 44, 83, 146–47, 174, 215, 237, 260
Postmodernism, 166
praxis, 10, 13–14, 63, 134, 220, 236, 247, 260, 274
prayer, 2, 7, 21, 26, 32–33, 50, 52, 57, 61, 63, 72, 76, 88, 92, 103, 109, 122–23, 129–31, 138, 141, 144, 163, 167–70, 172, 178, 204, 208–9, 216, 219, 223, 234, 254, 265, 275–76
preaching, 37, 69–70, 73–74, 86, 150, 193, 201, 236, 270
prophetic, 4, 18, 27, 29, 38–43, 45, 53, 60, 63–64, 74–75, 82, 89, 94, 99, 104, 111, 114–15, 127–28, 131, 158, 160, 199, 213, 222, 224, 226, 234, 237, 248, 257, 259, 265, 268, 274
protestant, 7, 48, 101, 108, 135, 146, 151, 193, 197, 247–48

rationality, 14–15, 73, 224
reason, 10, 33, 55, 74, 78, 87, 93, 103, 106, 121, 140, 145, 166, 226, 254
rebaptism, 195, 242–44
reconciliation, xiv, 31, 44, 63, 98, 106, 114, 127, 129, 136, 143, 145, 163, 167, 178, 181, 188, 207, 215, 217–21, 226, 229, 234, 236, 240–42, 244, 247, 253–55, 259, 265
redemption, 16, 37, 41, 76, 96, 112, 124, 191, 210–11, 218–19, 228, 231, 264, 269, 272
regeneration, 95, 97, 104, 160, 184, 189, 196, 202–3, 215
relationship, xiii, 2, 4–6, 8–10, 14, 19, 24, 27, 29, 34, 36–37, 42, 51, 55–56, 58, 63, 65, 85–86, 90, 93, 97–98, 110, 121, 128, 136, 138–39, 142–43, 147, 156, 161–62, 167, 169, 171, 179, 182, 184, 194–97, 200, 202, 204, 208, 211, 213, 216–18, 221, 231–33, 239–43, 245, 247, 249–50, 253, 258, 270, 274, 279

remembrance, 33–34, 120, 129–30, 137, 169, 179, 247
renewal, 7, 30, 62, 64, 77, 82, 92, 94, 97, 102–6, 109, 119, 136, 141, 157–58, 173, 178, 195–96, 209, 237, 241, 247, 257
repentance, 85, 89, 94, 102–3, 105, 124, 189, 197, 199, 202, 214, 218, 235, 244
restoration, 27, 64, 156, 171, 186, 218, 221, 224, 267
resurrection, xiv, 31, 33–35, 43, 49, 58, 62, 70, 73, 82, 89–90, 106, 114, 116, 122, 125, 127, 130, 148, 155, 158, 163, 169, 174, 181, 190, 200, 202, 204, 210, 215, 237, 241–42, 246, 250, 254, 263, 267, 273, 279
revelation, 14, 17–20, 47–48, 55, 58, 73–74, 78, 94, 112, 130, 145, 165, 167, 169, 174, 186, 195, 205, 248, 257
righteousness, 19, 41, 75, 77, 98, 122, 168, 182, 222, 231, 234, 251
rite, rites, 87–89, 94–95, 102, 123–24, 144, 147, 180, 183–84, 189–93, 195–96, 198–201, 204–5, 210, 213–15, 221, 245
ritual, rituals, 33–34, 73, 141, 143–44, 163, 165, 171, 182, 191–93, 196–97, 201–2, 204, 213, 247, 276
Robeck, Cecil M., x, 138, 147, 203, 244–45

sacrament, sacraments, 4, 7–8, 28–29, 34, 42–43, 45, 48, 53, 63, 65–66, 73, 82, 100–102, 105, 110–12, 123–29, 133, 136–37, 144, 147–48, 152, 154, 156, 160–61, 163, 168–69, 174–75, 182–84, 186–94, 196–200, 203, 205–6, 208–215, 227, 238, 243, 246, 248, 253, 258, 263, 265
sacramental, xv, 2–3, 5, 7–9, 13, 24, 43, 46, 50–52, 54, 58, 72, 81–83, 88–89, 98–101, 108–110, 116, 120, 123, 125–28, 133–37, 139, 144–45, 147–49, 151–54, 156, 160–61, 169, 172, 183–86, 188, 190–93, 195–97, 200, 205, 208–211, 213–16, 223–24, 230, 243–44, 248, 250, 260, 265, 277, 280
salvation, xiv, 12, 18, 20, 27, 33, 36, 41–44, 54, 61, 66, 69–70, 73–74, 81–82, 86, 88–89, 95–96, 101, 104–6, 114–15, 122, 125, 129, 136–37, 148, 151, 167, 175, 184–85, 188–89, 191, 195, 201, 206–7, 212–15, 222, 228, 231, 235, 238, 248, 258, 260–61, 265, 275–76
sanctification, 49, 63, 72, 92, 97, 135, 143, 157, 160, 175, 188, 206, 210, 248
Sandidge, Jerry L., 130, 141, 203, 244–45
Schleiermacher, Friedrich, 1, 87, 273
Schlink, Edmund, 3, 50, 197–99
Schmemann, Alexander, 169, 186–87, 208–9, 211
Schweizer, Eduard, 68–69, 88–89, 171
Scripture, iv, 4, 9–12, 14, 16–20, 26–27, 40, 44, 53, 56–57, 68, 78, 87, 95, 106, 135, 143, 156, 164, 167, 169–71, 174, 183, 185, 192–93, 196, 222, 232, 250–51, 269, 279
service, 29, 32, 34–35, 45, 49–51, 67, 69, 72, 74, 77–78, 88, 102, 106, 108, 111, 126–27, 133, 144, 146–47, 149, 152, 159–61, 163, 167, 181–82, 187, 206, 208, 210, 215, 231, 244, 248, 259–61, 263–65, 276
sign, ix, 27, 29, 42, 52–53, 62, 72, 74, 85–86, 92, 96, 99–101, 107–8, 111, 121–22, 124–27, 129, 137, 148–49, 151–53, 158, 162, 184, 191, 195–97, 202, 205–6, 214, 223–24, 229, 235, 246–47, 251, 253, 263
singing, 75, 145, 172, 179, 232
Smith, James K. A., 141–42, 164–66, 170–72, 178–79, 186–87, 201–2, 206–7, 220, 274
solidarity, 30, 134, 173, 212–13, 220, 227, 234, 236, 253, 266, 272, 275

sonship, 57–58, 76, 81, 87, 114, 123, 130
speech, 11, 73, 76, 78, 89, 115, 145, 168, 179, 199, 206, 224, 226, 240
spirituality, x, xiii, 2, 5, 8, 10–11, 13, 18, 20–21, 31, 34, 37, 46, 50, 52–53, 56, 62, 67, 74–75, 81, 90, 92, 97, 101, 103, 115, 120, 131, 138–44, 146–47, 152, 155–56, 159, 172, 180, 186, 216, 221, 223, 228, 238–40, 261–62, 265, 272
strangers, 33, 78, 216, 227–28, 247
Stronstad, Roger, 96, 260
structure, 18, 33, 38, 47, 52–53, 67–68, 82, 104, 117–19, 122, 126, 132, 137, 143, 157–58, 173, 192, 196, 207, 213, 225, 241, 262, 276
suffering, 21, 26–29, 47, 50, 62, 73, 98, 133, 135, 163, 170, 216, 222, 238, 240–42, 247, 259, 264
Supper, the Lord's, 33, 35, 65, 89, 129–31, 167, 175, 177, 183, 185, 192, 206, 208, 210–12, 263
symbol, symbolic, 24, 52, 71, 86, 100, 122–23, 147–48, 160, 172, 189, 196, 201–2, 206, 210–11, 214, 218, 224, 238, 250, 258, 265

Table, Lord's 20, 35, 66, 82, 128–29, 131, 156, 161, 163, 181, 206–7, 210, 215, 236, 241, 246–49, 251, 253, 255, 263, 267
Tangen, Karl Inge, x, 37, 83, 231–32
Tanner, Mary E., 13, 30, 238
teaching, 4, 32, 34–36, 44, 48, 55, 58–60, 67–68, 73, 77, 87–89, 113, 151, 157, 167, 173, 176, 179, 190, 204, 217, 258
temple, 4, 21, 25, 29–30, 35–36, 41, 109, 133, 185, 187, 209, 260
temptation, 12, 38, 56, 63, 99, 102–3, 158, 181, 217, 221, 242
Thiselton, Anthony C., 18, 44, 55, 60, 61, 86
Tillich, Paul, 123, 151
tongues, 9, 75–77, 80–81, 92, 95, 98, 100–101, 105, 118, 132–33, 141–42, 148–49, 151–54, 158, 160, 171, 173, 193, 196, 198, 225–27, 250, 254, 260–61, 271
trinitarian, 5, 13, 20, 24, 30, 37, 46, 55–56, 81, 91, 93, 104, 121, 135, 139, 156, 159, 175, 179, 191, 203, 206, 214, 227, 263, 271
Trinity, 1–2, 21, 25, 34, 36–37, 55, 111, 128, 158, 174–75, 220, 222–23, 227, 230, 258–59, 264
truth, 11, 14, 17, 19, 34, 36, 48, 109, 114, 116, 165, 173, 177–78, 182, 219, 230, 253, 255, 262, 267, 274, 279
Turner, Max, 11–12, 85

unity, x, 2, 4, 6, 9, 20, 23, 29, 31, 37, 46–48, 50–51, 54, 59, 65, 70, 78–79, 93, 108, 110–11, 113, 116–17, 123, 130, 140, 145, 158, 190, 193, 203, 208, 223, 227, 235–36, 242, 244–49, 251–58, 260, 264–68, 272–75, 279

Vanhoozer, Kevin J., 14, 20, 252
vision, xi, 24, 36–37, 51, 53, 71, 82, 159, 163, 167, 171, 181, 195, 213, 224–25, 227–28, 230, 247, 250, 257–58
Volf, Miroslav, 51–52, 55–56, 64–67, 99, 128–29, 159
Vondey, Wolfgang, 246–47
vulnerable, 18, 21, 25, 38, 41, 51, 78, 102, 149, 174, 219, 222, 266

water, 32–33, 79, 84, 86, 88, 92, 101, 105–6, 119, 124–25, 144, 184, 186, 188–89, 192, 194–97, 199–206, 212, 214–15, 242–43, 245
Wenk, Matthias, x, 61, 63–64, 115, 253, 265, 271–72
Wesley, John, Wesleyan, 37, 143, 265
Wilken, Robert L., 31–32, 34, 194, 208
Williams, Rowan, 62, 93, 168, 213, 265–66
women, x, xiii, 30–31, 52, 67, 71, 110, 113, 118, 122, 174, 200, 222, 225, 228–29, 234, 238–40, 259
worldview, 52, 63, 141–42, 151, 165, 171–72, 179–80

worship, vii, 8–9, 21–22, 24–26, 31–32, 34–35, 37, 43–44, 46, 49, 52–53, 59, 65, 72, 74–75, 79, 82, 98, 100–101, 106, 109, 111, 119, 122, 126–27, 129–30, 138–39, 141–45, 147, 151–55, 159–84, 186–87, 192, 201, 203, 206, 209–210, 214, 224, 230–34, 241, 251, 256, 258–60, 262, 266, 271, 275–76, 279

Yong, Amos, x, 9, 13–14, 44, 46, 63, 139–40, 163, 172–73, 183, 203–4, 211–12, 226–30, 239, 254, 260

Zizioulas, John D., 6, 8, 108–9, 116–18, 125, 127–29, 131, 134–35
Zwingli, Zwinglian, 100, 151, 211

www.ingramcontent.com/pod-product-compliance
Lightning Source LLC
Chambersburg PA
CBHW050620300426
44112CB00012B/1585